THE
CAMBRIDGE EDITION OF
THE LETTERS AND WORKS OF
D. H. LAWRENCE

ENGLAND, MY ENGLAND

AND OTHER STORIES

D. H. LAWRENCE

EDITED BY
BRUCE STEELE

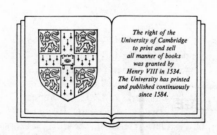

The right of the
University of Cambridge
to print and sell
all manner of books
was granted by
Henry VIII in 1534.
The University has printed
and published continuously
since 1584.

CAMBRIDGE UNIVERSITY PRESS

CAMBRIDGE
NEW YORK   PORT CHESTER
MELBOURNE   SYDNEY

Published by the Press Syndicate of the University of Cambridge
The Pitt Building, Trumpington Street, Cambridge CB2 1RP
40 West 20th Street, New York, NY 10011, USA
10 Stamford Road, Oakleigh, Melbourne 3166, Australia

Printed in Great Britain at the University Press, Cambridge

British Library cataloguing in publication data

Lawrence, D. H. (David Herbert), *1885–1930*
England, my England and other stories. – (The Cambridge edition of the letters and works of D. H. Lawrence)
I. Title   II. Steele, Bruce   III. Series
823′.912[F]

Library of Congress cataloguing in publication data
Lawrence, D. H. (David Herbert), 1885–1930.
England, my England and other stories.
(The Cambridge edition of the letters and works of D. H. Lawrence)
I. Steele, Bruce.   II. Title.   III. Series:
Lawrence, D. H. (David Herbert), 1885–1930. Works. 1979.
PR6023.A93E5   1990   823′.912   88-35341
ISBN 0 521 35267 3 hard covers
ISBN 0 521 35814 0 paperback

CE

CONTENTS

GENERAL EDITORS' PREFACE

D. H. Lawrence is one of the great writers of the twentieth century – yet the texts of his writings, whether published during his lifetime or since, are, for the most part, textually corrupt. The extent of the corruption is remarkable; it can derive from every stage of composition and publication. We know from study of his MSS that Lawrence was a careful writer, though not rigidly consistent in matters of minor convention. We know also that he revised at every possible stage. Yet he rarely if ever compared one stage with the previous one, and overlooked the errors of typists or copyists. He was forced to accept, as most authors are, the often stringent house-styling of his printers, which overrode his punctuation and even his sentence-structure and paragraphing. He sometimes overlooked plausible printing errors. More important, as a professional author living by his pen, he had to accept, with more or less good will, stringent editing by a publisher's reader in his early days, and at all times the results of his publishers' timidity. So the fear of Grundyish disapproval, or actual legal action, led to bowdlerisation or censorship from the very beginning of his career. Threats of libel suits produced other changes. Sometimes a publisher made more changes than he admitted to Lawrence. On a number of occasions in dealing with American and British publishers Lawrence produced texts for both which were not identical. Then there were extraordinary lapses like the occasion when a compositor turned over two pages of MS at once, and the result happened to make sense. This whole story can be reconstructed from the introductions to the volumes in this edition; cumulatively they will form a history of Lawrence's writing career.

The Cambridge edition aims to provide texts which are as close as can now be determined to those he would have wished to see printed. They have been established by a rigorous collation of extant manuscripts and typescripts, proofs and early printed versions; they restore the words, sentences, even whole pages omitted or falsified by editors or compositors; they are freed from printing-house conventions which were imposed on Lawrence's style; and interference on the part of frightened publishers has been eliminated. Far from doing violence to the texts Lawrence would

vii

have wished to see published, editorial intervention is essential to recover them. Though we have to accept that some cannot now be recovered in their entirety because early states have not survived, we must be glad that so much evidence remains. Paradoxical as it may seem, the outcome of this recension will be texts which differ, often radically and certainly frequently, from those seen by the author himself.

Editors have adopted the principle that the most authoritative form of the text is to be followed, even if this leads sometimes to a 'spoken' or a 'manuscript' rather than a 'printed' style. We have not wanted to strip off one house-styling in order to impose another. Editorial discretion has been allowed in order to regularise Lawrence's sometimes wayward spelling and punctuation in accordance with his most frequent practice in a particular text. A detailed record of these and other decisions on textual matters, together with the evidence on which they are based, will be found in the textual apparatus or an occasional explanatory note. These give significant deleted readings in manuscripts, typescripts and proofs; and printed variants in forms of the text published in Lawrence's lifetime. We do not record posthumous corruptions, except where first publication was posthumous.

In each volume, the editor's introduction relates the contents to Lawrence's life and to his other writings; it gives the history of composition of the text in some detail, for its intrinsic interest, and because this history is essential to the statement of editorial principles followed. It provides an account of publication and reception which will be found to contain a good deal of hitherto unknown information. Where appropriate, appendixes make available extended draft manuscript readings of significance, or important material, sometimes unpublished, associated with a particular work.

Though Lawrence is a twentieth-century writer and in many respects remains our contemporary, the idiom of his day is not invariably intelligible now, especially to the many readers who are not native speakers of British English. His use of dialect is another difficulty, and further barriers to full understanding are created by now obscure literary, historical, political or other references and allusions. On these occasions explanatory notes are supplied by the editor; it is assumed that the reader has access to a good general dictionary and that the editor need not gloss words or expressions that may be found in it. Where Lawrence's letters are quoted in editorial matter, the reader should assume that his manuscript is alone the source of eccentricities of phrase or spelling. An edition of the letters is still in course of publication: for this reason only the date and recipient of a letter will be given if it has not so far been printed in the Cambridge edition.

ACKNOWLEDGEMENTS

For their generous help in the preparation of this volume I wish to express my thanks to the following people:

Mrs Christian Hardie and members of her family for information about Greatham and the Lucas family; Mr George Lazarus for permission to use manuscript material in his possession and for hospitality at an early stage of my work; Mrs Bridget Pugh for information about Nottingham; Mr Best, Local History Librarian of the Nottingham Central Library; Mr Frank Van Straten, Director of the Performing Arts Museum of Victoria; staff of the Nottingham University Library; Ms Cathy Henderson and staff at the Harry Ransom Humanities Research Center, University of Texas; Dr Paul Eggert; Mr Ray Mainsbridge; Miss Lorraine Bullock and Mrs Mary Steele for expert research assistance.

To James T. Boulton, Michael Black and John Worthen, of the Editorial Board of the Cambridge edition of Lawrence, I express thanks for their wise and helpful comments, and especially to Lindeth Vasey for her astute and patient assistance with editorial detail.

I acknowledge the support of the Australian Research Grants Scheme in providing research assistance, and of Monash University in granting me a period of leave and travel assistance.

For permission to use materials in their possession I am grateful to the following institutions: New York Public Library; Nottinghamshire County Libraries; Stanford University; University of California at Berkeley; University of Illinois at Urbana-Champaign; University of Indiana, Charles H. Smith Collection; University of Nottingham; University of Texas at Austin; Yale University.

October 1988   B.S.

CHRONOLOGY

11 September 1885	Born in Eastwood, Nottinghamshire
September 1898–July 1901	Pupil at Nottingham High School
1902–1908	Pupil teacher; student at University College, Nottingham
7 December 1907	First publication: 'A Prelude', in *Nottinghamshire Guardian*
October 1908	Appointed as teacher at Davidson Road School, Croydon
November 1909	Publishes five poems in *English Review*
3 December 1910	Engagement to Louie Burrows; broken off on 4 February 1912
9 December 1910	Death of his mother, Lydia Lawrence
19 January 1911	*The White Peacock* published in New York (20 January in London)
19 November 1911	Ill with pneumonia; resigns his teaching post on 28 February 1912
March 1912	Meets Frieda Weekley; they elope to Germany on 3 May
23 May 1912	*The Trespasser*
September 1912–March 1913	At Gargnano, Lago di Garda, Italy
February 1913	*Love Poems and Others*
29 May 1913	*Sons and Lovers*
19 June 1913	Arrive in London
10–29 July 1913	At Broadstairs, Kent
28 July 1913	Sends 'The Primrose Path' manuscript to Douglas Clayton
August–September 1913	In Germany, Switzerland and Italy
October 1913–June 1914	At Fiascherino on the Gulf of Spezia
31 October 1913	Finishing 'The Mortal Coil'
July 1914–January 1915	In London and Buckinghamshire
13 July 1914	Marries Frieda Weekley in London
25 July 1914	Asks Clayton for another copy of 'The Primrose Path'
26 November 1914	*The Prussian Officer and Other Stories*
January–July 1915	At Greatham, Sussex
6 June 1915	Sends 'England, My England' and letter 'from an American' to J. B. Pinker

8 June 1915	Asks Clayton for a third copy of 'The Primrose Path'
by 13 July 1915	*English Review* buys 'England, My England'
August 1915–February 1916	In London
30 September 1915	*The Rainbow*; suppressed by court order on 13 November
October 1915	'England, My England' in *English Review*
29 October 1915	Finishing 'The Thimble'
30 October 1915	Sends 'The Thimble' manuscript to Lady Cynthia Asquith
2 November 1915	Sends 'The Thimble', returned from Lady Cynthia, to Pinker
5 November 1915	Hears of *The Rainbow* suppression
March 1916	Settle at Higher Tregerthen, Cornwall
June 1916	*Twilight in Italy*
July 1916	*Amores*
12 July 1916	Hears that MSS, probably including 'The Mortal Coil', are being returned from Italy
by 9 September 1916	Receives offer from *Seven Arts* to publish stories
31 October 1916	Sends rewritten 'The Mortal Coil' to Pinker
6 November 1916	Sends 'The Prodigal Husband' ('Samson and Delilah') to Pinker
13 November 1916	Sends revised typescript of 'The Mortal Coil' to Pinker
17 November 1916	Sends revised typescript of 'Samson and Delilah' to Pinker (noting new title); 'The Miracle' ('The Horse-Dealer's Daughter') is 'on hand'
11 December 1916	Receives acceptance of 'The Thimble' by *Seven Arts*
12 January 1917	Sends 'The Miracle' to Pinker
by 20 January 1917	*English Review* accepts 'Samson and Delilah'
March 1917	'Samson and Delilah' in *English Review* (June in *Lantern*); 'The Thimble' in *Seven Arts*
April 1917	'England, My England' in *Metropolitan*
July 1917	'The Mortal Coil' in *Seven Arts*
15 October 1917	After twenty-one months' residence in Cornwall, ordered to leave by military authorities
October 1917–November 1919	In London, Berkshire and Derbyshire
26 November 1917	*Look! We Have Come Through!*
26–30 August 1918	In the Forest of Dean with Carswells
October 1918	*New Poems*
November 1918	At Middleton-by-Wirksworth, Derbyshire
23 November 1918	Completes 'John Thomas' ('Tickets Please') and 'The Blind Man'
4 December 1918	Sends 'The Blind Man' to Pinker

15 January 1919	Sends 'Wintry Peacock' to Pinker and receives 'Tickets Please' typescript from him
6 March 1919	Invited by Middleton Murry to contribute to *Athenæum*
mid-March 1919	Writes 'Adolf' and 'Rex'
April 1919	'Tickets Please' in *Strand* (August in *Metropolitan* as 'The Eleventh Commandment')
3 April 1919	Murry rejects 'Adolf' (and possibly 'Rex')
25 April 1919	Arrive Chapel Farm Cottage, Hermitage, Berkshire
14 May 1919	Sends 'Fanny and Annie' ('The Last Straw') to Pinker
19 May 1919	Sends 'Monkey Nuts' to Pinker
? June–July 1919	Writes 'You Touched Me' ('Hadrian')
by 18 June 1919	Receives typescript of 'Monkey Nuts' from Pinker
14 November 1919	Leaves England
November 1919–March 1920	To Italy, then Capri and Sicily
20 November 1919	*Bay*
27 December 1919	Decides to leave Pinker's agency
8 February 1920	Asks Pinker to return manuscripts
16 February 1920	Asks Robert Mountsier to act as his American agent
8 March 1920–February 1922	At Fontana Vecchia, Taormina, Sicily
9 March 1920	Receives two bundles of manuscripts from Pinker
10 March 1920	Sends 'Wintry Peacock' to Michael Sadleir
by 24 March 1920	Carl Hovey requests a story for *Metropolitan* ('Wintry Peacock')
29 April 1920	'You Touched Me' ('Hadrian') in *Land and Water*
by 30 May 1920	*Dial* accepts 'Adolf'
20 June 1920	Sends 'Rex' to Richard Aldington for *Dial*
27 June 1920	Notes *Metropolitan*'s acceptance of 'Wintry Peacock'
July 1920	'The Blind Man' in *English Review* (7 August in *Living Age*)
23 July 1920	Sends 'Fanny and Annie' ('The Last Straw') to Mountsier for possible simultaneous publication in England and USA
September 1920	'Adolf' in *Dial*
by 1 September 1920	Receives cheque for 'Wintry Peacock' from *Metropolitan*
9 November 1920	Private publication of *Women in Love* (New York)
25 November 1920	*The Lost Girl*
by 9 December 1920	Receives *Dial* proofs of 'Rex' from Robert Mountsier
February 1921	'Rex' in *Dial*

CUE-TITLES

A. Manuscript locations

Lazarus	Mr George Lazarus
NCL	Nottinghamshire County Libraries
NYPL	New York Public Library
Smith	Charles H. Smith Collection, University of Indiana
StaU	Stanford University
UCB	University of California at Berkeley
UIll	University of Illinois at Urbana-Champaign
UN	University of Nottingham
UT	University of Texas at Austin
YU	Yale University

B. Printed works

(The place of publication, here and throughout, is London unless otherwise stated.)

Letters, i.	James T. Boulton, ed. *The Letters of D. H. Lawrence*. Volume I. Cambridge: Cambridge University Press, 1979.
Letters, ii.	George J. Zytaruk and James T. Boulton, eds. *The Letters of D. H. Lawrence*. Volume II. Cambridge: Cambridge University Press, 1981.
Letters, iii.	James T. Boulton and Andrew Robertson, eds. *The Letters of D. H. Lawrence*. Volume III. Cambridge: Cambridge University Press, 1984.
Letters, iv.	Warren Roberts, James T. Boulton and Elizabeth Mansfield, eds. *The Letters of D. H. Lawrence*. Volume IV. Cambridge: Cambridge University Press, 1987.
Letters, v.	James T. Boulton and Lindeth Vasey, eds. *The Letters of D. H. Lawrence*. Volume V. Cambridge: Cambridge University Press, 1989.
Nehls, i.	Edward Nehls, ed. *D. H. Lawrence: A Composite Biography*. Volume I. Madison: University of Wisconsin Press, 1957.
OED	Sir James A. H. Murray and others, eds. *A New English Dictionary on Historical Principles*. 10 volumes. Oxford: Clarendon Press, 1884–1928.
OED Supplement	R. W. Burchfield, ed. *A Supplement to the Oxford English Dictionary*. 4 volumes. Oxford: Clarendon Press, 1972–86.

Phoenix Edward D. McDonald, ed. *Phoenix: The Posthumous Papers of D. H. Lawrence*. New York: Viking Press, 1936.

Phoenix II Warren Roberts and Harry T. Moore, eds. *Phoenix II: Uncollected, Unpublished and Other Prose Works by D. H. Lawrence*. Heinemann, 1968.

Roberts Warren Roberts. *A Bibliography of D. H. Lawrence*. 2nd edn. Cambridge: Cambridge University Press, 1982.

Tedlock, *Lawrence MSS* E. W. Tedlock. *The Frieda Lawrence Collection of D. H. Lawrence Manuscripts: A Descriptive Bibliography*. Albuquerque: University of New Mexico, 1948.

INTRODUCTION

INTRODUCTION

D. H. Lawrence wrote and revised the fourteen stories collected in this volume between July 1913 and January 1922. All but one, 'The Primrose Path', first appeared in British or American periodicals between 1915 and 1922; five of them were published on both sides of the Atlantic during that period. They are listed here in order of composition and with the date and location of their first publication.

The Primrose Path	July 1913	*England, My England,* 1922
The Mortal Coil	October 1913	*Seven Arts,* July 1917
England, My England	June 1915	*English Review,* October 1915
The Thimble	October 1915	*Seven Arts,* March 1917
Samson and Delilah	November 1916	*English Review,* March 1917
The Horse-Dealer's Daughter	January 1917	*English Review,* April 1922
Tickets Please	November 1918	*Strand,* April 1919
The Blind Man	December 1918	*English Review,* July 1920
Wintry Peacock	January 1919	*Metropolitan,* August 1921
Adolf	March 1919	*Dial,* September 1920
Rex	March 1919	*Dial,* February 1921
The Last Straw [Fanny and Annie]	May 1919	*Hutchinson's Story Magazine,* November 1921
Monkey Nuts	May 1919	*Sovereign,* August 1922
Hadrian [You Touched Me]	July 1919	*Land and Water,* April 1920

'England, My England', 'Samson and Delilah', 'Tickets Please' and 'The Blind Man' were also published in American magazines after their British publication. 'Wintry Peacock', first published in USA, was later included in a British anthology, *The New Decameron III*, in 1922. In the same year,

Lawrence's second collection *England, My England and Other Stories* was published in America. This volume brought together ten of the listed stories. Lawrence considered 'The Mortal Coil', 'The Thimble', 'Adolf' and 'Rex' for inclusion but finally omitted them for reasons discussed below.

The two pre-war stories 'The Primrose Path' and 'The Mortal Coil' were written in the six months following the publication of *Sons and Lovers* in May 1913. Lawrence and Frieda, who had not yet received her divorce from Ernest Weekley, were living abroad for most of this period, during which he made a number of attempts at writing his novel 'The Sisters', which was ultimately to become *The Rainbow* and *Women in Love*.[1] The first story was set in the Nottingham area, and the second was based on an episode from the early army life of Frieda's father in Germany. In 1914, when he compiled his first collection, *The Prussian Officer and Other Stories*,[2] Lawrence excluded both stories probably because neither had secured periodical publication; and besides, his only copy of 'The Mortal Coil' had been left in Italy.

Six of the stories in the present volume were written between 1915 and 1918, that 'nightmare' period when the Lawrences, depressed by the horror and corruption of the First World War, and at times harassed by the authorities, were living in near poverty mainly in Sussex, Cornwall, Berkshire and Derbyshire.[3] Yet only 'England, My England' deals directly with the war. It is true that the main characters in 'The Thimble' and 'The Blind Man' have been physically maimed by the war, but the stories concentrate on their struggles to re-establish themselves psychologically and emotionally when they have returned to their wives. 'Tickets Please' merely alludes to the war. Of the six stories written in 1919, 'Wintry Peacock', 'Monkey Nuts' and 'Hadrian' have characters who are or have been soldiers. But the stories in the present collection are, with two exceptions, concerned above all else with the relations between men and women, and only secondarily with war or the accidental circumstances of their lives. The others, 'Adolf' and 'Rex', are animal sketches, anecdotes from Lawrence's childhood. They were composed in 1919 in response to a request for uncontroversial articles from his friend John Middleton Murry, the newly appointed editor of the *Athenæum*, but were rejected by him.

---

[1] See *The Rainbow*, ed. Mark Kinkead-Weekes (Cambridge, 1989), and *Women in Love*, ed. David Farmer, Lindeth Vasey and John Worthen (Cambridge, 1987).
[2] See *The Prussian Officer and Other Stories*, ed. John Worthen (Cambridge, 1985), pp. xxvii–xxx.
[3] See *Kangaroo*, chap. XII, 'The Nightmare'.

Throughout the war years Lawrence's letters to his London agent, J. B. Pinker,[4] and others, note his repeated intentions to write more stories, but the difficulty in placing those he had completed did not encourage him. In the later war years and in 1919 he was very keen to find publication in America, believing more and more that his future as a writer lay there rather than in England. He was aided to some extent by his friend, the American journalist Robert Mountsier, whom he first met in 1916, and who in March 1920 agreed to become his American agent.[5] But publication was sporadic. The *Seven Arts* magazine, which readily accepted his work in 1917, did not long survive. The *Metropolitan* published 'Wintry Peacock', 'England, My England' and 'Tickets Please'; an obscure magazine, the *Lantern*, republished 'Samson and Delilah', but severely cut it. The more prestigious publication, the *Dial*, did not publish his work until 1920, and even this was due partly to the initiative and help of his friend, the author Richard Aldington.

Failure to find publishers was not the only reason for Lawrence's relatively sparse output of stories during the war years. He was at work on his two largest novels, *The Rainbow* (1915) and *Women in Love* (privately published 1920), and at various times during the same period he wrote and rewrote his 'philosophy'. This last endeavour produced the unpublished 'Study of Thomas Hardy' (written in 1914), 'The Crown' (partly published 1915), 'The Reality of Peace' (1917) and other versions now lost. From early 1917 he worked on the essays which became *Studies in Classic American Literature* (1923). During 1918 he began *Aaron's Rod* (1922), and, moving into a new field altogether, in the summer and winter of 1918–19 he wrote the school text-book *Movements in European History* (1921).[6]

Back in the summer of 1914, Lawrence had returned to England from Italy to be married. He and Frieda anticipated a visit of perhaps three months, but the outbreak of war in August prevented them from leaving England. It was the end of 1919 before they were free to return to southern Europe. Lawrence, disillusioned after the harrowing experience of the

---

[4] James Brand Pinker (1863–1922), DHL's agent from July 1914 to December 1919.
[5] Robert Mountsier (1888–1972) met DHL in Cornwall in November. See also *Letters*, iii. 16–17, 476, 566.
[6] See *Study of Thomas Hardy and Other Essays*, ed. Bruce Steele (Cambridge, 1985), *Reflections on the Death of a Porcupine and Other Essays*, ed. Michael Herbert (Cambridge, 1987), *Aaron's Rod*, ed. Mara Kalnins (Cambridge, 1988); also *Studies in Classic American Literature* (to be published by Cambridge University Press) and *Movements in European History*, ed. Philip Crumpton (Cambridge, 1989).

war, saw his departure from England in the autumn of that year as a significant break from his homeland. He was to return only on brief visits thereafter.

For the next two years, the Lawrences lived principally in Sicily in the villa Fontana Vecchia above Taormina. In December 1919, as if to complete the break with his country, Lawrence decided to end his association with his English agent. His letter to Pinker on 27 December from Capri suggests that the two breaks were linked in his mind: 'We are here for a time – moving out of Europe before long, I hope. I think, there is not much point in our remaining bound to one another. . .What bit of work I have to place, I like to place myself' (iii. 439).[7]

A fortnight later, on receiving Pinker's compliance, Lawrence wrote again, this time about manuscripts: 'What things you have to return to me, please tell me' (iii. 453). On 6 February 1920 he noted in his diary the receipt from Pinker of a 'list of stories to be returned: Mortal Coil, Samson & Delilah, Miracle, At the Gates, Thimble, Bay, John Thomas, Fox, Wintry Peacock, Fanny & Annie, Monkey Nuts, You Touched Me', and reminding himself to enquire about other story manuscripts – among them 'Primrose Path'.[8] A diary entry two days later notes 'asked Pinker for MS. on his list'. While Lawrence refers to these thirteen items with character-istic imprecision as 'MS', some were typescripts which Pinker had had made to submit to publishers. In fact five works from the list had already been published, and not all were stories. *Bay* was a volume of poems (published November 1919) and 'At the Gates' (never published and now unlocated) was a late version of Lawrence's philosophy. Of the eleven stories in Pinker's possession, only four had been published by February 1920,[9] and in the next two years Lawrence would continue his efforts to place the others.

During 1920 and 1921 Lawrence was chiefly occupied in writing *The Lost Girl*, arranging its publication and that of *Women in Love*, writing *Mr Noon*[10] and *Fantasia of the Unconscious* (1922), completing *Aaron's Rod* and revising *Movements in European History* and arranging the collection of poems *Birds, Beasts and Flowers* (1923). With all this work on hand, he

---

[7] Bracketed references within the text are by volume and page to volumes ii–v of *The Letters of D. H. Lawrence*, ed. James T. Boulton *et al.* (Cambridge, 1981–9).

[8] Tedlock, *Lawrence MSS* 89 (text quoted from original MS at UCB, Roberts E93). See p. xxv and footnote 16 below for two other stories DHL requested.

[9] The four published stories were: 'The Mortal Coil', 'Samson and Delilah', 'The Thimble', 'John Thomas' ('Tickets Please').

[10] See *The Lost Girl*, ed. John Worthen (Cambridge, 1981) and *Mr Noon*, ed. Lindeth Vasey (Cambridge, 1984).

found no time for short fiction until October 1921, when he wrote 'The Captain's Doll', a longer form of story which he called a 'novelette' (iv. 143).

Throughout this productive period of residence in southern Europe, Lawrence frequently expressed in letters his desire not only to have done with England, but – in degrees ranging from longing to desperation – to set sail away from Europe altogether.[11] It is against this background – 'I feel one comes unstuck from England – from all the past – as if one would never go back' (iii. 488) – and his imminent departure from Europe that Lawrence finally began preparing his stories for a collection.

In September 1920, Mountsier had suggested a volume of short stories. Lawrence replied that he would 'begin to collect short stories for a book, as you suggest' (iii. 613); but, despite this apparent resolve, he remained more intent on placing his unpublished stories in magazines, particularly in America. There was a financial benefit in this procedure: periodical publication would offer substantial fees – more than one if he could find publication in both an American and a British magazine. Once a story was in volume-form, there would be no such fees, only the likelihood of a much lower royalty income for at most a year or two. It was therefore prudent to publish first in magazines and afterwards in book-form. Consequently it was late in 1921, when his hope of leaving Europe was at last moving towards reality, that Lawrence set himself to the task. Having completed the revision of *Fantasia of the Unconscious*, he told Mountsier that he intended to accept an invitation to join his American friends Earl and Achsah Brewster in Ceylon. In the same letter he wrote: 'The next thing, I think I will collect my short stories for a book, ready, so that my MSS are in order' (iv. 96). A month later he told Earl Brewster: 'I have been busy getting my MSS into order. . .so that I can clear out and be free. So I have brought the short stories up to the scratch, ready for a volume. . .' (iv. 126).

Getting his manuscripts into order involved in most cases considerable revision, and for some stories, complete rewriting. An entry in his diary for 26 October 1921 suggests that he had originally envisaged only one volume – 'a book of stories';[12] but five weeks later, the stories had themselves evolved somewhat differently. On 1 December he wrote to Mountsier that he was sending him 'The Fox', 'The Captain's Doll', 'Samson and Delilah', 'Fanny and Annie', 'The Blind Man', '"Hadrian" –

[11] See, e.g. *Letters*, iii. 418, 491–2, 504, etc. For his proposed expedition to the South Seas, see Compton Mackenzie, *My Life and Times: Octave Five 1915–1923* (1966), pp. 165, 184ff.

[12] Tedlock, *Lawrence MSS* 93.

(originally "You Touched Me")', 'Monkey Nuts' and 'The Horse-Dealer's Daughter', and added:

> I hope you have kept a copy of 'Wintry Peacock', from the *Metropolitan*.
> I shall send duplicates to Curtis Brown when I hear from you. I am doing a third long story – 'The Thimble' – to go with 'Fox' and 'Captain's Doll' in one volume. – Then I have three stories still to send you, enough to make up a volume of Short Stories. I want 'The Fox', 'The Thimble', and 'The Captain's Doll' to be one volume by themselves. . .[13]

Of the 'three stories still to send', 'Tickets Please' and 'The Primrose Path', both retyped after his revision, were posted to Mountsier on 12 December, and 'England, My England', much expanded and retyped, a month later. He had thus arrived at two volumes: the three longer stories – 'These I call the three novelettes' – and a book of ten short stories (iv. 143–4, 148). Mountsier could now negotiate American publication with Thomas Seltzer, who had published *Women in Love* the year before. For the short stories, Lawrence did not mention the order and only suggested that the volume 'begin with "Tickets Please" and perhaps. . .bear that title' (iv. 150).

The English edition of the short stories was not so simple a matter and was subject to an even longer delay than Lawrence at the time expected (iv. 155). He had reluctantly engaged Curtis Brown in London, having found it too difficult to work without an agent, and therefore forwarded copy for the English edition to him on 12 December 1921, as he had foreshadowed to Mountsier. He sent 'duplicate' revised versions of the following stories:

Samson and Delilah	Monkey Nuts
Fanny and Annie	The Horse-Dealer's Daughter
The Blind Man	Tickets Please
Hadrian (You Touched Me)	The Primrose Path

and noted that he had still to finish 'England, My England' (iv. 143–4). In the same letter, Lawrence said that his English publisher Martin Secker wanted 'a book of short stories quick, for the spring. I think better let him have these little stories – not the three novelettes.'

The Curtis Brown list was made up of only nine stories: Lawrence omitted 'Wintry Peacock' because Basil Blackwell, the Oxford publisher,

---

[13] *Letters*, iv. 134. See also ibid., 150 and diary entry for 9 January 1922 (Tedlock, *Lawrence MSS* 95). Albert Curtis Brown (1866–1945) became DHL's London agent in April 1921. The second volume was published by Martin Secker in 1923 as *The Ladybird* and contained 'The Ladybird' (formerly 'The Thimble'), 'The Fox' and 'The Captain's Doll'; the American edition was published by Thomas Seltzer the same year as *The Captain's Doll*.

had previously accepted the story for inclusion in his *New Decameron III* and his contract prevented other publication until the end of 1923 (iv. 169). When Lawrence sent the collection of stories to Mountsier for American publication, he believed that the Blackwell agreement was not effective in the United States, and so asked Mountsier to include the story, using the *Metropolitan* version. In answer to Mountsier's enquiry, Blackwell in fact released the story to him for a 'nominal fee' of two guineas.[14]

Allowing for the possibility that Secker's English volume would need additional material in place of 'Wintry Peacock', Lawrence had reassured Curtis Brown when sending the others: 'I think these will be quite enough short stories.[15] If not there are two animal sketches, "Rex" and "Adolf", which I can send. Both have appeared in *The Dial* in America' (iv. 144). But Lawrence did not persevere with this idea: in January 1922 he told Mountsier, 'Have written to Curtis Brown that they shall keep "Adolf" and "Rex" apart, for a possible animal sketch-book later' (iv. 169). No other sketches were written and these two remained uncollected in Lawrence's lifetime.

When preparing his collection, Lawrence must have considered the other stories he asked Pinker to return to him in 1920: 'The Witch à la Mode', 'Once—!' and 'The Mortal Coil'. The first two, dating from 1911 and 1912 respectively, were still unpublished, and it is uncertain whether they were in Pinker's possession at that time.[16] 'The Mortal Coil', rewritten in 1916, had been published in America, but Lawrence perhaps rejected its German subject as out of key with his collection of English stories.

The nature of Lawrence's revisions to the stories intended for the collection is not uniformly clear, since so few manuscripts and typescripts have survived. In the case of 'Wintry Peacock', which Lawrence asked Mountsier to forward direct to Seltzer in the *Metropolitan* printing, there was no opportunity for further revision at all. This makes the *Metropolitan* copy useful in determining what happened to the texts of the stories in the collection: since the differences between it and Seltzer's text show the nature and extent of the editing of Seltzer's copy, distinctions can be

---

[14] See *Letters*, iv. 117, 134; diary entry for 29 December 1921 (Tedlock, *Lawrence MSS* 95); letter from Basil Blackwell to Mountsier, 12 June 1922, UT.

[15] Martin Secker had already noted that the nine stories sent him would make a volume of barely 200 pages. (Letter from Secker to Curtis Brown, 5 July 1922, UIll).

[16] See p. xxii and *Love Among the Haystacks and Other Stories*, ed. John Worthen (Cambridge, 1987), pp. xxiiff. and xxxivff.

surmised in the other stories between what is probably editorial, or from the printer, and what is Lawrence's own revision.[17]

Five stories in the collection were sufficiently revised to need retyping. Lawrence's diary records a Mrs Carmichael, in Florence, as having typed 'Samson and Delilah', 'The Horse-Dealer's Daughter', 'Tickets Please', 'The Primrose Path' and 'England, My England'.[18] She produced the duplicate typescripts, all now unlocated, which he sent to Mountsier and Curtis Brown. For the remaining stories Lawrence must have used either existing typescripts, probably those provided by Pinker when the stories were first written, or the proofs or printed texts of periodical versions. The evidence relating to each story is discussed below in the section on 'Texts'.

Lawrence's rewriting of 'England, My England', the last story to be completed, took longer than he anticipated, and he finished it on 21 or 22 December (iv. 150). On receiving duplicate typescripts of the new version from Mrs Carmichael, he despatched them to both Curtis Brown and Mountsier on 9 January (iv. 159, 155–6). This was the last Lawrence had to do with the book before publication. In a little over a month he and Frieda were on board ship for Ceylon.

Publication

The first offer to publish a collection of Lawrence's short stories had come from Basil Blackwell, probably in October 1921.[19] Then, the following month, Lawrence reported to Curtis Brown: 'Jonathan Cape asked me if I had any book of short things to offe[r]' (iv. 129). He enclosed with this letter one from Secker making yet another proposal: 'I should like to do your collection of short stories, on the understanding of course that it does not count as a novel under the contract. Please send me the material & it can be published in February or so.'[20] Lawrence's comment on this proposal was that 'February would be too soon. . .I want to try the magazines, particularly in America. – If Secker is going to be cautious, so am I.'

In January 1922 Lawrence heard that Blackwell was still keen to

---

[17] In this story Seltzer, his editor or his printer deleted the *Metropolitan*'s editorial subtitle, replaced dialect 'ower' with 'over' and changed 'seeming' to 'seemingly'. (See Textual apparatus entries for 86:2 and 88:1). In 16 cases dashes were removed in favour of regular punctuation – full-stops or exclamation marks; 9 commas were inserted, 3 deleted; and there were 5 other punctuation changes. Italics were added once and omitted twice. The words 'forever', 'today' and 'valley-side' were house-styled to 'for ever', 'to-day' and 'valleyside'.

[18] Tedlock, *Lawrence MSS* 93–5. [19] See p. xxxix.

[20] Secker to DHL, 18 November 1921, UIll.

publish, and asked Curtis Brown whether he should let him have the volume 'failing Secker' (iv. 159). Since negotiations were still proceeding with Secker a fortnight later, it can be concluded that Curtis Brown was not in favour of a change of publisher. On 21 January Lawrence was suggesting to Secker, as he had to Mountsier, that 'Tickets Please' should be the volume title: 'I had thought of that. It fits pretty well' (iv. 173). It was not until February that he signed the agreement with Secker, but on the understanding that publication would not be before 'next autumn'. He wanted simultaneous publication in England and USA, and asked Mountsier to arrange it with Curtis Brown (iv. 187). He was to be disappointed.

Seltzer, in New York, having received the full contents of the volume from Mountsier, proposed publication in autumn 1922. His edition proceeded without any further reference to Lawrence. It is unlikely that he tried to contact Lawrence again: only months before, Lawrence had complained to Mountsier of Seltzer's reluctance to send him proofs of *Sea and Sardinia* (iv. 107). In any case, contact would have been difficult, for between February and September 1922 the Lawrences were travelling to Ceylon and Australia en route to USA. Thus the first edition of *England, My England and Other Stories* was published in New York on 24 October 1922, Seltzer having decided the title of the volume, the arrangement of the stories and a number of textual details. In November, Lawrence affirmed to Mountsier that he had seen no proofs (iv. 328).

One month before the American publication, Lawrence, now in New Mexico, received a letter from Secker pointing out that he was unable to publish an equivalent volume to Seltzer's because of Blackwell's hold on 'Wintry Peacock'. Without it, the book would be too short. In any case, Secker felt it better to defer the stories – which he wanted to call 'The Blind Man and Other Stories' – until after the publication of the three novelettes.[21] Lawrence replied: 'I might do you another short story to fill up your "Blind Man" book. Seltzer is calling it *England my England*. Let me know about this' (iv. 299). But he was clearly disenchanted with the English market and drew Secker's attention to the paucity of his English income: 'England makes me about £120 a year; if I got no more than that I should have to whistle my way across the globe.' Against this, he said, Hearst's had paid him $1,000 for the serial publication in America of 'The Captain's Doll'. 'If America will accept me and England wont, I belong to America' (iv. 298–9).

By March 1923, Secker had decided finally to defer the stories until 1924. He informed Curtis Brown that he would be publishing five

21 Secker to DHL, 25 July 1922, Ulll.

Lawrence books in 1923 and felt that this was enough for one year.[22] At the same time, of course, the further delay meant that 'Wintry Peacock' could be included. Blackwell had indicated to him that the story would be free after 1 September 1923.[23] Secker's edition of *England, My England* appeared in January 1924, fifteen months after the American edition.

Not only was Secker's volume identical in title and contents to Seltzer's, it seems actually to have been typeset from the American text and not from the typescripts Lawrence had sent through Curtis Brown. This can be shown in two ways. In the first place, Lawrence's practice on other occasions in correcting duplicate typescripts invariably introduced substantive variants between them.[24] In a book of stories it would be expected that the number of such variants would be considerable, and moreover would produce variant readings in the five stories for which there were duplicate typescripts. Between Seltzer's and Secker's editions, however, there are only two substantive variants which are not clearly printing errors, and these two are more typical of editorial interference than of authorial change.[25]

Secondly, as setting-copy for the English editions of both *Fantasia of the Unconscious* and *Studies in Classic American Literature*, published before and just after *England, My England*, Secker had given his printer copies of Seltzer's editions.[26] It is highly probable, therefore, that he did the same for the story volume. This would give Seltzer's edition (A1) clear priority over Secker's (E1). Seltzer's volume title and his order of contents are followed in the present edition. Despite his earlier preference for 'Tickets Please', Lawrence appears to have offered no objection to the title after publication. In marked contrast to his angry reaction to Garnett's inter-

---

[22] Secker to Curtis Brown, 13 March 1923, UIll. Secker published *The Ladybird* in March, *Psychology and the Unconscious* in July, *Fantasia of the Unconscious* and *Kangaroo* in September, and *Birds, Beasts and Flowers* in November 1923.

[23] On 5 October 1922 Secker acknowledged a letter from Basil Blackwell, adding 'I will take it then that I am at liberty to include "The Wintry Peacock". . .any time after September 1 1923' (UIll). DHL's belief that the story would not be free until the end of 1923 was presumably based on his calculation of eighteen months from the *Decameron* publication in June 1922. Blackwell was either calculating from the date of the agreement or accommodating Secker by reducing the period by three months.

[24] See for instance *The Boy in the Bush*, ed. Paul Eggert (Cambridge, 1990), p. xxxvi.

[25] Roberts A23. Typesetting errors appear in the Textual apparatus at e.g., 38:34 67:18, 56:33; editorial correction can be seen at e.g., 27:24 and 111:5. The two substantive variants are 'back of her' (A1) for 'behind her' (E1) [10:1], 'night' (A1) for 'evening' (E1) [60:9]. But an English editor might deem 'back of' an Americanism, although DHL does use it (e.g. in *Kangaroo*, chap. II). The second case might also be interpreted as transatlantic assimilation.

[26] Secker to Curtis Brown, 13 March 1923, UIll.

ference with the title of 'The Prussian Officer',[27] he had been receptive to Secker's suggested title 'The Blind Man'. He gave no firm indication of a preferred order for the stories in the volume.[28]

Reception

Although it was published at the height of Lawrence's career and in his most prolific period, *England, My England and Other Stories* attracted comparatively little separate attention. The post-war period had produced large numbers of short stories of high quality, which prompted at least one reviewer to reflect:

It may be that this is a day of swift flights and short spurts: that the genius of the moment is too distracted to admit of the long. . .narrative. . .and that a generation that produces nothing worthy of note in that form may nevertheless prove to have excelled in a different, though no less difficult, art – that of the short story.[29]

Almost all reviewers agreed that Lawrence was among the few great short-story writers of the time.

The first review appeared in the *New York Times Book Review* a month after publication. There was praise not only for the narrative and descriptive skill shown in the stories but for their subtlety, 'an evasive quality underlying yet penetrating the texture of the exterior plot'.[30] Even when apparently simple they are 'intensely complex, composed of innumerable tiny fibres of thought and feeling and instinct'. This review assumes an informed following of Lawrence among those American readers he had been so eager to attract. 'That the stories are all written in a flexible style of fine shadings and swift, delicate strokes is a mere matter of course to everyone who is at all familiar with Mr. Lawrence's work.' This review is long and quite detailed, referring to six of the ten stories, and pointing out the demands they make on the reader. The reward, it concludes, lies in 'a fruitful and long-enduring source of pleasure'.

In a review which also discussed *Fantasia of the Unconscious* and Seltzer's popular edition of *Women in Love*, Ben Lucien Burman in the *Nation* gave most space to *England, My England*. It was 'indubitably a great book', the

---

[27] See *The Prussian Officer*, ed. Worthen, pp. xxxii–xxxiii.
[28] While it is true that the numbering of the stories is identical in the lists DHL sent to Mountsier and to Curtis Brown on 1 and 12 December 1921, this is more suggestive of an inventory than a preferred order, since there is no instruction to keep that order.
[29] Filson Young, *New York Times Book Review*, 10 February 1924, p. 2.
[30] 19 November 1922, pp. 13–14. Reprinted in *D. H. Lawrence: The Critical Heritage*, ed. R. P. Draper (1970), pp. 189–90.

work of an artist 'who makes men's souls alive'.[31] He noted that 'constantly there is an uncanny feeling of disaster, of death to come, as though some fiendish gas of war – with which most of the sketches are intimately concerned – had spread out and seized all mortals in its bitter and poisonous embrace'. A similar point was made by the *Literary Digest International Book Review*: 'not one of these falls into the category of the war story; the scene of each is laid in England, and it is the influence of conditions brought about by the War which is described and not the War itself'.[32] This reviewer also noted the strain of fear apparent elsewhere in Lawrence – 'the occasionally conscious, more often subconscious, fear of woman as an implacable, possessive, devastating force'.

To the *Yale Review* for July 1923, Rebecca West contributed an article reviewing four short-story collections under the title 'The Present Plight of the Artist'.[33] She devoted only one tight paragraph to *England, My England*. While Lawrence is insulated from 'the evil effects of the day by absolute genius', she argued, he nevertheless commits flaws of taste – 'a peppering of French and Italian mars the decorum of an English page' – and he often writes 'in a slovenly way': the end of 'The Primrose Path', for instance, is abrupt 'with the most incredible artlessness'. On the other hand 'his genius triumphs' in 'Wintry Peacock', 'Samson and Delilah' and 'Fanny and Annie' – 'these are masterpieces'. She concluded that Lawrence's 'metaphysical system which he has devised for himself', while personally satisfying to him, 'undoubtedly limits his scope'. In this collection it leads to the monotonous theme of 'sex-antagonism and its sudden conversion into love as if it were a chemical change set up by the intensity of the antagonism'.

The publication of Secker's edition, fifteen months after the American one, brought a second notice in the *New York Times Book Review*. Filson Young from London commended the book to American readers as representative of 'the new generation's attitude toward the England of today'.[34] He also praised its 'grim, ironic humor' and the solid strength of the stories.

The Times Literary Supplement reviewer, A. S. McDowall, with an allusion to Wordsworth, recognised Lawrence as 'a master in delineating those swift or gradual tides of feeling which are none the less powerful for being felt in the blood before they are felt along the heart, and thus barely

---

[31] 17 January 1923, pp. 73–4.   [32] March 1923, pp. 52–3.
[33] Pp. 844–50 (for DHL see pp. 848–9). The other volumes are: Katharine Fullerton Gerould's *Valiant Dust*, Aldous Huxley's *Mortal Coils* and Virginia Woolf's *Monday or Tuesday*.
[34] 10 February 1924, p. 2.

grasped by consciousness. He can make us see like that the strange affinities of love and hate as points in one vibrating field of magnetism set up by men and women.'[35] Yet in this book the reader is too often unable to believe what he is being told 'because the climax comes with a sudden, straining paradox', and 'while feeling that things might have happened so, we want Mr. Lawrence to explain'. 'You Touched Me' and 'Samson and Delilah' are specifically cited. While praising the beauty and vividness of the stories, the reviewer is forced to conclude that 'these stories are certainly not "pleasant," and their author has a way of closing the escapes for us'. Lawrence seems fettered by the short-story form in this collection, whereas he succeeds most brilliantly in the 'little novels' like 'The Ladybird'.

In the *Nation and Athenæum*, Emily B. C. Jones (wife of F. L. Lucas) began a review of five volumes of stories by comparing Lawrence and Sherwood Anderson. She noted three things they shared: 'a passionate interest in psychological adventures', especially those involving instinct or the unconscious; an inclination to minimise the role of intellect in human life; and 'a tendency to fumbling repetitions'.[36] Lawrence's faults in this respect, however, 'are the faults of a giant'. 'To have read these pages is to have experienced something with an actuality, an intensity, a stimulation of one's faculties which is the appanage of real art.'

The strongest note of dissent came from J. B. Priestley, who reviewed six volumes of stories for the *London Mercury*. Lawrence's limitations are closing in on him, Priestley wrote. His principal limitation is his presentation only of 'those sensitive, rebellious and irrational spirits' who 'wish to walk alone, but have not the strength and hardness to be entirely self-dependent and complete'.[37] His control of the short-story form is not as successful as it is of the longer 'Ladybird' form. 'The story that gives the volume its title has merit, but is huddled towards the close, and suggests that the author began it and partly developed it with a much longer story in his mind. A later tale, *The Wintry Peacock*, shows the Lawrence manner at its best, and the other things, some of them verging on the comic, hover between failure and success.'

Reviewers of the *New Decameron III*, in which 'Wintry Peacock' appeared in slightly altered form, were unanimous in their praise of Lawrence's contribution. The *Saturday Review* remarked: 'we had occasion recently to mention in these columns the growth of the new English short story in the hands primarily of Miss Katherine Mansfield, Mr D. H.

[35] 24 January 1924, p. 50. [36] 23 February 1924, pp. 738–9.
[37] March 1924, pp. 546–8.

Lawrence and Mr Coppard. The greatest of these three is undoubtedly Mr Lawrence, who stands isolated, without precedent and progeny.'[38]

In comparison with the largely unsympathetic reception afforded his first collection of stories, *The Prussian Officer*, the response to *England, My England* indicated that Lawrence was now accepted on both sides of the Atlantic as an established writer – controversial, erratic, tedious perhaps, but above all brilliant, and to be neither dismissed nor overlooked.[39]

Texts

'England, My England'

Lawrence had completed the first version of this story by 6 June 1915 (ii. 345). He was living at the time in Greatham, Sussex, on the estate of Wilfrid Meynell and his family at the invitation of Meynell's daughter Viola. The story draws much detail both from the place and from members of the Meynell family, particularly the daughter Madeline and her husband Perceval Lucas. Lawrence, aware of the close relationship of his characters to their living models, once described the work as 'a story about the Lucases' (ii. 386). It gave offence to the family, and when Percy Lucas was killed in France a year later, Lawrence momentarily wished the story 'at the bottom of the sea', but quickly recovered his faith in it.[40]

Uncharacteristically, he appears to have composed this story on his typewriter, as Lady Cynthia Asquith observed in her diary: 'Lawrence has taken to a typewriter – there was a war story coming to life on it.'[41] Probably with its anti-war sentiments in mind, Lawrence told Pinker in a letter accompanying his typescript: 'I send you a story, which England will not publish, I am afraid, but which America may' (ii. 354). He was wrong. The *English Review* bought the story a month later, in July 1915, and published it in the October issue (Per1) (ii. 364, 406). Although the *Metropolitan* in New York had expressed interest in Lawrence at this time, and in August had cabled Pinker urgently requesting a story for October

---

[38] 24 June 1922, pp. 659–60.

[39] See *The Prussian Officer*, ed. Worthen, pp. xxxiii–xxxvi. *England, My England* was also favourably reviewed by Louis Kantor in the *New York Tribune*, 24 December 1922, p. 23, by Arthur W. Colton in the *New York Evening Post Literary Review*, 10 February 1923, p. 447, and by Humbert Wolfe in the *Weekly Westminster*, 23 February 1924, p. 532.

[40] *Letters*, ii. 635–6. See also Explanatory notes on 5:1, 6:32, 7:15, 18:23, 19:13, 22:19, 30:15.

[41] *Letters*, ii. 354 n. 4. Lady Cynthia (1887–1960) was the daughter-in-law of the Prime Minister, Herbert Asquith. She became a close friend and correspondent of the Lawrences. DHL had typed the first 7pp. of *The Rainbow* himself in November 1914 (Roberts E331a) and the first 368pp. of *Women in Love* in 1916 (Roberts E441d).

publication, Pinker did not send them 'England, My England'. Lawrence's typescript, perhaps the only copy, was already with the *English Review*. The story Pinker sent, though unnamed in the surviving correspondence, was probably 'The Primrose Path'. It was rejected.[42] The *Metropolitan* (Per2) eventually published 'England, My England' in April 1917, the month in which the United States entered the War.

Lawrence's typescript has not survived but a set of uncorrected galley proofs from the *English Review* (Roberts E114.5) has. He sent these proofs to his old Eastwood friend William Hopkin shortly before publication. Hopkin did not like the story but kept the proofs.[43] They thus contain the version closest to the story as Lawrence submitted it. In comparison, the version finally published in the *English Review* shows that Lawrence, quite typically, had made some thirty-four revisions to the proofs, many of them single words, but including one passage of sixteen words. Overall the story is shorter by 120 words, but it is not clear whether Lawrence himself made the deletions, as in some cases seems likely, or whether they were made editorially.[44]

The *Metropolitan* version shows that, for its copy, Lawrence made revisions to the same initial state of the story represented by the Hopkin proofs, but possibly in the form of a typescript. Much that was revised or deleted for the *English Review* remains unchanged in the *Metropolitan*, but there are more than seventy verbal revisions and several deletions quite independent of the *English Review* version. Moreover these changes extend through the whole story and in places make subtle alterations to both narrative and characterisation. Thus there are in effect two markedly different periodical forms of this first version of 'England, My England'. In the appendix to the present edition the story is reproduced from the Hopkin proofs as the earliest recoverable version. The variants from both periodical versions are given in the accompanying Textual apparatus.

When it came to the collection, Lawrence left 'England, My England' until last and revised it most comprehensively. He wrote to Mountsier on 21 December 1921: 'I am finishing today or tomorrow, D. V. – the last of the short stories – "England, My England"' (iv. 150). At the end of the month he was still waiting for the typescripts from Mrs Carmichael, and did not despatch the final copies to Curtis Brown and Mountsier until 9

---

[42] *Letters*, ii. 348, 354. *Metropolitan* (Carl Hovey) to Pinker, 3 August 1915; *Metropolitan* (Sonya Levien) to Pinker, 30 November 1915; NYPL. See also p. xliv.

[43] *Letters*, ii. 391, 402. The proofs are at NCL.

[44] For cuts made by the *English Review* to 'The Prussian Officer' ['Honour and Arms'] in 1914, see *The Prussian Officer*, ed. Worthen, pp. xxxviii–xxxix.

January.[45] It is perhaps significant that he was at the same time converting his other early war story, 'The Thimble', into the novella 'The Ladybird'. The new 'England, My England', while not quite a novella, grew to more than twice the length of the 1915 story, being reconceived in much the way that 'The Thimble' was. But the revision is not consistent throughout: the pre-war section is almost totally reworked and developed to five times its earlier length while the ending is much reduced. The comparatively schematised psychology of the 1915 version is refined, the horror and melodrama of the final scene are removed and the writing is altogether tauter and more economical. From remaining traces of the earlier version, it would seem that Lawrence had readings from both earlier published versions to hand when rewriting.[46] Only the published texts – Seltzer (A1) and Secker (E1) – of this final version survive, and A1 has been taken as the base-text for this edition.

'Tickets Please'

At Hermitage in November 1918, Lawrence, frustrated in his attempts to write essays on education for *The Times Literary Supplement*, turned to short stories. Late in the month he told Pinker that he had done three – 'The Fox', 'John Thomas' (later 'Tickets Please') and 'The Blind Man' (iii. 299). He sent the manuscripts of the first two to Katherine Mansfield for her to read and to send on to Pinker (iii. 307, 309, 319). This she had done by Christmas, and Lawrence received typescripts from Pinker on 15 January 1919 (iii. 320). 'Tickets Please' gained its setting from, and probably was suggested by, the tramway between Ripley and Eastwood which Lawrence had used late in 1917 and in 1918 (iii. 300).

The original title of the story was 'John Thomas' after the central male character John Thomas Raynor. Lawrence had more than once remarked to Pinker that he was unlikely to write a story acceptable to the popular and somewhat strait-laced *Strand* magazine (ii. 348, 419; iii. 155, 221). But the *Strand*, remarkably, did accept this story and published it in April 1919 (Per1). The rather prim editing of it was characteristic: the suggestive title had been changed to '"Tickets, Please!"', the inspector's name to John Joseph, and his nickname deleted. When in August the *Metropolitan* magazine in USA published the story (Per2), the title was changed to 'The

---

[45] *Letters*, iv. 153, 159. See also diary entry for 9 January 1922 (Tedlock, *Lawrence MSS* 95).
[46] E.g. A1 follows Per2 in 'fierce seclusion. . .savage peace of the commons' (Per1 'tense seclusion. . .peace. . .') but follows Per1 in 'our own men' (Per2 'Englishmen') (5:25, 31:31). It is probable that DHL was working from a typescript now lost.

Eleventh Commandment', the inspector's name left intact and the nickname 'Jontom' included.[47] It is unlikely that these changes were made with Lawrence's knowledge and approval. Given his poverty, and his desire to enter the American market, he would scarcely have demurred at the mild censorship, however much he might privately have fumed. There are, nevertheless, sufficient substantive differences between Per1 and Per2 of an uncontroversial kind to indicate that, as he often did, Lawrence corrected Pinker's typescript and its carbon copy differently. Since neither typescripts nor manuscript survive, these two divergent periodical versions are closest to the original form of the story.

When Pinker returned Lawrence's manuscripts in early 1920, Lawrence listed the story as 'John Thomas',[48] which suggests that he still had his original title in mind. When revising the story for his collection, however, he accepted the *Strand* title, even suggesting it as the volume title.[49] However, the number of agreements between Per2 and A1 indicate that he used the *Metropolitan* text for his revisions. To this he made numerous changes, most extensively to the ending. It was retyped by Mrs Carmichael, and Lawrence posted the new typescripts to his agents on 12 December.[50] None of this material has survived and Per2 is taken as the base-text for this edition. It is collated with Per1 which, despite its editing of the text, retains some of Lawrence's distinctive forms. The substantive changes in A1 are adopted. In letters Lawrence used 'Tickets Please' (without punctuation) and this form of the title has been adopted.

'The Blind Man'

Lawrence's good friend and later his biographer, Catherine Carswell, recalled Lawrence telling this story in the kitchen of the Vicarage at Upper Lydbrook in Monmouthshire, where he and Frieda were holidaying with the Carswells in August 1918.[51] He had completed the writing of it by 23 November, but did not plan to send it to Pinker until after he had returned

---

[47] For the significance of these changes see Explanatory notes on 34:1, 36:21. It is not clear whether DHL or the *Metropolitan* editor provided the nickname 'Jontom'. The 'Coddy' of A1 is DHL's.

[48] Diary entry for 6 February 1920 (Tedlock, *Lawrence MSS* 89).

[49] See above p. xxvii. It is possible that the new title was DHL's but there is no evidence either way.

[50] Diary entry for 12 December 1921 (Tedlock, *Lawrence MSS* 94); *Letters*, iv. 143–4. DHL's letter to Curtis Brown, dated 7 December, was not sent until 12 December when the 'Tickets Please' typescript was ready. A postscript and the office date of receipt stamp confirm this.

[51] Catherine Carswell, *The Savage Pilgrimage* (1932), pp. 105–6.

to Middleton on the 28th (iii. 298–9). Soon afterwards he commented to Katherine Mansfield that 'if one is to do fiction now, one must cross the threshold of the human psyche. . . .I've done "The Blind Man" – the end queer and ironical. – I realise *how* many people are just rotten at the quick' (iii. 302–3).

The story was sent to Pinker on 4 December (iii. 301) but eighteen months passed before the *English Review* published it in July 1920 – six months after Lawrence and Pinker had parted professional company. In December that year Lawrence heard from Mountsier in New York that the story had also appeared in the *Living Age* on 7 August (iii. 633, 635, 645). Believing this to be Pinker's doing, Lawrence sent a 'sharp letter to him' saying that he had received no payment for either publication (iii. 633, 690). Pinker replied that he had 'nothing to do with this' (iii. 650, 690). The following March Lawrence was still uncertain of the facts, and unpaid to boot: 'Did Harrison do it all on his own? And is he not going to pay for the story? It must have appeared in *The English Review* simultaneously with the American copy.'[52] Whether Lawrence ever received satisfaction on these points is not known. His attempt to manage his affairs without an agent frequently brought difficulties of this kind. Publication was in fact virtually simultaneous, but the *Living Age* acknowledged the *English Review* as its source.[53] Apart from American spelling, house-styling and one variant ('uplifted' for 'uptilted', 58:24) the two texts are identical, confirming that the American version was set from the *English Review*. Lawrence made two very small changes to the story for the collection, most probably on a copy of the *English Review*, as it did not require retyping by Mrs Carmichael. Since this version (Per1) has one stage less house-styling than A1,[54] it is taken as the base-text for this edition, and Lawrence's changes are incorporated.

'Monkey Nuts'

This is the story Lawrence sent to Pinker on 19 May 1919; its composition can therefore be dated from that month when Lawrence was at Chapel Farm Cottage in Hermitage, Berkshire (iii. 360, 365). This places it immediately after 'The Last Straw' ('Fannie and Annie') (see below) in order of composition. Pinker returned the 'MS' to Lawrence by 18 June

[52] *Letters*, iii. 690. Austin Harrison was the editor of the *English Review*.
[53] '[*The English Review*]' appears above the title (p. 358).
[54] See p. xxviii and footnote 25. Four distinctive agreements between Per1 and A1 and only two one-word differences suggest that DHL used Per1 as copy for Seltzer.

(iii. 365), having first had a typescript made, as Lawrence had instructed him to do. Pinker was unable to place the story, and it must have been the typescript that he returned to Lawrence in Sicily in February 1920.[55] Early in April 1922 Lawrence heard from Curtis Brown that *Hutchinson's Story Magazine* was to take the story, but the offer came to nothing (iv. 219–20).

No manuscripts or typescripts are known to exist, so that it is not possible to determine whether Lawrence made any alterations to the story in 1921 before the collection. He does not list it as having been retyped by Mrs Carmichael but was able to send copies to Curtis Brown and Mountsier in December 1921. 'Monkey Nuts' was first published in America in the *Sovereign* on 22 August 1922 (Per), only two months before A1.

This dual publication in America in 1922 suggests that more than one typescript was in existence. No doubt Mountsier or Seltzer had duplicates made for circulation to periodicals from the copy Lawrence had sent him. If so, the three or four substantive variants between A1 and Per were probably introduced by either a typist or an editor, and so would not represent Lawrence's own variant corrections to independent typescripts. He saw the proofs of neither publication. House-styling, copy-editing and setting errors are evident in both texts.

In the absence of authorial copy, Per is preferred to A1 as the base-text. Stylistically, in its use of 'pictures' rather than 'movies' (66:31), 'That's what I call cruel, now' rather than 'That's cruel of you' (70:3) and 'I may do' rather than the repetitive 'I may go' (68:26), it seems closer to Lawrence's usage, and occasionally, though not always, it reflects his characteristic punctuation. Per is collated with A1.

'Wintry Peacock'

Except for a brief visit to his sister Ada Clark in Ripley for Christmas, Lawrence and Frieda spent the whole of the winter 1918–19 at Mountain Cottage, Middleton. It was here early in January 1919 that Lawrence wrote 'Wintry Peacock'. He was finishing it on 9 January, and ready to forward the manuscript to Pinker for typing – if he considered it worth while – on 15 January (iii. 319–20). Lawrence's letters report the heavy snowfalls and bitter wintry conditions in that part of Derbyshire, which is the setting for the story (iii. 308, 312, 318). A letter of 17 April 1925 confirms the identification in the Middleton district of some geographical

---

[55] Diary entry for 6 February 1920 (Tedlock, *Lawrence MSS* 89).

details in the story.[56] The manuscript (Roberts E437a) is in a school exercise-book, the cover of which is inscribed: D. H. Lawrence, Middleton, Wirksworth. Both the cover and the first page of the manuscript have the title 'Wintry Peacock'.

Nothing further is known of the story until February 1920 – the time of Lawrence's imminent break with Pinker. Then in Sicily, Lawrence had received a request from Michael Sadleir for a short story to be included in a 'new review' he was to edit from Oxford (iii. 473–4). Having acknowledged receipt of his remaining 'manuscripts' from Pinker on 9 March 1920, Lawrence 'Sent Wintry Peacock to Michael Sadler' the following day. On 14 March he returned a signed agreement with the publisher of the review, Humphrey Milford, who was to pay £10 for the story.[57]

Ten days later, Lawrence received a request for a story from Carl Hovey of the *Metropolitan* magazine in New York. Having, it seems, no further copy on hand, Lawrence asked Sadleir to have a new typescript of 'Wintry Peacock' made and sent to Hovey, and to charge him (Lawrence) for both typing and postage (iii. 493). He noted on 27 June that Hovey had written agreeing to buy the story for $250. Reporting this to Sadleir, he added that he was 'curious to see your new magazine' (iii. 559); but Sadleir's review project had been abandoned. Subsequently, on 20 October, Lawrence noted the receipt of the '£10. for unused Wintry Peacock – Engl[and]'.[58] Rather than have Lawrence's story retyped for America, Sadleir simply sent on his copy, having no immediate use for it. Although Lawrence had received the *Metropolitan*'s cheque by 1 September (iii. 590), the magazine did not publish 'Wintry Peacock' until 21 August 1921, by which time it had gained an editorial sub-title – 'The Lance-Corporal Comes Home from the War' – and two illustrations by Robert W. Stewart.

A month before, in July, Seltzer had received two proof copies of the *Metropolitan* text and wrote to Mountsier: '*The Wintry Peacock* they tell me will be published in August. I secured two copies and sent one to Michael Sadler in London and the other to Lawrence. . .'[59] While he acknowledged receipt of his copy on 30 July 1921, Lawrence evidently did not correct these proofs before publication (iv. 58). There would scarcely have been time. On the surviving proof copy (Roberts E437c) there are five corrections of a routine nature, certainly in Lawrence's hand, one of

[56] *Letters*, v. 243. DHL was replying to an enquiry by Hermann Augustine Piehler, a writer of travel books. See also Explanatory note on 77:5.

[57] *Letters*, iii. 485, iv. 31; Tedlock, *Lawrence MSS* 89.   [58] Tedlock, *Lawrence MSS* 91.

[59] *D. H. Lawrence: Letters to Thomas and Adele Seltzer*, ed. Gerald M. Lacy (Santa Barbara, 1976), p. 210.

which was not made in the *Metropolitan* text as published. This copy was in fact the one Seltzer had sent to Sadleir who then used it as setting-copy for the *Decameron* version of the story discussed below.

There are considerable differences between the manuscript and the *Metropolitan* text. Most are unquestionably authorial revisions. Lawrence has been at pains to refine his depiction of the Goytes; for instance, the published text heightens the witch-like characteristics of Mrs Goyte and removes details about her background and her position as merely a farming woman. The last scene between the narrator and Lance-Corporal Goyte is largely rewritten. It is known that Lawrence made extensive revisions to the story in a typescript which cannot now be located.[60] Whether he did so in Middleton (on receipt of Pinker's typescript) or later in Sicily is uncertain. A long opening passage in the manuscript describing Tible and its surroundings, and recounting two earlier meetings with Mrs Goyte, is totally omitted from the published text. At first sight this might appear to have been editorial cutting: most, but not all, of the backward references to the deleted matter have been adjusted – 'She saw me' for 'She recognised me' (77:21), for example, but 'the. . .bonnet' (77:23), implying previous identification, remains. There is, however, no reason to doubt that the removal of the slightly garrulous preamble to the story formed part of Lawrence's own revision. The deletion is in tune with the other changes. He seems not to have complained of editorial mutilation of 'Wintry Peacock' as he did on finding that 'Hadrian' ('You Touched Me') had been seriously cut by *Land and Water* magazine (see below); and he accepted the *Metropolitan* version as setting-copy for both the *Decameron* and the collection.

By October 1921, a change had taken place on the British publishing scene. Writing to Mountsier, Lawrence said:

I don't feel much like work. Am collecting short stories to make a book any time, and to get my MSS in order. Basil Blackwell of Oxford asked me if I couldn't give *him* a vol. of short stories. You know he is doing 'Wintry Peacock' in his *New Decameron* series – in January presumably – and I engaged not to put this story into a volume for another year. (iv, 103)

After the failure of the original review scheme, Sadleir had been appointed editor of *New Decameron III* for Blackwell. Recalling 'Wintry Peacock', for which Lawrence had already been paid a fee, he wrote directly to

---

[60] Lawrence Clark Powell, *The Manuscripts of D. H. Lawrence: A Descriptive Catalogue* (Los Angeles, 1937), p. 24: '35. Wintry Peacock/ Corrected typescript. . .Many pages completely rewritten between the lines in Lawrence's hand.' This typescript was given by Frieda Lawrence to her lawyer in 1938.

Lawrence with a proposal to use the story in the *Decameron*.[61] Lawrence, however, was in Germany at this time and his papers were in Sicily. Both he and Sadleir wrote to Mountsier for a copy of the *Metropolitan* version. But Mountsier was in London, and in the end the copy came to Sadleir from Seltzer.[62]

The *New Decameron* series differed from other short-story anthologies in that it offered a linking narrative between the stories which were contributed by various authors. It was a latter-day imitation of both Boccaccio (whence the title) and Chaucer (in the development of a narrative link between the stories). Lawrence's story was the first of a group supposed to have fallen into the hands of a provincial French police officer – one of a number of manuscripts in English apparently written on wall-paper. The officer has them translated into French in order to satisfy himself that they are of no use in his investigations. In Chaucerian style 'Wintry Peacock' is given an additional sur-title 'The Poet's Tale' just as the one immediately following – 'Père Etienne' by Robert Keable – is given the title 'The Priest's Tale'. In view of this format, Sadleir required Lawrence to make some changes to his story on the set of the *Metropolitan* proofs (Roberts E437c) which Seltzer had sent him. He indicated in red ink the points at which Lawrence was to make the changes. Their effect was to remove all reference to the war: thus Alfred Goyte is no longer a lance-corporal who has been fighting in France, but a chauffeur engaged in driving his employer in Europe. Lawrence returned the copy to Sadleir 'with all the alterations to fit' on 9 August (iv. 67). For this story Blackwell paid an additional £21 in December 1921, and the *Decameron* was published on 15 June 1922.[63] Lawrence's agreement with Blackwell for 'Wintry Peacock' as a significant factor in the delay of the English edition of *England, My England* has already been discussed.[64]

For the version of the story to be included in his collection, Lawrence seems to have expected Mountsier to use the unchanged *Metropolitan* text since, on 1 December, under the list of stories he was sending, he expressed the hope that Mountsier had kept a copy of it (iv. 134). Since any further authorial revision was thus out of the question, 'Wintry Peacock' is the only story in the *England, My England* volume for which a copy at least of the setting-copy survives. As indicated above, it is thus possible to

---

[61] Michael Sadleir to DHL, 5 June 1921, Smith.
[62] Sadleir to Mountsier, 17 June 1921, Smith; *Letters*, iv. 31, 36.
[63] Roberts B10. DHL recorded receipt on 29 December 1921 (Tedlock, *Lawrence MSS* 95).
[64] *Letters*, iv. 262 n. and see above p. xxv.

ascertain the nature and extent of Seltzer's (or his printer's) editing of his copy.[65]

For this edition the *Metropolitan* text (Per), corrected for accidentals from the manuscript, is taken as base-text and collated with A1. The two lengthy passages from the manuscript discussed above, one deleted, one revised, are included in the Explanatory notes to the story.

'Hadrian' ['You Touched Me']

Nothing is known of the genesis of this story. It seems to date from late June or July 1919 just after Lawrence moved from Derbyshire to Hermitage in Berkshire. Having completed 'The Last Straw' ('Fanny and Annie') and 'Monkey Nuts', Lawrence promised Pinker 'I'll try and get more stories done' (iii. 365). The setting, based on Eastwood, links it with 'Adolf', 'Rex', 'Tickets Please' and 'The Last Straw' which were written between March and May 1919, while similarities in theme with 'The Fox', written late in November 1918, might suggest an even earlier date. In July 1919, however, Lawrence was contemplating cuts to 'The Fox' for publication. His decision that he could not shorten it, announced to Pinker with some warmth, shows that 'The Fox' was very much in his mind at the time (iii. 371, 373–4). At all events, Pinker had the story entitled 'You Touched Me' in his possession by the end of 1919, as he returned the manuscript (or typescript) to Lawrence in February 1920.

The story was published by *Land and Water* (Per) on 29 April 1920. Despite the late date, this could have been through Pinker's agency; but Lawrence may have placed the story himself. At Christmas 1919 in Capri, he had renewed his acquaintance with Compton Mackenzie, and indeed stayed in one of Mackenzie's houses on the island. He described Mackenzie as 'a man one can trust and like'.[66] Mackenzie may have suggested Hubert Foss, assistant editor of *Land and Water*, as a likely publisher of Lawrence's work. In March, Lawrence wrote to Mackenzie asking for the name and address of the '*Land and Water* man' for a friend – implying some prior discussion of Foss between them (iii. 480).

Neither the manuscript nor the typescripts of this story are located, but it seems that Lawrence did not make many changes to it for A1. In December 1921 he sent his revised copy to Mountsier, but to Curtis

---

[65] See above pp. xxv–xxvi and footnote 17.

[66] Sir Edward Compton Mackenzie, Scottish novelist. See also footnote 11 and *Letters*, iii. 476.

Brown he simply sent a *Land and Water* copy. Later, realising that it had been heavily cut, he arranged for Mountsier 'to send a true copy from America' (iv. 144), probably a typescript of his revised copy. A comparison of Per and A1 reveals that *Land and Water* cut some 300 words. On the other hand, among his own revisions in 1921, Lawrence appears to have removed one passage of 60 words which had appeared in the periodical text.[67] He drew the attention of both his agents to the new title: '"Hadrian" – originally "You Touched Me"', and again: '"You Touched Me" – re-christened "Hadrian"' (iv. 144–5). But this change was ignored by Seltzer, who retained the old title. While A1 is the base-text for this edition, Lawrence's final, preferred title has been adopted.

'Samson and Delilah'

Originally entitled 'The Prodigal Husband' in manuscript, this 'story. . .which I don't much care for', as Lawrence described it, was completed by 6 November 1916 at Higher Tregerthen in Cornwall (iii. 100, 22). Although he lived for some two years in Cornwall, this is his only story with a Cornish setting. Lawrence sent Pinker MS (Roberts E352.7), a small exercise-book, on 6 November. Pinker had it typed, and Lawrence returned the corrected typescript to him on 17 November, noting that he had 're-christened it' – presumably as 'Samson and Delilah' (iii. 34). The story, accepted by the *English Review* by 20 January 1917 (iii. 79), was published in the March issue (Per1). It was reprinted – heavily cut – by the *Lantern* in America in June (Per2).[68]

Lawrence made some changes to the story, particularly to its ending, when preparing it for the *England, My England* collection, possibly using both MS and Per1 in his revision.[69] It was one of the five stories retyped in Florence by Mrs Carmichael. The base-text for this edition is MS, which is incomplete by a leaf or two. It is emended from Per1 and A1.

---

[67] See Textual apparatus for 92:32.

[68] DHL had nothing to do with Per2 which was almost certainly reprinted from Per1. Pinker had made two typescripts from MS, one of which went to the *English Review*. The other was with the *Century Magazine*, which declined it, until May 1918 (*Century Magazine*, T. R. Smith, to Pinker, 8 May 1918, NYPL). In reprinting, Per2 cut almost 1000 words from the text and made many punctuation and spelling changes. Since it is of no value in establishing the transmission of the text, only its few substantive variants are noted in the apparatus.

[69] In A1, 9 substantive readings from MS are not in Per1, 5 from Per1 are not in MS, e.g. 'dark, young, expressionless' (MS), 'dark, living, young' (Per1); 'bright, mindless' (Per1), 'inexpressive' (MS) (110:27, 109:28).

'The Primrose Path'

This is the only story in the *England, My England* volume to come from Lawrence's pre-war period of short-story writing. During their return to England in 1913, the Lawrences were on holiday in July at Broadstairs, Kent. 'I have been grubbing away among the short stories', Lawrence noted. 'God, I shall be glad when it is done. . .We bathe, and I write among the babies of the foreshore: it is an innocent life, and a dull one' (ii. 48). The stories he was revising included several that were to be collected in *The Prussian Officer* volume in 1914. 'The Primrose Path', completed towards the end of the month, may have been begun in Italy. The first ten leaves of the manuscript (Roberts E322.7a) are from an Italian exercise-book. On the verso of some pages Frieda has written out exercises in the Italian language.

In a letter of 28 July Lawrence apologised to his typist Douglas Clayton for the 'very shocking' state of the manuscript, explaining: 'I hadn't an inch of paper when I began' (ii. 52). Lawrence had once given Katharine Clayton (Constance Garnett's younger sister) permission to 'alter anything that seems to you wrong – these MSS are *so* slovenly' (ii. 30). In this case the typescript (TS) her son Douglas produced (Roberts E322.7b) contains numerous changes in both punctuation and wording from MS which, while it is messy, is by no means illegible. Evidently Clayton believed he had authority to make alterations.[70]

Before returning to Europe the following month, Lawrence left both MS and TS with his old friend Edward Garnett. By December 1913, it would seem, Garnett had been unable to place the story, for Lawrence wrote to him gloomily: 'As for the "Primrose Path" – who *would* print it' (ii. 127). Nevertheless it may have been in the hope of its eventual periodical publication that Lawrence did not include it with the group he assembled for *The Prussian Officer* volume in 1914. In the same letter, he asked Garnett to return it to him 'some day when it is convenient'. This he evidently did not do, for in July 1914 Lawrence asked Clayton to send a new copy of the story to Pinker (ii. 201). Pinker was as unsuccessful in placing it as Garnett had been.

In June 1915, having just completed 'England, My England', Lawrence sent Pinker a letter he had received from an American editor. He did not indicate either the contents or the name of the sender (ii. 354). Two days later, evidently at Pinker's suggestion, Lawrence arranged with Clayton to

---

[70] For further evidence of Clayton's alterations see *The Prussian Officer*, ed. Worthen, p. xxxvi.

make yet another copy of 'The Primrose Path' (ii. 356). Then in August, Carl Hovey of the *Metropolitan* in New York cabled Pinker requesting a story from Lawrence for the October issue. Probably Hovey was the 'American' of Lawrence's letters in June, since the cable presumes that negotiations with Pinker were already established and indicates an immediate opening for publication. In this case, the new typing of 'The Primrose Path' would have been intended for Hovey. Lawrence's typescript of 'England, My England', the only other story currently available, had by this time gone to the *English Review*. Finally, the *Metropolitan* wrote to Pinker in November returning a story with the comment that 'the end is weak and rather pointless'.[71] Such a criticism, if in fact made of 'The Primrose Path', gives an indication of why it never found a publisher in Lawrence's lifetime.

Six years later, when calling in his manuscripts, he remembered the story and, on 17 October 1921, wrote to Garnett from Sicily asking him to return it (iv. 100). Garnett returned Clayton's 1913 TS which has Garnett's name and address on the title page. It arrived on 10 November (iv. 115). Because he had made revisions to it and because he needed two copies, Lawrence had the story retyped. At the beginning of December he sent copies to Mountsier and Curtis Brown.[72] These new typescripts have since disappeared but they included the seven changes in wording and one new sentence which Lawrence had added in ink to the 1913 TS.[73]

Clayton's interference with Lawrence's manuscript version in making TS was extensive – in all, 99 alterations in the typing, eleven of them substantive, some of them subtle in effect. When revising, Lawrence noticed only a very few: it was, after all, eight years since he had written the story and he did not have his MS. He was, characteristically, more concerned to make revisions to the story before him than to check the accuracy of a typescript. In 26 autograph markings on TS, about half are substantive revisions. Lawrence's MS has been taken as the base-text for this edition. It has been emended to include his revisions to TS and the later substantive changes which appear in A1. The Textual apparatus indicates the extent of Clayton's 'editing' of the manuscript.[74]

---

[71] See pp. xxxii–xxxiii and footnote 42. The Hovey cable is also in NYPL.
[72] Diary entries for 1 and 12 December 1921 (Tedlock, *Lawrence MSS* 94).
[73] See Textual apparatus for 124:20, 125:29, etc. It is possible, of course, that these changes had already been made in 1913.
[74] The two other TSS of this story (Roberts E322c and d) are later copies and have no value in establishing the text.

'The Horse-Dealer's Daughter'

Entitled 'The Miracle', this story was written at the end of 1916 when Lawrence was in Cornwall. It was probably the story he told Pinker he had 'on hand' as he was completing *Women in Love* in November (iii. 29). On 12 January 1917 he sent it to Pinker, commenting: 'I send you the MS. of another story – "The Miracle", which is beautiful and ends happily, so the swine of people ought to be very thankful for it' (iii. 74). Happy ending or not, no periodical took the story, and in 1920 it came back to Lawrence in Sicily after his break with Pinker.

Lawrence's diary for 26 October 1921 records the next stage of its development: 'Have written over The Miracle story, sent it to Mrs Carmichael to type – called now The Horse-Dealers Daughter.'[75] The completed typescript, presumably in two copies, was returned on 30 October and went along with other stories to Mountsier and to Curtis Brown.[76] Curtis Brown was able to place it with the *English Review* (Per) where it appeared in April 1922.

Lawrence received the proofs of this version in Ceylon on 11 April but wrote to the editor, Austin Harrison: 'I got the proofs of "The Horsedealer's Daughter" here this morning. No good sending them back – you'll have printed the thing doubtless by the time you get this' (iv. 226). It was the last contact that Lawrence had with the story. There are four substantive variants between Per and A1, all more likely to have been of typesetting or editorial rather than authorial origin. Neither the manuscript nor any of the typescripts has survived, and the *English Review* version is taken as the base-text for this edition. The story was reprinted from A1 in *The Best British Short Stories of 1923*, ed. J. O'Brien and John Cournos (Boston, 1923), pp. 175–93.

'The Last Straw' ['Fanny and Annie']

Lawrence had a similar lack of success with the periodical publication of 'Fanny and Annie' until 1921. Having completed the revisions of *Movements in European History* at Middleton, Derbyshire during April 1919, he wrote to Pinker 'that for the next six weeks I will write nothing but short stories, if the short stories will come. It's as good a promise as I can make' (iii. 355). Exactly a fortnight after this promise, on 14 May, he despatched

[75] Tedlock, *Lawrence MSS* 93; see also *Letters*, iv. 107.
[76] Tedlock, *Lawrence MSS* 93–4.

'Fanny and Annie' to Pinker with a note: 'I send you "Fanny and Annie". I hope it is the right sort. If you think it would be better with a different ending, I will write a different ending if you send the MS. back' (iii. 360).

Both this flurry of activity and his concern about the ending were Lawrence's response to a show of interest in his work by the *Cosmopolitan* magazine, the details of which Pinker had sent on. Nothing is known of the offer, but Lawrence evidently believed that his existing stories were 'not in their line'.[77] Neither, it seems, was 'Fanny and Annie'.

At the time of his break with Pinker, it may have been the manuscript that was returned to him in Sicily. When he sent the story to Mountsier in July 1920, he asked him to have it typed for simultaneous magazine publication in both USA and England (iii. 576). Three months later, in October, he reminded Mountsier emphatically *'You have the only copy'*, adding that it was not on offer to English publishers (iii. 613). Mountsier reported in December that the *Century* and the *Atlantic Monthly* had refused it, most likely because of its 'too Englishness' (iii. 644 n.). The previous August Lawrence had asked Mountsier to send a copy to J. C. Squire, editor of the *London Mercury*, but he also refused it (iii. 582, 681). Nevertheless, Squire was probably responsible for passing it on successfully to *Hutchinson's Story Magazine* the following year. Lawrence had corrected their proofs by 26 October,[78] and the story was published in the issue of 21 November 1921 (Per).

By this time Lawrence was noting: 'Book of stories nearly ready'.[79] It is clear from A1 that he made a number of significant changes to the text of 'Fanny and Annie' at this time, but there is no record of its having been retyped. As he had no previous typescripts, he probably used copies of the *Hutchinson's* version for the revision. On 29 December he notified Secker that he wanted the title changed to 'The Last Straw' (iv. 152), but seems not to have told Seltzer or Mountsier, so that the story retained his original title in A1.

For the present edition, Per is taken as the base-text; with Lawrence's revisions, it was probably the copy-text for A1. He had corrected the proofs of Per which retains many of his distinctive forms, particularly in direct speech. The base-text is emended from A1 to take account of his subsequent revisions, and Lawrence's final title is adopted.

[77] This offer is most likely to have been the 'Fanny & Annie' agreement which DHL forwarded to Mountsier on 23 July 1920, having received it along with others from Pinker (diary entry for 23 July 1920, Tedlock, *Lawrence MSS* 91).

[78] Tedlock, *Lawrence MSS* 93.

[79] Diary entry for 13 November 1921 (Tedlock, *Lawrence MSS* 94).

With its original title, 'Fanny and Annie' was the final story in the *England, My England* volume.

Uncollected Stories, 1913–22

'The Mortal Coil'

After their visit to England in the summer of 1913, the Lawrences returned to Italy where they settled in a 'lovely little 4 roomed cottage on a tiny little bay' at Lerici on 4 October 1913 (ii. 79). Soon after their arrival, Lawrence received a letter on behalf of Austin Harrison, editor of the *English Review*, offering him £15 apiece for his stories 'Honour and Arms' ('The Prussian Officer') and 'Vin Ordinaire' ('The Thorn in the Flesh'), and inviting him to submit one or two more stories 'on similar lines' (ii. 81 n., 82 and n. 2).[80] Commenting to Edward Garnett on this proposal, Lawrence suggested that Harrison be offered the story 'Once—!', and that for 'a fourth, I think I would write one I have had in my mind for a long time' (ii. 82). This was most probably 'The Mortal Coil', based on an incident in the life of Frieda's father, Friedrich Freiherr von Richthofen.[81] By 31 October, after a period of inactivity, Lawrence told Garnett that he was 'just finishing' the story, but that there was no further news of publication from the *English Review* (ii. 99). He completed the story by 2 November (ii. 99). Some time before 21 December Harrison confirmed his intention to publish 'the 4 soldier stories soon' (ii. 127), but in the end took only the first two. The manuscript of 'The Mortal Coil' was among those left in Italy when Lawrence returned to England in June 1914.

In September 1916, now in Cornwall, Lawrence received an invitation to submit short stories to a new little magazine, *Seven Arts*, to be published in New York. Two months earlier he had received a bundle of his manuscripts from Italy (ii. 630), among them 'one or two stories, that want doing up, and then are all right' (ii. 653). On 31 October he sent 'The Mortal Coil' to Pinker, 're-written from MS' which it seems he had just recently received. With a pun on the *Strand* magazine, which he believed would probably not take it, he added, 'It is a first-class story, one of my purest creations, but not destined, I fear, like the holy in the hymn, to land – On the golden Strand – Where the ransomed in glory we see. I really grieve when I send you still another unmarketable wretch of fiction' (ii. 669). Pinker had a typescript made, which Lawrence returned to him, after

---

[80] See also *The Prussian Officer*, ed. Worthen, pp. xxv, xxix and *Love Among the Haystacks*, ed. Worthen, pp. xxxv–xxxvi.

[81] See Martin Green, *The von Richthofen Sisters* (New York, 1974), pp. 12, 347.

revision, on 13 November (iii. 28). After the *English Review*, approached again by Pinker, refused to take the story, it was accepted by the *Seven Arts* – 'the cent-a-worders' in Lawrence's phrase – and was published there (Per) in July 1917 (ii. 670 and n. 2).

Neither Lawrence's manuscript nor the corrected typescript, which was the setting-copy for the *Seven Arts*, survives.[82] The story is known only in Per, which is thus the base-text for this edition; it was reprinted in 1968 in *Phoenix II*.

'The Thimble'

In August 1915, Lawrence had left the Meynell cottage in Greatham, Sussex and moved to London. From his new quarters in Hampstead he wrote to Lady Cynthia Asquith on 29 October 1915 that he was finishing a story, and confessed that he had included a portrait of her (ii. 418–19). When she received the completed manuscript two days later, she commented in her diary: 'I *was* amused to see the "word picture" of me. He has quite gratuitously put in the large feet' (ii. 420 and n. 1). This story was 'The Thimble'. On its return from Lady Cynthia, Lawrence sent it to Pinker on 2 November (ii. 426). Pinker had it typed but was unable to place the story until ten months later when the invitation came from the *Seven Arts* magazine. Pinker forwarded 'The Thimble' through his American agent, Paul R. Reynolds, and Lawrence reported its acceptance by the magazine on 11 December 1916 (iii. 50). It was published in the issue of March 1917 (Per), and Lawrence received a copy the following month (iii. 111).

When reviewing his stories in 1921, Lawrence saw possibilities in 'The Thimble' for development into a novelette, as he wrote to Mountsier: 'I am doing a third long story – "The Thimble" – to go with "Fox" and "Captain's Doll" in one volume...I want [these] to be one volume by themselves...' (iv. 134). On 9 January he sent typescripts of the story – now called 'The Ladybird' – to Mountsier and Curtis Brown.[83]

He had grown to dislike the first form of the story. In 1924 he recalled for his bibliographer, Edward McDonald, that 'there was a first (not very good) story, called "The Thimble", appeared in some out of the way

---

[82] The surviving typescript at UT (Roberts E246.8) is part of an uncorrected copy of Per made for possible inclusion in *Phoenix*.

[83] Tedlock, *Lawrence MSS* 95. See *The Ladybird* volume to be published by Cambridge University Press.

American magazine – can't remember its name – would rather like "The Thimble" to disappear into oblivion – but confess to it' (v. 104).

None of the typescripts of this story has survived but Lawrence's manuscript (Roberts E396.7a) has. This manuscript (MS), corrected for substantive changes from the *Seven Arts* text (Per), is the base-text for this edition. It is clear that Lawrence made one or two corrections to the typescript before returning it to Pinker, but he saw no proofs of the magazine version, which also shows evidence of house-styling.[84] 'The Thimble' was reprinted in *Phoenix II*.

'Adolf' and 'Rex'

These two sketches, based on childhood experiences, were probably written together in 1919. Early in March of that year, John Middleton Murry invited Lawrence to contribute to his fairly conservative magazine, the *Athenæum*. At first pleased by the invitation, Lawrence replied to Murry saying: 'I will try to be pleasant and a bit old-fashioned' (iii. 332). At the time, he had been so seriously ill with influenza and its complications that he had been moved from Mountain Cottage in Derbyshire to the home and care of his sister Ada Clarke in Ripley. Nevertheless, during his convalescence he told Koteliansky on 14 March that he had begun to write for the *Athenæum* (iii. 337). Among the works he began, and presumably continued after his return to Mountain Cottage on 17 March, were 'Adolf' and 'Rex'. Perhaps these recollections of childhood arose from Lawrence's being in the care of his favourite sister, Ada, and closer to his family than he had been for some years.

On 11 April, Murry published the first contribution from Lawrence, 'Whistling of Birds', but used a pseudonym – 'Grantorto'.[85] He had, one week before, declined 'with thanks' the other submissions (iii. 346). Murry later recollected that he had rejected 'Adolf', though from what he added, and Catherine Carswell also claimed, he rejected more than one piece.[86] There is no firm evidence that 'Rex' was among them, though given the close relationship of the subjects, it would seem likely that they were written and submitted at the same time. The earliest typescripts of each

---

84 E.g., see Textual apparatus for 192:31, 193:30.
85 *Athenæum*, 11 April 1919, pp. 167–8 and see *Reflections on the Death of a Porcupine*, ed. Herbert, pp. xxvii–xxviii, xli–xlii, 21–40.
86 J. Middleton Murry, *Reminiscences of D. H. Lawrence* (1933), pp. 96–8, 141ff.; Catherine Carswell, *The Savage Pilgrimage*, p. 108. Another probable reject was the essay 'Clouds', published in *Reflections on the Death of a Porcupine*, ed. Herbert, pp. 55–60.

story were done by the same typist and both carry Lawrence's own corrections: the typed carbon copy of 'Rex' (Roberts E349.5b), and the typescript of 'Adolf' (TS1, Roberts E3.3a). After Murry's refusal, Lawrence may have tried to place the two sketches elsewhere, but no record of his attempts has survived.

Early in 1920, the *Dial* made an approach to Lawrence, who was now living in Sicily, possibly through Richard Aldington.[87] Lawrence offered 'Adolf' which the editor, Scofield Thayer, accepted for $40 (£9-17-6)[88] and added a request for another contribution. On 30 May, Lawrence wrote a note to Aldington on the back of page 7 of the manuscript of 'Rex', offering it to the *Dial* and asking for the bill for making a typescript (iii. 536). An entry in Lawrence's diary for 20 June 1920 reads: 'Sent Richard Rex, to go with Adolf, for the Dial',[89] which suggests that for some reason he delayed sending the manuscript until three weeks after writing the note to Aldington. A typescript must subsequently have been made, but is now unlocated. Lawrence's manuscript (Roberts E349.5a) is marked for a wordcount and assessed at $50 at the top of page 1; it is not, however, marked for the printer and so was not used as the setting-copy. In the case of 'Adolf', the position is reversed. The manuscript of 'Adolf' is lost, but the *Dial* papers include a typescript (TS2, Roberts E3.3c) which is marked in detail for the printer. TS2 incorporated the autograph revisions to TS1 – possibly from a duplicate copy since it differs in some respects from TS1.

'Adolf' was published in the *Dial* for September 1920 (Per), and Lawrence recorded payment 'via Richard' on 26 July.[90] 'Rex' appeared in the issue of February 1921 (Per). Lawrence was pleased, and 'the money is very attractive' he told Aldington (iii. 536). The *Dial*'s editing of his stories was comparatively slight but of some importance, consisting mostly of the removal of Lawrence's emphases. That these excisions were the work of a copy-editor is evident from the typescript of 'Adolf' where all the underlining has been cancelled, thus removing Lawrence's careful pointing of the intonations of speech. Similar use of underlining is very clear in the manuscript of 'Rex'. In the printing there were some careless misreadings, even the omission of one sentence from 'Adolf'. If Lawrence corrected proofs of both stories, he can have made few corrections. He acknowledged receipt of the proofs of 'Rex' from Mountsier on 9

---

[87] A diary entry for 13 February 1920 (Tedlock, *Lawrence MSS* 89) records DHL's receipt of a letter from the editor of the *Dial*, Scofield Thayer, which may have been a request for a story. Payment for 'Adolf', however, was received 'via Richard' and negotiations with the *Dial* for 'Rex' were conducted through Aldington (see below).

[88] *Letters*, iii. 536 and n. and diary entry for 26 July 1920 (Tedlock, *Lawrence MSS* 91).

[89] Tedlock, *Lawrence MSS* 90.   [90] Tedlock, *Lawrence MSS* 91.

December 1920 and a copy of the published story on 28 February 1921 (iii. 634, 675).

Lawrence's proposal that 'Adolf' and 'Rex' might be included in the Secker edition of *England, My England* has already been discussed. Neither story appeared in collected form in Lawrence's lifetime. 'Adolf' was first published in England in the *New Keepsake for 1921* (E1) in December of that year, its source having apparently been close to an unedited version of the *Dial* typescript TS2. In 1931 the sketch replaced the early essay 'Rachel Annand Taylor' in Secker's English edition of *Young Lorenzo*, entitled *Early Life of D. H. Lawrence*.[91] 'Rex' appeared in *Stories from the Dial*, published in England by Jonathan Cape, in February 1924 (E1). Both were reprinted in *Phoenix*.

The base-text for 'Rex' in this edition is Lawrence's manuscript (MS). The absence of a manuscript for 'Adolf' makes it necessary to consider two typescripts. The earlier TS1 contains some typing errors but also Lawrence's autograph corrections and additions which appear in all later states except the *Early Life* text, for which either the manuscript or an uncorrected typescript appears to have been used. TS1, however, does not include Lawrence's underlinings which were reproduced in the later typescript (TS2) only to be removed editorially when it was being marked up as setting-copy for the *Dial* printer. These underlinings do appear in the *Keepsake* version. The base-text for 'Adolf' in this edition is TS1, and it is emended from TS2.

---

[91] See *Study of Thomas Hardy*, ed. Steele, pp. xlii–xliv, 143–8. The texts in *Early Life*, including 'Adolf', are unreliable in their treatment of the details of DHL's MSS and TSS.

ENGLAND, MY ENGLAND AND OTHER STORIES

Note on the texts

For two of the ten stories in *England, My England and Other Stories*, the base-texts in this edition are the first American edition (A1) published on 24 October 1922 by Thomas Seltzer. These stories are:

'England, My England': A1 is emended once from the first English edition (E1 except where otherwise indicated), published by Martin Secker in January 1924.

'Hadrian': A1 is emended from the text ('You Touched Me') in *Land and Water* (29 April 1920, pp. 25–9) (Per).

The base-texts for the remaining eight stories are:

'Tickets Please': Per2, the text in the *Metropolitan* (August 1919, pp. 26–8, 80), emended from A1 and collated with the text in the *Strand* (April 1919, pp. 287–93) (Per1) and with E1.

'The Blind Man': Per1, the text in the *English Review* (xxvii, July 1920, pp. 22–41), emended from A1 and collated with E1 and the *Living Age* (7 August 1920, pp. 358–370) (Per2).

'Monkey Nuts': Per, the text in the *Sovereign* (22 August 1922, pp. 229–36), emended from A1 and collated with E1.

'Wintry Peacock': Per, the text in the *Metropolitan* (21 August 1921, pp. 21–2, 48–9) emended from MS (Roberts E437a) in the possession of Mr George Lazarus. It is collated with A1, the version in *New Decameron*, pp. 123–46 (here E1), and Secker's *England, My England* (here E2).

'Samson and Delilah': MS (Roberts E352.7), located at UT, emended from A1 and the text in the *English Review* (xxiv, March 1917, pp. 209–24) (Per1) and collated with E1.

'The Primrose Path': MS (Roberts E322.7a), located at UN, emended from TS (Roberts E322.7b), located at UT, and A1, and collated with E1.

'The Horse-Dealer's Daughter': Per, the text in the *English Review* (April 1922), emended from A1 and collated with E1.

'The Last Straw': Per, the text ('Fanny and Annie') in *Hutchinson's Story Magazine* (21 November 1921, pp. 461–9), emended from A1 and collated with E1.

The base-texts for the four additional stories in this volume are:

'The Mortal Coil': Per, the only surviving text in the *Seven Arts* (July 1917, pp. 280–305).

'The Thimble': MS (Roberts E396.7a), located at StaU, emended from the text in the *Seven Arts* (March 1917, pp. 435–48) (Per).

'Adolf': TS1 (Roberts E3.3a), located at UT, emended from TS2 (Roberts E3.3c), located at YU and collated with the texts in the *Dial* (lxix, September 1920, pp. 269–76) (Per) and *The New Keepsake for 1921*, pp. 19–33 (here E1).

'Rex': MS (Roberts E349.5a), located at YU, emended from the text in the *Dial* (lxx, February 1921, pp. 169–76) (Per) and collated with TS (Roberts E349.5b), and the text in *Stories from The Dial*, pp. 37–52 (here E1).

The apparatus records all variants between the base-texts and the texts printed in this edition. It also records variants from all versions of the stories published in DHL's lifetime.

The following practice is followed:

1. Clearly inadvertent errors and obvious typesetter's errors, e.g. 'beautifiul', or the omission of inverted commas, are silently emended.

2. A1 and E1 consistently printed story-titles in bold capitals, and DHL sometimes put a full stop after titles in manuscript; emendation to upper and lower case type and deletion of full stops are not recorded.

3. Mr., Mrs. in 'Wintry Peacock' (A1), 'Samson and Delilah' (all printed versions), 'The Primrose Path' (TS, A1) and Mr, Mrs in 'The Blind Man' (E1), 'Hadrian' (E1), 'The Last Straw' (E1) are not recorded unless in conjunction with another variant.

4. The following variations are not recorded unless in conjunction with another variant: '-is-' and '-iz-', 'gray' and 'grey', 'labor' and 'labour', 'odor' and 'odour', 'whiskey' and 'whisky', 'favorite' and 'favourite', 'to-night' and 'tonight', 'to-morrow' and 'tomorrow', 'canceled' and 'cancelled', 'trammeling' and 'trammelling', 'quarreling' and 'quarrelling'.

5. In 'Tickets Please' the spellings 'Thermopylæ' (A1 and E1) for 'Thermopylae' and 'sha'n't' (Per1 and A1) are not recorded. In 'The Blind Man' the forms 'did n't', 'is n't' and 'you 're' in Per2 are not recorded.

6. In 'Samson and Delilah' only substantive variants from Per2 are recorded, see Introduction, p. xlii and Explanatory note on 108:13.

England, My England[*]

He was working on the edge of the common, beyond the small brook that ran in the dip at the bottom of the garden, carrying the garden path in continuation from the plank bridge on to the common. He had cut the rough turf and bracken, leaving the grey, dryish soil bare. 5
But he was worried because he could not get the path straight, there was a pleat between his brows. He had set up his sticks, and taken the sights between the big pine trees, but for some reason everything seemed wrong. He looked again, straining his keen blue eyes, that had a touch of the Viking in them, through the shadowy pine trees as 10
through a doorway, at the green-grassed garden-path rising from the shadow of alders by the log bridge up to the sunlit flowers. Tall white and purple columbines, and the butt-end of the old Hampshire cottage that crouched near the earth amid flowers, blossoming in the bit of shaggy wildness round about. 15

There was a sound of children's voices calling and talking: high, childish, girlish voices, slightly didactic and tinged with domineering: "If you don't come quick, nurse, I shall run out there to where there are snakes." And nobody had the *sang-froid* to reply: "Run then, little fool." It was always "No, darling. Very well, darling. In a 20
moment, darling. Darling, you *must* be patient."

His heart was hard with disillusion: a continual gnawing and resistance. But he worked on. What was there to do but submit!

The sunlight blazed down upon the earth, there was a vividness of flamy vegetation, of fierce seclusion amid the savage peace of the 25
commons. Strange how the savage England lingers in patches: as here, amid these shaggy gorse commons, and marshy, snake-infested places near the foot of the south downs. The spirit of place lingering on primeval, as when the Saxons[*] came, so long ago.

Ah, how he had loved it! The green garden path, the tufts of 30
flowers, purple and white columbines, and great oriental red poppies with their black chaps, and mulleins[*] tall and yellow: this flamy garden which had been a garden for a thousand years, scooped out in the little hollow among the snake-infested commons. He had made it

5

flame with flowers, in a sun cup under its hedges and trees. So old, so old a place! And yet he had re-created it.

The timbered cottage with its sloping, cloak-like roof was old and forgotten. It belonged to the old England of hamlets and yeomen.
5 Lost all alone on the edge of the common, at the end of a wide, grassy, briar-entangled lane shaded with oak, it had never known the world of to-day. Not till Egbert came with his bride. And he had come to fill it with flowers.

The house was ancient and very uncomfortable. But he did not
10 want to alter it. Ah, marvellous to sit there in the wide, black, time-old chimney, at night when the wind roared overhead, and the wood which he had chopped himself sputtered on the hearth! Himself on one side the angle, and Winifred on the other.

Ah, how he had wanted her: Winifred! She was young and
15 beautiful and strong with life, like a flame in sunshine. She moved with a slow grace of energy like a blossoming, red-flowered bush in motion. She, too, seemed to come out of the old England, ruddy, strong, with a certain crude, passionate quiescence and a hawthorn robustness. And he, he was tall and slim and agile, like an English
20 archer, with his long, supple legs and fine movements. Her hair was nut-brown and all in energic curls and tendrils. Her eyes were nut-brown, too, like a robin's for brightness. And he was white-skinned with fine, silky hair that had darkened from fair, and a slightly arched nose of an old country family. They were a beautiful
25 couple.

The house was Winifred's. Her father was a man of energy too. He had come from the north poor. Now he was moderately rich. He had bought this fair stretch of inexpensive land, down in Hampshire. Not far from the tiny church of the almost extinct hamlet stood his
30 own house, a commodious old farm-house standing back from the road across a bare grassed yard. On one side of this quadrangle was the long, long barn or shed* which he had made into a cottage for his youngest daughter Priscilla. One saw little blue-and-white check curtains at the long windows, and inside, overhead, the grand old
35 timbers of the high-pitched shed. This was Prissy's house. Fifty yards away was the pretty little new cottage which he had built for his daughter Magdalen, with the vegetable garden stretching away to the oak copse. And then away beyond the lawns and rose-trees of the house-garden went the track across a shaggy, wild grass space,
40 towards the ridge of tall black pines that grew on a dyke-bank,

through the pines and above the sloping little bog, under the wide, desolate oak trees, till there was Winifred's cottage crouching unexpectedly in front, so much alone, and so primitive.

It was Winifred's own house, and the gardens and the bit of common and the boggy slope were hers: her tiny domain. She had married just at the time when her father had bought the estate, about ten years before the war, so she had been able to come to Egbert with this for a marriage portion. And who was more delighted, he or she, it would be hard to say. She was only twenty at the time, and he was only twenty-one. He had about a hundred and fifty pounds a year of his own—and nothing else but his very considerable personal attractions. He had no profession: he earned nothing. But he talked of literature and music, he had a passion for old folk-music, collecting folk-songs and folk-dances, studying the Morris-dance and the old customs.* Of course in time he would make money in these ways.

Meanwhile youth and health and passion and promise. Winifred's father was always generous: but still, he was a man from the north with a hard head and a hard skin too, having received a good many knocks. At home he kept the hard head out of sight, and played at poetry and romance with his literary wife and his sturdy, passionate girls. He was a man of courage, not given to complaining, bearing his burdens by himself. No, he did not let the world intrude far into his home. He had a delicate, sensitive wife whose poetry won some fame in the narrow world of letters. He himself, with his tough old barbarian fighting spirit, had an almost child-like delight in verse, in sweet poetry, and in the delightful game of a cultured home. His blood was strong even to coarseness. But that only made the home more vigorous, more robust and Christmassy. There was always a touch of Christmas about him, now he was well off. If there was poetry after dinner, there were also chocolates, and nuts, and good little out-of-the-way things to be munching.

Well then, into this family came Egbert. He was made of quite a different paste. The girls and the father were strong-limbed, thick-blooded people, true English, as holly-trees and hawthorn are English. Their culture was grafted on to them, as one might perhaps graft a common pink rose on to a thorn-stem. It flowered oddly enough, but it did not alter their blood.

And Egbert was a born rose. The age-long breeding had left him with a delightful spontaneous passion. He was not clever, nor even

"literary." No, but the intonation of his voice, and the movement of his supple, handsome body, and the fine texture of his flesh and his hair, the slight arch of his nose, the quickness of his blue eyes would easily take the place of poetry. Winifred loved him, loved him, this
5 southerner, as a higher being. A *higher* being, mind you. Not a deeper. And as for him, he loved her in passion with every fibre of him. She was the very warm stuff of life to him.

Wonderful then, those days at Crockham Cottage, the first days, all alone save for the woman who came to work in the mornings.
10 Marvellous days, when she had all his tall, supple, fine-fleshed youth to herself, for herself, and he had her like a ruddy fire into which he could cast himself for rejuvenation. Ah, that it might never end, this passion, this marriage! The flame of their two bodies burnt again into that old cottage, that was haunted already by so much by-gone,
15 physical desire. You could not be in the dark room for an hour without the influences coming over you. The hot blood-desire of by-gone yeomen, there in this old den where they had lusted and bred for so many generations. The silent house, dark, with thick, timbered walls and the big black chimney-place, and the sense of secrecy.
20 Dark, with low, little windows, sunk into the earth. Dark, like a lair where strong beasts had lurked and mated, lonely at night and lonely by day, left to themselves and their own intensity for so many generations. It seemed to cast a spell on the two young people. They became different. There was a curious secret glow about them, a
25 certain slumbering flame hard to understand, that enveloped them both. They too felt that they did not belong to the London world any more. Crockham had changed their blood: the sense of the snakes that lived and slept even in their own garden, in the sun, so that he, going forward with the spade, would see a curious coiled brownish
30 pile on the black soil, which suddenly would start up, hiss, and dazzle rapidly away, hissing. One day Winifred heard the strangest scream from the flower-bed under the low window of the living room: ah, the strangest scream, like the very soul of the dark past crying aloud. She ran out, and saw a long brown snake on the flower-bed, and in
35 its flat mouth the one hind leg of a frog was striving to escape, and screaming its strange, tiny, bellowing scream. She looked at the snake, and from its sullen flat head it looked at her, obstinately. She gave a cry, and it released the frog and slid angrily away.

That was Crockham. The spear of modern invention had not
40 passed through it, and it lay there secret, primitive, savage as when

the Saxons first came. And Egbert and she were caught there, caught out of the world.

He was not idle, nor was she. There were plenty of things to be done, the house to be put into final repair after the workmen had gone, cushions and curtains to sew, the paths to make, the water to fetch and attend to, and then the slope of the deep-soiled, neglected garden to level, to terrace with little terraces and paths, and to fill with flowers. He worked away, in his shirt-sleeves, worked all day intermittently doing this thing and the other. And she, quiet and rich in herself, seeing him stooping and labouring away by himself, would come to help him, to be near him. He of course was an amateur—a born amateur. He worked so hard, and did so little, and nothing he ever did would hold together for long. If he terraced the garden, he held up the earth with a couple of long narrow planks that soon began to bend with the pressure from behind, and would not need many years to rot through and break and let the soil slither all down again in a heap towards the stream-bed. But there you are. He had not been brought up to come to grips with anything, and he thought it would do. Nay, he did not think there was anything else except little temporary contrivances possible, he who had such a passion for his old enduring cottage, and for the old enduring things of the by-gone England. Curious that the sense of permanency in the past had such a hold over him, whilst in the present he was all amateurish and sketchy.

Winifred could not criticise him. Town-bred, everything seemed to her splendid, and the very digging and shovelling itself seemed romantic. But neither Egbert nor she yet realised the difference between work and romance.

Godfrey Marshall, her father, was at first perfectly pleased with the ménage down at Crockham Cottage. He thought Egbert was wonderful, the many things he accomplished, and he was gratified by the glow of physical passion between the two young people. To the man who in London still worked hard to keep steady his modest fortune, the thought of this young couple digging away and loving one another down at Crockham Cottage, buried deep among the commons and marshes, near the pale-showing bulk of the downs, was like a chapter of living romance. And they drew the sustenance for their fire of passion from him, from the old man. It was he who fed their flame. He triumphed secretly in the thought. And it was to her father that Winifred still turned, as the one source of all surety

and life and support. She loved Egbert with passion. But back of her*
was the power of her father. It was the power of her father she
referred to, whenever she needed to refer. It never occurred to her to
refer to Egbert, if she were in difficulty or doubt. No, in all the *serious*
5   matters she depended on her father.

For Egbert had no intention of coming to grips with life. He had
no ambition whatsoever. He came from a decent family, from a
pleasant country home, from delightful surroundings. He should, of
course, have had a profession. He should have studied law or
10 entered business in some way. But no—that fatal three pounds a
week would keep him from starving as long as he lived, and he did
not want to give himself into bondage. It was not that he was idle. He
was always doing something, in his amateurish way. But he had no
desire to give himself to the world, and still less had he any desire to
15 fight his way in the world. No, no, the world wasn't worth it. He
wanted to ignore it, to go his own way apart, like a casual pilgrim
down the forsaken side-tracks. He loved his wife, his cottage and
garden. He would make his life there, as a sort of epicurean hermit.
He loved the past, the old music and dances and customs of old
20 England. He would try and live in the spirit of these, not in the spirit
of the world of business.

But often Winifred's father called her to London: for he loved to
have his children round him. So Egbert and she must have a tiny flat
in town, and the young couple must transfer themselves from time to
25 time from the country to the city. In town Egbert had plenty of
friends, of the same ineffectual sort as himself, tampering with the
arts, literature, painting, sculpture, music. He was not bored.

Three pounds a week, however, would not pay for all this.
Winifred's father paid. He liked paying. He made her only a very
30 small allowance, but he often gave her ten pounds—or gave Egbert
ten pounds. So they both looked on the old man as the mainstay.
Egbert didn't mind being patronised and paid for. Only when he felt
the family was a little *too* condescending, on account of money, he
began to get huffy.

35   Then of course children came: a lovely little blonde daughter with
a head of thistle-down. Everybody adored the child. It was the first
exquisite blonde thing that had come into the family, a little mite
with the white, slim, beautiful limbs of its father, and as it grew up
the dancing, dainty movement of a wild little daisy-spirit. No wonder
40 the Marshalls all loved the child: they called her Joyce. They

themselves had their own grace, but it was slow, rather heavy. They had everyone of them strong, heavy limbs and darkish skins, and they were short in stature. And now they had for one of their own this light little cowslip child. She was like a little poem in herself.

But nevertheless, she brought a new difficulty. Winifred must have a nurse for her. Yes, yes, there must be a nurse. It was the family decree. Who was to pay for the nurse? The grandfather—seeing the father himself earned no money. Yes, the grandfather would pay, as he had paid all the lying-in expenses. There came a slight sense of money-strain. Egbert was living on his father-in-law.

After the child was born, it was never quite the same between him and Winifred. The difference was at first hardly perceptible. But it was there. In the first place Winifred had a new centre of interest. She was not going to adore her child. But she had what the modern mother so often has in the place of spontaneous love: a profound sense of duty towards her child. Winifred appreciated her darling little girl, and felt a deep sense of duty towards her. Strange, that this sense of duty should go deeper than the love for her husband. But so it was. And so it often is. The responsibility of motherhood was the prime responsibility in Winifred's heart: the responsibility of wife-hood came a long way second.

Her child seemed to link her up again in a circuit with her own family. Her father and mother, herself, and her child, that was the human trinity for her. Her husband—? Yes, she loved him still. But that was like play. She had an almost barbaric sense of duty and of family. Till she married, her first human duty had been towards her father: he was the pillar, the source of life, the everlasting support. Now another link was added to the chain of duty: her father, herself, and her child.

Egbert was out of it. Without anything happening, he was gradually, unconsciously excluded from the circle. His wife still loved him, physically. But, but—he was *almost* the unnecessary party in the affair. He could not complain of Winifred. She still did her duty towards him. She still had a physical passion for him, that physical passion on which he had put all his life and soul. But—but—

It was for a long while an ever-recurring *but*. And then, after the second child, another blonde, winsome touching little thing, not so proud and flame-like as Joyce—after Annabel came, then Egbert began truly to realise how it was. His wife still loved him. But—and now the but had grown enormous—her physical love for him was of secondary importance to her. It became ever less important. After all, she had had it, this physical passion, for two years now. It was not this that one lived from. No, no—something sterner, realer.

5   She began to resent her own passion for Egbert—just a little she began to despise it. For after all there he was, he was charming, he was lovable, he was terribly desirable. But—but—oh the awful looming cloud of that *but!*—He did not stand firm in the landscape of her life like a tower of strength, like a great pillar of significance. No, 10 he was like a cat one has about the house, which will one day disappear and leave no trace. He was like a flower in the garden, trembling in the wind of life, and then gone, leaving nothing to show. As an adjunct, as an accessory, he was perfect. Many a woman would have adored to have him about her all her life, the most beautiful and 15 desirable of all her possessions. But Winifred belonged to another school.

The years went by, and instead of coming more to grips with life, he relaxed more. He was of a subtle, sensitive, passionate nature. But he simply *would* not give himself to what Winifred called life, *Work*. 20 No, he would not go into the world and work for money. No, he just would not. If Winifred liked to live beyond their small income—well, it was her look-out.

And Winifred did not really want him to go out into the world to work for money. Money became, alas, a word like a firebrand 25 between them, setting them both aflame with anger. But that is because we must talk in symbols. Winifred did not really care about money. She did not care whether he earned or did not earn anything. Only she knew she was dependent on her father for three-fourths of the money spent for herself and her children, and she let that be the 30 *casus belli*,* the drawn weapon between herself and Egbert.

What did she want?—what did she want? Her mother once said to her, with that characteristic touch of irony: "Well, dear, if it is your fate to consider the lilies, that toil not, neither do they spin,* that is one destiny among many others, and perhaps not so unpleasant as 35 most. Why do you take it amiss, my child?"

The mother was subtler than her children, they very rarely knew how to answer her. So Winifred was only more confused. It was not a question of lilies. At least, if it were a question of lilies, then her children were the little blossoms. They at least *grew*. Doesn't Jesus 40 say: "Consider the lilies *how they grow*." Good then, she had her growing babies. But as for that other tall, handsome flower of a father of theirs, he was full grown already, so she did not want to spend her life considering him in the flower of his days.

No, it was not that he didn't earn money. It was not that he was idle. He was *not* idle. He was always doing something, always working away, down at Crockham, doing little jobs. But oh dear, the little jobs—the garden paths—the gorgeous flowers—the chairs to mend, old chairs to mend!

It was that he stood for nothing. If he had done something unsuccessfully, and *lost* what money they had! If he had but striven with something. Nay, even if he had been wicked, a waster, she would have been more free. She would have had something to resist, at least. A waster stands for something, really. He says: "No, I will not aid and abet society in this business of increase and hanging together, I will upset the apple-cart as much as I can, in my small way." Or else he says: "No, I will *not* bother about others. If I have lusts, they are my own, and I prefer them to other people's virtues." So, a waster, a scamp, takes a sort of stand. He exposes himself to opposition and final castigation: at any rate in story-books.

But Egbert! What are you to do with a man like Egbert? He had no vices. He was really kind, nay generous. And he was not weak. If he had been weak Winifred could have been kind to him. But he did not even give her that consolation. He was not weak, and he did not want her consolation or her kindness. No thank you. He was of a fine passionate temper, and of a rarer steel than she. He knew it, and she knew it. Hence she was only the more baffled and maddened, poor thing. He, the higher, the finer, in his way the stronger, played with his garden and his old folk-songs and Morris-dances, just played, and let her support the pillars of the future on her own heart.

And he began to get bitter, and a wicked look began to come on his face. He did not give in to her; not he. There were seven devils inside his long, slim white body. He was healthy, full of restrained life. Yes, even he himself had to lock up his own vivid life inside himself, now she would not take it from him. Or rather, now that she only took it occasionally. For she had to yield at times. She loved him so, she desired him so, he was so exquisite to her, the fine creature that he was, finer than herself. Yes, with a groan she had to give in to her own unquenched passion for him. And he came to her then—ah terrible, ah wonderful, sometimes she wondered how either of them could live after the terror of the passion that swept between them. It

was to her as if pure lightning, flash after flash, went through every
fibre of her, till extinction came.

But it is the fate of human beings to live on. And it is the fate of
clouds that seem nothing but bits of vapour slowly to pile up, to pile
up and fill the heavens and blacken the sun entirely.

So it was. The love came back, the lightning of passion flashed
tremendously between them. And there was blue sky and gorgeous-
ness for a little while. And then, as inevitably, as inevitably, slowly the
clouds began to edge up again above the horizon, slowly, slowly to
lurk about the heavens, throwing an occasional cold and hateful
shadow: slowly, slowly to congregate, to fill the empyrean space.

And as the years passed, the lightning cleared the sky more and
more rarely, less and less the blue showed. Gradually the grey lid
sank down upon them, as if it would be permanent.

Why didn't Egbert do something, then? Why didn't he come to
grips with life? Why wasn't he like Winifred's father, a pillar of
society, even if a slender, exquisite column? Why didn't he go into
harness of some sort? Why didn't he take *some* direction?

Well, you can bring an ass to the water,* but you cannot make him
drink. The world was the water and Egbert was the ass. And he
wasn't having any. He couldn't: he just couldn't. Since necessity did
not force him to work for his bread and butter, he would not work for
work's sake. You can't make the columbine flowers nod in January,
nor make the cuckoo sing in England at Christmas. Why? It isn't his
season. He doesn't want to. Nay, he *can't* want to.

And there it was with Egbert. He couldn't link up with the world's
work, because the basic desire was absent from him. Nay, at the
bottom of him he had an even stronger desire: to hold aloof. To hold
aloof. To do nobody any damage. But to hold aloof. It was not his
season.

Perhaps he should not have married and had children. But you
can't stop the waters flowing.

Which held true for Winifred too. She was not made to endure
aloof. Her family tree was a robust vegetation that had to be stirring
and believing. In one direction or another her life *had* to go. In her
own home she had known nothing of this diffidence which she found
in Egbert, and which she could not understand, and which threw her
into such dismay. What was she to do, what was she to do, in face of
this terrible diffidence?

It was all so different in her own home. Her father may have had his own misgivings, but he kept them to himself. Perhaps he had no very profound belief in this world of ours, this society which we have elaborated with so much effort, only to find ourselves elaborated to death at last. But Godfrey Marshall was of tough, rough fibre, not without a vein of healthy cunning through it all. It was for him a question of winning through, and leaving the rest to heaven. Without having many illusions to grace him, he still *did* believe in heaven. In a dark and unquestioning way, he had a sort of faith: an acrid faith like the sap of some not-to-be-exterminated tree. Just a blind acrid faith as sap is blind and acrid, and yet pushes on in growth and in faith. Perhaps he was unscrupulous, but only as a striving tree is unscrupulous, pushing its single way in a jungle of others.

In the end, it is only this robust, sap-like faith which keeps man going. He may live on for many generations inside the shelter of the social establishment which he has erected for himself, as pear-trees and currant bushes would go on bearing fruit for many seasons, inside a walled garden, even if the race of man were suddenly exterminated. But bit by bit the wall-fruit-trees would gradually pull down the very walls that sustained them. Bit by bit every establishment collapses, unless it is renewed or restored by living hands, all the while.

Egbert could not bring himself to any more of this restoring or renewing business. He was not aware of the fact: but awareness doesn't help much, anyhow. He just couldn't. He had the stoic and epicurean quality of his old, fine breeding. His father-in-law, however, though he was not one bit more of a fool than Egbert, realised that since we are here we may as well live. And so he applied himself to his own tiny section of the social work, and to doing the best for his family, and to leaving the rest to the ultimate will of heaven. A certain robustness of blood made him able to go on. But sometimes even from him spurted a sudden gall of bitterness against the world and its make-up. And yet—he had his own will-to-succeed, and this carried him through. He refused to ask himself what the success would amount to. It amounted to the estate down in Hampshire, and his children lacking for nothing, and himself of some importance in the world: and *basta!*—Basta! Basta!

Nevertheless do not let us imagine that he was a common pusher. He was not. He knew as well as Egbert what disillusion meant. Perhaps in his soul he had the same estimation of success. But he had a certain acrid courage, and a certain will-to-power. In his own small circle he would emanate power, the single power of his own blind self. With all his spoiling of his children, he was still the father of the old English type. He was too wise to make laws and to domineer in the abstract. But he had kept, and all honour to him, a certain primitive dominion over the souls of his children, the old, almost magic prestige of paternity. There it was, still burning in him, the old smoky torch of paternal godhead.

And in the sacred glare of this torch his children had been brought up. He had given the girls every liberty, at last. But he had never really let them go beyond his power. And they, venturing out into the hard white light of our fatherless world, learned to see with the eyes of the world. They learned to criticise their father, even, from some effulgence of worldly white light, to see him as inferior. But this was all very well in the head. The moment they forgot their tricks of criticism, the old red glow of his authority came over them again. He was not to be quenched.

Let the psychoanalysts talk about father complex. It is just a word invented.* Here was a man who had kept alive the old red flame of fatherhood, fatherhood that had even the right to sacrifice the child to God, like Isaac.* Fatherhood that had life-and-death authority over the children: a great natural power. And till his children could be brought under some other great authority as girls; or could arrive at manhood and become themselves centres of the same power, continuing the same male mystery as men; until such time, willynilly, Godfrey Marshall would keep his children.

It had seemed as if he might lose Winifred. Winifred had *adored* her husband, and looked up to him as to something wonderful. Perhaps she had expected in him another great authority, a male authority greater, finer than her father's. For having once known the glow of male power, she would not easily turn to the cold white light of feminine independence. She would hunger, hunger all her life for the warmth and shelter of true male strength.

And hunger she might, for Egbert's power lay in the abnegation of power. He was himself the living negative of power. Even of responsibility. For the negation of power at last means the negation of responsibility. As far as these things went, he would confine himself to himself. He would try to confine his own *influence* even to himself. He would try as far as possible to abstain from influencing his children by assuming any responsibility for them. "A little child shall lead them—"* His child should lead, then. He would try not to make it go in any direction whatever. He would abstain from influencing it—Liberty!—

Poor Winifred was like a fish out of water in this liberty, gasping for the denser element which should contain her. Till her child came. And then she knew that she must be responsible for it, that she must have authority over it.

But here Egbert silently and negatively stepped in. Silently, negatively, but fatally he neutralised her authority over her children.

There was a third little girl born. And after this Winifred wanted no more children. Her soul was turning to salt.

So, she had charge of the children, they were her responsibility. The money for them had come from her father. She would do her very best for them, and have command over their life and death.— But no! Egbert would not take the responsibility. He would not even provide the money. But he would not let her have her way. Her dark, silent, passionate authority he would not allow. It was a battle between them, the battle between liberty and the old blood-power. And of course he won. The little girls loved him and adored him. "Daddy! Daddy!" They could do as they liked with him. Their mother would have ruled them. She would have ruled them passionately, with indulgence, with the old dark magic of parental authority, something looming and unquestioned and after all divine: if we believe in divine authority. The Marshalls did, being Catholic.

And Egbert, he turned her old dark, Catholic blood-authority into a sort of tyranny. He would not leave her her children. He stole them from her, and yet without assuming responsibility for them. He stole them from her, in emotion and spirit, and left her only to command their behaviour. A thankless lot for a mother. And her children adored him, adored him, little knowing the empty bitterness they were preparing for themselves when they too grew up to have husbands: husbands such as Egbert, adorable and null.

Joyce, the eldest, was still his favourite. She was now a quicksilver little thing of six years old. Barbara, the youngest, was a toddler of two years. They spent most of their time down at Crockham, because he wanted to be there. And even Winifred loved the place really. But now, in her frustrated and blinded state, it was full of menace for her children. The adders, the poison-berries, the brook, the marsh, the water that might not be pure—one thing and another. From mother and nurse it was a guerilla gunfire of commands, and blithe, quicksilver disobedience from the three blonde, never-still little

girls. Behind the girls was the father, against mother and nurse. And
so it was.

"If you don't come quick, nurse, I shall run out there to where
there are snakes."

5   "Joyce, you *must* be patient. I'm just changing Annabel."

There you are. There it was: always the same. Working away on
the common across the brook he heard it. And he worked on, just the
same.

Suddenly he heard a shriek, and he flung the spade from him and
10 started for the bridge, looking up like a startled deer.—Ah, there was
Winifred—Joyce had hurt herself. He went on up the garden.

"What is it?"

The child was still screaming—now it was—"Daddy! Daddy!
Oh—oh Daddy!" And the mother was saying:

15 "Don't be frightened, darling. Let mother look."

But the child only cried:

"Oh Daddy, Daddy, Daddy!"

She was terrified by the sight of the blood running from her own
knee.—Winifred crouched down, with her child of six in her lap, to
20 examine the knee. Egbert bent over also.

"Don't make such a noise, Joyce," he said irritably. "How did she
do it?"

"She fell on that sickle thing which you left lying about* after
cutting the grass," said Winifred, looking into his face with bitter
25 accusation as he bent near.

He had taken his handkerchief and tied it round the knee. Then
he lifted the still sobbing child in his arms, and carried her into the
house and upstairs to her bed. In his arms she became quiet. But his
heart was burning with pain and with guilt. He had left the sickle
30 there lying on the edge of the grass, and so his first-born child whom
he loved so dearly had come to hurt. But then it was an accident—it
was an accident. Why should he feel guilty— It would probably be
nothing, better in two or three days. Why take it to heart, why worry?
He put it aside.

35 The child lay on the bed in her little summer frock, her face very
white now after the shock. Nurse had come carrying the youngest
child: and little Annabel stood holding her skirt. Winifred, terribly
serious and wooden-seeming, was bending over the knee, from
which she had taken his blood-soaked handkerchief. Egbert bent
40 forward too, keeping more *sang froid* in his face than in his heart.

Winifred went all of a lump of seriousness, so he had to keep some reserve. The child moaned and whimpered.

The knee was still bleeding profusely—it was a deep cut right in the joint.

"You'd better go for the doctor, Egbert," said Winifred bitterly. 5

"Oh no! Oh no!" cried Joyce in a panic.

"Joyce, my darling, don't cry!" said Winifred, suddenly catching the little girl to her breast in a strange tragic anguish, the *Mater Dolorata.* Even the child was frightened into silence. Egbert looked at the tragic figure of his wife with the child at her breast, and turned 10 away. Only Annabel started suddenly to cry: "Joycey, Joycey, don't have your leg bleeding!"

Egbert rode four miles to the village* for the doctor. He could not help feeling that Winifred was laying it on rather. Surely the knee itself wasn't hurt! Surely not. It was only a surface cut. 15

The doctor was out. Egbert left the message and came cycling swiftly home, his heart pinched with anxiety. He dropped sweating off his bicycle and went into the house, looking rather small, like a man who is at fault. Winifred was upstairs sitting by Joyce, who was looking pale and important in bed, and was eating some tapioca 20 pudding. The pale, small, scared face of his child went to Egbert's heart.

"Doctor Wing was out. He'll be here about half-past two," said Egbert.

"I don't want him to come," whimpered Joyce. 25

"Joyce dear, you must be patient and quiet," said Winifred. "He won't hurt you. But he will tell us what to do to make your knee better quickly. That is why he must come."

Winifred always explained carefully to her little girls: and it always took the words off their lips for the moment. 30

"Does it bleed yet?" said Egbert.

Winifred moved the bedclothes carefully aside.

"I think not," she said.

Egbert stooped also to look.

"No, it doesn't," he said. Then he stood up with a relieved look on 35 his face. He turned to the child.

"Eat your pudding, Joyce," he said. "It won't be anything. You've only got to keep still for a few days."

"You haven't had your dinner, have you, Daddy?"

"Not yet." 40

"Nurse will give it to you," said Winifred.

"You'll be all right, Joyce," he said, smiling to the child and pushing the blonde hair aside off her brow. She smiled back winsomely into his face.

5 He went downstairs and ate his meal alone. Nurse served him. She liked waiting on him. All women liked him and liked to do things for him.

The doctor came—a fat country practitioner, pleasant and kind.

"What, little girl, been tumbling down, have you? There's a thing
10 to be doing, for a smart little lady like you! What! And cutting your knee! Tut-tut-tut! That *wasn't* clever of you, now was it? Never mind, never mind, soon be better. Let us look at it. Won't hurt you. Not the least in life. Bring a bowl with a little warm water, nurse. Soon have it all right again, soon have it all right."

15 Joyce smiled at him with a pale smile of faint superiority. This was *not* the way in which she was used to being talked to.

He bent down carefully looking at the little, thin, wounded knee of the child. Egbert bent over him.

"Oh dear, oh dear! Quite a deep little cut. Nasty little cut. Nasty
20 little cut. But never mind. Never mind, little lady. We'll soon have it better. Soon have it better, little lady. What's your name?"

"My name is Joyce," said the child distinctly.

"Oh really!" he replied. "Oh really! Well that's a fine name too, in my opinion. Joyce, eh?—And how old might Miss Joyce be? Can she
25 tell me that?"

"I'm six," said the child, slightly amused and very condescending.

"Six! There now. Add up and count as far as six, can you? Well that's a clever little girl, a clever little girl. And if she has to drink a spoonful of medicine, she won't make a murmur, I'll be bound. Not
30 like *some* little girls. What? Eh?"

"I take it if mother wishes me to," said Joyce.

"Ah, there now! That's the style! That's what I like to hear from a little lady in bed because she's cut her knee. That's the style—"

The comfortable and prolix doctor dressed and bandaged the
35 knee and recommended bed and a light diet for the little lady. He thought a week or a fortnight would put it right. No bones or ligatures damaged—fortunately. Only a flesh cut. He would come again in a day or two.

So Joyce was reassured and stayed in bed and had all her toys up.
40 Her father often played with her. The doctor came the third day. He

was fairly pleased with the knee. It was healing. It was healing—yes—yes. Let the child continue in bed. He came again after a day or two. Winifred was a trifle uneasy. The wound seemed to be healing on the top, but it hurt the child too much. It didn't look quite right. She said so to Egbert.

"Egbert, I'm sure Joyce's knee isn't healing properly."

"I think it is," he said. "I think it's all right."

"I'd rather Doctor Wing came again—I don't feel satisfied."

"Aren't you trying to imagine it worse than it really is?"

"You would say so, of course. But I shall write a post-card to Doctor Wing now."

The doctor came next day. He examined the knee. Yes, there was inflammation. Yes, there *might* be a little septic poisoning—there might. There might. Was the child feverish?

So a fortnight passed by, and the child *was* feverish, and the knee was more inflamed and grew worse and was painful, painful. She cried in the night, and her mother had to sit up with her. Egbert still insisted it was nothing really—it would pass. But in his heart he was anxious.

Winifred wrote again to her father. On Saturday the elderly man appeared. And no sooner did Winifred see the thick, rather short figure in its grey suit than a great yearning came over her.

"Father, I'm not satisfied with Joyce. I'm not satisfied with Doctor Wing."

"Well, Winnie dear, if you're not satisfied we must have further advice, that is all."

The sturdy, powerful elderly man went upstairs, his voice sounding rather grating through the house, as if it cut upon the tense atmosphere.

"How are you, Joyce darling?" he said to the child. "Does your knee hurt you? Does it hurt you, dear?"

"It does sometimes."—The child was shy of him, cold towards him.

"Well dear, I'm sorry for that. I hope you try to bear it, and not trouble mother too much."

There was no answer. He looked at the knee. It was red and stiff.

"Of course," he said, "I think we must have another doctor's opinion. And if we're going to have it, we had better have it at once. Egbert, do you think you might cycle in to Bingham for Doctor Wayne? I found him *very* satisfactory for Winnie's mother."

"I can go if you think it necessary," said Egbert.

"Certainly I think it necessary. Even if there *is* nothing, we can have peace of mind. Certainly I think it necessary. I should like Doctor Wayne to come this evening if possible."

5   So Egbert set off on his bicycle through the wind, like a boy sent on an errand, leaving his father-in-law a pillar of assurance, with Winifred.

Doctor Wayne came, and looked grave. Yes, the knee was certainly taking the wrong way. The child might be lame for life.

10   Up went the fire of fear and anger in every heart. Doctor Wayne came again the next day for a proper examination. And yes, the knee had really taken bad ways. It should be X-rayed. It was very important.

Godfrey Marshall walked up and down the lane with the doctor,
15   beside the standing motor-car: up and down, up and down in one of those consultations of which he had had so many in his life.

As a result he came indoors to Winifred.

"Well, Winnie dear, the best thing to do is to take Joyce up to London,* to a nursing home where she can have proper treatment.
20   Of course this knee has been allowed to go wrong. And apparently there is a risk that the child may even lose her leg. What do you think, dear? You agree to our taking her up to town and putting her under the best care?"

"Oh father, you *know* I would do anything on earth for her."

25   "I know you would, Winnie darling. The pity is that there has been this unfortunate delay already. I can't think what Doctor Wing was doing. Apparently the child is in danger of losing her leg. Well then, if you will have everything ready, we will take her up to town to-morrow. I will order the large car from Denley's to be here at ten.
30   Egbert, will you take a telegram at once to Doctor Jackson? It is a small nursing home for children and for surgical cases, not far from Baker Street. I'm sure Joyce will be all right there."

"Oh father, can't I nurse her myself!"

"Well, darling, if she is to have proper treatment, she had best be
35   in a home. The X-ray treatment, and the electric treatment, and whatever is necessary."

"It will cost a great deal—" said Winifred.

"We can't think of cost, if the child's leg is in danger—or even her life. No use speaking of cost," said the elder man impatiently.

40   And so it was. Poor Joyce, stretched out on a bed in the big closed

motor-car—the mother sitting by her head, the grandfather in his short grey beard and a bowler hat, sitting by her feet, thick and implacable in his responsibility,—they rolled slowly away from Crockham, and from Egbert who stood there bareheaded and a little ignominious, left behind. He was to shut up the house and bring the rest of the family back to town, by train, the next day.

Followed a dark and bitter time. The poor child. The poor, poor child, how she suffered, an agony and a long crucifixion in that nursing home. It was a bitter six weeks which changed the soul of Winifred for ever. As she sat by the bed of her poor, tortured little child, tortured with the agony of the knee and the still worse agony of these diabolic, but perhaps necessary modern treatments, she felt her heart killed and going cold in her breast. Her little Joyce, her frail, brave, wonderful little Joyce, frail and small and pale as a white flower! Ah, how had she, Winifred, dared to be so wicked, so wicked, so careless, so sensual!

"Let my heart die! Let my woman's heart of flesh die! Saviour, let my heart die. And save my child. Let my heart die from the world and from the flesh. Oh, destroy my heart that is so wayward. Let my heart of pride die. Let my heart die."

So she prayed beside the bed of her child. And like the Mother with the seven swords in her breast, slowly her heart of pride and passion died in breast, bleeding away. Slowly it died, bleeding away, and she turned to the Church for comfort, to Jesus, to the Mother of God, but most of all, to that great and enduring institution, the Roman Catholic Church. She withdrew into the shadow of the Church. She was a mother with three children. But in her soul she died, her heart of pride and passion and desire bled to death, her soul belonged to her church, her body belonged to her duty as a mother.

Her duty as a wife did not enter. As a wife she had no sense of duty: only a certain bitterness towards the man with whom she had known such sensuality and distraction. She was purely the *Mater Dolorata*. To the man she was closed as a tomb.

Egbert came to see his child. But Winifred seemed to be always seated there, like the tomb of his manhood and his fatherhood. Poor Winifred: she was still young, still strong and ruddy and beautiful like a ruddy hard flower of the field. Strange—her ruddy, healthy face, so sombre, and her strong, heavy, full-blooded body, so still. She, a nun! Never. And yet the gates of her heart and soul had shut in his face with a slow, resonant clang, shutting him out for ever. There was no need for her to go into a convent. Her will had done it.

And between this young mother and this young father lay the crippled child, like a bit of pale silk floss on the pillow, and a little white pain-quenched face. He could not bear it. He just could not bear it. He turned aside. There was nothing to do but to turn aside. He turned aside, and went hither and thither, desultory. He was still attractive and desirable. But there was a little frown between his brow as if he had been cleft there with a hatchet: cleft right in, for ever, and that was the stigma.

The child's leg was saved: but the knee was locked stiff. The fear now was lest the lower leg should wither, or cease to grow. There must be long-continued massage and treatment, daily treatment, even when the child left the nursing home. And the whole of the expense was borne by the grandfather.

Egbert now had no real home. Winifred with the children and nurse was tied to the little flat in London. He could not live there: he could not contain himself. The cottage was shut-up—or lent to friends. He went down sometimes to work in his garden and keep the place in order. Then with the empty house around him at night, all the empty rooms, he felt his heart go wicked. The sense of frustration and futility, like some slow, torpid snake, slowly bit right through his heart. Futility, futility, futility: the horrible marsh-poison went through his veins and killed him.

As he worked in the garden in the silence of day he would listen for a sound. No sound. No sound of Winifred from the dark inside of the cottage: no sound of children's voices from the air, from the common, from the near distance. No sound, nothing but the old dark marsh-venomous atmosphere of the place. So he worked spasmodically through the day, and at night made a fire and cooked some food, alone.

He was alone. He himself cleaned the cottage and made his bed. But his mending he did not do. His shirts were slit on the shoulders, when he had been working, and the white flesh showed through. He would feel the air and the spots of rain on his exposed flesh. And he would look again across the common, where the dark, tufted gorse was dying to seed, and the bits of cat-heather were coming pink in tufts, like a sprinkling of sacrificial blood.

His heart went back to the savage old spirit of the place: the desire for old gods, old, lost passions, the passion of the cold-blooded, darting snakes that hissed and shot away from him, the mystery of blood-sacrifices, all the lost, intense sensations of the primeval people of the place, whose passions seethed in the air still, from those long days before the Romans came. The seethe of a lost, dark passion in the air. The presence of unseen snakes.

A queer, baffled, half-wicked look came on his face. He could not stay long at the cottage. Suddenly he must swing on to his bicycle and go—anywhere. Anywhere, away from the place. He would stay a few days with his mother in the old home. His mother adored him and grieved as a mother would. But the little, baffled, half-wicked smile curled on his face, and he swung away from his mother's solicitude as from everything else.

Always moving on—from place to place, friend to friend: and always swinging away from sympathy. As soon as sympathy, like a soft hand, was reached out to touch him, away he swerved, instinctively, as a harmless snake swerves and swerves and swerves away from an outstretched hand. Away he must go. And periodically he went back to Winifred.

He was terrible to her now, like a temptation. She had devoted herself to her children and her church. Joyce was once more on her feet; but, alas! lame, with iron supports to her leg, and a little crutch. It was strange how she had grown into a long, pallid, wild little thing. Strange that the pain had not made her soft and docile, but had brought out a wild, almost menad temper in the child. She was seven, and long and white and thin, but by no means subdued. Her blonde hair was darkening. She still had long sufferings to face, and, in her own childish consciousness, the stigma of her lameness to bear.

And she bore it. An almost menad courage seemed to possess her, as if she were a long, thin, young weapon of life. She acknowledged all her mother's care. She would stand by her mother for ever. But some of her father's fine-tempered desperation flashed in her.

When Egbert saw his little girl limping horribly—not only limping but lurching horribly in crippled, childish way, his heart again hardened with chagrin, like steel that is tempered again. There was a tacit understanding between him and his little girl: not what we would call love, but a weapon-like kinship. There was a tiny touch of irony in his manner towards her, contrasting sharply with Winifred's heavy, unleavened solicitude and care. The child flickered back to him with an answering little smile of irony and recklessness: an odd flippancy which made Winifred only the more sombre and earnest.

The Marshalls took endless thought and trouble for the child,
5 searching out every means to save her limb and her active freedom. They spared no effort and no money, they spared no strength of will. With all their slow, heavy power of will they willed that Joyce should save her liberty of movement, should win back her wild, free grace. Even if it took a long time to recover, it should be recovered.

10 So the situation stood. And Joyce submitted, week after week, month after month, to the tyranny and pain of the treatment. She acknowledged the honorable effort on her behalf. But her flamy reckless spirit was her father's. It was he who had all the glamour for her. He and she were like members of some forbidden secret society
15 who know one another but may not recognize one another. Knowledge they had in common, the same secret of life, the father and the child. But the child stayed in the camp of her mother, honourably, and the father wandered outside like Ishmael,* only coming sometimes to sit in the home for an hour or two, an evening or two beside
20 the camp fire, like Ishmael, in a curious silence and tension, with the mocking answer of the desert speaking out of his silence, and annulling the whole convention of the domestic home.

His presence was almost an anguish to Winifred. She prayed against it. That little cleft between his brow, that flickering, wicked
25 little smile that seemed to haunt his face, and above all, the triumphant loneliness, the Ishmael quality. And then the erectness of his supple body, like a symbol. The very way he stood, so quiet, so insidious, like an erect, supple symbol of life, the living body, confronting her downcast soul, was torture to her. He was like a
30 supple living idol moving before her eyes, and she felt if she watched him she was damned.

And he came and made himself at home in her little home. When he was there, moving in his own quiet way, she felt as if the whole great law of sacrifice, by which she had elected to live, were annulled.
35 He annulled by his very presence the laws of her life. And what did he substitute? Ah, against that question she hardened herself in recoil.

It was awful to her to have to have him about—moving about in his shirt-sleeves, speaking in his tenor, throaty voice to the children.
40 Annabel simply adored him, and he teased the little girl. The baby

Barbara was not sure of him. She had been born a stranger to him. But even the nurse, when she saw his white shoulder of flesh through the slits of his torn shirt, thought it a shame.

Winifred felt it was only another weapon of his against her.

"You have other shirts—why do you wear that old one that is all   5
torn, Egbert?" she said.

"I may as well wear it out," he said subtly.

He knew she would not offer to mend it for him. She *could* not. And no, she would not. Had she not her own gods to honour? And could she betray them, submitting to his Baal and Ashtaroth?* And it   10
was terrible to her, his unsheathed presence, that seemed to annul her and her faith, like another revelation. Like a gleaming idol evoked against her, a vivid life-idol that might triumph.

He came and he went—and she persisted. And then the great war broke out. He was a man who could not go to the dogs. He could not   15
dissipate himself. He was pure-bred in his Englishness, and even when he would have liked to be vicious, he could not.

So when the war broke out his whole instinct was against it: against war. He had not the faintest desire to overcome any foreigners or to help in their death. He had no conception of   20
Imperial England, and Rule Britannia was just a joke to him. He was a pure-blooded Englishman, perfect in his race, and when he was truly himself he could no more have been aggressive on the score of his Englishness than a rose can be aggressive on the score of its rosiness.   25

No, he had no desire to defy Germany and to exalt England. The distinction between German and English was not for him the distinction between good and bad. It was the distinction between blue water-flowers and red or white bush-blossoms: just difference. The difference between the wild boar and the wild bear. And a man   30
was good or bad according to his nature, not according to his nationality.

Egbert was well-bred, and this was part of his natural understanding. It was merely unnatural to him to hate a nation *en bloc*. Certain individuals he disliked, and others he liked, and the mass he knew   35
nothing about. Certain deeds he disliked, certain deeds seemed natural to him, and about most deeds he had no particular feeling.

He had, however, the one deepest pure-bred instinct. He recoiled inevitably from having his feelings dictated to him by the mass feeling. His feelings were his own, his understanding was his own,   40 and he would never go back on either, willingly. Shall a man become inferior to his own true knowledge and self, just because the mob expects it of him?

What Egbert felt subtly and without question, his father-in-law felt also, in a rough, more combative way. Different as the two men were, they were two real Englishmen, and their instincts were almost the same.

And Godfrey Marshall had the world to reckon with. There was German military aggression, and the English non-military idea of liberty and the "conquests of peace"*—meaning industrialism. Even if the choice between militarism and industrialism were a choice of evils, the elderly man asserted his choice of the latter, perforce. He whose soul was quick with the instinct of power.

Egbert just refused to reckon with the world. He just refused even to decide between German militarism and British industrialism. He chose neither. As for atrocities, he despised the people who committed them, as inferior criminal types. There was nothing national about crime.

And yet, war! War! Just war! Not right or wrong, but just war itself. Should he join? Should he give himself over to war? The question was in his mind for some weeks. Not because he thought England was right and Germany wrong. Probably Germany was wrong, but he refused to make a choice. Not because he felt inspired. No. But just—war.

The deterrent was, the giving himself over into the power of other men, and into the power of the mob-spirit of a democratic army. Should he give himself over? Should he make over his own life and body to the control of something which he *knew* was inferior, in spirit, to his own self? Should he commit himself into the power of an inferior control? Should he? Should he betray himself?

He was going to put himself into the power of his inferiors, and he knew it. He was going to subjugate himself. He was going to be ordered about by petty *canaille** of non-commissioned officers—and even commissioned officers. He who was born and bred free. Should he do it?

He went to his wife, to speak to her.

"Shall I join up, Winifred?"

She was silent. Her instinct also was dead against it. And yet a certain profound resentment made her answer:

"You have three children dependent on you. I don't know whether you have thought of that."

It was still only the third month of the war, and the old pre-war ideas were still alive.

"Of course. But it won't make much difference to them. I shall be earning a shilling a day, at least."

"You'd better speak to father, I think," she replied heavily.

Egbert went to his father-in-law. The elderly man's heart was full of resentment.

"I should say," he said rather sourly, "it is the best thing you could do."

Egbert went and joined up immediately, as a private soldier. He was drafted into the light artillery.

Winifred now had a new duty towards him: the duty of a wife towards a husband who is himself performing his duty towards the world. She loved him still. She would always love him, as far as earthly love went. But it was duty she now lived by. When he came back to her in khaki, a soldier, she submitted to him as a wife. It was her duty. But to his passion she could never again fully submit. Something prevented her, for ever: even her own deepest choice.

He went back again to camp. It did not suit him to be a modern soldier. In the thick, gritty, hideous khaki his subtle physique was extinguished as if he had been killed. In the ugly intimacy of the camp his thoroughbred sensibilities were just degraded. But he had chosen, so he accepted. An ugly little look came on to his face, of a man who has accepted his own degradation.

In the early spring Winifred went down to Crockham to be there when primroses were out, and the tassels hanging on the hazel-bushes. She felt something like a reconciliation towards Egbert, now he was a prisoner in camp most of his days. Joyce was wild with delight at seeing the garden and the common again, after the eight or nine months of London and misery. She was still lame. She still had the irons up her leg. But she lurched about with a wild, crippled agility.

Egbert came for a week-end, in his gritty, thick, sand-paper khaki and puttees and the hideous cap. Nay, he looked terrible. And on his face a slightly impure look, a little sore on his lip, as if he had eaten too much or drunk too much or let his blood become a little unclean. He was almost uglily healthy, with the camp life. It did not suit him.

Winifred waited for him in a little passion of duty and sacrifice, willing to serve the soldier, if not the man. It only made him feel a little more ugly inside. The week-end was torment to him: the memory of the camp, the knowledge of the life he led there; even the sight of his own legs in that abhorrent khaki. He felt as if the hideous cloth went into his blood and made it gritty and dirty. Then Winifred so ready to serve the *soldier*, when she repudiated the man. And this made the grit worse between his teeth. And the children running around playing and calling in the rather mincing fashion of children who have nurses and governesses and literature in the family. And Joyce so lame! It had all become unreal to him, after the camp. It only set his soul on edge. He left at dawn on the Monday morning, glad to get back to the realness and vulgarity of the camp.

Winifred would never meet him again at the cottage—only in London, where the world was with them. But sometimes he came alone* to Crockham, perhaps when friends were staying there. And then he would work awhile in his garden. This summer still it would flame with blue anchusas and big red poppies, the mulleins would sway their soft, downy erections in the air: he loved mulleins: and the honeysuckle would stream out scent like memory, when the owl was whooing. Then he sat by the fire with the friends and with Winifred's sisters, and they sang the folk-songs. He put on thin civilian clothes, and his charm and his beauty and the supple dominancy of his body glowed out again. But Winifred was not there.

At the end of the summer he went to Flanders, into action. He seemed already to have gone out of life, beyond the pale of life. He hardly remembered his life any more, being like a man who is going to take a jump from a height, and is only looking to where he must land.

He was twice slightly wounded, in two months. But not enough to put him off duty for more than a day or two. They were retiring again, holding the enemy back. He was in the rear—three machine-guns. The country was all pleasant, war had not yet trampled it. Only the air seemed shattered, and the land awaiting death. It was a small, unimportant action in which he was engaged.

The guns were stationed on a little bushy hillock just outside a village. But occasionally, it was difficult to say from which direction came the sharp crackle of rifle-fire, and beyond, the far-off thud of cannon. The afternoon was wintry and cold.

A lieutenant stood on a little iron platform at the top of the ladders, taking the sights and giving the aim, calling in a high, tense, mechanical voice. Out of the sky came the sharp cry of the directions, then the warning numbers, then "Fire!" The shot went, the piston of the gun sprang back, there was a sharp explosion, and a very faint film of smoke in the air. Then the other two guns fired, and there was a lull. The officer was uncertain of the enemy's position. The thick clump of horse-chestnut trees below was without change. Only in the far distance the sound of heavy firing continued, so far off as to give a sense of peace.

The gorse bushes on either hand were dark, but a few sparks of flowers showed yellow. He noticed them almost unconsciously as he waited, in the lull. He was in his shirt-sleeves, and the air came chill on his arms. Again his shirt was slit on the shoulders, and the flesh showed through. He was dirty and unkempt. But his face was quiet. So many things go out of consciousness before we come to the end of consciousness.

Before him, below, was the highroad, running between high banks of grass and gorse. He saw the whitish, muddy tracks and deep scores in the road, where the part of the regiment had retired. Now all was still. Sounds that came, came from the outside. The place where he stood was still silent, chill, serene; the white church among the trees beyond seemed like a thought only.

He moved into a lightning-like mechanical response at the sharp cry from the officer overhead. Mechanism, the pure mechanical action of obedience at the guns. Pure mechanical action at the guns. It left the soul unburdened, brooding in dark nakedness. In the end, the soul is alone, brooding on the face of the uncreated flux, as a bird on a dark sea.

Nothing could be seen but the road, and a crucifix knocked slanting and the dark, autumnal fields and woods. There appeared three horsemen on a little eminence, very small, on the crest of a ploughed field. They were our own men. Of the enemy, nothing.

The lull continued. Then suddenly came sharp orders, and a new direction of the guns, and an intense, exciting activity. Yet at the centre the soul remained dark and aloof, alone.

But even so, it was the soul that heard the new sound: the new, deep "papp!" of a gun that seemed to touch right upon the soul. He kept up the rapid activity at the machine-gun, sweating. But in his soul was the echo of the new, deep sound, deeper than life.

And in confirmation came the awful faint whistling of a shell, advancing almost suddenly into a piercing, tearing shriek that would

tear through the membrane of life. He heard it in his ears, but he heard it also in his soul, in tension. There was relief when the thing had swung by and struck, away beyond. He heard the hoarseness of its explosion, and the voice of the soldier calling to the horses. But he
5   did not turn round to look. He only noticed a twig of holly with red berries fall like a gift on to the road below.

Not this time, not this time. Whither thou goest I will go.* Did he say it to the shell, or to whom? Whither thou goest I will go. Then, the faint whistling of another shell dawned, and his blood became
10 small and still to receive it. It drew nearer, like some horrible blast of wind; his blood lost consciousness. But in the second of suspension he saw the heavy shell swoop to earth, into the rocky bushes on the right, and earth and stones poured up into the sky. It was as if he heard no sound. The earth and stones and fragments of bush fell to
15 earth again, and there was the same unchanging peace. The Germans had got the aim.

Would they move now? Would they retire? Yes. The officer was giving the last lightning-rapid orders to fire before withdrawing. A shell passed unnoticed in the rapidity of action. And then, into the
20 silence, into the suspense where the soul brooded, finally crashed a noise and a darkness and a moment's flaming agony and horror. Ah, he had seen the dark bird flying towards him, flying home this time. In one instant life and eternity went up in a conflagration of agony, then there was a weight of darkness.

25 When faintly something began to struggle in the darkness, a consciousness of himself, he was aware of a great load and a clanging sound. To have known the moment of death! And to be forced, before dying, to review it. So, fate, even in death.

There was a resounding of pain. It seemed to sound from the
30 outside of his consciousness: like a loud bell clanging very near. Yet he knew it was himself. He must associate himself with it. After a lapse and a new effort, he identified a pain in his head, a large pain that clanged and resounded. So far he could identify himself with himself. Then there was a lapse.

35 After a time he seemed to wake up again, and waking, to know that he was at the front, and that he was killed. He did not open his eyes. Light was not yet his. The clanging pain in his head rang out the rest of his consciousness. So he lapsed away from consciousness, in unutterable sick abandon of life.

40 Bit by bit, like a doom, came the necessity to know. He was hit in the head. It was only a vague surmise at first. But in the swinging of

the pendulum of pain, swinging ever nearer and nearer, to touch him into an agony of consciousness and a consciousness of agony, gradually the knowledge emerged—he must be hit in the head—hit on the left brow; if so, there would be blood—was there blood?— could he feel blood in his left eye? Then the clanging seemed to burst the membrane of his brain, like death-madness.

Was there blood on his face? Was hot blood flowing? Or was it dry blood congealing down his cheek? It took him hours even to ask the question: time being no more than an agony in darkness, without measurement.

A long time after he had opened his eyes he realised he was seeing something—something, something, but the effort to recall what was too great. No, no; no recall!

Were they the stars in the dark sky? Was it possible it was stars in the dark sky? Stars? The world? Ah, no, he could not know it! Stars and the world were gone for him, he closed his eyes. No stars, no sky, no world. No, no! The thick darkness of blood alone. It should be one great lapse into the thick darkness of blood in agony.

Death, oh death! The world all blood, and the blood all writhing with death. The soul like the tiniest little light out on a dark sea, the sea of blood. And the light guttering, beating, pulsing in a windless storm, wishing it could go out, yet unable.

There had been life. There had been Winifred and his children. But the frail death-agony effort to catch at straws of memory, straws of life from the past, brought on too great a nausea. No, no! No Winifred, no children. No world, no people. Better the agony of dissolution ahead than the nausea of the effort backwards. Better the terrible work should go forward, the dissolving into the black sea of death, in the extremity of dissolution, than that there should be any reaching back towards life. To forget! To forget! Utterly, utterly to forget, in the great forgetting of death. To break the core and the unit of life, and to lapse out on the great darkness. Only that. To break the clue, and mingle and commingle with the one darkness, without afterwards or forwards. Let the black sea of death itself solve the problem of futurity. Let the will of man break and give up.

What was that? A light! A terrible light! Was it figures? Was it legs of a horse colossal—colossal above him: huge, huge?

The Germans heard a slight noise, and started. Then, in the glare of a light-bomb, by the side of the heap of earth thrown up by the shell, they saw the dead face.

Tickets Please*

There is in the Midlands a single-line tramway system* which boldly leaves the county town and plunges off into the black, industrial countryside, up hill and down dale, through the long, ugly villages of workmen's houses, over canals and railways, past churches perched high and nobly over the smoke and shadows, through stark, grimy, cold little market-places, tilting away in a rush past cinemas and shops down to the hollow where the collieries are, then up again, past a little rural church, under the ash trees, on in a rush to the terminus,* the last little ugly place of industry, the cold little town that shivers on the edge of the wild, gloomy country beyond. There the green and creamy-coloured tram-car seems to pause and purr with curious satisfaction. But in a few minutes—the clock on the turret of the Co-operative Wholesale Society's Shops* gives the time—away it starts once more on the adventure. Again there are the reckless swoops downhill, bouncing the loops: again the chilly wait in the hill-top market-place:* again the breathless slithering round the precipitous drop under the church: again the patient halts at the loops, waiting for the outcoming car: so on and on, for two long hours, till at last the city looms beyond the fat gas works, the narrow factories draw near, we are in the sordid streets of the great town, once more we sidle to a standstill at our terminus, abashed by the great crimson and cream-coloured city cars,* but still perky, jaunty, somewhat dare-devil, green as a jaunty sprig of parsley out of a black colliery garden.

To ride on these cars is always an adventure. Since we are in war-time, the drivers are men unfit for active service: cripples and hunchbacks. So they have the spirit of the devil in them.* The ride becomes a steeplechase. Hurray!—we have leapt in a clean jump over the canal bridges—now for the four-lane corner. With a shriek and a trail of sparks we are clear again. To be sure, a tram often leaps the rails—but what matter! It sits in a ditch till other trams come to haul it out. It is quite common for a car packed with one solid mass of living people to come to a dead halt in the midst of unbroken

34

blackness, the heart of nowhere on a dark night, and for the driver and the girl conductor to call—"All get off—car's on fire." Instead, however, of rushing out in a panic, the passengers stolidly reply: "Get on—get on. We're not coming out. We're stopping where we are. Push on, George." So till flames actually appear. 5

The reason for this reluctance to dismount is that the nights are howlingly cold, black, and wind-swept, and a car is a haven of refuge. From village to village the miners travel, for a change of cinema, of girl, of pub. The trams are desperately packed. Who is going to risk himself in the black gulf outside, to wait perhaps an hour for another 10 tram, then to see the forlorn notice—"Depot Only"—because there is something wrong: or to greet a unit of three bright cars all so tight with people that they sail past with a howl of derision. Trams that pass in the night.*

This, the most dangerous tram service in England, as the authori- 15 ties themselves declare with pride, is entirely conducted by girls and driven by rash young men, a little crippled, or by delicate young men, who creep forward in terror. The girls are fearless young hussies. In their ugly blue uniforms, skirts up to their knees, shapeless old peaked caps on their heads, they have all the *sang froid* of an old 20 non-commissioned officer. With a tram packed with howling colli- ers, roaring hymns downstairs and a sort of antiphony of obscenities upstairs, the lasses are perfectly at their ease. They pounce on the youths who try to evade their ticket-machine. They push off the men at the end of their distance. They are not going to be done in the 25 eye—not they. They fear nobody—and everybody fears them.

"Halloa, Annie!"

"Halloa, Ted!"

"Oh, mind my corn, Miss Stone. It's my belief you've got a heart of stone, for you've trod on it again." 30

"You should keep it in your pocket," replies Miss Stone, and she goes sturdily upstairs in her high boots.

"Tickets, please."

She is peremptory, suspicious, and ready to hit first. She can hold her own against ten thousand. The step of that tram-car is her 35 Thermopylae.*

Therefore, there is a certain wild romance aboard these cars—and in the sturdy bosom of Annie herself. The time for soft romance is in the morning, between ten o'clock and one, when things are rather slack: that is, except market day and Saturday. Then Annie has time 40

to look about her. Then she often hops off her car and into a shop where she has spied something, while her driver chats in the main road. There is very good feeling between the girls and the drivers. Are they not companions in peril, shipmates aboard this careering
5　vessel of a tram-car, for ever rocking on the waves of a stormy land.

Then, also, during the easy hours, the inspectors are most in evidence. For some reason, everybody employed in this tram-service is young: there are no grey heads. It would not do. Therefore the inspectors are of the right age, and one, the chief, is also good-
10　looking. See him stand on a wet gloomy morning, in his long oil-skin, his peaked cap well down over his eyes, waiting to board a car. His face is ruddy, his small brown moustache is weathered, he has a faint impudent smile. Fairly tall and agile, even in his water-proof, he springs aboard a car and greets Annie.

15　"Halloa, Annie—keeping the wet out?"

"Trying to."

There are only two people in the car. Inspecting is soon over. Then for a long and impudent chat on the foot-board—a good, easy, twelve-mile chat.

20　The inspector's name is John Thomas Raynor: always called John Thomas, except sometimes, in malice, Coddy.* His face sets in fury when he is addressed, from a distance, with this abbreviation. There is considerable scandal about John Thomas in half a dozen villages. He flirts with the girl conductors in the morning, and walks out with
25　them in the dark night, when they leave their tram-car at the depôt. Of course the girls quit the service frequently. Then he flirts and walks out with the new-comer: always providing she is sufficiently attractive, and that she will consent to walk. It is remarkable, however, that most of the girls are quite comely, they are all young,
30　and this roving life aboard the car gives them a sailor's dash and recklessness. What matter how they behave when the ship is in port. Tomorrow they will be aboard again.

Annie, however, was something of a tartar, and her sharp tongue had kept John Thomas at arm's length for many months. Perhaps,
35　therefore, she liked him all the more: for he always came up smiling, with impudence. She watched him vanquish one girl, then another. She could tell by the movement of his mouth and eyes, when he flirted with her in the morning, that he had been walking out with this lass, or the other, the night before. A fine Cock-of-the-walk he was.
40　She could sum him up pretty well.

In their subtle antagonism, they knew each other like old friends, they were as shrewd with one another almost as man and wife. But Annie had always kept him sufficiently at arm's length. Besides, she had a boy of her own.

The Statutes fair,* however, came in November, at Bestwood. It happened that Annie had the Monday night off. It was a drizzling ugly night, yet she dressed herself up and went to the fair ground. She was alone, but she expected soon to find a pal of some sort.

The roundabouts were veering round and grinding out their music, the side shows were making as much commotion as possible. In the cocoa-nut shies there were no cocoa-nuts, but artificial war-time substitutes, which the lads declared were fastened into the irons. There was a sad decline in brilliance and luxury. None the less, the ground was muddy as ever, there was the same crush, the press of faces lighted up by the flares and the electric lights, the same smell of naphtha and [of new-]fried* potatoes, and of electricity.

Who should be the first to greet Miss Annie, on the show ground, but John Thomas. He had a black overcoat buttoned up to his chin, and a tweed cap pulled down over his brows, his face between was ruddy and smiling and hardy as ever. She knew so well the way his mouth moved.

She was very glad to have a "boy." To be at the Statutes without a fellow was no fun. Instantly, like the gallant he was, he took her on the Dragons, grim-toothed, round-about switchbacks. It was not nearly so exciting as a tram-car, actually. But then, to be seated in a shaking green dragon, uplifted above the sea of bubble faces, careering in a rickety fashion in the lower heavens, whilst John Thomas, leaned over her, his cigarette in his mouth, was after all the right style. She was a plump, quick, alive little creature. So she was quite excited and happy.

John Thomas made her stay on for the next round. And therefore she could hardly for shame repulse him when he put his arm round her and drew her a little nearer to him, in a very warm and cuddly manner. Besides, he was fairly discreet, he kept his movement as hidden as possible. She looked down, and saw that his red, clean hand was out of sight of the crowd. And they knew each other so well. So they warmed up to the fair.

After the dragons they went on the horses. John Thomas paid each time, so she could but be complaisant. He of course sat astride on the outer horse—named "Black Bess"—and she sat sideways,

towards him, on the inner horse—named "Wildfire." But of course
John Thomas was not going to sit discreetly on "Black Bess,"
holding the brass bar. Round they spun and heaved, in the light. And
round he swung on his wooden steed, flinging one leg across her
5   mount, and perilously tipping up and down, across the space, half
lying back, laughing at her. He was perfectly happy, she was afraid
her hat was on one side, but she was excited.

He threw quoits on a table, and won her two large, pale blue
hat-pins. And then, hearing the noise of the cinema,* announcing
10 another performance, they climbed the boards and went in.

Of course, during these performances, pitch darkness falls from
time to time, when the machine goes wrong. Then there is a wild
whooping, and a loud smacking of simulated kisses. In these
moments John Thomas drew Annie towards him. After all, he had a
15 wonderfully warm, cosy way of holding a girl with his arm, he seemed
to make such a nice fit. And after all it was pleasant to be so held: so
very comforting and cosy and nice. He leaned over her and she felt
his breath on her hair, she knew he wanted to kiss her on the lips.
And after all, he was so warm and she fitted in to him so softly. After
20 all, she wanted him to touch her lips.

But the light sprang up, she also started electrically, and put her
hat straight. He left his arm lying nonchalant behind her. Well, it was
fun, it was exciting to be at the Statutes with John Thomas.

When the cinema was over they went for a walk across the dark,
25 damp fields. He had all the arts of love-making. He was especially
good at holding a girl, when he sat with her on a stile in the black,
drizzling darkness. He seemed to be holding her in space, against his
own warmth and gratification. And his kisses were soft and slow and
searching.

30 So Annie walked out with John Thomas, though she kept her own
boy dangling in the distance. Some of the tram-girls chose to be
huffy. But there, you must take things as you find them, in this life.

There was no mistake about it, Annie liked John Thomas a good
deal. She felt so rich and warm in herself, whenever he was near.
35 And John Thomas really liked Annie, more than usual. The soft,
melting way in which she could flow into a fellow, as if she melted
into his very bones, was something rare and good. He fully
appreciated this.

But with a developing acquaintance there began a developing
40 intimacy. Annie wanted to consider him a person, a man, she wanted

to take an intelligent interest in him, and to have an intelligent
response. She did not want a *mere* nocturnal presence: which was
what he was so far. And she prided herself that he could not leave
her.

Here she made a mistake. John Thomas intended to remain a 5
nocturnal presence, he had no idea of becoming an all-round
individual to her. When she started to take an intelligent interest in
him and his life and his character, he sheered off. He hated
intelligent interest. And he knew that the only way to stop it was to
avoid it. The possessive female was aroused in Annie. So he left 10
her.

It was no use saying she was not surprised. She was at first
startled, thrown out of her count. For she had been so *very* sure of
holding him. For a while she was staggered, and everything became
uncertain to her. Then she wept with fury, indignation, desolation 15
and misery. Then she had a spasm of despair. And then, when he
came, still impudently, on to her car, still familiar, but letting her
see by the movement of his head that he had gone away to somebody else, for the time being, and was enjoying pastures new, then
she determined to have her own back. 20

She had a very shrewd idea what girls John Thomas had taken
out. She went to Nora Purdy. Nora was a tall, rather pale, but
well-built girl, with beautiful yellow hair. She was rather secretive.

"Hey!" said Annie, accosting her: then softly: "Who's John
Thomas on with now?" 25

"I don't know," said Nora.

"Why tha does," said Annie, ironically lapsing into dialect. "Tha
knows as well as I do."

"Well, I do then," said Nora. "It isn't me, so don't bother."

"It's Cissy Meakin, isn't it?" 30

"It is for all I know."

"Hasn't he got a face on him!"* said Annie. "I don't half like his
cheek! I could knock him off the foot-board when he comes round
at me."

"He'll get dropped on* one of these days," said Nora. 35

"Ay, he will when somebody makes up their mind to drop it on
him. I should like to see him taken down a peg or two, shouldn't
you?"

"I shouldn't mind," said Nora.

"You've got quite as much cause to as I have," said Annie. "But 40 we'll drop on him one of these days, my girl. What? Don't you want to?"

"I don't mind," said Nora.

But as a matter of fact, Nora was much more vindictive than
5 Annie.

One by one Annie went the round of the old flames. It so happened that Cissy Meakin left the tramway service in quite a short time. Her mother made her leave. Then John Thomas was on the *qui vive*. He cast his eyes over his old flock. And his eyes lighted on
10 Annie. He thought she would be safe now. Besides, he liked her.

She arranged to walk home with him on Sunday night. It so happened that her car would be in the depôt at half-past nine: the last car would come in at 10.15. So John Thomas was to wait for her there.

15 At the depôt the girls had a little waiting-room of their own. It was quite rough, but cosy, with a fire and an oven and a mirror, and table and wooden chairs. The half dozen girls who knew John Thomas only too well had arranged to take service this Sunday afternoon. So as the cars began to come in, early, the girls dropped in to the
20 waiting-room. And instead of hurrying off home, they sat round the fire and had a cup of tea. Outside was the darkness and lawlessness of war-time.

John Thomas came on the car after Annie, at about a quarter to ten. He poked his head easily into the girls' waiting-room.

25 "Prayer meeting?" he asked.

"Ay," said Laura Sharp. "Ladies only."

"That's me!" said John Thomas. It was one of his favourite exclamations.

"Shut the door, boy," said Muriel Baggaley.

30 "On which side of me?" said John Thomas.

"Which tha likes," said Polly Birkin.*

He had come in, and closed the door behind him. The girls moved in their circle, to make a place for him near the fire. He took off his great-coat and pushed back his hat.

35 "Who handles the tea-pot?" he said.

Nora Purdy silently poured him out a cup of tea.

"Want a bit o' my bread and drippin'?" said Muriel Baggaley to him.

"Ay, give us a bit."

40 And he began to eat his piece of bread.

"There's no place like home, girls," he said.

They all looked at him as he uttered this piece of impudence. He seemed to be sunning himself in the presence of so many damsels.

"Especially if you're not afraid to go home in the dark," said Laura Sharp.

"Me! By myself I am."

They sat till they heard the last tram come in. In a few minutes, Emma Houselay entered.

"Come on, my old duck," cried Polly Birkin.

"It *is* perishing," said Emma, holding her fingers to the fire.

"'But—I'm afraid to, go home in, the dark,'" sang Laura Sharp, the tune having got into her mind.*

"Who're you going with tonight, John Thomas?" asked Muriel Baggaley, coolly.

"Tonight?" said John Thomas. "Oh, I'm going home by myself, tonight—all on my lonely-O."*

"That's me!" said Nora Purdy, using his own ejaculation.

The girls laughed shrilly.

"Me as well, Nora," said John Thomas.

"Don't know what you mean," said Laura.

"Yes, I'm toddling," said he, rising and reaching for his overcoat.

"Nay," said Polly. "We're all here waiting for you."

"We've got to be up in good time in the morning," he said, in the benevolent official manner.

They all laughed.

"Nay," said Muriel, "don't leave us all lonely, John Thomas. Take one!"

"I'll take the lot, if you like," he responded gallantly.

"That you won't, either," said Muriel. "Two's company, seven's too much of a good thing."

"Nay, take one," said Laura. "Fair and square, all above board, and say which one."

"Ay," cried Annie, speaking for the first time. "Pick, John Thomas, let's hear thee."

"Nay," he said. "I'm going home quiet tonight. Feeling good, for once."

"Whereabouts?" said Annie. "Take a good un, then. But tha's got to take one of us!"

"Nay, how can I take one," he said, laughing uneasily. "I don't want to make enemies."

"You'd only make *one*," said Annie.

"The chosen *one*," added Laura.

"Oh ay! Who said girls!" exclaimed John Thomas, again turning, as if to escape. "Well, good-night."

5   "Nay, you've got to make your pick," said Muriel. "Turn your face to the wall, and say which one touches you. Go on—we shall only just touch your back—one of us—go on—turn your face to the wall, and don't look, and say which one touches you."

He was uneasy, mistrusting them. Yet he had not the courage to 10 break away. They pushed him to a wall and stood him there with his face to it. Behind his back they all grimaced, tittering. He looked so comical. He looked around uneasily.

"Go on!" he cried.

"You're looking—you're looking!" they shouted.

15   He turned his head away. And suddenly, with a movement like a swift cat, Annie went forward and fetched him a box on the side of the head that sent his cap flying, and himself staggering. He started round.

But at Annie's signal they all flew at him, slapping him, pinching 20 him, pulling his hair, though more in fun than in spite or anger. He however saw red. His blue eyes flamed with strange fear as well as fury, and he butted through the girls to the door. It was locked. He wrenched at it. Roused, alert, the girls stood round and looked at him. He faced them, at bay. At that moment they were rather 25 horrifying to him, as they stood in their short uniforms. He was distinctly afraid.

"Come on, John Thomas! Come on! Choose!" said Annie.

"What are you after? Open the door," he said.

"We sha'n't—not till you've chosen," said Muriel.

30   "Chosen what?" he said.

"Chosen the one you're going to marry," she replied.

He hesitated a moment:—

"Open the blasted door," he said, "and get back to your senses." He spoke with official authority.

35   "You've got to choose," cried the girls.

"Come on!" cried Annie, looking him in the eye. "Come on! Come on!"

He went forward, rather vaguely. She had taken off her belt, and swinging it, she fetched him a sharp blow over the head, with the 40 buckle end. He sprang and seized her. But immediately the other

girls rushed upon him, pulling and tearing and beating him. Their
blood was now thoroughly up. He was their sport now. They were
going to have their own back, out of him. Strange, wild creatures,*
they hung on him and rushed at him to bear him down. His tunic was
torn right up the back. Nora had hold at the back of his collar, and   5
was actually strangling him. Luckily the button burst. He struggled
in a wild frenzy of fury and terror, almost mad terror. His tunic was
simply torn off his back, his shirt-sleeves were torn away, his arms
were naked. The girls rushed at him, clenched their hands on him
and pulled at him: or they rushed at him and pushed him, butted him   10
with all their might: or they struck him wild blows. He ducked and
cringed and struck sideways. They became more intense.

At last he was down. They rushed on him, kneeling on him. He
had neither breath nor strength to move. His face was bleeding with
a long scratch, his brow was bruised.   15

Annie knelt on him, the other girls knelt and hung on to him.
Their faces were flushed, their hair wild, their eyes were all glittering
strangely. He lay at last quite still, with face averted, as an animal lies
when it is defeated and at the mercy of the captor. Sometimes his eye
glanced back at the wild faces of the girls. His breast rose heavily, his 20
wrists were torn.

"Now then, my fellow!" gasped Annie at length. "Now
then—now——"

At the sound of her terrifying, cold triumph, he suddenly started
to struggle as an animal might, but the girls threw themselves upon   25
him with unnatural strength and power, forcing him down.

"Yes—now then—!" gasped Annie at length.

And there was a dead silence, in which the thud of heart-beating
was to be heard. It was a suspense of pure silence in every soul.

"Now you know where you are," said Annie.   30

The sight of his white, bare arm maddened the girls. He lay in a
kind of trance of fear and antagonism. They felt themselves filled
with supernatural strength.

Suddenly Polly started to laugh—to giggle wildly—helplessly—
and Emma and Muriel joined in. But Annie and Nora and Laura   35
remained the same, tense, watchful, with gleaming eyes. He winced
away from these eyes.

"Yes," said Annie, in a curious low tone, secret and deadly. "Yes!
You've got it now! *You* know what you've done, don't you?—You
know what you've done."   40

He made no sound nor sign, but lay with bright, averted eyes, and averted, bleeding face.

"You ought to be *killed*, that's what you ought," said Annie, tensely. "You ought to be *killed*." And there was a terrifying lust in her voice.

Polly was ceasing to laugh, and giving long-drawn Oh-h-hs and sighs as she came to herself.

"He's got to choose," she said vaguely.

"Oh, yes, he has," said Laura, with vindictive decision.

"Do you hear—do you hear?" said Annie. And with a sharp movement, that made him wince, she turned his face to her.

"Do you hear?" she repeated, shaking him.

But he was quite dumb. She fetched him a sharp slap on the face. He started, and his eyes widened. Then his face darkened with defiance, after all.

"Do you hear?" she repeated.

He only looked at her with hostile eyes.

"Speak!" she said, putting her face devilishly near his.

"What?" he said, almost overcome.

"You've got to *choose*!" she cried, as if it were some terrible menace, and as if it hurt her that she could not exact more.

"What?" he said, in fear.

"Choose your girl, Coddy. You've got to choose her now. And you'll get your neck broken if you play any more of your tricks, my boy. You're settled now."

There was a pause. Again he averted his face. He was cunning in his overthrow. He did not give in to them really—no, not if they tore him to bits.

"All right then," he said, "I choose Annie." His voice was strange and full of malice. Annie let go of him as if he had been a hot coal.

"He's chosen Annie!" said the girls in chorus.

"Me!" cried Annie. She was still kneeling, but away from him. He was still lying prostrate, with averted face. The girls grouped uneasily around.

"Me!" repeated Annie, with a terrible bitter accent.

Then she got up, drawing away from him with strange disgust and bitterness.

"I wouldn't touch him," she said.

But her face quivered with a kind of agony, she seemed as if she would fall. The other girls turned aside. He remained lying on the floor, with his torn clothes and bleeding, averted face.

"Oh, if he's chosen——" said Polly.

"I don't want him—he can choose again," said Annie, with the same rather bitter hopelessness.

"Get up," said Polly, lifting his shoulder. "Get up."

He rose slowly, a strange, ragged dazed creature. The girls eyed him from a distance, curiously, furtively, dangerously.

"Who wants him?" cried Laura roughly.

"Nobody," they answered, with contempt. Yet each one of them waited for him to look at her, hoped he would look at her. All except Annie, and something was broken in her.

He, however, kept his face closed and averted from them all. There was a silence of the end. He picked up the torn pieces of his tunic, without knowing what to do with them. The girls stood about uneasily, flushed, panting, tidying their hair and their dress unconsciously, and watching him. He looked at none of them. He espied his cap in a corner, and went and picked it up. He put it on his head, and one of the girls burst into a shrill, hysteric laugh at the sight he presented. He, however, took no heed, but went straight to where his overcoat hung on a peg. The girls moved away from contact with him as if he had been an electric wire. He put on his coat and buttoned it down. Then he rolled his tunic-rags into a bundle, and stood before the locked door, dumbly.

"Open the door, somebody," said Laura.

"Annie's got the key," said one.

Annie silently offered the key to the girls. Nora unlocked the door.

"Tit for tat, old man," she said. "Show yourself a man, and don't bear a grudge."

But without a word or sign he had opened the door and gone, his face closed, his head dropped.

"That'll learn him," said Laura.

"Coddy!" said Nora.

"Shut up, for God's sake!" cried Annie fiercely, as if in torture.

"Well, I'm about ready to go, Polly. Look sharp!" said Muriel.

The girls were all anxious to be off. They were tidying themselves hurriedly, with mute, stupefied faces.

The Blind Man

Isabel Pervin* was listening for two sounds—for the sound of wheels on the drive outside and for the noise of her husband's footsteps in the hall. Her dearest and oldest friend, a man who seemed almost 5 indispensable to her living, would drive up in the rainy dusk of the closing November day. The trap had gone to fetch him from the station. And her husband, who had been blinded in Flanders, and who had a disfiguring mark on his brow, would be coming in from the out-houses.

10 He had been home for a year now. He was totally blind. Yet they had been very happy. The Grange* was Maurice's own place. The back was a farmstead, and the Wernhams, who occupied the rear premises, acted as farmers. Isabel lived with her husband in the handsome rooms in front. She and he had been almost entirely alone 15 together since he was wounded. They talked and sang and read together in a wonderful and unspeakable intimacy. Then she reviewed books for a Scottish newspaper,* carrying on her old interest, and he occupied himself a good deal with the farm. Sightless, he could still discuss everything with Wernham, and he 20 could also do a good deal of work about the place, menial work, it is true, but it gave him satisfaction. He milked the cows, carried in the pails, turned the separator, attended to the pigs and horses. Life was still very full and strangely serene for the blind man, peaceful with the almost incomprehensible peace of immediate contact in dark-25 ness. With his wife he had a whole world, rich and real and invisible.

They were newly and remotely happy. He did not even regret the loss of his sight in these times of dark, palpable joy. A certain exultance swelled his soul.

But as time wore on, sometimes the rich glamour would leave 30 them. Sometimes, after months of this intensity, a sense of burden overcame Isabel, a weariness, a terrible *ennui*, in that silent house approached between a colonnade of tall-shafted pines. Then she felt she would go mad, for she could not bear it. And sometimes he had devastating fits of depression, which seemed to lay waste his whole

46

being. It was worse than depression—a black misery, when his own life was a torture to him, and when his presence was unbearable to his wife. The dread went down to the roots of her soul as these black days recurred. In a kind of panic she tried to wrap herself up still further in her husband. She forced the old spontaneous cheerfulness and joy to continue. But the effort it cost her was almost too much. She knew she could not keep it up. She felt she would scream with the strain, and would give anything, anything, to escape. She longed to possess her husband utterly; it gave her inordinate joy to have him entirely to herself. And yet, when again he was gone in a black and massive misery, she could not bear him, she could not bear herself; she wished she could be snatched away off the earth altogether, anything rather than live at this cost.

Dazed, she schemed for a way out. She invited friends, she tried to give him some further connection with the outer world. But it was no good. After all their joy and suffering, after their dark, great year of blindness and solitude and unspeakable nearness, other people seemed to them both shallow, prattling, rather impertinent. Shallow prattle seemed presumptuous. He became impatient and irritated, she was wearied. And so they lapsed into their solitude again. For they preferred it.

But now, in a few weeks' time, her second baby would be born. The first had died, an infant, when her husband first went out to France. She looked with joy and relief to the coming of the second. It would be her salvation. But also she felt some anxiety. She was thirty years old, her husband was a year younger. They both wanted the child very much. Yet she could not help feeling afraid. She had her husband on her hands, a terrible joy to her, and a terrifying burden. The child would occupy her love and attention. And then, what of Maurice? What would he do? If only she could feel that he, too, would be at peace and happy when the child came! She did so want to luxuriate in a rich, physical satisfaction of maternity. But the man, what would he do? How could she provide for him, how avert those shattering black moods of his, which destroyed them both?

She sighed with fear. But at this time Bertie Reid* wrote to Isabel. He was her old friend, a second or third cousin, a Scotchman, as she was a Scotchwoman. They had been brought up near to one another, and all her life he had been her friend, like a brother, but better than her own brothers. She loved him—though not in the marrying sense. There was a sort of kinship between them, an affinity. They understood one another instinctively. But Isabel would never have thought of marrying Bertie. It would have seemed like marrying in her own family.

Bertie was a barrister and a man of letters, a Scotchman of the intellectual type, quick, ironical, sentimental, and on his knees before the woman he adored but did not want to marry. Maurice Pervin was different. He came of a good old country family—the Grange was not a very great distance from Oxford. He was passionate, sensitive, perhaps over-sensitive, wincing—a big fellow with heavy limbs and a forehead that flushed painfully. For his mind was slow, as if drugged by the strong provincial blood that beat in his veins. He was very sensitive to his own mental slowness, his feelings being quick and acute. So that he was just the opposite to Bertie, whose mind was much quicker than his emotions, which were not so very fine.

From the first the two men did not like each other. Isabel felt that they *ought* to get on together. But they did not. She felt that if only each could have the clue to the other there would be such a rare understanding between them. It did not come off, however. Bertie adopted a slightly ironical attitude, very offensive to Maurice, who returned the Scotch irony with English resentment, a resentment which deepened sometimes into stupid hatred.

This was a little puzzling to Isabel. However, she accepted it in the course of things. Men were made freakish and unreasonable. Therefore, when Maurice was going out to France for the second time, she felt that, for her husband's sake, she must discontinue her friendship with Bertie. She wrote to the barrister to this effect. Bertram Reid simply replied that in this, as in all other matters, he must obey her wishes, if these were indeed her wishes.

For nearly two years nothing had passed between the two friends. Isabel rather gloried in the fact: she had no compunction. She had one great article of faith, which was, that husband and wife should be so important to one another, that the rest of the world simply did not count. She and Maurice were husband and wife. They loved one another. They would have children. Then let everybody and everything else fade into insignificance outside this connubial felicity. She professed herself quite happy and ready to receive Maurice's friends. She was happy and ready: the happy wife, the ready woman in possession. Without knowing why, the friends retired abashed, and came no more. Maurice, of course, took as much satisfaction in this connubial absorption as Isabel did.

He shared in Isabel's literary activities, she cultivated a real interest in agriculture and cattle-raising. For she, being at heart perhaps an emotional enthusiast, always cultivated the practical side of life, and prided herself on her mastery of practical affairs. Thus the husband and wife had spent the five years of their married life. The last had been one of blindness and unspeakable intimacy. And now Isabel felt a great indifference coming over her, a sort of lethargy. She wanted to be allowed to bear her child in peace, to nod by the fire and drift vaguely, physically, from day to day. Maurice was like an ominous thunder-cloud. She had to keep waking up to remember him.

When a little note from Bertie, asking if he were to put up a tombstone to their dead friendship, and speaking of the real pain he felt on account of her husband's loss of sight, she felt a pang, a fluttering agitation of re-awakening. And she read the letter to Maurice.

"Ask him to come down," he said.

"Ask Bertie to come here!" she re-echoed.

"Yes—if he wants to."

Isabel paused for a few moments.

"I know he wants to—he'd only be too glad," she replied. "But what about you, Maurice? How would you like it?"

"I should like it."

"Well—in that case—— But I thought you didn't care for him——"

"Oh, I don't know. I might think different of him now," the blind man replied. It was rather abstruse to Isabel.

"Well, dear," she said, "if you're quite sure——"

"I'm sure enough. Let him come," said Maurice.

So Bertie was coming, coming this evening, in the November rain and darkness. Isabel was agitated, racked with her old restlessness and indecision. She had always suffered from this pain of doubt, just an agonising sense of uncertainty. It had begun to pass off, in the lethargy of maternity. Now it returned, and she resented it. She struggled as usual to maintain her calm, composed, friendly bearing, a sort of mask she wore over all her body.

A woman had lighted a tall lamp beside the table, and spread the cloth. The long dining-room was dim, with its elegant but rather severe pieces of old furniture. Only the round table glowed softly under the light. It had a rich, beautiful effect. The white cloth glistened and dropped its heavy, pointed lace corners almost to the carpet, the china was old and handsome, creamy-yellow, with a blotched pattern of harsh red and deep blue, the cups large and bell-shaped, the teapot gallant. Isabel looked at it with superficial appreciation.

5   Her nerves were hurting her. She looked automatically again at the high, uncurtained windows. In the last dusk she could just perceive outside a huge fir-tree swaying its boughs: it was as if she thought it rather than saw it. The rain came flying on the window panes. Ah, why had she no peace? These two men, why did they tear

10 at her? Why did they not come—why was there this suspense?

She sat in a lassitude that was really suspense and irritation. Maurice, at least, might come in—there was nothing to keep him out. She rose to her feet. Catching sight of her reflection in a mirror, she glanced at herself with a slight smile of recognition, as if she were

15 an old friend to herself. Her face was oval and calm, her nose a little arched. Her neck made a beautiful line down to her shoulder. With hair knotted loosely behind, she had something of a warm, maternal look. Thinking this of herself, she arched her eyebrows and her rather heavy eye-lids, with a little flicker of a smile, and for a moment

20 her grey eyes looked amused and wicked, a little sardonic, out of her transfigured Madonna face.

Then, resuming her air of womanly patience—she was really fatally self-determined—she went with a little jerk towards the door. Her eyes were slightly reddened.

25 She passed down the wide hall, and through a door at the end. Then she was in the farm premises. The scent of dairy, and of farm-kitchen, and of farm-yard and of leather almost overcame her: but particularly the scent of dairy. They had been scalding out the pans. The flagged passage in front of her was dark, puddled and wet.

30 Light came out from the open kitchen door. She went forward and stood in the doorway. The farm-people were at tea, seated at a little distance from her, round a long, narrow table, in the centre of which stood a white lamp. Ruddy faces, ruddy hands holding food, red mouths working, heads bent over the tea-cups: men, land-girls,

35 boys: it was tea-time, feeding-time. Some faces caught sight of her. Mrs. Wernham, going round behind the chairs with a large black tea-pot, halting slightly in her walk, was not aware of her for a moment. Then she turned suddenly.

"Oh, is it Madam!" she exclaimed. "Come in, then, come in!

40 We're at tea." And she dragged forward a chair.

"No, I won't come in," said Isabel. "I'm afraid I interrupt your meal."

"No—no—not likely, Madam, not likely."

"Hasn't Mr. Pervin come in, do you know?"

"I'm sure I couldn't say! Missed him, have you, Madam?"

"No, I only wanted him to come in," laughed Isabel, as if shyly.

"Wanted him, did ye? Get up, boy—get up, now——"

Mrs. Wernham knocked one of the boys on the shoulder. He began to scrape to his feet, chewing largely.

"I believe he's in top stable," said another face from the table.

"Ah! No, don't get up. I'm going myself," said Isabel.

"Don't you go out of a dirty night like this. Let the lad go. Get along wi' ye, boy," said Mrs. Wernham.

"No, no," said Isabel, with a decision that was always obeyed. "Go on with your tea, Tom. I'd like to go across to the stable, Mrs. Wernham."

"Did ever you hear tell!" exclaimed the woman.

"Isn't the trap late?" asked Isabel.

"Why, no," said Mrs. Wernham, peering into the distance at the tall, dim clock. "No, Madam—we can give it another quarter or twenty minutes yet, good—yes, every bit of a quarter."

"Ah! It seems late when darkness falls so early," said Isabel.

"It do, that it do. Bother the days, that they draw in so," answered Mrs. Wernham. "Proper miserable!"

"They are," said Isabel, withdrawing.

She pulled on her overshoes, wrapped a large Tartan shawl around her, put on a man's felt hat, and ventured out along the causeways of the first yard. It was very dark. The wind was roaring in the great elms behind the outhouses. When she came to the second yard the darkness seemed deeper. She was unsure of her footing. She wished she had brought a lantern. Rain blew against her. Half she liked it, half she felt unwilling to battle.

She reached at last the just visible door of the stable. There was no sign of a light anywhere. Opening the upper half, she looked in: into a simple well of darkness. The smell of horses, and ammonia, and of warmth was startling to her, in that full night. She listened with all her ears, but could hear nothing save the night, and the stirring of a horse.

"Maurice!" she called, softly and musically, though she was afraid. "Maurice—are you there?"

Nothing came from the darkness. She knew the rain and wind blew in upon the horses, the hot animal life. Feeling it wrong, she entered the stable, and drew the lower half of the door shut, holding the upper part close. She did not stir, because she was aware of the
5 presence of the dark hind-quarters of the horses, though she could not see them, and she was afraid. Something wild stirred in her heart.

She listened intensely. Then she heard a small noise in the distance—far away, it seemed—the chink of a pan, and a man's voice
10 speaking a brief word. It would be Maurice, in the other part of the stable. She stood motionless, waiting for him to come through the partition door. The horses were so terrifyingly near to her, in the invisible.

The loud jarring of the inner door-latch made her start; the door
15 was opened. She could hear and feel her husband entering and invisibly passing among the horses near to her, in darkness as they were, actively intermingled. The rather low sound of his voice as he spoke to the horses came velvety to her nerves. How near he was, and how invisible! The darkness seemed to be in a strange swirl of violent
20 life, just upon her. She turned giddy.

Her presence of mind made her call, quietly and musically:

"Maurice! Maurice—dea-ar!"

"Yes," he answered. "Isabel?"

She saw nothing, and the sound of his voice seemed to touch her.
25 "Hello!" she answered cheerfully, straining her eyes to see him. He was still busy, attending to the horses near her, but she saw only darkness. It made her almost desperate.

"Won't you come in, dear?" she said.

"Yes, I'm coming. Just half a minute. *Stand over—now!* Trap's not
30 come, has it?"

"Not yet," said Isabel.

His voice was pleasant and ordinary, but it had a slight suggestion of the stable to her. She wished he would come away. Whilst he was so utterly invisible, she was afraid of him.
35 "How's the time?" he asked.

"Not yet six," she replied. She disliked to answer into the dark. Presently he came very near to her, and she retreated out of doors.

"The weather blows in here," he said, coming steadily forward, feeling for the doors. She shrank away. At last she could dimly see
40 him.

"Bertie won't have much of a drive," he said, as he closed the doors.

"He won't indeed!" said Isabel calmly, watching the dark shape at the door.

"Give me your arm, dear," she said.

She pressed his arm close to her, as she went. But she longed to see him, to look at him. She was nervous. He walked erect, with face rather lifted, but with a curious tentative movement of his powerful, muscular legs. She could feel the clever, careful, strong contact of his feet with the earth, as she balanced against him. For a moment he was a tower of darkness to her, as if he rose out of the earth.

In the house-passage he wavered, and went cautiously, with a curious look of silence about him as he felt for the bench. Then he sat down heavily. He was a man with rather sloping shoulders, but with heavy limbs, powerful legs that seemed to know the earth. His head was small, usually carried high and light. As he bent down to unfasten his gaiters and boots, he did not look blind. His hair was brown and crisp, his hands were large, reddish, intelligent, the veins stood out in the wrists; and his thighs and knees seemed massive. When he stood up his face and neck were surcharged with blood, the veins stood out on his temples. She did not look at his blindness.

Isabel was always glad when they had passed through the dividing door into their own regions of repose and beauty. She was a little afraid of him, out there in the animal grossness of the back. His bearing also changed, as he smelt the familiar indefinable odour that pervaded his wife's surroundings, a delicate, refined scent, very faintly spicy. Perhaps it came from the pot-pourri bowls.

He stood at the foot of the stairs, arrested, listening. She watched him, and her heart sickened. He seemed to be listening to fate.

"He's not here yet," he said. "I'll go up and change."

"Maurice," she said, "you're not wishing he wouldn't come, are you?"

"I couldn't quite say," he answered. "I feel myself rather on the *qui vive*."

"I can see you are," she answered. And she reached up and kissed his cheek. She saw his mouth relax into a slow smile.

"What are you laughing at?" she said, roguishly.

"You consoling me," he answered.

"Nay," she answered. "Why should I console you? You know we

love each other—you know *how* married we are! What does anything else matter?"

"Nothing at all, my dear."

He felt for her face, and touched it, smiling.

5   "*You're* all right, aren't you?" he asked, anxiously.

"I'm wonderfully all right, love," she answered. "It's you I am a little troubled about, at times."

"Why me?" he said, touching her cheeks delicately with the tips of his fingers. The touch had an almost hypnotising effect on her.

10   He went away upstairs. She saw him mount into the darkness, unseeing and unchanging. He did not know that the lamps on the upper corridor were unlighted. He went on into the darkness with unchanging step. She heard him in the bath-room.

Pervin moved about almost unconsciously in his familiar sur-
15   roundings, dark though everything was. He seemed to know the presence of objects before he touched them. It was a pleasure to him to rock thus through a world of things, carried on the flood in a sort of blood-prescience. He did not think much or trouble much. So long as he kept this sheer immediacy of blood-contact with the
20   substantial world he was happy, he wanted no intervention of visual consciousness. In this state there was a certain rich positivity, bordering sometimes on rapture. Life seemed to move in him like a tide lapping, lapping, and advancing, enveloping all things darkly. It was a pleasure to stretch forth the hand and meet the unseen object,
25   clasp it, and possess it in pure contact. He did not try to remember, to visualise. He did not want to. The new way of consciousness substituted itself in him.

The rich suffusion of this state generally kept him happy, reaching its culmination in the consuming passion for his wife. But at times
30   the flow would seem to be checked and thrown back. Then it would beat inside him like a tangled sea, and he was tortured in the shattered chaos of his own blood. He grew to dread this arrest, this throw-back, this chaos inside himself, when he seemed merely at the mercy of his own powerful and conflicting elements. How to get
35   some measure of control or surety, this was the question. And when the question rose maddening in him, he would clench his fists as if he would *compel* the whole universe to submit to him. But it was in vain. He could not even compel himself.

To-night, however, he was still serene, though little tremors of
40   unreasonable exasperation ran through him. He had to handle the razor very carefully, as he shaved, for it was not at one with him, he

was afraid of it. His hearing also was too much sharpened. He heard the woman lighting the lamps on the corridor, and attending to the fire in the visitors' room. And then, as he went to his room, he heard the trap arrive. Then came Isabel's voice, lifted and calling, like a bell ringing:

"Is it you, Bertie? Have you come?"

And a man's voice answered out of the wind:

"Hello, Isabel! There you are."

"Have you had a miserable drive? I'm so sorry we couldn't send a closed carriage. I can't see you at all, you know."

"I'm coming. No, I liked the drive—it was like Perthshire. Well, how are you? You're looking fit as ever, as far as I can see."

"Oh, yes," said Isabel. "I'm wonderfully well. How are you? Rather thin, I think——"

"Worked to death—everybody's old cry. But I'm all right, Ciss. How's Pervin?—isn't he here?"

"Oh, yes, he's upstairs changing. Yes, he's awfully well. Take off your wet things; I'll send them to be dried."

"And how are you both, in spirits? He doesn't fret?"

"No—no, not at all. No, on the contrary, really. We've been wonderfully happy, incredibly. It's more than I can understand—so wonderful: the nearness, and the peace——"

"Ah! Well, that's awfully good news——"

They moved away. Pervin heard no more. But a childish sense of desolation had come over him, as he heard their brisk voices. He seemed shut out—like a child that is left out. He was aimless and excluded, he did not know what to do with himself. The helpless desolation came over him. He fumbled nervously as he dressed himself, in a state almost of childishness. He disliked the Scotch accent in Bertie's speech, and the slight response it found on Isabel's tongue. He disliked the slight purr of complacency in the Scottish speech. He disliked intensely the glib way in which Isabel spoke of their happiness and nearness. It made him recoil. He was fretful and beside himself like a child, he had almost a childish nostalgia to be included in the life circle. And at the same time he was a man, dark and powerful and infuriated by his own weakness. By some fatal flaw, he could not be by himself, he had to depend on the support of another. And this very dependence enraged him. He hated Bertie Reid, and at the same time he knew the hatred was nonsense, he knew it was the outcome of his own weakness.

He went downstairs. Isabel was alone in the dining-room. She watched him enter, head erect, his feet tentative. He looked so strong-blooded and healthy, and, at the same time, cancelled. Cancelled—that was the word that flew across her mind. Perhaps it was his scar suggested it.

5 "You heard Bertie come, Maurice?" she said.

"Yes—isn't he here?"

"He's in his room. He looks very thin and worn."

"I suppose he works himself to death."

A woman came in with a tray—and after a few minutes Bertie
10 came down. He was a little dark man, with a very big forehead, thin, wispy hair, and sad, large eyes. His expression was inordinately sad—almost funny. He had odd, short legs.

Isabel watched him hesitate under the door, and glance nervously at her husband. Pervin heard him and turned.

15 "Here you are, now," said Isabel. "Come, let us eat."

Bertie went across to Maurice.

"How are you, Pervin?" he said, as he advanced.

The blind man stuck his hand out into space, and Bertie took it.

"Very fit. Glad you've come," said Maurice.

20 Isabel glanced at them, and glanced away, as if she could not bear to see them.

"Come," she said. "Come to table. Aren't you both awfully hungry? I am, tremendously."

"I'm afraid you waited for me," said Bertie, as they sat down.

25 Maurice had a curious monolithic way of sitting in a chair, erect and distant. Isabel's heart always beat when she caught sight of him thus.

"No," she replied to Bertie. "We're very little later than usual. We're having a sort of high tea, not dinner. Do you mind? It gives us
30 such a nice long evening, uninterrupted."

"I like it," said Bertie.

Maurice was feeling, with curious little movements, almost like a cat kneading her bed, for his plate, his knife and fork, his napkin. He was getting the whole geography of his cover into his consciousness.
35 He sat erect and inscrutable, remote-seeming. Bertie watched the static figure of the blind man, the delicate tactile discernment of the large, ruddy hands, and the curious mindless silence of the brow, above the scar. With difficulty he looked away, and without knowing what he did, picked up a little crystal bowl of violets from the table,
40 and held them to his nose.

"They are sweet-scented," he said. "Where do they come from?"

"From the garden—under the windows," said Isabel.

"So late in the year—and so fragrant! Do you remember the violets under Aunt Bell's south wall?"

The two friends looked at each other and exchanged a smile, Isabel's eyes lighting up.

"Don't I?" she replied. "*Wasn't* she queer!"

"A curious old girl," laughed Bertie. "There's a streak of freakishness in the family, Isabel."

"Ah—but not in you and me, Bertie," said Isabel. "Give them to Maurice, will you?" she added, as Bertie was putting down the flowers. "Have you smelled the violets, dear? Do!—they are so scented."

Maurice held out his hand, and Bertie placed the tiny bowl against his large, warm-looking fingers. Maurice's hand closed over the thin white fingers of the barrister. Bertie carefully extricated himself. Then the two watched the blind man smelling the violets. He bent his head and seemed to be thinking. Isabel waited.

"Aren't they sweet, Maurice?" she said at last, anxiously.

"Very," he said. And he held out the bowl. Bertie took it. Both he and Isabel were a little afraid, and deeply disturbed.

The meal continued. Isabel and Bertie chatted spasmodically. The blind man was silent. He touched his food repeatedly, with quick, delicate touches of his knife-point, then cut irregular bits. He could not bear to be helped. Both Isabel and Bertie suffered: Isabel wondered why. She did not suffer when she was alone with Maurice. Bertie made her conscious of a strangeness.

After the meal the three drew their chairs to the fire, and sat down to talk. The decanters were put on a table near at hand. Isabel knocked the logs on the fire, and clouds of brilliant sparks went up the chimney. Bertie noticed a slight weariness in her bearing.

"You will be glad when your child comes now, Isabel?" he said.

She looked up to him with a quick, wan smile.

"Yes, I shall be glad," she answered. "It begins to seem long. Yes, I shall be very glad. So will you, Maurice, won't you?" she added.

"Yes, I shall," replied her husband.

"We are both looking forward so much to having it," she said.

"Yes, of course," said Bertie.

He was a bachelor, three or four years older than Isabel. He lived in beautiful rooms overlooking the river, guarded by a faithful

Scottish man-servant. And he had his friends among the fair sex—not lovers, friends. So long as he could avoid any danger of courtship or marriage, he adored a few good women with constant and unfailing homage, and he was chivalrously fond of quite a
5   number. But if they seemed to encroach on him, he withdrew and detested them.

Isabel knew him very well, knew his beautiful constancy, and kindness, also his incurable weakness, which made him unable ever to enter into close contact of any sort. He was ashamed of himself,
10 because he could not marry, could not approach women physically. He wanted to do so. But he could not. At the centre of him he was afraid, helplessly and even brutally afraid. He had given up hope, had ceased to expect any more that he could escape his own weakness. Hence he was a brilliant and successful barrister, also a
15 *littérateur* of high repute, a rich man, and a great social success. At the centre he felt himself neuter, nothing.

Isabel knew him well. She despised him even while she admired him. She looked at his sad face, his little short legs, and felt contempt of him. She looked at his dark grey eyes, with their uncanny, almost
20 childlike intuition, and she loved him. He understood amazingly— but she had no fear of his understanding. As a man she patronised him.

And she turned to the impassive, silent figure of her husband. He sat leaning back, with folded arms, and face a little uptilted. His
25 knees were straight and massive. She sighed, picked up the poker, and again began to prod the fire, to rouse the clouds of soft brilliant sparks.

"Isabel tells me," Bertie began suddenly, "that you have not suffered unbearably from the loss of sight."
30 Maurice straightened himself to attend, but kept his arms folded.

"No," he said, "not unbearably. Now and again one struggles against it, you know. But there are compensations."

"They say it is much worse to be stone deaf," said Isabel.

"I believe it is," said Bertie. "Are there compensations?" he
35 added, to Maurice.

"Yes. You cease to bother about a great many things." Again Maurice stretched his figure, stretched the strong muscles of his back, and leaned backwards, with uplifted face.

"And that is a relief," said Bertie. "But what is there in place of
40 the bothering? What replaces the activity?"

There was a pause. At length the blind man replied, as out of a negligent, unattentive thinking:

"Oh, I don't know. There's a good deal when you're not active."

"Is there?" said Bertie. "What, exactly? It always seems to me that when there is no thought and no action, there is nothing."

Again Maurice was slow in replying.

"There is something," he replied. "I couldn't tell you what it is."

And the talk lapsed once more, Isabel and Bertie chatting gossip and reminiscence, the blind man silent.

At length Maurice rose restlessly, a big, obtrusive figure. He felt tight and hampered. He wanted to go away.

"Do you mind," he said, "if I go and speak to Wernham?"

"No—go along, dear," said Isabel.

And he went out. A silence came over the two friends. At length Bertie said:

"Nevertheless, it is a great deprivation, Cissie."

"It is, Bertie. I know it is."

"Something lacking all the time," said Bertie.

"Yes, I know. And yet—and yet—Maurice is right. There is something else, something *there*, which you never knew was there, and which you can't express."

"What is there?" asked Bertie.

"I don't know—it's awfully hard to define it—but something strong and immediate. There's something strange in Maurice's presence—indefinable—but I couldn't do without it. I agree that it seems to put one's mind to sleep. But when we're alone I miss nothing; it seems awfully rich, almost splendid, you know."

"I'm afraid I don't follow," said Bertie.

They talked desultorily. The wind blew loudly outside, rain chattered on the window-panes, making a sharp drum-sound, because of the closed, mellow-golden shutters inside. The logs burned slowly, with hot, almost invisible small flames. Bertie seemed uneasy, there were dark circles round his eyes. Isabel, rich with her approaching maternity, leaned looking into the fire. Her hair curled in odd, loose strands, very pleasing to the man. But she had a curious feeling of old woe in her heart, old, timeless night-woe.

"I suppose we're all deficient somewhere," said Bertie.

"I suppose so," said Isabel wearily.

"Damned, sooner or later."

"I don't know," she said, rousing herself. "I feel quite all right, you know. The child coming seems to make me indifferent to everything, just placid. I can't feel that there's anything to trouble about, you know."

"A good thing, I should say," he replied slowly.

5   "Well, there it is. I suppose it's just Nature. If only I felt I needn't trouble about Maurice, I should be perfectly content——"

"But you feel you must trouble about him?"

"Well—I don't know——" She even resented this much effort.

The night passed slowly. Isabel looked at the clock.

10   "I say," she said. "It's nearly ten o'clock. Where can Maurice be? I'm sure they're all in bed at the back. Excuse me a moment."

She went out, returning almost immediately.

"It's all shut up and in darkness," she said. "I wonder where he is. He must have gone out to the farm——"

15   Bertie looked at her.

"I suppose he'll come in," he said.

"I suppose so," she said. "But it's unusual for him to be out now."

"Would you like me to go out and see?"

"Well—if you wouldn't mind. I'd go, but——" She did not want
20   to make the physical effort.

Bertie put on an old overcoat and took a lantern. He went out from the side door. He shrank from the wet and roaring night. Such weather had a nervous effect on him: too much moisture everywhere made him feel almost imbecile. Unwilling, he went through it all. A
25   dog barked violently at him. He peered in all the buildings. At last, as he opened the upper door of a sort of intermediate barn, he heard a grinding noise, and looking in, holding up his lantern, saw Maurice, in his shirt-sleeves, standing listening, holding the handle of a turnip-pulper. He had been pulping sweet roots, a pile of which lay
30   dimly heaped in a corner behind him.

"That you, Wernham?" said Maurice, listening.

"No, it's me," said Bertie.

A large, half-wild grey cat was rubbing at Maurice's leg. The blind man stooped to rub its sides. Bertie watched the scene, then
35   unconsciously entered and shut the door behind him. He was in a high sort of barn-place, from which, right and left, ran off the corridors in front of the stalled cattle. He watched the slow, stooping motion of the other man, as he caressed the great cat.

Maurice straightened himself.

40   "You came to look for me?" he said.

"Isabel was a little uneasy," said Bertie.

"I'll come in. I like messing about doing these jobs."

The cat had reared her sinister, feline length against his leg, clawing at his thigh affectionately. He lifted her claws out of his flesh.

"I hope I'm not in your way at all at the Grange here," said Bertie, rather shy and stiff.

"My way? No, not a bit. I'm glad Isabel has somebody to talk to. I'm afraid it's I who am in the way. I know I'm not very lively company. Isabel's all right, don't you think? She's not unhappy, is she?"

"I don't think so."

"What does she say?"

"She says she's very content—only a little troubled about you."

"Why me?"

"Perhaps afraid that you might brood," said Bertie, cautiously.

"She needn't be afraid of that." He continued to caress the flattened grey head of the cat with his fingers. "What I am a bit afraid of," he resumed, "is that she'll find me a dead weight, always alone with me down here."

"I don't think you need think that," said Bertie, though this was what he feared himself.

"I don't know," said Maurice. "Sometimes I feel it isn't fair that she's saddled with me." Then he dropped his voice curiously. "I say," he asked, secretly struggling, "is my face much disfigured? Do you mind telling me?"

"There is the scar," said Bertie, wondering. "Yes, it is a disfigurement. But more pitiable than shocking."

"A pretty bad scar, though," said Maurice.

"Oh, yes."

There was a pause.

"Sometimes I feel I am horrible," said Maurice, in a low voice, talking as if to himself. And Bertie actually felt a quiver of horror.

"That's nonsense," he said.

Maurice again straightened himself, leaving the cat.

"There's no telling," he said. Then again, in an odd tone, he added: "I don't really know you, do I?"

"Probably not," said Bertie.

"Do you mind if I touch you?"

The lawyer shrank away instinctively. And yet, out of very philanthropy, he said, in a small voice: "Not at all."

But he suffered as the blind man stretched out a strong, naked hand to him. Maurice accidentally knocked off Bertie's hat.

"I thought you were taller," he said, starting. Then he laid his hand on Bertie Reid's head, closing the dome of the skull in a soft,
5 firm grasp, gathering it, as it were; then, shifting his grasp and softly closing again, with a fine, close pressure, till he had covered the skull and the face of the smaller man, tracing the brows, and touching the full, closed eyes, touching the small nose and the nostrils, the rough, short moustache, the mouth, the rather strong chin. The hand of the
10 blind man grasped the shoulder, the arm, the hand of the other man. He seemed to take him, in the soft, travelling grasp.

"You seem young," he said quietly, at last.

The lawyer stood almost annihilated, unable to answer.

"Your head seems tender, as if you were young," Maurice
15 repeated. "So do your hands. Touch my eyes, will you?—touch my scar."

Now Bertie quivered with revulsion. Yet he was under the power of the blind man, as if hypnotised. He lifted his hand, and laid the fingers on the scar, on the scarred eyes. Maurice suddenly covered
20 them with his own hand, pressed the fingers of the other man upon his disfigured eye-sockets, trembling in every fibre, and rocking slightly, slowly, from side to side. He remained thus for a minute or more, whilst Bertie stood as if in a swoon, unconscious, imprisoned.

Then suddenly Maurice removed the hand of the other man from
25 his brow, and stood holding it in his own.

"Oh, my God," he said, "we shall know each other now, shan't we? We shall know each other now."

Bertie could not answer. He gazed mute and terror-struck, overcome by his own weakness. He knew he could not answer. He
30 had an unreasonable fear, lest the other man should suddenly destroy him. Whereas Maurice was actually filled with hot, poignant love, the passion of friendship. Perhaps it was this very passion of friendship which Bertie shrank from most.

"We're all right together now, aren't we?" said Maurice. "It's all
35 right now, as long as we live, so far as we're concerned?"

"Yes," said Bertie, trying by any means to escape.

Maurice stood with head lifted, as if listening. The new delicate fulfilment of mortal friendship had come as a revelation and surprise to him, something exquisite and unhoped-for. He seemed to be
40 listening to hear if it were real.

Then he turned for his coat.

"Come," he said, "we'll go to Isabel."

Bertie took the lantern and opened the door. The cat disappeared. The two men went in silence along the causeways. Isabel, as they came, thought their footsteps sounded strange. She looked up pathetically and anxiously for their entrance. There seemed a curious elation about Maurice. Bertie was haggard, with sunken eyes.

"What is it?" she asked.

"We've become friends," said Maurice, standing with his feet apart, like a strange colossus.

"Friends!" re-echoed Isabel. And she looked again at Bertie. He met her eyes with a furtive, haggard look; his eyes were as if glazed with misery.

"I'm so glad," she said, in sheer perplexity.

"Yes," said Maurice.

He was indeed so glad. Isabel took his hand with both hers, and held it fast.

"You'll be happier now, dear," she said.

But she was watching Bertie. She knew that he had one desire—to escape from this intimacy, this friendship, which had been thrust upon him. He could not bear it that he had been touched by the blind man, his insane reserve broken in. He was like a mollusc whose shell is broken.

Monkey Nuts[*]

At first Joe thought the job O. K.[*] He was loading hay on the trucks, along with Albert, the corporal. The two men were pleasantly billeted in a cottage[*] not far from the station; they were their own masters; for Joe never thought of Albert as a master. And the little sidings of the tiny village station was as pleasant a place as you could wish for. On one side, beyond the line, stretched the woods: on the other, the near side, across a green smooth field red houses were dotted among flowering apple trees. The weather being sunny, work being easy, Albert a real good pal, what life could be better! After Flanders it was heaven itself.

Albert, the corporal, was a clean-shaven, shrewd-looking fellow of about forty. He seemed to think his one aim in life was to be full of fun and nonsense. In repose, his faced looked a little withered, old. He was a very good pal to Joe, steady, decent, and grave under all his "mischief"; for his mischief was only his laborious way of skirting his own ennui.

Joe was much younger than Albert—only twenty-three. He was a tallish, quiet youth, pleasant-looking. He was of slightly better class than his corporal, more personable. Careful about his appearance, he shaved every day. "I haven't got much of a face," said Albert. "If I was to shave every day like you, Joe, I should have none."

There was plenty of life in the little goods-yard: three porter youths, a continual come and go of farm wagons bringing hay, wagons with timber from the woods, coal carts loading at the trucks. The black coal seemed to make the place sleepier, hotter. Round the big white gate the station-master's children played and his white chickens walked, whilst the station-master himself, a young man getting too fat, helped his wife to peg out the washing on the clothes line in the meadow.

The great boat-shaped wagons came up from Playcross[*] with the hay. At first the farm-men waggoned it. On the third day one of the land-girls[*] appeared with the first load, drawing to a standstill easily at the head of her two great horses. She was a buxom girl, young, in

linen overalls and gaiters. Her face was ruddy, she had large blue
eyes.

"Now, that's the waggoner for us boys," said the corporal
loudly.

"Whoa!" she said to her horses; and then to the corporal, "Which
boys do you mean?"

"We are the pick of the bunch. That's Joe, my pal.—Don't you let
on that my name's Albert," said the corporal to his private. "I'm the
corporal."

"And I'm Miss Stokes,"* said the land-girl coolly, "if that's all the
boys you are."

"You know you couldn't want more, Miss Stokes," said Albert
politely. Joe, who was bare-headed, whose grey flannel sleeves were
rolled up to the elbow, and whose shirt was open at the breast, looked
modestly aside as if he had no part in the affair.

"Are you on this job regular, then?" said the corporal to Miss
Stokes.

"I don't know for sure," she said, pushing a piece of hair under
her hat, and attending to her splendid horses.

"Oh, make it a certainty!" said Albert.

She did not reply. She turned and looked over the two men coolly.
She was pretty, moderately blonde, with crisp hair, a good skin, and
large blue eyes. She was strong too, and the work went on leisurely
and easily.

"Now," said the corporal, stopping as usual to look round,
"pleasant company makes work a pleasure—don't hurry it, boys."
He stood on the truck surveying the world. That was one of his great
and absorbing occupations: to stand and look out on things in
general. Joe, also standing on the truck, also turned round to look
what was to be seen. But he could not become blankly absorbed as
Albert could.

Miss Stokes watched the two men from under her broad felt hat.
She had seen hundreds of Alberts, khaki soldiers standing in loose
attitudes absorbed in watching nothing in particular. She had seen
also a good many Joes, quiet, good-looking young soldiers with
half-averted faces. But there was something in the turn of Joe's head,
and something in his quiet, tender-looking form, young and
fresh—which attracted her eye. As she watched him closely from
below, he turned as if he felt her, and his dark-blue eye met her
straight, light-blue gaze. He faltered and turned aside again and

looked as if he were going to fall off the truck. A slight flush mounted under the girl's full, ruddy face. She liked him.

Always after this when she came into the sidings with her team it was Joe she looked for. She acknowledged to herself that she was 5 sweet on him. But Albert did all the talking. He was so full of fun and nonsense. Joe was a very shy bird, very brief and remote in his answers. Miss Stokes was driven to indulge in repartee with Albert, but she fixed her magnetic attention on the younger fellow. Joe would talk with Albert, and laugh at his jokes but Miss Stokes could 10 get little out of him. She had to depend on her silent forces. They were more effective than might be imagined.

Suddenly, on Saturday afternoon at about two o'clock, Joe received a bolt from the blue—a telegram:

"Meet me Belbury Station 6 p.m. to-day.—M. S."

15 He knew at once who M. S. was. His heart melted, he felt weak as if he had had a blow.

"What's the trouble, boy?" asked Albert anxiously.

"No—no trouble—it's to meet somebody." Joe lifted his dark-blue eyes in confusion towards his corporal.

20 "Meet somebody!" repeated the corporal, watching his young pal with keen blue eyes. "It's all right, then, nothing wrong?"

"No—nothing wrong. I'm not going," said Joe.

Albert was old and shrewd enough to see that nothing more should be said before the housewife. He also saw that Joe did not 25 want to take him into confidence. So he held his peace, though he was piqued.

The two soldiers went into town, smartened up. Albert knew a fair number of the boys round about; there would be plenty of gossip in the market-place, plenty of lounging in groups on the Bath Road, 30 watching the Saturday evening shoppers. Then a modest drink or two, and the pictures.* They passed an agreeable, casual, nothing-in-particular evening, with which Joe was quite satisfied. He thought of Belbury Station, and of M. S. waiting there. He had not the faintest intention of meeting her. And he had not the faintest intention of 35 telling Albert.

And yet, when the two men were in their bedroom, half undressed, Joe suddenly held out the telegram to his corporal, saying: "What d'you think of that?"

Albert was just unbuttoning his braces. He desisted, took the 40 telegram form, and turned towards the candle to read it.

"Meet me Belbury Station 6 p.m. to-day. M. S." he read, *sotto voce.*
His face took on its fun-and-nonsense look.

"Who's M. S.?" he asked, looking shrewdly at Joe.

"You know as well as I do," said Joe, non-committal.

"M. S.," repeated Albert. "Blamed if I know, boy. Is it a woman?"   5

The conversation was carried on in tiny voices, for fear of
disturbing the householders.

"I don't know," said Joe, turning. He looked full at Albert, the two
men looked straight into each other's eyes. There was a lurking grin
in each of them.   10

"Well I'm—*blamed!*" said Albert at last, throwing the telegram
down emphatically on the bed.

"Wha-at?" said Joe, grinning rather sheepishly, his eyes clouded
none the less.

Albert sat on the bed and proceeded to undress, nodding his head   15
with mock gravity all the while. Joe watched him foolishly.

"What?" he repeated faintly.

Albert looked up at him with a knowing look.

"If that isn't coming it quick,* boy!" he said. "What the blazes—
what ha' you bin doing?"   20

"Nothing!" said Joe.

Albert slowly shook his head as he sat on the side of the bed.

"Don't happen to me when *I've* bin doin' nothing," he said. And
he proceeded to pull off his stockings.

Joe turned away, looking at himself in the mirror as he unbuttoned   25
his tunic.

"You didn't want to keep the appointment?" Albert asked, in a
changed voice, from the bedside.

Joe did not answer for a moment. Then he said:

"I made no appointment."   30

"I'm not saying you did, boy. Don't be nasty about it. I mean you
didn't want to answer the—unknown person's summons—shall I put
it that way?"

"No," said Joe.

"What was the deterring motive?" asked Albert, who was now   35
lying on his back in bed.

"Oh," said Joe, suddenly looking round rather haughtily, "I didn't
want to." He had a well-balanced head, and could take on a sudden
distant bearing.

"Didn't want to—didn't cotton on,* like. Well—*they be artful, the*   40 *women*—" he mimicked his landlord. "Come on into bed, boy. Don't loiter about as if you'd lost something."

Albert turned over, to sleep.

On Monday Miss Stokes turned up as usual, striding beside her team. Her "whoa!" was resonant and challenging, she looked up at the truck as her steeds came to a standstill. Joe had turned aside, and had his face averted from her. She glanced him over—save for his slender succulent tenderness she would have despised him. She sized him up in a steady look. Then she turned to Albert, who was looking down at her and smiling in his mischievous turn. She knew his aspects by now. She looked straight back at him, though her eyes were hot. He saluted her.

"Beautiful morning, Miss Stokes."

"Very!" she replied.

"Handsome is as handsome looks,"* said Albert.

Which produced no response.

"Now Joe, come on here," said the corporal. "Don't keep the ladies waiting—it's the sign of a weak heart."

Joe turned, and the work began. Nothing more was said for the time being. As the week went on, all parties became more comfortable. Joe remained silent, averted, neutral, a little on his dignity. Miss Stokes was off-hand and masterful. Albert was full of mischief.

The great theme was a circus, which was coming to the market town on the following Saturday.

"You'll go to the circus, Miss Stokes?" said Albert.

"I may do. Are you going?"

"Certainly. Give us the pleasure of escorting you."

"No thanks."

"That's what I call a flat refusal—what, Joe? You don't mean that you have no liking for our company, Miss Stokes?"

"Oh, I don't know," said Miss Stokes. "How many are there of you?"

"Only me and Joe."

"Oh, is that all?" she said satirically.

Albert was a little nonplussed.

"Isn't that enough for you?" he asked.

"Too many by half," blurted out Joe, jeeringly, in a sudden fit of uncouth rudeness that made both the others stare.

"Oh, I'll stand out of the way, boy, if that's it," said Albert to Joe. Then he turned mischievously to Miss Stokes. "He wants to know what M. stands for," he said confidentially.

"Monkeys," she replied, turning to her horses.

"What's M. S.?" said Albert.

"Monkey nuts," she retorted, leading off her team.

Albert looked after her a little discomfited. Joe had flushed dark, and cursed Albert in his heart.

On the Saturday afternoon the two soldiers took the train into town. They would have to walk home. They had tea at six o'clock, and lounged about till half-past seven. The circus* was in a meadow near the river—a great red-and-white striped tent. Caravans stood at the side. A great crowd of people was gathered round the ticket caravan.

Inside the tent the lamps were lighted, shining on a ring of faces, a great circular bank of faces round the green grassy centre. Along with some comrades, the two soldiers packed themselves on a thin plank seat, rather high. They were delighted with the flaring lights, the wild effect. But the circus performance did not affect them deeply. They admired the lady in black velvet with rose-purple legs, who leapt so neatly on to the galloping horse, they watched the feats of strength and laughed at the clown. But they felt a little patronising, they missed the sensational drama of the cinema.*

Half-way through the performance Joe was electrified to see the face of Miss Stokes not very far from him. There she was, in her khaki and her felt hat, as usual; he pretended not to see her. She was laughing at the clown; she also pretended not to see him. It was a blow to him, and it made him angry. He would not even mention it to Albert. Least said, soonest mended. He liked to believe she had not seen him. But he knew, fatally, that she had.

When they came out it was nearly eleven o'clock; a lovely night, with a moon and tall, dark noble trees: a magnificent May night. Joe and Albert laughed and chaffed with the boys. Joe looked round frequently to see if he were safe from Miss Stokes. It seemed so.

But there were six miles to walk home. At last the two soldiers set off, swinging their canes. The road was white between tall hedges, other stragglers were passing out of the town towards the villages, the air was full of pleased excitement.

They were drawing near to the village, when they saw a dark figure ahead. Joe's heart sank with pure fear. It was a figure wheeling a bicycle—a land-girl—Miss Stokes. Albert was ready with his nonsense. Miss Stokes had a puncture.

"Let me wheel the rattler,"* said Albert.

"Thank you," said Miss Stokes. "You *are* kind."

"Oh, I'd be kinder than that, if you'd show me how," said Albert.

"Are you sure?" said Miss Stokes.

"Doubt my words?" said Albert. "That's what I call cruel, now, Miss Stokes."

5   Miss Stokes walked between them, close to Joe.

"Have you been to the circus?" she asked him.

"Yes," he replied mildly.

"Have *you* been?" Albert asked her.

"Yes. I didn't see you," she replied.

10   "What!—you say so! Didn't see us! Didn't think us worth looking at," began Albert. "Aren't I as handsome as the clown, now? And you didn't as much as glance in our direction? I call it a downright oversight."

"I never *saw* you," reiterated Miss Stokes. "I didn't know you saw 15 me."

"That makes it worse," said Albert.

The road passed through a belt of dark pine wood. The village, and the branch road, was very near. Miss Stokes put out her fingers and felt for Joe's hand, as it swung at his side. To say he was 20 staggered is to put it mildly. Yet he allowed her softly to clasp his fingers for a few moments. But he was a mortified youth.

At the cross-roads they stopped—Miss Stokes should turn off.* She had another mile to go.

"You'll let us see you home," said Albert.

25   "Do me a kindness," she said. "Put my bike in your shed, and take it to Baker's on Monday, will you?"

"I'll sit up all night and mend it for you, if you like."

"No thanks. And Joe and I'll walk on."

"Oh—ho! Oh—ho!" sang Albert. "Joe! Joe! What do you say to 30 that, now, boy? Aren't you in luck's way? And I get the bloomin' old bike for my pal! Consider it again, Miss Stokes."

Joe turned aside his face, and did not speak.

"Oh, well! I wheel the grid,* do I? I leave you, boy——"

"I'm not keen on going any further," barked out Joe in an uncouth 35 voice. "She bain't my choice."

The girl stood silent, and watched the two men.

"There now!" said Albert. "Think o' that. If it was *me* now—" But he was uncomfortable. "Well, Miss Stokes, have me," he added.

Miss Stokes stood quite still, neither moved nor spoke. And so the 40 three remained for some time at the lane end. At last Joe began kicking the ground—then he suddenly lifted his face. At that moment Miss Stokes was at his side. She put her arm delicately round his waist.

"Seems I'm the one extra, don't you think?" Albert inquired of the high bland moon. 5

Joe had dropped his head and did not answer. Miss Stokes stood with her arm lightly round his waist. Albert bowed, saluted, and bade good-night. He walked away, leaving the two standing.

Miss Stokes put a light pressure on Joe's waist, and drew him down the road. They walked in silence. The night was full of 10 scent—wild cherry, the first bluebells. Still they walked in silence. A nightingale was singing. They approached nearer, and nearer, till they stood close by his dark bush. The powerful notes sounded from the cover, almost like flashes of light—then the interval of silence—then the moaning notes, almost like a dog faintly howling, 15 followed by the long, rich trill and flashing notes. Then a short silence again.

Miss Stokes turned at last to Joe. She looked up at him, and in the moonlight he saw her faintly smiling. He felt maddened, but helpless. Her arm was round his waist, she drew him closely to her 20 with a soft pressure that made all his bones rotten.

Meanwhile Albert was waiting at home. He put on his overcoat, for the fire was out, and he had had malarial fever. He looked fitfully at the *Daily Mirror* and the *Daily Sketch*,* but he saw nothing. It seemed a long time. He began to yawn widely, even to nod. At last 25 Joe came in.

Albert looked at him keenly. The young man's brow was black, his face sullen.

"All right, boy?" asked Albert.

Joe merely grunted for a reply. There was nothing more to be got 30 out of him. So they went to bed.

Next day Joe was silent, sullen. Albert could make nothing of him. He proposed a walk after tea.

"I'm going somewhere," said Joe.

"Where—monkey-nuts?" asked the corporal. 35

But Joe's brow only became darker.

So the days went by. Almost every evening Joe went off alone, returning late. He was sullen, taciturn, and had a hang-dog look, a curious way of dropping his head and looking dangerously from under his brows. And he and Albert did not get on so well any more 40 with one another. For all his fun and nonsense, Albert was really irritable, soon made angry. And Joe's stand-offish sulkiness and complete lack of confidence riled him, got on his nerves. His fun and nonsense took a biting, sarcastic turn, at which Joe's eyes glittered occasionally, though the young man turned unheeding aside. Then again Joe would be full of odd, whimsical fun, outshining Albert himself.

Miss Stokes still came to the station with the wain—Monkey-nuts, Albert called her, though not to her face. For she was very clear and good-looking; almost she seemed to gleam. And Albert was a tiny bit afraid of her. She very rarely addressed Joe whilst the hay-loading was going on, and that young man always turned his back to her. He seemed thinner, and his limber figure looked more slouching. But still it had the tender attractive appearance, especially from behind. His tanned face, a little thinned and darkened, took a handsome, slightly sinister look.

"Come on, Joe!" the corporal urged sharply one day. "What're you doing, boy? Looking for beetles on the bank?"

Joe turned round swiftly, almost menacing, to work.

"He's a different fellow these days, Miss Stokes," said Albert to the young woman. "What's got him? Is it monkey-nuts that don't suit him, do you think?"

"Choked with chaff, more like!" she retorted. "It's as bad as feeding a threshing machine, to have to listen to some folks."

"As bad as what?" said Albert. "You don't mean *me*, do you, Miss Stokes?"

"No," she cried. "I don't mean you."

Joe's face became dark-red during these sallies, but he said nothing. He would eye the young woman curiously, as she swung so easily at the work, and he had some of the look of a dog which is going to bite.

Albert, with his nerves on edge, began to find the strain rather severe. The next Saturday evening, when Joe came in more black-browed than ever, he watched him, determined to have it out with him.

When the boy went upstairs to bed, the corporal followed him. He closed the door behind him carefully, sat on the bed and watched the younger man undressing. And for once he spoke in a natural voice, neither chaffing nor commanding.

"What's gone wrong, boy?"

Joe stopped a moment as if he had been shot. Then he went on unwinding his puttees and did not answer or look up.

"You can hear, can't you?" said Albert, nettled.

"Yes, I can hear," said Joe, stooping over his puttees till his face was purple.   5

"Then why don't you answer?"

Joe sat up. He gave a long, sideways look at the corporal. Then he lifted his eyes and stared at a crack in the ceiling.

The corporal watched these movements shrewdly.

"And *then* what?" he asked ironically.   10

Again Joe turned and stared him in the face. The corporal smiled very slightly, but kindly.

"There'll be murder done one of these days," said Joe, in a quiet, unimpassioned voice.

"So long as it's by daylight—" replied Albert. Then he went over, 15 sat down by Joe, put his hand on his shoulder affectionately, and continued: "What is it, boy? What's gone wrong? You can trust me, can't you?"

Joe turned and looked curiously at the face so near to his.

"It's nothing, that's all," he said laconically.   20

Albert frowned.

"Then who's going to be murdered?—and who's going to do the murdering?—me or you—which is it, boy?" He smiled gently at the stupid youth, looking straight at him all the while into his eyes. Gradually the stupid, hunted, glowering look died out of Joe's eyes. 25 He turned his head aside, gently, as one rousing from a spell.

"I don't want her," he said, with fierce resentment.

"Then you needn't have her," said Albert. "What do you go for, boy?"

But it wasn't as simple as all that. Joe made no remark.   30

"She's a smart-looking girl. What's wrong with her, my boy? I should have thought you were a lucky chap, myself."

"I don't want 'er!" Joe barked, with ferocity and resentment.

"Then tell her so and have done," said Albert. He waited a while. There was no response. "Why don't you?" he added.   35

"Because I don't," confessed Joe, sulkily.

Albert pondered—rubbed his head.

"You're too soft-hearted, that's where it is, boy. You want your mettle dipping in cold water to temper it.* You're too soft-hearted——"   40

He laid his arm affectionately across the shoulders of the younger man. Joe seemed to yield a little towards him.

"When are you going to see her again?" Albert asked. For a long time there was no answer.

5 "When is it, boy?" persisted the softened voice of the corporal.

"To-morrow," confessed Joe.

"Then let me go," said Albert. "Let me go, will you?"

The morrow was Sunday, a sunny day, but a cold evening. The sky was grey, the new foliage very green, but the air was chill and
10 depressing. Albert walked briskly down the white road towards Beeley.* He crossed a larch plantation, and followed a narrow by-road, where blue speedwell flowers fell from the banks into the dust. He walked, swinging his cane, with mixed sensations. Then having gone a certain length, he turned and began to walk in the
15 opposite direction.

So he saw a young woman approaching him. She was wearing a wide hat of grey straw, and a loose, swinging dress of nigger-grey velvet. She walked with slow inevitability. Albert faltered a little as he approached her. Then he saluted her, and his roguish, slightly
20 withered skin flushed. She was staring straight into his face.

He fell in by her side, saying impudently:

"Not so nice for a walk as it was, is it?"

She only stared at him. He looked back at her.

"You've seen me before, you know," he said, grinning slightly.
25 "Perhaps you never noticed me. Oh, I'm quite nice looking, in a quiet way, you know. What——?"

But Miss Stokes did not speak: she only stared with large, icy blue eyes at him. He became self-conscious, lifted up his chin, walked with his nose in the air, and whistled at random. So they went down
30 the quiet, deserted grey lane. He was whistling the air:

"I'm Gilbert, the filbert, the colonel of the nuts."*

At last she found her voice:

"Where's Joe?"

"He thought you'd like a change; they say variety's the salt of
35 life*—that's why I'm mostly in pickle."

"Where is he?"

"Am I my brother's keeper?* He's gone his own ways."

"Where?"

"Nay, how am I to know! Not so far but he'll be back for supper."
40 She stopped in the middle of the lane. He stopped, facing her.

"Where's Joe?" she asked.

He struck a careless attitude, looked down the road, this way and that, lifted his eyebrows, pushed his khaki cap on one side and answered:

"He is not conducting the service to-night: he asked me if I'd officiate."

"Why hasn't he come?"

"Didn't want to, I expect. *I* wanted to."

She stared him up and down, and he felt uncomfortable in his spine, but maintained his air of nonchalance. Then she turned slowly on her heel, and started to walk back. The corporal went at her side.

"You're not going back, are you?" he pleaded. "Why, me and you, we should get on like a house on fire."

She took no heed, but walked on. He went uncomfortably at her side, making his funny remarks from time to time. But she was as if stone deaf. He glanced at her, and to his dismay saw the tears running down her cheeks. He stopped suddenly, and pushed back his cap.

"I say, you know—" he began.

But she was walking on like an automaton, and he had to hurry after her.

She never spoke to him. At the gate of her farm she walked straight in, as if he were not there. He watched her disappear. Then he turned on his heel, cursing silently, puzzled, lifting off his cap to scratch his head.

That night, when they were in bed, he remarked:

"Say, Joe, boy, strikes me you're well-off without Monkey-nuts. Gord love us, beans ain't in it."*

So they slept in amity. But they waited with some anxiety for the morrow.

It was a cold morning, a grey sky shifting in a cold wind, and threatening rain. They watched the wagon come up the road and through the yard gates. Miss Stokes was with her team as usual: her "Whoa!" rang out like a war-whoop.

She faced up at the truck where the two men stood.

"Joe?" she called, to the averted figure which stood up in the wind.

"What?" He turned unwillingly.

She made a queer movement, lifting her head slightly in a sipping, half-inviting, half-commanding gesture. And Joe was crouching already to jump off the truck to obey her, when Albert put his hand on his shoulder.

"Half a minute, boy! Where are you off? Work's work, and nuts is nuts. You stop here."

5   Joe slowly straightened himself.

"Joe?" came the woman's clear call from below.

Again Joe looked at her. But Albert's hand was on his shoulder, detaining him. He stood half-averted, with his tail between his legs.

"Take your hand off him, you," said Miss Stokes.

10   "Yes, Major," retorted Albert satirically.

She stood and watched.

"Joe!" Her voice rang for the third time.

Joe turned and looked at her, and a slow, jeering smile gathered on his face.

15   "Monkey nuts!" he replied, in a tone mocking her call.

She turned white—dead white. The men thought she would fall. Albert began yelling to the porters up the line to come and help with the load. He could yell like any non-commissioned officer upon occasion.

20   Some way or other the wagon was unloaded, the girl was gone. Joe and his corporal looked at one another and smiled slowly. But they had a weight on their minds, they were afraid.

They were reassured, however, when they found that Miss Stokes came no more with the hay. As far as they were concerned, she had
25   vanished into oblivion. And Joe felt more relieved even than he had felt when he heard the firing cease, after the news had come that the armistice* was signed.

Wintry Peacock*

There was thin, crisp snow on the ground, the sky was blue, the wind very cold, the air clear. Farmers were just turning out the cows for an hour or so in the mid-day, and the smell of cow-sheds was unendurable as I entered Tible.* I noticed the ash-twigs up in the sky 5 were pale and luminous, passing into the blue. And then I saw the peacocks. There they were in the road before me, three of them, and tail-less, brown, speckled birds, with dark-blue necks and ragged crests. They stepped archly over the filigree snow, and their bodies moved with slow motion, like small, light, flat-bottomed boats. I 10 admired them, they were curious. Then a gust of wind caught them, heeled them over as if they were three frail boats, opening their feathers like ragged sails. They hopped and skipped with discomfort, to get out of the draught of the wind. And then, in the lee of the walls, they resumed their arch, wintry motion, light and unballasted now 15 their tails were gone, indifferent. They were indifferent to my presence. I might have touched them. They turned off to the shelter of an open shed.

As I passed the end of the upper house, I saw a young woman just coming out of the back door. I had spoken to her in the summer.* She 20 recognised me at once, and waved to me. She was carrying a pail, wearing a white apron that was longer than her preposterously short skirt, and she had on the cotton bonnet. I took off my hat to her and was going on. But she put down her pail and darted with a swift, furtive movement after me. 25

"Do you mind waiting a minute?" she said. "I'll be out in a minute."

She gave me a slight, odd smile, and ran back. Her face was long and sallow and her nose rather red. But her gloomy black eyes softened caressively to me for a moment, with that momentary 30 humility which makes a man lord of the earth.

I stood in the road, looking at the fluffy, dark-red young cattle that mooed and seemed to bark at me. They seemed happy, frisky cattle, a little impudent, and either determined to go back into

the warm shed, or determined not to go back. I could not decide
which.

Presently the woman came forward again, her head rather ducked.
But she looked up at me and smiled, with that odd, immediate
5   intimacy, something witch-like and impossible.

"Sorry to keep you waiting," she said. "Shall we stand in this
cart-shed—it will be more out of the wind."

So we stood among the shafts of the open cart-shed, that faced the
road. Then she looked down at the ground, a little sideways, and I
10 noticed a small black frown on her brows. She seemed to brood for a
moment. Then she looked straight into my eyes, so that I blinked and
wanted to turn my face aside. She was searching me for something
and her look was too near. The frown was still on her keen, sallow
brow.

15 "Can you speak French?" she asked me, abruptly.

"More or less," I replied.

"I was supposed to learn it at school," she said. "But I don't know
a word." She ducked her head and laughed, with a slightly ugly
grimace and a rolling of her black eyes.

20 "No good keeping your mind full of scraps," I answered.

But she had turned aside her sallow, long face, and did not hear
what I said. Suddenly again she looked at me. She was searching.
And at the same time she smiled at me, and her eyes looked softly,
darkly, with infinite trustful humility into mine. I was being cajoled.

25 "Would you mind reading a letter for me, in French," she said,
her face immediately black and bitter-looking. She glanced at me,
frowning.

"Not at all," I said.

"It's a letter to my husband," she said, still scrutinising.

30 I looked at her, and didn't quite realise. She looked too far into
me, my wits were gone. She glanced round. Then she looked at me
shrewdly. She drew a letter from her pocket, and handed it to me. It
was addressed from France* to Lance-Corporal Goyte, at Tible. I
took out the letter and began to read it, as mere words. "Mon cher*
35 Alfred"—it might have been a bit of a torn newspaper. So I followed
the script: the trite phrases of a letter from a French-speaking girl to
an English soldier. "I think of you always, always. Do you think
sometimes of me."—And then I vaguely realised that I was reading a
man's private correspondence. And yet, how could one consider
40 these trivial, facile French phrases private! Nothing more trite and

vulgar in the world, than such a love-letter—no newspaper more obvious.

Therefore I read with a callous heart the effusions of the Belgian damsel. But then I gathered my attention. For the letter went on "Notre cher petit bébé—our dear little baby was born a week ago. 5 Almost I died, knowing you were far away, and perhaps forgetting the fruit of our perfect love. But the child comforted me. He has the smiling eyes and virile air of his English father. I pray to the Mother of Jesus to send me the dear father of my child, that I may see him with my child in his arms, and that we may be united in holy family 10 love. Ah, my Alfred, can I tell you how I miss you, how I weep for you. My thoughts are with you always, I think of nothing but you, I live for nothing but you and our dear baby. If you do not come back to me soon, I shall die, and our child will die. But no. You cannot come back to me. But I can come to you. I can come to England with 15 our child. If you do not wish to present me to your good mother and father, you can meet me in some town, some city, for I shall be so frightened to be alone in England with my child, and no one to take care of us. Yet I must come to you, I must bring my child, my little Alfred, to his father, the big, beautiful Alfred that I love so much. 20 Oh, write and tell me where I shall come. I have some money, I am not a penniless creature. I have money for myself and my dear baby— —"

I read to the end. It was signed: "Your very happy and still more unhappy Elise." I suppose I must have been smiling. 25

"I can see it makes you laugh," said Mrs Goyte, sardonically. I looked up at her.

"It's a love-letter, I know that," she said. "There's too many 'Alfreds' in it."

"One too many," I said. 30

"Oh yes.—And what does she say—Eliza?—We know her name's Eliza, that's another thing." She grimaced a little, looking up at me with a mocking laugh.

"Where did you get this letter?" I said.

"Post-man gave it me last week." 35

"And is your husband at home?"

"I expect him home tonight. He's been wounded, you know, and we've been applying for him home. He was home about six weeks ago—he's been in Scotland since then.—Oh, he was wounded in the leg. Yes, he's all right, a great strapping fellow. But he's lame, he 40

limps a bit. He expects he'll get his discharge—but I don't think he
will.—We married? We've been married six years—and he joined up
the first day of the war.—Oh, he thought he'd like the life. He'd been
through the South African War.*—No, he was sick of it, fed up.—I'm
5   living with his father and mother.—I've no home of my own now. My
people had a big farm—over a thousand acres—in Oxfordshire. Not
like here—no.—Oh, they're very good to me, his father and mother.
Oh yes, they couldn't be better. They think more of me than of their
own daughters.—But it's not like being in a place of your own, is it?
10 You can't *really* do as you like.—No, there's only me and his father
and mother at home.—Before the war? Oh, he was anything. He's
had a good education—but he liked the farming better.—Then he
was a chauffeur. That's how he knew French. He was driving a
gentleman in France for a long time—"
15   At this point the peacocks came round the corner on a puff of
wind.
     "Hello Joey!" she called, and one of the birds came forward, on
delicate legs. Its grey speckled back was very elegant, it rolled its full,
dark-blue neck as it moved to her. She crouched down. "Joey dear,"
20 she said, in an odd, saturnine caressive voice. "You're bound to find
me, aren't you." She put her face forward, and the bird rolled his
neck, almost touching her face with his beak, as if kissing her.
     "He loves you," I said.
     She twisted her face up at me with a laugh.
25   "Yes," she said, "he loves me, Joey does—"—then, to the
bird—"and I love Joey, don't I? I *do* love Joey." And she smoothed
his feathers for a moment. Then she rose, saying: "He's an
affectionate bird."
     I smiled at the roll of her 'bu-rrd.'*
30   "Oh yes, he is," she protested. "He came with me from my home
seven years ago. Those others are his descendants—but they're not
like Joey—*are they, dee-urrr?*" Her voice rose at the end with a
witch-like cry.
     Then she forgot the birds in the cart-shed, and turned to business
35 again.
     "Won't you read that letter?" she said. "Read it, so that I know
what it says."
     "It's rather behind his back," I said.
     "Oh, never mind him," she cried. "He's been behind my back
40 long enough—all these four years. If he never did no worse things

behind my back than I do behind his, he wouldn't have cause to grumble.—You read me what it says."

Now I felt a distinct reluctance to do as she bid, and yet I began—'My dear Alfred.'

"I guessed that much," she said. "Eliza's dear Alfred—" She laughed. "How do you say it in French? *Eliza?*"

I told her, and she repeated the name with great contempt—*Elise.*

"Go on," she said. "You're not reading."

So I began—"'I have been thinking of you sometimes—have you been thinking of me—'"

"Of several others as well, besides her, I'll wager," said Mrs Goyte.

"Probably not," said I, and continued—"'A dear little baby was born here a week ago. Ah, can I tell you my feelings when I take my darling little brother into my arms—'"

"I'll bet it's *his*," cried Mrs Goyte.

"No," I said. "It's her mother's."

"Don't you believe it," she cried. "It's a blind. You mark me, it's her own right enough—and his."

"No," I said, "it's her mother's.—'He has sweet smiling eyes, but not like your beautiful English eyes—'"

She suddenly struck her hand on her skirt with a wild motion, and bent down, doubled with laughter. Then she rose and covered her face with her hand.

"I'm forced to laugh at the beautiful English eyes," she said.

"Aren't his eyes beautiful?" I asked.

"Oh yes—*very*.—Go on!—*Joey dear, dee-urr Joey!*"—this to the peacock.

"—Er—'We miss you very much. We all miss you. We wish you were here to see the darling baby. Ah, Alfred, how happy we were when you stayed with us. We all loved you so much. My mother will call the baby Alfred so that we shall never forget you—'"

"Of course it's his right enough," cried Mrs Goyte.

"No," said I. "It's the mother's. Er—'My mother is very well. My father came home yesterday—on leave. He is delighted with his son, my little brother, and wishes to have him named after you, because you were so good to us all in that terrible time, which I shall never forget. I must weep now when I think of it. Well, you are far away in England, and perhaps I shall never see you again. How did you find your dear mother and father?—I am so happy that your wound is better, and that you can nearly walk—'"

"How did he find his dear *wife*!" cried Mrs Goyte.—"He never told her he had one.—Think of taking the poor girl in like that!"

5 "'We are all so pleased when you write to us. Yet now you are in England you will forget the family you served so well—'"

"A bit too well—*Eh Joey*!—" cried the wife.

"'If it had not been for you we should not be alive now, to grieve and to rejoice in this life, that is so hard for us. But we have recovered
10 some of our losses, and no longer feel the burden of poverty. The little Alfred is a great comfort to me. I hold him to my breast and think of the big, good Alfred, and I weep to think that those times of suffering were perhaps the times of a great happiness that is gone for ever—'"

15 "Oh, but isn't it a shame, to take a poor girl in like that!" cried Mrs Goyte. "Never to let on that he was married, and raise her hopes.—I call it beastly, I do."

"You don't know," I said. "You know how anxious women are to fall in love, wife or no wife. How could he help it, if she was
20 determined to fall in love with him?"

"He could have helped it if he'd wanted."

"Well," I said. "We aren't all heroes."

"Oh, but that's different!—The big, good Alfred!—did ever you hear such Tommy-rot in your life!—Go on—what does she say at
25 the end?"

"Er—'We shall be pleased to hear of your life in England.—We all send many kind regards to your good parents. I wish you all happiness for your future days. Your very affectionate and ever-grateful Elise.'"

30 There was silence for a moment, during which Mrs Goyte remained with her head dropped, sinister and abstracted. Suddenly she lifted her face, and her eyes flashed.

"Oh, but I call it beastly, I call it mean, to take a girl in like that."

"Nay," I said. "Probably he hasn't taken her in at all. Do you think
35 those French girls are such poor innocent things? I guess she's a great deal more downy* than he."

"Oh, he's one of the biggest fools that ever walked," she cried.

"There you are!" said I.

"But it's his child right enough," she said.

40 "I don't think so," said I.

"I'm sure of it."

"Oh well," I said,—"if you prefer to think that way."

"What other reason has she for writing like that—"

I went out into the road and looked at the cattle.

"Who is this driving the cows?" I said.

She too came out.

"It's the boy from the next farm," she said.

"Oh well," said I, "those Belgian girls! You never know where their letters will end.—And after all, it's his affair—you needn't bother."

"Oh—!" she cried, with rough scorn—"it's not *me* that bothers. But it's the nasty meanness of it—me writing him such loving letters"—she put her hand before her face and laughed malevolently—"and sending him parcels all the time. You bet he fed that gurrl on my parcels—I know he did. It's just like him.—I'll bet they laughed together over my letters. I'll bet anything they did——"

"Nay," said I. "He'd* burn your letters for fear they'd give him away."

There was a black look on her yellow face.—Suddenly a voice was heard calling. She poked her head out of the shed, and answered coolly:

"All right!" Then turning to me: "That's his mother looking after me."

She laughed into my face, witch-like, and we turned down the road.

When I awoke, the morning after this episode, I found the house darkened with deep, soft snow, which had blown against the large west windows, covering them with a screen. I went outside, and saw the valley all white and ghastly below me, the trees beneath black and thin looking like wire, the rock-faces dark between the glistering shroud, and the sky above sombre, heavy, yellowish-dark, much too heavy for this world below of hollow bluey whiteness, figured with black. I felt I was in a valley of the dead. And I sensed I was a prisoner, for the snow was everywhere deep, and drifted in places. So all the morning I remained indoors, looking up the drive at the shrubs so heavily plumed with snow, at the gateposts raised high with a foot or more of extra whiteness. Or I looked down into the white-and-black valley, that was utterly motionless and beyond life, a hollow sarcophagus.

Nothing stirred the whole day—no plume fell off the shrubs, the

valley was as abstracted as a groove* of death. I looked over at the tiny, half-buried farms away on the bare uplands beyond the valley hollow, and I thought of Tible in the snow, of the black, witch-like little Mrs Goyte. And the snow seemed to lay one bare to influences I
5 wanted to escape.

In the faint glow of half-clear light that came about four o'clock in the afternoon, I was roused to see a motion in the snow away below, near where the thorn-trees stood very black and dwarfed, like a little savage group, in the dismal white. I watched closely. Yes, there was a
10 flapping and a struggle—a big bird, it must be, labouring in the snow. I wondered. Our biggest birds, in the valley, were the large hawks that often hung flickering opposite my windows, level with me, but high above some prey on the steep valley-side. This was much too big for a hawk—too big for any known bird. I searched in my mind
15 for the largest English wild birds, geese, buzzards.

Still it laboured and strove, then was still, a dark spot, then struggled again. I went out of the house and down the steep slope, at risk of breaking my leg between the rocks. I knew the ground so well—and yet I got well shaken before I drew near the thorn-trees.
20 Yes, it was a bird. It was Joey. It was the grey-brown peacock with a blue neck. He was snow-wet and spent.

"Joey—Joey de-urr!" I said, staggering unevenly towards him. He looked so pathetic, rowing and struggling in the snow, too spent to rise, his blue neck stretching out and lying sometimes on the snow,
25 his eye closing and opening quickly, his crest all battered.

"Joey dee-urr! Dee-urr!" I said caressingly to him. And at last he lay still, blinking, in the surged and furrowed snow, whilst I came near and touched him, stroked him, gathered him under my arm. He stretched his long, wetted neck away from me as I held him, none the
30 less he was quiet in my arm, too tired, perhaps, to struggle. Still he held his poor, crested head away from me, and seemed sometimes to droop, to wilt, as if he might suddenly die.

He was not so heavy as I expected, yet it was a struggle to get up to the house with him again. We set him down, not too near the fire,
35 and gently wiped him with cloths. He submitted, only now and then stretching his soft neck away from us, avoiding us helplessly. Then we set warm food by him. I put it to his beak, tried to make him eat. But he ignored it. He seemed to be ignorant of what we were doing, recoiled inside himself inexplicably. So we put him in a basket with
40 cloths, and left him crouching oblivious. His food we put near him.

The blinds were drawn, the house was warm, it was night. Sometimes he stirred, but mostly he huddled still, leaning his queer crested head on one side. He touched no food, and took no heed of sounds or movements. We talked of brandy or stimulants. But I realised we had best leave him alone.

In the night however we heard him thumping about. I got up anxiously with a candle. He had eaten some food, and scattered more, making a mess. And he was perched on the back of a heavy arm-chair. So I concluded he was recovered, or recovering.

The next day was clear, and the snow had frozen, so I decided to carry him back to Tible. He consented, after various flappings, to sit in a big fish-bag with his battered head peeping out with wild uneasiness. And so I set off with him, slithering down into the valley, making good progress down in the pale shadow beside the rushing waters, then climbing painfully up the arrested white valley-side, plumed with clusters of young pine trees, into the paler white radiance of the snowy, upper regions, where the wind cut fine. Joey seemed to watch all the time with wide, anxious, unseeing eye, brilliant and inscrutable. As I drew near to Tible township, he stirred violently in the bag, though I do not know if he had recognised the place. Then, as I came to the sheds, he looked sharply from side to side, and stretched his neck out long. I was a little afraid of him. He gave a loud, vehement yell, opening his sinister beak, and I stood still, looking at him as he struggled in the bag, shaken myself by his struggles, yet not thinking to release him.

Mrs Goyte came darting past the end of the house, her head sticking forward in sharp scrutiny. She saw me, and came forward.

"Have you got Joey!" she cried sharply, as if I were a thief.

I opened the bag, and he flopped out, flapping as if he hated the touch of the snow, now. She gathered him up, and put her lips to his beak. She was flushed and handsome, her eyes bright, her hair slack, thick, but more witch-like than ever. She did not speak.

She had been followed by a grey-haired woman with a round, rather sallow face and a slightly hostile bearing.

"Did you bring him with you, then?" she asked sharply. I answered that I had rescued him the previous evening.

From the background slowly approached a slender man with a grey moustache and large patches on his trousers.

"You've got 'im back 'gain, Ah see," he said to his daughter-in-law. His wife explained how I had found Joey.

"Ah," went on the grey man. "It wor our Alfred scarred him off, back your life.—He must 'a flyed ower t'valley.—Tha ma' thank thy stars as 'e wor fun, Maggie, 'e'd a bin froze.—They a bit nesh,* you know," he concluded, to me.

5   "They are," I answered. "This isn't their country."

"No, it isna," replied Mr Goyte. He spoke very slowly and deliberately, quietly, as if the soft pedal were always down in his voice. He looked at his daughter-in-law as she crouched, flushed and dark, before the peacock, which would lay its long blue neck for 10 a moment along her lap. In spite of his grey moustache and thin grey hair, the elderly man had a face young and almost delicate, like a young man's. His blue eyes twinkled with some inscrutable source of pleasure, his skin was fine and tender, his nose delicately arched. His grey hair being slightly ruffled, he had a debonair look, as of a youth 15 who is in love.

"We mun tell 'im it's come," he said slowly, and turning, he called: "Alfred—Alfred! Wheer's ter gotten to?"

Then he turned again to the group.

"Get up then, Maggie, lass, get up wi' thee. Tha ma'es too much 20 o' th' bod."

A young man approached, wearing rough khaki and knee-breeches. He was Danish looking, broad at the loins.

"'E's come back then," said the father to the son—"least-wise, he's bin browt back. 'E flyed ower ter Griff Low."*

25   The son looked at me. He had a devil-may-care bearing, his cap on one side, his hands stuck in the front pockets of his breeches. But he said nothing.

"Shall you come in a minute, Master?" said the elderly woman, to me.

30   "Ay, come in an' ha'e a cup o' tea or summat. You'll do wi' summat, carryin' that bod. Come on, Maggie wench, let's go in."

So we went indoors, into the rather stuffy, overcrowded living room, that was too cosy, and too warm. The son followed last, standing in the doorway. The father talked to me. Maggie put out the 35 tea-cups. The mother went into the dairy again.

"Tha'lt rouse thysen up a bit again, now, Maggie," the father-in-law said—and then to me: "'Er's not bin very bright sin' Alfred come whoam, an' the bod flyed awee. 'E come whoam a Wednesday night, Alfred did.—But ay, you knowed, didna yer.—Ay, 'e comed 'a

Wednesday—an' I reckon there wor a bit of a to-do between 'em, worn't they, Maggie?"

He twinkled maliciously to his daughter-in-law, who was flushed brilliant and handsome.

"Oh, be quiet father. You're wound up, by the sound of you," she said to him, as if crossly. But she could never be cross with him.

"'Er's got 'er colour back this mornin'," continued the father-in-law slowly. "It's bin heavy weather wi' us this last two days. Ay—er's bin north-east sin 'er seed you a Wednesday."

"Father, do stop talking. You'd wear the leg off an iron pot. I can't think where you've found your tongue, all of a sudden," said Maggie, with caressive sharpness.

"Ah'n found it wheer I lost it.—Aren't goin' ter come in an' sit thee down, Alfred—?"

But Alfred turned and disappeared.

"'E's got th' monkey on 's back, ower this letter job," said the father secretly to me. "Mother, 'er knows nowt about it. Lot o' tom-foolery, isn't it? Ay! What's good o' makkin' a peck o' trouble ower what's far enough off, an' ned niver come no nigher. No—not a smite* o' use.—That's what I tell 'er. 'Er should ta'e no notice on't.—Ay, what can y' expect."

The mother came in again, and the talk became general. Maggie flashed her eyes at me from time to time, complacent and satisfied, moving among the men. I paid her little compliments, which she did not seem to hear. She attended to me with a kind of sinister, witch-like graciousness, her dark head ducked between her shoulders, at once humble and powerful. She was happy as a child attending to her father-in-law and to me. But there was something ominous between her eyebrows, as if a dark moth were settled there: and something ominous in her bent, hulking bearing.

She sat on a low stool by the fire, near her father-in-law. Her head was dropped, she seemed in a state of abstraction. From time to time she would suddenly recover, and look up at us, laughing and chatting. Then she would forget again. Yet in her hulked, black forgetting she seemed very near to us.*

The door having been opened, the peacock came slowly in, prancing calmly. He went near to her, and crouched down, coiling his blue neck. She glanced at him, but almost as if she did not observe him. The bird sat silent, seeming to sleep, and the woman

also sat hulked and silent, seeming oblivious. Then once more there
was a heavy step, and Alfred entered. He looked at his wife, and he
looked at the peacock crouching by her. He stood large in the
doorway, his hands stuck in front of him, in his breeches pockets.
5 Nobody spoke. He turned on his heel and went out again.

I rose also to go. Maggie started as if coming to herself.

"Must you go?" she asked, rising and coming near to me, standing
in front of me, twisting her head sideways and looking up at me.
"Can't you stop a bit longer?—We can all be cosy today, there's
10 nothing to do outdoors." And she laughed, showing her teeth oddly.
She had a long chin.

I said I must go. The peacock uncoiled and coiled again his long
blue neck, as he lay on the hearth. Maggie still stood close in front of
me, so that I was acutely aware of my waistcoat buttons.

15 "Oh well," she said, "you'll come again, won't you? Do come
again."

I promised.

"Come to tea one day—yes, do!"

I promised—one day.

20 The moment I went out of her presence I ceased utterly to exist
for her—as utterly as I ceased to exist for Joey. With her curious
abstractedness, she forgot me again immediately. I knew it as I left
her. Yet she seemed almost in physical contact with me while I was
with her.

25 The sky was all pallid again, yellowish, when I went out, there was
no sun, the snow was blue and cold. I hurried away down the hill,
musing on Maggie. The road made a loop down the sharp face of the
slope. As I went crunching over the laborious snow I became aware
of a figure striding down the steep scarp, to intercept me. It was a
30 man with his hands in front of him, half stuck in his breeches
pockets, and his shoulders square—a real farmer of the hills: Alfred,
of course. He waited for me by the stone fence.

"Excuse me," he said, as I came up.

I came to a halt in front of him, and looked into his sullen blue
35 eyes. He had a certain odd haughtiness on his brows. But his blue
eyes stared insolently at me.

"Do you know anything about a letter—in French—that my wife
opened—a letter of mine—?"

"Yes," said I. "She asked me to read it to her."

40 He looked square at me. He did not know exactly how to feel.

"What was there in it?" he asked.

"Why?" I said. "Don't you know?"

"She makes out she's burnt it," he said.

"Without showing it you?" I asked.

He nodded slightly. He seemed to be meditating as to what line of action he should take. He wanted to know the contents of the letter: he must know: and therefore he must ask me, for evidently his wife had taunted him. At the same time, no doubt, he would like to wreak untold vengeance on my unfortunate person. So he eyed me, and I eyed him, and neither of us spoke. He did not want to repeat his request to me. And yet I only looked at him, and considered.

Suddenly he threw back his head and glanced down the valley. Then he changed his position—he was a horse-soldier. Then he looked at me more confidentially.

"She burnt the blasted thing before I saw it," he said.

"Well," I answered slowly, "she doesn't know herself what was in it."

He continued to watch me narrowly. I grinned to myself.

"I didn't like to read her out what there was in it," I continued.

He suddenly flushed so that the veins in his neck stood out, and he stirred again uncomfortably.

"The Belgian girl said her baby had been born a week ago, and that they were going to call it Alfred," I told him.

He met my eyes. I was grinning. He began to grin, too.

"Good luck to her," he said.

"Best of luck," said I.

"And what did you tell *her*?" he asked.

"That the baby belonged to the old mother—that it was brother to your girl, who was writing to you as a friend of the family."

He stood smiling, with the long, subtle malice of a farmer.

"And did she take it in?" he asked.

"As much as she took anything else."

He stood grinning fixedly. Then he broke into a short laugh.

"Good for *her*!" he exclaimed cryptically.

And then he laughed aloud once more, evidently feeling he had won a big move in his contest with his wife.

"What about the other woman?" I asked.

"Who?"

"Elise."

"Oh"—he shifted uneasily—"she was all right——"

"You'll be getting back to her," I said.

He looked at me. Then he made a grimace with his mouth.

"Not me," he said. "Back your life it's a plant."

"You don't think the *cher petit bébé* is a little Alfred?"

5   "It might be," he said.

"Only might?"

"Yes—an' there's lots of mites in a pound of cheese." He laughed boisterously but uneasily.

"What did she say, exactly?" he asked.

10 I began to repeat, as well as I could, the phrases of the letter:

"'*Mon cher Alfred— Figure-toi comme je suis désolée——*'"*

He listened with some confusion. When I had finished all I could remember, he said:

"They know how to pitch you out a letter, those Belgian lasses."

15 "Practice," said I.

"They get plenty," he said.

There was a pause.

"Oh well," he said. "I've never got that letter, anyhow."

The wind blew fine and keen, in the sunshine, across the snow. I

20 blew my nose and prepared to depart.

"And *she* doesn't know anything?" he continued, jerking his head up the hill in the direction of Tible.

"She knows nothing but what I've said—that is, if she really burnt the letter."

25 "I believe she burnt it," he said, "for spite. She's a little devil, she is. But I shall have it out with her." His jaw was stubborn and sullen. Then suddenly he turned to me with a new note.

"Hey!" he said. "Why didn't you wring that b— peacock's neck—that b— Joey?"

30 "Why?" I said. "What for?"

"I hate the brute," he said. "I had a shot at him——"

I laughed. He stood and mused.

"Poor little Elise," he murmured.*

"Was she small—*petite*?" I asked.

35 He jerked up his head.

"No," he said. "Rather tall."

"Taller than your wife, I suppose."

Again he looked into my eyes. And then once more he went off into a loud burst of laughter that made the still, snow-deserted valley

40 clap again.

"God, it's a knock-out," he said, thoroughly amused.

Then he stood at ease, one foot out, his hands in his breeches pocket, in front of him, his head thrown back, a handsome figure of a man.

"But I'll do that blasted Joey in—" he mused.   5

I ran down the hill, shouting also with laughter.

Hadrian
[You Touched Me]*

The Pottery House* was a square, ugly, brick house girt in by the wall
that enclosed the whole grounds of the pottery itself. To be sure, a
privet hedge partly masked the house and its grounds from the
pottery-yard and works: but only partly. Through the hedge could
be seen the desolate yard, and the many-windowed, factory-like
pottery, over the hedge could be seen the chimneys and the
out-houses. But inside the hedge, a pleasant garden and lawn sloped
down to a willow pool, which had once supplied the works.

The pottery itself was now closed, the great doors of the yard
permanently shut. No more the great crates, with yellow straw
showing through, stood in stacks by the packing shed. No more the
drays drawn by great horses rolled down the hill with a high load. No
more the pottery-lasses in their clay-coloured overalls, their faces
and hair splashed with grey fine mud, shrieked and larked with the
men. All that was over.

"We like it much better—oh, much better—quieter," said
Matilda Rockley.

"Oh, yes," assented Emmie Rockley, her sister.

"I'm sure you do," agreed the visitor.

But whether the two Rockley girls really liked it better, or whether
they only imagined they did, is a question. Certainly their lives were
much more grey and dreary now that the grey clay had ceased to
spatter its mud and silt its dust over the premises. They did not quite
realise how they missed the shrieking, shouting lasses, whom they
had known all their lives and disliked so much.

Matilda and Emmie were already old maids. In a thorough
industrial district, it is not easy for the girls who have expectations
above the common to find husbands. The ugly industrial town was
full of men, young men who were ready to marry. But they were all
colliers or pottery-hands, mere workmen. The Rockley girls would
have about ten thousand pounds each when their father died: ten
thousand pounds' worth of profitable house-property. It was not to
be sneezed at: they felt so themselves, and refrained from sneezing

92

away such a fortune on any mere member of the proletariat.
Consequently, bank-clerks or nonconformist clergymen or even
school-teachers having failed to come forward, Matilda had begun to
give up all idea of ever leaving the Pottery House.

Matilda was a tall, thin, graceful fair girl, with a rather large nose. 5
She was the Mary to Emmie's Martha:* that is, Matilda loved
painting and music, and read a good many novels, whilst Emmie
looked after the housekeeping. Emmie was shorter, plumper than
her sister, and she had no accomplishments. She looked up to
Matilda, whose mind was naturally refined and sensible. 10

In their quiet, melancholy way, the two girls were happy. Their
mother was dead. Their father was ill also. He was an intelligent man
who had had some education, but preferred to remain as if he were
one with the rest of the working people. He had a passion for music
and played the violin pretty well. But now he was getting old, he was 15
very ill, dying of a kidney disease. He had been rather a heavy
whiskey-drinker.

This quiet household, with one servant-maid, lived on year after
year in the Pottery House. Friends came in, the girls went out, the
father drank himself more and more ill. Outside in the street there 20
was a continual racket of the colliers and their dogs and children. But
inside the pottery wall was a deserted quiet.

In all this ointment there was one little fly. Ted Rockley, the father
of the girls, had had four daughters, and no son. As his girls grew, he
felt angry at finding himself always in a household of women. He 25
went off to London and adopted a boy out of a Charity Institution.
Emmie was fourteen years old, and Matilda sixteen, when their
father arrived home with his prodigy, the boy of six, Hadrian.

Hadrian was just an ordinary boy from a Charity Home, with
ordinary brownish hair and ordinary bluish eyes and of ordinary 30
rather cockney speech. The Rockley girls—there were three at home
at the time of his arrival—had resented his being sprung on them.
He, with his watchful, charity-institution instinct, knew this at once.
Though he was only six years old, Hadrian had a subtle, jeering look
on his face when he regarded the three young women. They insisted 35
he should address them as Cousin: Cousin Flora, Cousin Matilda,
Cousin Emmie. He complied, but there seemed a mockery in his
tone.

The girls, however, were kind-hearted by nature. Flora married
and left home. Hadrian did very much as he pleased with Matilda 40

and Emmie, though they had certain strictnesses. He grew up in the Pottery House and about the Pottery premises, went to an elementary school, and was invariably called Hadrian Rockley. He regarded Cousin Matilda and Cousin Emmie with a certain laconic indiffer-
5 ence, was quiet and reticent in his ways. The girls called him sly, but that was unjust. He was merely cautious, and without frankness. His Uncle, Ted Rockley, understood him tacitly, their natures were somewhat akin. Hadrian and the elderly man had a real but unemotional regard for one another.

10 When he was thirteen years old the boy was sent to a High School in the County town. He did not like it. His Cousin Matilda had longed to make a little gentleman of him, but he refused to be made. He would give a little contemptuous curve to his lip, and take on a shy, charity-boy grin, when refinement was thrust upon him. He
15 played truant from the High School, sold his books, his cap with its badge, even his very scarf and pocket-handkerchief, to his schoolfellows, and went raking off heaven knows where with the money. So he spent two very unsatisfactory years.

When he was fifteen he announced that he wanted to leave
20 England to go to the Colonies. He had kept touch with the Home. The Rockleys knew that, when Hadrian made a declaration, in his quiet, half-jeering manner, it was worse than useless to oppose him. So at last the boy departed, going to Canada under the protection of the Institution to which he had belonged. He said good-bye to the
25 Rockleys without a word of thanks, and parted, it seemed without a pang. Matilda and Emmie wept often to think of how he left them: even on their father's face a queer look came. But Hadrian wrote fairly regularly from Canada. He had entered some electricity works near Montreal, and was doing well.

30 At last, however, the war came. In his turn, Hadrian joined up and came to Europe. The Rockleys saw nothing of him. They lived on, just the same, in the Pottery House. Ted Rockley was dying of a sort of dropsy, and in his heart he wanted to see the boy. When the armistice* was signed, Hadrian had a long leave, and wrote that he
35 was coming home to the Pottery House.

The girls were terribly fluttered. To tell the truth, they were a little afraid of Hadrian. Matilda, tall and thin, was frail in her health, both girls were worn with nursing their father. To have Hadrian, a young man of twenty-one, in the house with them, after he had left them so
40 coldly five years before, was a trying circumstance.

They were in a flutter. Emmie persuaded her father to have his bed made finally in the morning-room downstairs, whilst his room upstairs was prepared for Hadrian. This was done, and preparations were going on for the arrival, when, at ten o'clock in the morning the young man suddenly turned up, quite unexpectedly. Cousin Emmie, with her hair bobbed up in absurd little bobs round her forehead, was busily polishing the stair-rods, while Cousin Matilda was in the kitchen washing the drawing-room ornaments in a lather, her sleeves rolled back on her thin arms, and her head tied up oddly and coquettishly in a duster.

Cousin Matilda blushed deep with mortification when the self-possessed young man walked in with his kit-bag, and put his cap on the sewing machine. He was little and self-confident, with a curious neatness about him that still suggested the Charity Institution. His face was brown, he had a small moustache, he was vigorous enough in his smallness.

"*Well*, is it Hadrian!" exclaimed Cousin Matilda, wringing the lather off her hands. "We didn't expect you till to-morrow."

"I got off Monday night," said Hadrian, glancing round the room.

"Fancy!" said Cousin Matilda. Then, having dried her hands, she went forward, held out her hand, and said:

"How are you?"

"Quite well, thank you," said Hadrian.

"You're quite a man,' said Cousin Matilda.

Hadrian glanced at her. She did not look her best: so thin, so large-nosed, with that pink-and-white checked duster tied round her head. She felt her disadvantage. But she had had a good deal of suffering and sorrow, she did not mind any more.

The servant entered—one that did not know Hadrian.

"Come and see my father," said Cousin Matilda.

In the hall they roused Cousin Emmie like a partridge from cover. She was on the stairs pushing the bright stair-rods into place. Instinctively her hand went to the little knobs, her front hair bobbed on her forehead.

"Why!" she exclaimed, crossly. "What have you come today for?"

"I got off a day earlier," said Hadrian, and his man's voice so deep and unexpected was like a blow to Cousin Emmie.

"Well, you've caught us in the midst of it," she said, with resentment. Then all three went into the middle room.

Mr. Rockley was dressed—that is, he had on his trousers and

socks—but he was resting on the bed, propped up just under the window, from whence he could see his beloved and resplendent garden, where tulips and apple-trees were ablaze. He did not look as ill as he was, for the water puffed him up, and his face kept its colour.

5 His stomach was much swollen. He glanced round swiftly, turning his eyes without turning his head. He was the wreck of a handsome, well-built man.

Seeing Hadrian, a queer, unwilling smile went over his face. The young man greeted him sheepishly.

10 "You wouldn't make a life-guardsman," he said. "Do you want something to eat?"

Hadrian looked round—as if for the meal.

"I don't mind," he said.

"What shall you have—egg and bacon?" asked Emmie shortly.

15 "Yes, I don't mind," said Hadrian.

The sisters went down to the kitchen, and sent the servant to finish the stairs.

"Isn't he *altered?*" said Matilda, *sotto voce.*

"Isn't he!" said Cousin Emmie. "*What* a little man!"

20 They both made a grimace, and laughed nervously.

"Get the frying-pan," said Emmie to Matilda.

"But he's as cocky as ever," said Matilda, narrowing her eyes and shaking her head knowingly, as she handed the frying-pan.

"Mannie!"* said Emmie sarcastically. Hadrian's new-fledged,

25 cock-sure manliness evidently found no favour in her eyes.

"Oh, he's not bad," said Matilda. "You don't want to be prejudiced against him."

"I'm not prejudiced against him, I think he's all right for looks," said Emmie, "but there's too much of the little mannie about him."

30 "Fancy catching us like this," said Matilda.

"They've no thought for anything," said Emmie with contempt. "You go up and get dressed, our Matilda. I don't care about him. I can see to things, and you can talk to him. I shan't."

"He'll talk to my father," said Matilda, meaningful.

35 "*Sly*—!" exclaimed Emmie, with a grimace.

The sisters believed that Hadrian had come hoping to get something out of their father—hoping for a legacy. And they were not at all sure he would not get it.

Matilda went upstairs to change. She had thought it all out how

40 she would receive Hadrian, and impress him. And he had caught her

with her head tied up in a duster, and her thin arms in a basin of lather. But she did not care. She now dressed herself most scrupulously, carefully folded her long, beautiful, blonde hair, touched her pallor with a little rouge, and put her long string of exquisite crystal beads over her soft green dress. Now she looked elegant, like a heroine in a magazine illustration, and almost as unreal.

She found Hadrian and her father talking away. The young man was short of speech as a rule, but he could find his tongue with his "uncle." They were both sipping a glass of brandy, and smoking, and chatting like a pair of old cronies. Hadrian was telling about Canada. He was going back there when his leave was up.

"You wouldn't like to stop in England, then?" said Mr. Rockley.

"No, I wouldn't stop in England," said Hadrian.

"How's that? There's plenty of electricians here," said Mr. Rockley.

"Yes. But there's too much difference between the men and the employers over here—too much of that for me," said Hadrian.

The sick man looked at him narrowly, with oddly smiling eyes.

"That's it, is it?" he replied.

Matilda heard and understood. "So that's your big idea, is it, my little man," she said to herself. She had always said of Hadrian that he had no proper *respect* for anybody or anything, that he was sly and *common*. She went down to the kitchen for a *sotto voce* confab with Emmie.

"He thinks a rare lot of himself!" she whispered.

"He's somebody, he is!" said Emmie with contempt.

"He thinks there's too much difference between masters and men, over here," said Matilda.

"Is it any different in Canada?" asked Emmie.

"Oh yes—democratic," replied Matilda. "He thinks they're all on a level over there."

"Ay, well he's over here now," said Emmie drily, "so he can keep his place."

As they talked they saw the young man sauntering down the garden, looking casually at the flowers. He had his hands in his pockets, and his soldier's cap neatly on his head. He looked quite at his ease, as if in possession. The two women, fluttered, watched him through the window.

"We know what he's come for," said Emmie churlishly. Matilda looked a long time at the neat khaki figure. It had something of the charity-boy about it still; but now it was a man's figure, laconic, charged with plebeian energy. She thought of the derisive passion in his voice as he had declaimed against the propertied classes, to her father.

5   "You don't know, Emmie. Perhaps he's not come for that," she rebuked her sister. They were both thinking of the money.

They were still watching the young soldier. He stood away at the bottom of the garden, with his back to them, his hands in his pockets, looking into the water of the willow pond. Matilda's dark-blue eyes

10 had a strange, full look in them, the lids, with the faint blue veins showing, dropped rather low. She carried her head light and high, but she had a look of pain. The young man at the bottom of the garden turned and looked up the path. Perhaps he saw them through the window. Matilda moved into shadow.

15   That afternoon their father seemed weak and ill. He was easily exhausted. The doctor came, and told Matilda that the sick man might die suddenly at any moment—but then he might not. They must be prepared.

So the day passed, and the next. Hadrian made himself at home.

20 He went about in the morning in his brownish jersey and his khaki trousers, collarless, his bare neck showing. He explored the pottery premises, as if he had some secret purpose in so doing, he talked with Mr. Rockley, when the sick man had strength. The two girls were always angry when the two men sat talking together like cronies. Yet

25 it was chiefly a kind of politics they talked.

On the second day after Hadrian's arrival, Matilda sat with her father in the evening. She was drawing a picture which she wanted to copy. It was very still, Hadrian was gone out somewhere, no one knew where, and Emmie was busy. Mr. Rockley reclined on his bed,

30 looking out in silence over his evening-sunny garden.

"If anything happens to me, Matilda," he said, "you won't sell this house—you'll stop here——"

Matilda's eyes took their slightly haggard look as she stared at her father.

35   "Well, we couldn't do anything else," she said.

"You don't know what you might do," he said. "Everything is left to you and Emmie, equally. You do as you like with it—only don't sell this house, don't part with it."

"No," she said.

40   "And give Hadrian my watch and chain, and a hundred pounds

out of what's in the bank—and help him if he ever wants helping. I haven't put his name in the will."

"Your watch and chain, and a hundred pounds—yes. But you'll be here when he goes back to Canada, father."

"You never know what'll happen," said her father.

Matilda sat and watched him, with her full, haggard eyes, for a long time, as if tranced. She saw that he knew he must go soon—she saw like a clairvoyant.

Later on she told Emmie what her father had said about the watch and chain and the money.

"What right has *he*"—*he*—meaning Hadrian—"to my father's watch and chain—what has it to do with him? Let him have the money, and get off," said Emmie. She loved her father.

That night Matilda sat late in her room. Her heart was anxious and breaking, her mind seemed entranced. She was too much entranced even to weep, and all the time she thought of her father, only her father. At last she felt she must go to him.

It was near midnight. She went along the passage and to his room. There was a faint light from the moon outside. She listened at his door. Then she softly opened and entered. The room was faintly dark. She heard a movement on the bed.

"Are you asleep?" she said softly, advancing to the side of the bed.

"Are you asleep?" she repeated gently, as she stood at the side of the bed. And she reached her hand in the darkness to touch his forehead. Delicately, her fingers met the nose and the eyebrows, she laid her fine, delicate hand on his brow. It seemed fresh and smooth—very fresh and smooth. A sort of surprise stirred her, in her entranced state. But it could not waken her. Gently, she leaned over the bed and stirred her fingers over the low-growing hair on his brow.

"Can't you sleep to-night?" she said.

There was a quick stirring in the bed. "Yes, I can," a voice answered. It was Hadrian's voice. She started away. Instantly, she was wakened from her late-at-night trance. She remembered that her father was downstairs, that Hadrian had his room. She stood in the darkness as if stung.

"Is that you, Hadrian?" she said. "I thought it was my father." She was so startled, so shocked, that she could not move. The young man gave an uncomfortable laugh, and turned in his bed.

At last she got out of the room. When she was back in her own room, in the light, and her door was closed, she stood holding up her hand that had touched him, as if it were hurt. She was almost too shocked, she could not endure.

"Well," said her calm and weary mind, "it was only a mistake, why take any notice of it."

But she could not reason her feelings so easily. She suffered, feeling herself in a false position. Her right hand, which she had laid so gently on his face, on his fresh skin, ached now, as if it were really injured. She could not forgive Hadrian for the mistake: it made her dislike him deeply.

Hadrian too slept badly. He had been awakened by the opening of the door, and had not realised what the question meant. But the soft, straying tenderness of her hand on his face startled something out of his soul. He was a charity boy, aloof and more or less at bay. The fragile exquisiteness of her caress startled him most, revealed unknown things to him.

In the morning she could feel the consciousness in his eyes, when she came downstairs. She tried to bear herself as if nothing at all had happened, and she succeeded. She had the calm self-control, self-indifference, of one who has suffered and borne her suffering. She looked at him from her darkish, almost drugged blue eyes, she met the spark of consciousness in his eyes, and quenched it. And with her long, fine hand she put the sugar in his coffee.

But she could not control him as she thought she could. He had a keen memory stinging his mind, a new set of sensations working in his consciousness. Something new was alert in him. At the back of his reticent, guarded mind he kept his secret alive and vivid. She was at his mercy, for he was unscrupulous, his standard was not her standard.

He looked at her curiously. She was not beautiful, her nose was too large, her chin was too small, her neck was too thin. But her skin was clear and fine, she had a high-bred sensitiveness. This queer, brave, high-bred quality she shared with her father. The charity boy could see it in her tapering fingers, which were white and ringed. The same glamour that he knew in the elderly man he now saw in the woman. And he wanted to possess himself of it, he wanted to make himself master of it. As he went about through the old pottery-yard, his secretive mind schemed and worked. To be master of that strange soft delicacy such as he had felt in her hand upon his face,—this was what he set himself towards. He was secretly plotting.

He watched Matilda as she went about, and she became aware of his attention, as of some shadow following her. But her pride made her ignore it. When he sauntered near her, his hands in his pockets, she received him with that same commonplace kindliness which mastered him more than any contempt. Her superior breeding 5 seemed to control him. She made herself feel towards him exactly as she had always felt: he was a young boy who lived in the house with them, but was a stranger. Only, she dared not remember his face under her hand. When she remembered that, she was bewildered. Her hand had offended her, she wanted to cut it off. And she wanted, 10 fiercely, to cut off the memory in him. She assumed she had done so.

One day, when he sat talking with his "uncle," he looked straight into the eyes of the sick man, and said:

"But I shouldn't like to live and die here in Rawsley."*

"No—well—you needn't," said the sick man. 15

"Do you think Cousin Matilda likes it?"

"I should think so."

"I don't call it much of a life," said the youth. "How much older is she than me, Uncle?"

The sick man looked at the young soldier. 20

"A good bit," he said.

"Over thirty?" said Hadrian.

"Well, not so much. She's thirty-two."

Hadrian considered a while.

"She doesn't look it," he said. 25

Again the sick father looked at him.

"Do you think she'd like to leave here?" said Hadrian.

"Nay, I don't know," replied the father, restive.

Hadrian sat still, having his own thoughts. Then in a small, quiet voice, as if he were speaking from inside himself, he said: 30

"I'd marry her if you wanted me to."

The sick man raised his eyes suddenly, and stared. He stared for a long time. The youth looked inscrutably out of the window.

"*You!*" said the sick man, mocking, with some contempt. Hadrian turned and met his eyes. The two men had an inexplicable under- 35 standing.

"If you wasn't against it," said Hadrian.

"Nay," said the father, turning aside, "I don't think I'm against it. I've never thought of it. But— But Emmie's the youngest."

He had flushed, and looked suddenly more alive. Secretly he 40 loved the boy.

"You might ask her," said Hadrian.

The elder man considered.

"Hadn't you better ask her yourself?" he said.

"She'd take more notice of you," said Hadrian.

5   They were both silent. Then Emmie came in.

For two days Mr. Rockley was excited and thoughtful. Hadrian went about quietly, secretly, unquestioning. At last the father and daughter were alone together. It was very early morning, the father had been in much pain. As the pain abated, he lay still, thinking.

10   "Matilda!" he said suddenly, looking at his daughter.

"Yes, I'm here," she said.

"Ay! I want you to do something——"

She rose in anticipation.

"Nay, sit still.—I want you to marry Hadrian——"

15   She thought he was raving. She rose, bewildered and frightened.

"Nay, sit you still, sit you still. You hear what I tell you."

"But you don't know what you're saying, father."

"Ay, I know well enough.—I want you to marry Hadrian, I tell you."

20   She was dumbfounded. He was a man of few words.

"You'll do what I tell you," he said.

She looked at him slowly.

"What put such an idea in your mind?" she said proudly.

"He did."

25   Matilda almost looked her father down, her pride was so offended.

"Why, it's disgraceful," she said.

"Why?"

She watched him slowly.

"What do you ask me for?" she said. "It's disgusting."

30   "The lad's sound enough," he replied, testily.

"You'd better tell him to clear out," she said coldly.

He turned and looked out of the window. She sat flushed and erect, for a long time. At length her father turned to her, looking really malevolent.

35   "If you won't," he said, "you're a fool, and I'll make you pay for your foolishness, do you see?"

Suddenly a cold fear gripped her. She could not believe her senses. She was terrified and bewildered. She stared at her father, believing him to be delirious, or mad, or drunk. What could she
40 do?

"I tell you," he said. "I'll send for Whittle to-morrow if you don't. You shall neither of you have anything of mine."

Whittle was the solicitor. She understood her father well enough: he would send for his solicitor, and make a will leaving all his property to Hadrian: neither she nor Emmie should have anything. It 5
was too much. She rose and went out of the room, up to her own room, where she locked herself in.

She did not come out for some hours. At last, late at night, she confided in Emmie.

"The sliving* demon, he wants the money," said Emmie. "My 10
father's out of his mind."

The thought that Hadrian merely wanted the money was another blow to Matilda. She did not love the impossible youth—but she had not yet learned to think of him as a thing of evil. He now became hideous to her mind. 15

Emmie had a little scene with her father next day.

"You don't mean what you said to our Matilda yesterday, do you, father?" she asked aggressively.

"Yes," he replied.

"What, that you'll alter your will?" 20
"Yes."

"You won't," said his angry daughter.

But he looked at her with a malevolent little smile.

"Annie!" he shouted. "Annie!"

He had still power to make his voice carry. The servant maid came 25
in from the kitchen.

"Put your things on, and go down to Whittle's office, and say I want to see Mr. Whittle as soon as he can, and will he bring a will-form."

The sick man lay back a little—he could not lie down. His 30
daughter sat as if she had been struck. Then she left the room.

Hadrian was pottering about in the garden. She went straight down to him.

"Here," she said. "You'd better get off. You'd better take your things and go from here, quick." 35

Hadrian looked slowly at the infuriated girl.

"Who says so?" he asked.

"*We* say so—get off, you've done enough mischief and damage."

"Does Uncle say so?"

"Yes, he does." 40

"I'll go and ask him."

But like a fury Emmie barred his way.

"No, you needn't. You needn't ask him nothing at all. We don't want you, so you can go."

5   "Uncle's boss here."

"A man that's dying, and you crawling round and working on him for his money!—you're not fit to live."

"Oh!" he said. "Who says I'm working for his money?"

"I say. But my father told our Matilda, and *she* knows what you are.
10 *She* knows what you're after. So you might as well clear out, for all you'll get—gutter-snipe!"

He turned his back on her, to think. It had not occurred to him that they would think he was after the money. He *did* want the money—badly. He badly wanted to be an employer himself, not one
15 of the employed. But he knew, in his subtle, calculating way, that it was not for money he wanted Matilda. He wanted both the money and Matilda. But he told himself the two desires were separate, not one. He could not do with Matilda, *without* the money. But he did not want her *for* the money.

20   When he got this clear in his mind, he sought for an opportunity to tell it her, lurking and watching. But she avoided him. In the evening the lawyer came. Mr. Rockley seemed to have a new access of strength—a will was drawn up, making the previous arrangements wholly conditional. The old will held good, if Matilda would consent
25 to marry Hadrian. If she refused then at the end of six months the whole property passed to Hadrian.

Mr. Rockley told this to the young man, with malevolent satisfaction. He seemed to have a strange desire, quite unreasonable, for revenge upon the women who had surrounded him for so long, and
30 served him so carefully.

"Tell her in front of me," said Hadrian.

So Mr. Rockley sent for his daughters.

At last they came, pale, mute, stubborn. Matilda seemed to have retired far off, Emmie seemed like a fighter ready to fight to the
35 death. The sick man reclined on the bed, his eyes bright, his puffed hand trembling. But his face had again some of its old, bright handsomeness. Hadrian sat quiet, a little aside: the indomitable, dangerous charity boy.

"There's the will," said their father, pointing them to the paper.
40 The two women sat mute and immovable, they took no notice.

"Either you marry Hadrian, or he has everything," said the father with satisfaction.

"Then let him have everything," said Matilda coldly.

"He's not! He's not!" cried Emmie fiercely. "He's not going to have it. The gutter-snipe!"

An amused look came on her father's face.

"You hear that, Hadrian," he said.

"I didn't offer to marry Cousin Matilda for the money," said Hadrian, flushing and moving in his seat.

Matilda looked at him slowly, with her dark-blue, drugged eyes. He seemed a strange little monster to her.

"Why, you liar, you know you did," cried Emmie.

The sick man laughed. Matilda continued to gaze strangely at the young man.

"She knows I didn't," said Hadrian.

He too had his courage, as a rat has indomitable courage in the end. Hadrian had some of the neatness, the reserve, the underground quality of the rat. But he had perhaps the ultimate courage, the most unquenchable courage of all.

Emmie looked at her sister.

"Oh, well," she said. "Matilda—don't you bother. Let him have everything, we can look after ourselves."

"I know he'll take everything," said Matilda abstractedly.

Hadrian did not answer. He knew in fact that if Matilda refused him he would take everything, and go off with it.

"A clever little mannie—!" said Emmie, with a jeering grimace.

The father laughed noiselessly to himself. But he was tired. . . .

"Go on then," he said. "Go on, let me be quiet."

Emmie turned and looked at him.

"You deserve what you've got," she said to her father bluntly.

"Go on," he answered mildly. "Go on."

Another night passed—a night nurse sat up with Mr. Rockley. Another day came. Hadrian was there as ever, in his woollen jersey and coarse khaki trousers and bare neck. Matilda went about, frail and distant, Emmie black-browed in spite of her blondness. They were all quiet, for they did not intend the mystified servant to learn everything.

Mr. Rockley had very bad attacks of pain, he could not breathe. The end seemed near. They all went about quiet and stoical, all unyielding. Hadrian pondered within himself. If he did not marry

Matilda he would go to Canada with twenty thousand pounds. This was itself a very satisfactory prospect. If Matilda consented he would have nothing—she would have her own money.

Emmie was the one to act. She went off in search of the solicitor and brought him home with her. There was an interview, and Whittle tried to frighten the youth into withdrawal—but without avail. Then clergyman and relatives were summoned—but Hadrian stared at them and took no notice. It made him angry, however.

He wanted to catch Matilda alone. Many days went by, and he was not successful: she avoided him. At last, lurking, he surprised her one day as she came to pick gooseberries, and he cut off her retreat. He came to the point at once.

"You don't want me then?" he said, in his subtle, insinuating voice.

"I don't want to speak to you," she said, averting her face.

"You put your hand on me, though," he said. "You shouldn't have done that, and then I should never have thought of it. You shouldn't have touched me."

"If you were anything decent, you'd know that was a mistake, and forget it," she said.

"I know it was a mistake—but I shan't forget it. If you wake a man up, he can't go to sleep again because he's told to."

"If you had any decent feeling in you, you'd have gone away," she replied.

"I didn't want to," he replied.

She looked away into the distance. At last she asked:

"What do you persecute me for, if it isn't for the money? I'm old enough to be your mother. In a way I've been your mother."

"Doesn't matter," he said. "You've been no mother to me. Let us marry and go out to Canada—you might as well—you've touched me."

She was white and trembling. Suddenly she flushed with anger.

"It's so *indecent*," she said.

"How?" he retorted. "You touched me."

But she walked away from him. She felt as if he had trapped her. He was angry and depressed, he felt again despised.

That same evening, she went into her father's room.

"Yes," she said suddenly. "I'll marry him."

Her father looked up at her. He was in pain, and very ill.

"You like him now, do you?" he said, with a faint smile.

She looked down into his face, and saw death not far off. She turned and went coldly out of the room.

The solicitor was sent for, preparations were hastily made. In all the interval Matilda did not speak to Hadrian, never answered him if he addressed her. He approached her in the morning.

"You've come round to it, then?" he said, giving her a pleasant look from his twinkling, almost kindly eyes. She looked down at him and turned aside. She looked down on him both literally and figuratively. Still he persisted, and triumphed.

Emmie raved and wept, the secret flew abroad. But Matilda was silent and unmoved, Hadrian was quiet and satisfied, and nipped with fear also. But he held out against his fear. Mr. Rockley was very ill, but unchanged.

On the third day the marriage took place. Matilda and Hadrian drove straight home from the registrar, and went straight into the room of the dying man. His face lit up with a clear twinkling smile.

"Hadrian,—you've got her?" he said, a little hoarsely.

"Yes," said Hadrian, who was pale round the gills.

"Ay, my lad, I'm glad you're mine," replied the dying man. Then he turned his eyes closely on Matilda.

"Let's look at you, Matilda," he said. Then his voice went strange and unrecognisable. "Kiss me," he said.

She stooped and kissed him. She had never kissed him before, not since she was a tiny child. But she was quiet, very still.

"Kiss him," the dying man said.

Obediently, Matilda put forward her mouth and kissed the young husband.

"That's right! That's right!" murmured the dying man.

Samson and Delilah[*]

A man got down from the motor-omnibus that runs from Penzance to St. Just-in-Penwith,[*] and turned northwards, uphill towards the Polestar. It was only half-past six, but already the stars were out, a
5   cold little wind was blowing from the sea, and the crystalline, three-pulse flash of the lighthouse below the cliffs[*] beat rhythmically in the first darkness.

    The man was alone. He went his way unhesitating, but looked from side to side with cautious curiosity. Tall, ruined power-houses of
10   tin-mines[*] loomed in the darkness from time to time, like remnants of some by-gone civilisation. The lights of many miners' cottages scattered on the hilly darkness, twinkled desolate in their disorder, yet twinkled with the lonely homeliness of the Celtic night.[*]

    He tramped steadily on, always watchful with curiosity. He was a
15   tall, well-built man, apparently in the prime of life. His shoulders were square and rather stiff, he leaned forwards a little as he went, from the hips, like a man who must stoop to lower his height. But he did not stoop his shoulders: he bent his straight back from the hips.

20   Now and again short, stumpy, thick-legged figures of Cornish miners passed him, and he invariably gave them goodnight, as if to insist that he was on his own ground. He spoke with the west-Cornish intonation. And as he went along the dreary road, looking now at the lights of the dwellings on land, now at the lights away to
25   sea, vessels veering round in sight of the Longships Lighthouse, the whole of the Atlantic Ocean in darkness and space between him and America, he seemed a little excited and pleased with himself, watchful, thrilled, veering along in a sense of mastery and of power in conflict.

30   The houses began to close on the road, he was entering the straggling, formless, desolate mining village, that he knew of old. On the left was a little space set back from the road, and cosy lights of an inn. There it was. He peered up at the sign: "The Tinners Rest."[*] But he could not make out the name of the proprietor. He listened.

There was excited talking and laughing, a woman's voice laughing shrilly among the men's.

Stooping a little, he entered the warmly-lit bar. The lamp was burning, a buxom woman rose from the white-scrubbed deal table where the black and white and red cards were scattered, and several men, miners, lifted their faces from the game.

The stranger went to the counter, averting his face. His cap was pulled down over his brow.

"Good-evening!" said the landlady, in her rather ingratiating voice.

"Good-evening.—A glass of ale."

"A glass of ale," repeated the landlady suavely. "Cold night—but bright."

"Yes," the man assented, laconically. Then he added, when nobody expected him to say any more: "Seasonable weather."

"Quite seasonable, quite," said the landlady. "Thank you."

The man lifted his glass straight to his lips, and emptied it. He put it down again on the zinc counter with a click.

"Let's have another," he said.

The woman drew the beer, and the man went away with his glass to the second table, near the fire. The woman, after a moment's hesitation, took her seat again at the table with the card-players. She had noticed the man: a big fine fellow, well dressed, a stranger. But he spoke with that Cornish-Yankee accent she accepted as the natural twang among the miners.

The stranger put his foot on the fender and looked into the fire. He was handsome, well-coloured, with well-drawn Cornish eye-brows and the usual dark, bright, mindless Cornish eyes. He seemed abstracted in thought. Then he watched the card-party.

The woman was buxom and healthy, with dark hair and small, quick brown eyes. She was bursting with life and vigour, the energy she threw into the game of cards excited all the men, they shouted, and laughed, and the woman held her breast, shrieking with laughter.

"Oh my, it'll be the death o' me," she panted. "Now come on, Mr Trevorrow, play fair. Play fair, I say, or I s'll put the cards down."

"Play fair! Why who's played unfair!" ejaculated Mr Trevorrow. "Do you mean t'accuse me, as I haven't played fair, Mrs Nankervis?"

"I do. I say it and I mean it. Haven't you got the Queen of

Spades?—Now come on, no dodging round me. *I* know you've got
that queen, as well as I know my name's Alice."

"Well—if your name's Alice, you'll have to have it—"

"Ay now—what did I say! Did ever you see such a man? My word,
but your Missis must be easy took in, by the looks of things."

And off she went into peals of laughter. She was interrupted by the
entrance of four men in khaki, a short, stumpy sergeant, of middle
age, a young corporal, and two young privates. The woman leaned
back in her chair.

"Oh my!" she cried. "If there isn't the boys back: looking
perished, I believe—"

"Perished, Ma!" exclaimed the sergeant. "Not yet."

"Near enough," said a young private, uncouthly.

The woman got up.

"I'm sure you are, my dears.—You'll be wanting your suppers, I'll
be bound."

"We could do with 'em."

"Let's have a wet first," said the sergeant.

The woman bustled about getting the drinks. The soldiers moved
to the fire, spreading out their hands.

"Have your suppers in here, will you?" she said. "Or in the
kitchen."

"Let's have it here," said the sergeant. "More cosier—*if* you don't
mind."

"You shall have it where you like, boys, where you like."

She disappeared. In a minute a girl of about sixteen came in. She
was tall and fresh, with dark, young, expressionless eyes, and
well-drawn brows, and the immature softness and mindlessness of
the sensuous Celtic type.

"Ho—Maryann! Evenin' Maryann! How's Maryann, now!" came
the multiple greeting.

She replied to everybody in a soft voice, a strange, soft *aplomb** that
was very attractive. And she moved round with rather mechanical,
attractive movements, as if her thoughts were elsewhere. But she had
always this dim far-awayness in her bearing: a sort of modesty. The
strange man by the fire watched her curiously. There was an alert,
inquisitive, mindless curiosity on his well-coloured face.

"I'll have a bit of supper with you, if I might," he said.

She looked at him, with her clear, unreasoning eyes, just like the
eyes of some non-human creature.

"I'll ask mother," she said. Her voice was soft-breathing, gently sing-song.

When she came in again:

"Yes," she said, almost whispering. "What will you have?"

"What have you got?" he said, looking up in to her face.   5

"There's cold meat—"

"That's for me, then."

The stranger sat at the end of the table, and ate with the tired, quiet soldiers. Now, the landlady was interested in him. Her brow was knit rather tense, there was a look of panic on her large, healthy 10
face, but her small brown eyes were fixed most dangerously. She was a big woman, but her eyes were small and tense. She drew near the stranger. She wore a rather loud-patterned flannelette blouse, and a dark skirt.

"What will you have to drink with your supper?" she asked, and 15
there was a new, dangerous note in her voice.

He moved uneasily.

"Oh, I'll go on with ale."

She drew him another glass. Then she sat down on the bench at the table with him and the soldiers, and fixed him with her attention. 20

"You've come from St. Just, have you?" she said.

He looked at her with those clear, dark, inscrutable Cornish eyes, and answered at length:

"No, from Penzance."

"Penzance!—But you're not thinking of going back there 25
tonight?"

"No—no."

He still looked at her with those wide, clear eyes that seemed like very bright agate. Her anger began to rise. It was seen on her brows. Yet her voice was still suave and deprecating.   30

"I *thought* not.—But you're not living in these parts, are you?"

"No—no, I'm not living here." He was always slow in answering, as if something intervened between him and any outside question.

"Oh, I see," she said, "you've got relations down here."

Again he looked straight into her eyes, as if looking her into 35
silence.

"Yes," he said.

He did not say any more. She rose with a flounce. The anger was tight on her brow. There was no more laughing and card-playing that evening, though she kept up her motherly, suave, good- 40 humoured way with the men. But they knew her, they were all afraid of her.

The supper was finished, the table cleared, the stranger did not go. Two of the young soldiers went off to bed, with their cheery:

5   "Goodnight, Ma. Goodnight, Maryann."

The stranger talked a little to the sergeant, about the war, which was in its first year, about the New Army,* a fragment of which was quartered in this district, about America.

The landlady darted looks at him from her small eyes, minute by 10 minute the electric storm swelled in her bosom, as still he did not go. She was quivering with suppressed, violent passion, something frightening and abnormal. She could not sit still for a moment. Her heavy form seemed to flash with sudden, involuntary movements as the minutes passed by, and still he sat there, and the tension on her 15 heart grew unbearable. She watched the hands of the clock move on. Three of the soldiers had gone to bed, only the crop-headed, terrier-like old sergeant remained.

The landlady sat behind the bar fidgeting spasmodically with the newspaper. She looked again at the clock. At last it was five minutes 20 to ten.

"Gentlemen—the enemy!" she said, in her diminished, furious voice. "Time, please. Time, my dears. And goodnight all!"

The men began to drop out, with a brief goodnight. It was a minute to ten. The landlady rose.

25   "Come," she said. "I'm shutting the door."

The last of the miners passed out. She stood stout and menacing, holding the door. Still the stranger sat on by the fire, his black overcoat opened, smoking.

"We're closed now, Sir," came the perilous, narrowed voice of the 30 landlady.

The little, dog-like, hard-headed sergeant touched the arm of the stranger.

"Closing-time," he said.

The stranger turned round in his seat, and his quick-moving, 35 dark, jewel-like eyes went from the sergeant to the landlady.

"I'm stopping here tonight," he said, in his laconic, Cornish-Yankee accent.

The landlady seemed to tower. Her eyes lifted strangely, frightening.

40   "Oh indeed!" she cried. "Oh indeed!—And whose orders are those, may I ask?"

He looked at her again.

"My orders," he said.

Involuntarily she shut the door, and advanced like a great, dangerous bird. Her voice rose, there was a touch of hoarseness in it.

5

"And what might *your* orders be, if you please?" she cried. "Who might *you* be, to give orders in my house?"

He sat still, watching her.

"You know who I am," he said. "At least, I know who you are."

"Oh do you! Oh do you! And who am *I* then, if you'll be so good as to tell me?"

10

He stared at her with his bright, dark eyes.

"You're my Missis, you are," he said. "And you know it, as well as I do."

She started as if something had exploded in her. Her eyes lifted and flared madly.

15

"*Do* I know it indeed!" she cried. "I know no such thing! I know no such thing! Do you think a man's going to walk into this bar, and tell me off-hand I'm his Missis, and I'm going to believe him?—I say to you, whoever you may be, you're mistaken. I know myself for no Missis of yours, and I'll thank you to go out of this house, this minute, before I get those that will put you out."

20

The man rose to his feet, stretching his head towards her a little. He was a handsomely built Cornishman in the prime of life.

"What you say, eh? You don't know me?" he said, in his sing-song voice, emotionless, but rather smothered and pressing: it reminded one of the girl's. "I should know *you* anywhere, you see. I should! I shouldn't have to look twice to know you, you see. You see, now, don't you?"

25

The woman was baffled.

30

"So you may say," she replied, staccato. "So you may say. That's easy enough. My name's known, and respected, by most people for ten miles round.—But I don't know *you*." Her voice ran to sarcasm. "I can't say I know *you*. You're a *perfect* stranger to me, and I don't believe I've ever set eyes on you before tonight."

35

Her voice was very flexible and sarcastic.

"Yes you have," replied the man, in his reasonable way. "Yes you have. Your name's my name, and that girl Maryann is my girl; she's my daughter. You're my Missis right enough. As sure as I'm Willie Nankervis."

40

He spoke as if it were an accepted fact. His face was handsome, with a strange, watchful alertness and a fundamental fixity of intention that maddened her.

"You villain!" she cried. "You villain, to come to this house and dare to speak to me. You villain, you downright rascal!"

5 He looked at her.

"Ay," he said unmoved. "All that." He was uneasy before her. Only he was not afraid of her. There was something impenetrable about him, like his eyes, which were as bright as agate.

She towered, and drew near to him menacingly.

10 "You're going out of this house, aren't you—" she stamped her foot in sudden madness "*this minute!*"

He watched her. He knew she wanted to strike him.

"No," he said, with suppressed emphasis. "I've told you, I'm stopping here."

15 He was afraid of her personality, but it did not alter him. She wavered. Her small, tawny-brown eyes concentrated in a point of vivid, sightless fury, like a tiger's. The man was wincing, but he stood his ground. Then she bethought herself. She would gather her forces.

20 "We'll see whether you're stopping here," she said. And she turned, with a curious, frightening lifting of her eyes, and surged out of the room. The man, listening, heard her go upstairs, heard her tapping at a bedroom door, heard her saying: "Do you mind coming down a minute, boys! I want you, I'm in trouble."

25 The man in the bar took off his cap and his black overcoat, and threw them on the seat behind him. His black hair was short and touched with grey at the temples. He wore a well-cut, well-fitting suit of dark-grey, American in style, and a turn-down collar. He looked well-to-do, a fine, solid figure of a man. The rather rigid look

30 of the shoulders came from his having had his collar-bone twice broken in the mines.

The little terrier of a sergeant, in dirty khaki, looked at him furtively.

"She's your missis?" he asked, jerking his head in the direction of

35 the departed woman.

"Yes, she is," barked the man. "She's that, sure enough."

"Not seen her for a long time, haven't ye?"

"Sixteen years come March month."

"Hm!"

40 And the sergeant laconically resumed his smoking.

The landlady was coming back, followed by the three young soldiers, who entered rather sheepishly, in trousers and shirt and stocking-feet. The woman stood histrionically at the end of the bar, and exclaimed:

"That man refuses to leave the house, claims he's stopping the night here. You know very well I have no bed, don't you? And this house doesn't accommodate travellers. Yet he's going to stop in spite of all!—But not while I've a drop of blood in my body, that I declare with my dying breath.—And not if you men are worth the name of men, and will help a woman as has no one to help her."

Her eyes sparkled, her face was flushed pink. She was drawn up like an Amazon.

The young soldiers did not quite know what to do. They looked at the man, they looked at the sergeant, one of them looked down and fastened his braces on the second button.

"What say, sergeant?" asked one whose face twinkled for a little devilment.

"Man says he's husband to Mrs Nankervis," said the sergeant.

"He's no husband of mine. I declare I never set eyes on him before this night. It's a dirty trick, nothing else, it's a dirty trick."

"Why you're a liar, saying you never set eyes on me before," barked the man near the hearth. "You're married to me, and that girl Maryann you had by me—well enough you know it."

The young soldiers looked on in delight, the sergeant smoked unperturbed.

"Yes," sang the landlady, slowly shaking her head in supreme sarcasm, "it sounds very pretty, doesn't it! But you see we don't believe a word of it, and *how* are you going to prove it?" She smiled nastily.

The man watched in silence for a moment, then he said:

"It wants no proof."

"Oh yes, but it does! Oh yes but it does, sir, it wants a lot of proving!" sang the landlady's sarcasm. "We're not such gulls as all that, to swallow your words whole."

But he stood unmoved near the fire, she stood with one hand resting on the zinc-covered bar, the sergeant sat with legs crossed, smoking, on the seat half way between them, the three young soldiers in their shirts and braces stood wavering in the gloom behind the bar. There was silence.

"Do you know anything of the whereabouts of your husband, Mrs

Nankervis?—Is he still living?" asked the sergeant, in his judicious fashion.

Suddenly the landlady began to cry, great, scalding tears, that left the young men aghast.

5   "I know nothing of him," she sobbed, feeling for her pocket-handkerchief. "He left me when Maryann was a baby, went mining to America, and after about six months never wrote a line nor sent me a penny bit. I can't say whether he's alive or dead, the villain.— All I've heard of him's to the bad—and I've heard nothing for years

10 an' all, now." She sobbed violently.

The golden-skinned, handsome man near the fire watched her as she wept. He was frightened, he was troubled, he was bewildered, but none of his emotions altered him underneath.

There was no sound in the room but the violent sobbing of the
15 landlady. The men, one and all, were overcome.

"Don't you think as you'd better go, for tonight?" said the sergeant to the man, with sweet reasonableness. "You'd better leave it a bit, and arrange something between you.—You can't have much claim on a woman, I should imagine, if it's how she says. And you've come
20 down on her a bit too sudden-like."

The landlady sobbed heart-brokenly. The man watched her large breasts shaken. They seemed to cast a spell over his mind.

"How I've treated her, that's no matter!" he replied. "I've come back, and I'm going to stop in my own home,—for a bit, anyhow.
25 There you've got it."

"A dirty action," said the sergeant, his face flushing dark. "A dirty action, to come, after deserting a woman for that number of years, and want to force yourself on her! A dirty action—as isn't allowed by the law."

30 The landlady wiped her eyes.

"Never you mind about law nor nothing," cried the man, in a strange, strong voice. "I'm not moving out of this public tonight."

The woman turned to the soldiers behind her, and said, in a wheedling, sarcastic tone:

35 "Are we going to stand it, boys?—Are we going to be done like this, Sergeant Thomas, by a scoundrel and a bully as has led a life beyond *mention*, in those American mining-camps, and then wants to come back and make havoc of a poor woman's life and savings, after having left her with a baby in arms to struggle as best she
40 might?—It's a crying shame if nobody will stand up for me—a crying shame—!"

The soldiers, and the little sergeant, were bristling. The woman stooped and rummaged under the counter for a minute. Then, unseen to the man away near the fire, she threw out a plaited grass rope, such as is used for binding bales, and left it lying near the feet of the young soldiers, in the gloom at the back of the bar.

Then she rose and fronted the situation.

"Come now," she said to the man, in a reasonable, coldly-coaxing tone, "put your coat on and leave us alone. Be a man, and not worse than a brute of a German.—You can get a bed easy enough in St. Just, and if you've nothing to pay for it with, sergeant would lend you a couple of shillings, I'm sure he would."

All eyes were fixed on the man. He was looking down at the woman like a creature spell-bound or possessed by some devil's own intention.

"I've got money of my own," he said. "Don't you be frightened for your money, I've plenty of that, for the time."

"Well then," she coaxed, in a cold, almost sneering propitiation, "put your coat on and go where you're wanted—be a *man*, not a brute of a German."

She had drawn quite near to him, in her challenging coaxing intentness. He looked down at her with his bewitched face.

"No I shan't," he said. "I shan't do no such thing.—*You'll* put me up for tonight."

"Shall I!" she cried. And suddenly she flung her arms round him, hung on to him with all her powerful weight, calling to the soldiers: "Get the rope boys,* and fasten him up. Alfred—John, quick now——"

The man reared, looked round with maddened eyes, and heaved his powerful body. But the woman was powerful also, and very heavy, and was clenched with the determination of death. Her face, with its exulting, horribly vindictive look, was turned up to him from his own breast, he reached back his head frantically, to get away from it. Meanwhile the young soldiers, after having watched this frightful Laocoon* swaying for a moment, stirred, and the malicious one darted swiftly with the rope. It was tangled a little.

"Give me the end here!" cried the sergeant.

Meanwhile the big man heaved and struggled, swung the woman round against the seat and the table, in his convulsive effort to get free. But she pinned down his arms like a cuttle-fish wreathed heavily upon him. And he heaved and swayed, and they crashed about the room, the soldiers hopping, the furniture bumping.

The young soldier had got the rope once round, the brisk sergeant helping him. The woman sank heavily lower, they got the rope round several times. In the struggle the victim fell over against the table. The ropes tightened till they cut his arms. The woman clung to his
5   knees. Another soldier ran in a flash of genius, and fastened the strange man's feet with a pair of braces. Seats had crashed over, the table was thrown against the wall, but the man was bound, his arms pinned against his sides, his feet tied. He lay half fallen, sunk against the table, still for a moment.

10   The woman rose, and sank, faint, on to the seat against the wall. Her breast heaved, she could not speak, she thought she was going to die. The bound man lay against the over-turned table, his coat all twisted and pulled up beneath the ropes, leaving the loins exposed. The soldiers stood around, a little dazed, but excited with the row.

15   The man began to struggle again, heaving instinctively against the ropes, taking great deep breaths. His face, with its golden skin, flushed dark and surcharged, he heaved again. The great veins in his neck stood out. But it was no good, he went relaxed. Then again, suddenly, he jerked his feet.

20   "Another pair of braces, William," cried the excited soldier. He threw himself on the legs of the bound man, and managed to fasten the knees. Then again there was stillness. They could hear the clock tick.

The woman looked at the prostrate figure, the strong, straight
25   limbs, the strong back bound in subjection, the wide-eyed face that reminded her of a calf tied in a sack in a cart, only its head stretched dumbly backwards. And she triumphed.

The bound-up body began to struggle again. She watched fascinated the muscles working, the shoulders, the hips, the large,
30   clean thighs. Even now he might break the ropes. She was afraid. But the lively young soldier sat on the shoulders of the bound man, and after a few perilous moments, there was stillness again.

"Now," said the judicious sergeant, to the bound man, "if we untie you, will you promise to go off and make no more trouble."
35   "You'll not untie him in here," cried the woman. "I wouldn't trust him as far as I could blow him."

There was silence.

"We might carry him outside, and undo him there," said the soldier. "Then we could get the policeman, if he made any more
40   bother."

"Yes," said the sergeant. "We could do that." Then again, in an altered, almost severe tone, to the prisoner: "If we undo you outside, will you take your coat and go without creating any more disturbance?"

But the prisoner would not answer, he only lay with wide, dark, bright eyes, like a bound animal. There was a space of perplexed silence.

"Well then, do as you say," said the woman irritably. "Carry him out amongst you, and let us shut up the house."

They did so. Picking up the bound man, the four soldiers staggered clumsily into the silent square in front of the inn, the woman following with the cap and the overcoat. The young soldiers quickly unfastened the braces from the prisoner's legs, and they hopped indoors. They were in their stocking-feet, and outside the stars flashed cold. They stood in the doorway watching. The man lay quite still on the cold ground.

"Now," said the sergeant, in a subdued voice, "I'll loosen the knot, and he can work himself free, if you'll go in, Missis."

She gave a last look at the dishevelled, bound man, as he sat on the ground. Then she went indoors, followed quickly by the sergeant. Then they were heard locking and barring the door.

The man seated on the ground outside worked and strained at the rope. But it was not so easy to undo himself even now. So, with hands bound, making an effort, he got on his feet, and went and worked the cord against the rough edge of an old wall. The rope, being of a kind of plaited grass, soon frayed and broke, and he freed himself. He had various contusions. His arms were hurt and bruised from the bonds. He rubbed them slowly. Then he pulled his clothes straight, stooped, put on his cap, struggled into his overcoat, and walked away.

The stars were very brilliant. Clear as crystal the beam from the lighthouse under the cliffs struck rhythmically on the night. Dazed, the man walked along the road past the church-yard. Then he stood leaning up against a wall, for a long time.

He was roused because his feet were so cold. So he pulled himself together, and turned again in the silent night, back towards the inn. The bar was in darkness. But there was a light in the kitchen. He hesitated. Then, very quietly, he tried the door.

He was surprised to find it open. He entered, and quietly closed it behind him. Then he went down the step past the bar-counter, and

through to the lighted doorway of the kitchen. There sat his wife, planted in front of the range, where a furze fire was burning. She sat in a chair full in front of the range, her knees wide apart on the fender. She looked over her shoulder at him as he entered, but she
5 did not speak. Then she stared in the fire again.

It was a small, narrow kitchen. He dropped his cap on the table, that was covered with yellowish American cloth,* and took a seat with his back to the wall, near the oven. His wife still sat with her knees apart, her feet on the steel fender, and stared into the fire,
10 motionless. Her skin was smooth and rosy in the firelight. Everything in the house was very clean and bright. The man sat silent too, his head dropped. And thus they remained.

It was a question who would speak first. The woman leaned forward and poked the ends of the sticks in between the bars of the
15 range. He lifted his head and looked at her.

"Others gone to bed, have they?" he asked.

But she remained closed in silence.

"'S a cold night, out," he said, as if to himself.

And he laid his large, yet well-shaped workman's hand on the top
20 of the stove, that was polished black and smooth as velvet. She would not look at him, yet she glanced out of the corners of her eyes.

His eyes were fixed brightly on her, the pupils large and electric like those of a cat.

"I should have picked you out among thousands," he said.
25 "Though you're bigger than I'd have believed. Fine flesh you've made."

She was silent for some time. Then she turned in her chair upon him.

"What do you think of yourself," she said, "coming back on me
30 like *this* after over fifteen year?—You don't think I've not heard of you, neither, in Butte City* and elsewhere?"

He was watching her with his clear, translucent, unchallenged eyes.

"Yes," he said. "Chaps comes an' goes.—I've heard tell of you
35 from time to time."

She drew herself up.

"And what lies have you heard about *me*?" she demanded superbly.

"I dunno as I've heard any lies at all—'sept as you was getting on
40 very well, like."

His voice ran warily and detached. Her anger stirred again in her, violently. But she subdued it, because of the danger there was in him, and more, perhaps, because of the beauty of his head and his level-drawn brows, which she could not bear to forfeit.

"That's more than I can say of *you*," she said. "I've heard more   5
harm than good about *you*."

"Ay, I dessay,"* he said, looking in the fire. It was a long time since he had seen the furze burning, he said to himself. There was a silence, during which she watched his face.

"Do you call yourself a *man*?" she said, more in contemptuous   10
reproach than in anger. "Leave a woman as you've left me, you don't care to what!—and then to turn up in *this* fashion, without a word to say for yourself."

He stirred in his chair, planted his feet apart, and resting his arms on his knees, looked steadily into the fire, without answering. So   15
near to her was his head, and the close black hair, she could scarcely refrain from starting away, as if it would bite her.

"Do you call that the action of a *man*!" she repeated.

"No," he said, reaching and poking the bits of wood into the fire with his finger, "I didn't call it anything, as I know of. It's no good   20
calling things by any names whatsoever, as I know of."

She watched him in his actions. There was a longer and longer pause between each speech, though neither knew it.

"I *wonder* what you think of yourself!" she exclaimed, with vexed emphasis. "I *wonder* what sort of a fellow you take yourself to be!"   25
She was really perplexed as well as angry.

"Well," he said, lifting his head to look at her, "I guess I'll answer for my own faults, if everybody else'll answer for theirs."

Her heart beat fiery hot as he lifted his face to her. She breathed heavily, averting her face, almost losing her self-control.   30

"And what do you take *me* to be?" she cried, in real helplessness.

His face was lifted watching her, watching her soft, averted face, and the softly heaving mass of her breasts.

"I take you," he said, with that laconic truthfulness which exercised such power over her, "to be the deuce of a fine woman—   35
darn me if you're not as fine a built woman as I've seen, handsome with it as well. I shouldn't have expected you to put on such handsome flesh: 'struth* I shouldn't."

Her heart beat fiery hot, as he watched her with those bright agate eyes, fixedly.   40

"Been very handsome to *you*, for fifteen years, my sakes!" she replied.

He made no answer to this, but sat with his bright, quick eyes upon her.

5   Then he rose. She started involuntarily. But he only said, in his laconic, measured way:

"It's warm in here now."

And he pulled off his overcoat, throwing it on the table. She sat as if slightly cowed, whilst he did so.

10   "Them ropes has given my arms something, by Ga-ard,"* he drawled, feeling his arms with his hands.

Still she sat in her chair before him, slightly cowed.

"You was sharp, wasn't you, to catch me like that, eh?" he smiled slowly. "By Ga-ard, you had me fixed proper, proper you had. Damn 15   me, you* fixed me up proper—proper, you did."

He leaned forwards in his chair towards her.

"I don't think no worse of you for it, no, darned if I do. Fine pluck in a woman's what I admire. That I do, indeed."

She only gazed into the fire.

20   "We fet* from the start, we did. And my word, you begin again quick the minute you see me, you did. Darn me, you was too sharp for me. A darn fine woman, puts up a darn good fight. Darn me if I could find a woman in all the darn States as could get me down like that. Wonderful fine woman you be, truth to say, at this minute."

25   She only sat glowering into the fire.

"As grand a pluck as a man could wish to find in a woman, true as I'm here," he said, reaching forward his hand and tentatively touching her between her full, warm breasts, quietly.

She started, and seemed to shudder. But his hand insinuated itself 30   between her breasts, as she continued to gaze in the fire.

"And don't you think I've come back here a-begging," he said. "I've more than *one* thousand pounds to my name, I have. And a bit of a fight for a how-de-do pleases me, that it do. But that doesn't mean as you're going to deny as you're my Missis . . ."

The Primrose Path*

A young man came out of the Victoria station,* looking undecidedly at the taxi-cabs, dark-red and black, pressing against the curb under the glass roof. Several men in greatcoats and brass buttons jerked themselves erect to catch his attention, at the same time keeping an eye on the other people as they filtered through the open doorways of the station. Berry however was occupied by one of the men, a big, burly fellow whose blue eyes glared back and whose red-brown moustache bristled in defiance.

"Do you *want* a cab, Sir?" the man asked, in a half-mocking, challenging voice.

Berry hesitated still.

"Are you Daniel Sutton?" he asked.

"Yes," replied the other defiantly, as if* with uneasy conscience.

"Then you are my uncle,"* said Berry.

They were alike in colouring, and somewhat in features, but the taxi driver was a powerful, well-fleshed man who glared at the world aggressively, being really on the defensive against his own heart. His nephew, of the same height, was thin, well-dressed, quiet and indifferent in his manner. And yet they were obviously kin.

"And who the devil are you?" asked the taxi driver.

"I'm Daniel Berry," replied the nephew.

"Well I'm damned—never saw you since you were a kid." Rather awkwardly, at this late hour, the two shook hands. "How are you, lad?"

"All right. I thought you were in Australia."

"Been back three months—bought a couple of these damned things—"

He kicked the tyre of his taxicab in affectionate disgust. There was a moment's silence.

"Oh, but I'm going back out there. I can't stand this cankering, rotten-hearted hell of a country any more.—You want to come out to Sydney with me, lad. That's the place for you—beautiful place, oh, you could wish for nothing better. And money in it, too.—How's your mother?"

"She died at Christmas,"* said the young man.

"Dead! What!—Our Anna!" The big man's eyes stared, and he
5 recoiled in fear. "God, lad," he said, "that's three of 'em gone!"*

The two men looked away at the people passing along the pale grey pavements, under the wall of Trinity Church.*

"Well, strike me lucky!" said the taxi driver at last, out of breath. "She wor th' best o' th' bunch of 'em.—I see nowt nor hear nowt
10 from any of 'em—they're not worth it, I'll be damned if they are:—our sermon-lapping* Adela and Maud,—" he looked scornfully at his nephew.—"But she was the best of 'em, our Anna was, that's a fact."

He was talking because he was afraid.

15 "An' after a hard life like she'd had. How old was she, lad?"

"Fifty five."

"Fifty five—" He hesitated. Then, in a rather hushed voice, he asked the question that frightened him. "And what was it then?"

"Cancer."

20 "Cancer again—like Julia! I never knew there was cancer in our family.—Oh my good God, our poor Anna, after the life she'd had!—What lad, do you see any God at the back of that?—I'm damned if I do."

He was glaring, very blue eyed and fierce, at his nephew. Berry
25 lifted his shoulders slightly.

"God?" went on the taxi-driver, in a curious, intense tone. "You've only to look at the folk in the street to know there's nothing keeps it going but gravitation. Look at 'em. Look at him!"—A mongrel-looking man was nosing past. "Wouldn't *he* murder you for
30 your watch-chain, but that he's afraid of society. He's got it *in* him.—Look at 'em."

Berry watched the towns-people go by, and, sensitively feeling his uncle's antipathy, it seemed he was watching a sort of *danse macabre** of ugly criminals.

35 "Did ever you see such a God-forsaken crew creeping about. It gives you the very horrors to look at 'em. I sit in this damned car and watch 'em, till, I can tell you, I feel like running the cab amuck among 'em, and running myself to kingdom come—"

Berry wondered at this outburst. He knew his uncle was the
40 black-sheep, the youngest, the darling, of his mother's family. He

knew him to be at outs with respectability, mixing with the looser, sporting type, all betting and drinking and showing dogs and birds, and racing. As a critic of life, however, he did not know him. But the young man felt curiously understanding. "He uses words like I do, he talks nearly as I talk, except that I shouldn't say those things. But I might feel like that, in myself, if I went a certain road—"*

"I've got to go to Watmore,"* he said. "Can you take me?"

"When d'you want to go?" asked the uncle fiercely.

"Now."

"Come on then. What d'yer stand gassin' on th' causeway for?"

The nephew took his seat beside the driver. The cab began to quiver, then it started forward with a whirr. The uncle, his hands and feet acting mechanically, kept his blue eyes fixed on the highroad into whose traffic the car was insinuating its way. Berry felt curiously as if he were sitting beside an older development of himself. His mind went back to his mother. She had been twenty years older than this brother of hers, whom she had loved so dearly.—"He was one of the most affectionate little lads, and such a curly head! I could never have believed he would grow into the great, coarse bully he is for he's nothing else. My father made a God of him—well, it's a good thing his father is dead. He got in with that sporting gang, that's what did it. Things were made too easy for him, and so he thought of no one but himself, and this is the result."

Not that Daniel Sutton* was so very black a sheep. He had lived idly till he was eighteen, then had suddenly married a young, beautiful girl with clear brows and dark grey eyes, a factory girl. Having taken her to live with his parents, he, lover of dogs and pigeons, went on to the staff of a sporting paper. But his wife was without uplift or warmth. Though they made money enough, their house was dark and cold and uninviting. He had two or three dogs, and the whole attic was turned into a great pigeon-house. He and his wife lived together roughly, with no warmth, no refinement, no touch of beauty anywhere, except that she was beautiful. He was a blustering, impetuous man, she was rather cold in her soul, did not care about anything very much, was rather capable and close with money. And she had a common accent in her speech. He outdid her a thousand times in coarse language, and yet that cold twang in her voice tortured him with shame that he stamped down in bullying and in becoming more violent in his own speech.

Only his dogs adored him, and to them, and to his pigeons, he talked with rough, yet curiously tender caresses, while they leaped and fluttered for joy.

After he and his wife had been married for seven years a little girl was born to them, then later, another. But the husband and wife drew no nearer together. She had an affection for her children almost like a cool governess. He had an emotional man's fear of sentiment, which helped to nip his wife from putting out any shoots. He treated his children roughly, and pretended to think it a good job when one was adopted by a well-to-do maternal aunt. But in his soul he hated his wife that she could give away one of his children. For after her cool fashion, she loved him. With a chaos of a man such as he, she had no chance of being anything but cold and hard, poor thing. For she did love him.

In the end he fell absurdly and violently in love with a rather sentimental young woman who read Browning. He made his wife an allowance, and established a new ménage with the young lady, shortly after emigrating with her to Australia. Meanwhile his wife had gone to live with a publican, a widower, with whom she had had one of those curious, tacit understandings of which quiet women are capable, something like an arrangement for provision in the future.

This was as much as the nephew knew. He sat beside his uncle, wondering how things stood at the present. They raced lightly out past the cemetery* and along the boulevard, then turned into the rather grimy country. The mud flew out on either side, there was a fine mist of rain which blew in their faces. Berry covered himself up.

In the lanes the high hedges shone black with rain. The silvery grey sky, faintly dappled, spread wide over the low, green land. The elder man glanced fiercely up the road, then turned his red face to his nephew.

"And how're you going on, lad?" he said loudly. Berry noticed that his uncle was slightly uneasy of him. It made him also uncomfortable. The elder man had evidently something pressing on his soul.

"Who are you living with in town?" asked the nephew. "Have you gone back to Aunt Maud?"

"No," barked the uncle. "She wouldn't have me. I offered to—I wanted to—but she wouldn't."

"You're alone then?"

"No, I'm not alone."

He turned and glared with his fierce blue eyes at his nephew, but said no more for some time. The car ran on through the mud, under the wet wall of the park.

"That other devil tried to poison me," suddenly shouted the elder man. "The one I went to Australia with."—At which, in spite of himself, the younger smiled in secret.

"How was that?" he asked.

"Wanted to get rid of me. She got in with another fellow on the ship.—By Jove, I was bad."

"Where?—on the ship?"

"No," bellowed the other. "No. That was in Wellington, New Zealand. I was bad, and got lower an' lower—couldn't think what was up. I could hardly crawl about. As certain as I'm here, she was poisoning me, to get to th' other chap—I'm certain of it."

"And what did you do?"

"I cleared out—went to Sydney—"

"And left her?"

"Yes, I thought begod, I'd better clear out if I wanted to live—."

"And you were all right in Sydney?"

"Better in no time.—I *know* she was putting poison in my coffee—"

"Hm!"

There was a glum silence. The driver stared at the road ahead, fixedly, managing the car as if it were a live thing. The nephew felt that his uncle was afraid, quite stupefied with fear, fear of life, of death, of himself.

"You're in rooms, then?" asked the nephew.

"No, I'm in a house of my own," said the uncle defiantly, "wi' th' best little woman in th' Midlands. She's a marvel—Why don't you come an' see us—"

"I will. Who is she?"

"Oh, she's a good girl—a beautiful little thing. I was clean gone on her first time I saw her. An' she was on me. Her mother lives with us—respectable girl, none o' your—"

"And how old is she?"

"How old is she?—she's twenty one—"

"Poor thing."

"*She's* right enough."

"You'd marry her—getting a divorce—?"

"I shall marry her—"

There was a little antagonism between the two men.

"Where's Aunt Maud?" asked the younger.

"She's at the Railway Arms—we passed it, just against Rollin's Mill Crossing.*—They sent me a note this morning to go an' see her when I can spare time—She's got consumption."

5   "Good Lord. Are you going?"

"Yes—"

But again Berry felt that his uncle was afraid.

The young man got through his commission in the village, had a drink with his uncle at the inn, and the two were returning home.
10   The elder man's subject of conversation was Australia. As they drew near the town, they grew silent, thinking both of the public-house. At last they saw the gates of the railway crossing were closed before them.

"Shan't you call?" asked Berry, jerking his head in the direction of
15   the inn, which stood at the corner between two roads, its sign hanging under a bare horse-chestnut tree in front.

"I might as well. Come in an' have a drink," said the uncle.

It had been raining all the morning, so shallow pools of water lay about. A brewer's wagon, with wet barrels and warm-smelling
20   horses, stood near the door of the inn. Everywhere seemed silent, but for the rattle of trains at the crossing. The two men went uneasily up the steps and into the bar. The place was paddled with wet feet, empty. As the bar-man was heard approaching, the uncle asked, in his usual bluster slightly hushed by fear:

25   "What yer goin' ta have, lad? Same as last time?"

A man entered, evidently the proprietor. He was good-looking, with a long, heavy face and quick dark eyes. His glance at Sutton was swift, a start, a recognition, and a withdrawal into heavy neutrality.

30   "How are yer, Dan?" he said, scarcely troubling to speak.

"—Are yer, George?" replied Sutton, hanging back. "My nephew, Dan Berry.—Give us Red Seal,* George."

The publican nodded to the younger man, and set the glasses on the bar. He pushed forward the two glasses, then leaned back in the
35   dark corner behind the bar, his arms folded, evidently preferring to get back from the watchful eyes of the nephew.

"'s luck," said Sutton.

The publican nodded in acknowledgment. Sutton and his nephew drank.

40   "Why the hell you don't get that road mended out there in

Cinderhill—,"* said Sutton fiercely, pushing back his driver's cap and showing his short-cut, bristling hair.

"They can't find in their hearts to pull it up," replied the publican, laconically.

"Find in their hearts! They want settin' in barrows an' runnin' up 5 and down it till they cried for mercy."

Sutton put down his glass. The publican renewed it with a sure hand, at ease in whatsoever he did. Then he leaned back against the bar. He wore no coat. He stood with arms folded, his chin on his chest, his long moustache hanging. His back was round and slack, so 10 that the lower part of his abdomen stuck forward, though he was not stout. His cheek was healthy, brown red, and he was muscular. Yet there was about him this physical slackness, a reluctance in his slow, sure movements. His eyes were keen under his dark brows, but reluctant also, as if he were gloomily apathetic. 15

There was a halt. The publican evidently would say nothing. Berry looked at the mahogany bar-counter, slopped with beer, at the whiskey-bottles on the shelves. Sutton, his cap pushed back, showing a white brow above a weather-reddened face, rubbed his cropped hair uneasily. 20

The publican glanced round suddenly. It seemed that only his dark eyes moved.

"Going up?" he asked.

And something, perhaps his eyes, indicated the unseen bed-chamber. 25

"Ay—that's what I came for," replied Sutton, shifting nervously from one foot to the other. "She been asking for me?"

"This morning," replied the publican, neutral.

Then he put up a flap of the bar, and turned away through the dark doorway behind. Sutton, pulling off his cap, showing a round, 30 short-cropped head which now was ducked forward, followed after him, the buttons holding the strap of his great-coat behind glittering for a moment.

They climbed the dark stairs, the husband placing his feet carefully, because of his big boots. Then he followed down the 35 passage, trying vaguely to keep a grip on his bowels, which seemed to be melting away, and definitely wishing for a neat brandy. The publican opened a door. Sutton, big and burly in his great-coat, went past him.

The bedroom seemed light and warm after the passage. There 40

was a red eiderdown on the bed. Then, making an effort, Sutton
turned his eyes to see the sick woman. He met her eyes direct, dark,
dilated. It was such a shock he almost started away. For a second he
remained in torture, as if some invisible flame were playing on him to
5   reduce his bones and fuse him down. Then he saw the sharp white
edge of her jaw, and the black hair beside the hollow cheek. With a
start he went towards the bed.

"Hello Maud," he said. "Why, what yer been doin'—!"

The publican stood at the window with his back to the bed. The
10 husband, like one condemned but on the point of starting away,
stood by the bedside staring in horror at his wife, whose dilated grey
eyes, nearly all black now, watched him wearily, as if she were
looking at something a long way off.

Going exceedingly pale, he jerked up his head and stared at the
15 wall over the pillows. There was a little coloured picture of a bird
perched on a bell, and a nest among ivy-leaves beneath. It appealed
to him, made him wonder, roused a feeling of childish magic in him.
They were wonderfully fresh, green ivy-leaves, and nobody had seen
the nest among them, save him.

20 Then suddenly he looked down again at the face on the bed, to try
and recognise it. He knew the white brow and the beautiful clear
eyebrows. That was his wife, with whom he had passed his youth:
flesh of his flesh, his, himself. Then those tired eyes, which met his
again from a long way off, disturbed him till he did not know where
25 he was. Only the sunken cheeks, and the mouth that seemed to
protrude now were foreign to him, and filled him with horror. It
seemed he lost his identity. He was the young husband of the woman
with the clear brows; he was the married man fighting with her
whose eyes watched him, a little indifferently, from a long way off;
30 and he was a child in horror of that protruding mouth.

There came a crackling sound of her voice. He knew she had
consumption of the throat, and braced himself hard to bear the
noise.

"What was it, Maud?" he asked in panic.

35 Then the broken, crackling voice came again. He was too terrified
of the sound of it to hear what was said. There was a pause.

"You'll take Winnie,"* the publican's voice interpreted, from the
window.

"Don't you bother, Maud, I'll take her," he said, stupefying his
40 mind so as not to understand.

He looked curiously round the room. It was not a bad bedroom, light and warm. There were many medicine bottles aggregated in a corner of the wash-stand—and a bottle of three-star brandy, half full. There were also photographs of strange people on the chest of drawers. It was not a bad room.

Again he started as if he were shot. She was speaking. He bent down, but did not look at her.

"Be good to her," she whispered.

When he realised her meaning, that he should be good to their child when the mother was gone, a blade went through his flesh.

"I'll be good to her Maud, don't you bother," he said, beginning to feel shaky.

He looked again at the picture of the bird. It perched cheerfully under a blue sky, with robust, jolly ivy leaves near. He was gathering his courage to depart. He looked down, but struggled hard not to take in the sight of his wife's face.

"I s'll come again, Maud," he said. "I hope you'll go on all right. Is there anything as you want?"

There was an almost imperceptible shake of the head from the sick woman, making his heart melt swiftly again. Then, dragging his limbs, he got out of the room and down the stairs.

The landlord came after him.

"I'll let you know if anything happens," the publican said, still laconic, but with his eyes dark and swift.

"Ay, a' right," said Sutton blindly. He looked round for his cap, which he had had all the time in his hand. Then he got out of doors.

In a moment the uncle and nephew were in the car jolting on the level crossing. The elder man seemed as if something tight in his brain made him open his eyes wide, and stare. He held the steering wheel firmly. He knew he could steer accurately, to a hair's breadth. Glaring fixedly ahead, he let the car go, till it bounded over the uneven road. There were three coal-carts in a string. In an instant the car grazed past them, almost biting the kerb on the other side. Sutton aimed his car like a projectile, staring ahead. He did not want to know, to think, to realise, he wanted to be only the driver of that quick taxi.

The town drew near, suddenly. There were allotment gardens, with dark-purple twiggy fruit-trees and wet alleys between the hedges. Then suddenly the streets of dwelling houses whirled close, and the car was climbing the hill, with an angry whirr,—up—up—till they rode out onto the crest and could see the tram-cars, dark-red and yellow, threading their way round the corner below, and all the traffic roaring between the shops.

"Got anywhere to go?" asked Sutton of his nephew.

5   "I was going to see one or two people."

"Come an' have a bit o' dinner with us," said the other.

Berry knew that his uncle wanted to be distracted, so that he should not think nor realise. The big man was running hard away from the horror of realisation.

10   "All right," Berry agreed.

The car went quickly through the town. It ran up a long street nearly into the country again. Then it pulled up at a house that stood alone, below the road.

"I s'll be back in ten minutes," said the uncle.

15   The car went on to the garage. Berry stood curiously at the top of the stone stairs that led from the high-road down to the level of the house, an old, stone place. The garden was dilapidated. Broken fruit-trees leaned at a sharp angle down the steep bank. Right across the dim grey atmosphere, in a kind of valley on the edge of the town,

20   new suburb-patches showed pinkish on the dark earth. It was a kind of unresolved borderland.

Berry went down the steps. Through the broken black fence of the orchard, long grass showed yellow. The place seemed deserted. He knocked, then knocked again. An elderly woman appeared. She

25   looked like a house-keeper. At first she said suspiciously that Mr Sutton was not in.

"My uncle just put me down. He'll be in in ten minutes," replied the visitor.

"Oh are you the Mr Berry who is related to him?" exclaimed the

30   elderly woman. "Come in—come in."

She was at once kindly and a little bit servile. The young man entered. It was an old house, rather dark, and sparsely furnished. The elderly woman sat nervously on the edge of one of the chairs in a drawing-room that looked as if it were furnished from dismal relics

35   of dismal homes, and there was a little straggling attempt at conversation. Mrs Greenwell was evidently a working class woman unused to service or to any formality.

Presently she gathered up courage to invite her visitor into the dining room. There from the table under the window rose a tall slim

40   girl with a cat in her arms. She was evidently a little more ladylike

than was habitual to her, but she had a gentle, delicate, small nature.
Her brown hair almost covered her ears, her dark lashes came down
in shy awkwardness over her beautiful blue eyes. She shook hands in
a frank way, yet she was shrinking. Evidently she was not sure how
her position would affect her visitor. And yet she was assured in 5
herself, shrinking and timid as she was.

"She must be a good deal in love with him," thought Berry.

Both women glanced shamefacedly at the roughly laid table.
Evidently they ate in a rather rough and ready fashion.

Elaine—she had this poetic name*—fingered her cat timidly, not 10
knowing what to say or to do, unable even to ask her visitor to sit
down. He noticed how her skirt hung almost flat on her hips. She
was young, scarce developed, a long, slender thing. Her colouring
was warm and exquisite.

The elder woman bustled out to the kitchen. Berry fondled the 15
terrier dogs that had come curiously to his heels, and glanced out of
the window at the wet, deserted orchard.

This room too was not well furnished, and rather dark. But there
was a big red fire.

"He always has fox terriers," he said. 20

"Yes," she answered, showing her teeth in a smile.

"Do you like them too?"

"Yes." She glanced down at the dogs. "I like Tam better than
Sally—"

Her speech always tailed off into an awkward silence. 25

"We've been to see Aunt Maud," said the nephew.

Her eyes, blue and scared and shrinking, met his.

"Dan had a letter," he explained. "She's very bad."

"Isn't it horrible!" she exclaimed, her face crumpling up with
fear. 30

The old woman, evidently a hard-used, rather down-trodden
workman's wife, came in with two soup-plates. She glanced
anxiously to see how her daughter was progressing with the visitor.

"Mother, Dan's been to see Maud," said Elaine, in a quiet voice
full of fear and trouble. 35

The old woman looked up anxiously, in question.

"I think she wanted him to take the child. She's very bad, I
believe," explained Berry.

"Oh, we should take Winnie!" cried Elaine. But both women
seemed uncertain, wavering in their position. Already Berry could 40

see that his uncle had bullied them, as he bullied everybody. But they were used to unpleasant men, and seemed to keep at a distance.

"Will you have some soup?" asked the mother, humbly.

She evidently did the work. The daughter was to be a lady, more
5   or less; always dressed and nice for when Sutton came in.

They heard him heavily running down the steps outside. The dogs got up. Elaine seemed to forget the visitor. It was as if she came into life. Yet she was nervous and afraid. The mother stood as if ready to exculpate herself.

10   Sutton burst open the door. Big, blustering, wet in his immense grey coat, he came into the dining room.*

"Hello!" he said to his nephew, "making yourself at home?"

"Oh yes," replied Berry.

"Hello Jack," he said to the girl. "Got owt to grizzle about?"

15   "What for?" she asked, in a clear, half challenging voice, that had that peculiar twang, almost petulant, so female and so attractive. Yet she was defiant like a boy.

"It's a wonder if you haven't," growled Sutton. And, with a really intimate movement, he stooped down and fondled his dogs, though
20   paying no attention to them. Then he stood up, and remained with feet apart on the hearthrug, his head ducked forward, watching the girl. He seemed abstracted, as if he could only watch her. His great-coat hung open, so that she could see his figure, simple and human in the great husk of cloth. She stood nervously with her
25   hands behind her, glancing at him, unable to see anything else. And he was scarcely conscious but of her. His eyes were still strained and staring, and as they followed the girl, when, long-limbed and languid, she moved away, it was as if he saw in her something impersonal, the female, not the woman.

30   "Had your dinner?" he asked.

"We were just going to have it," she replied, with the same curious little vibration in her voice, like the twang of a string.

The mother entered, bringing a saucepan from which she ladled soup into three plates.

35   "Sit down, lad," said Sutton. "You sit down, Jack, an' give me mine here."

"Oh aren't you coming to table?" she complained.

"No, I tell you," he snarled, almost pretending to be disagreeable. But she was slightly afraid even of the pretence. Which pleased and
40   relieved him. He stood on the hearthrug eating his soup noisily.

"Aren't you going to take your coat off?" she said. "It's filling the place full of steam."

He did not answer, but, with his head bent forward over the plate, ate his soup hastily, to get it done with. When he put down his empty plate, she rose and went to him.

"Do take your coat off, Dan," she said, and she took hold of the breast of his coat, trying to push it back over his shoulder. But she could not. Only the stare in his eyes changed to a glare as her hand moved over his shoulder. He looked down into her eyes. She became pale, rather frightened-looking, and she turned her face away, and it was drawn slightly with love and fear and misery. She tried again to put off his coat, her thin wrists pulling at it. He stood solidly planted, and did not look at her, but stared straight in front. She was playing with passion, afraid of it, and really wretched because it left her, the person, out of count. Yet she continued. And there came into his bearing, into his eyes, the curious smile of passion, pushing away even the death-horror. It was life stronger than death in him. She stood close to his breast. Their eyes met, and she was carried away.

"Take your coat off, Dan," she said coaxingly, in a low tone meant for no one but him. And she slid her hands on his shoulder, and he yielded, so that the coat was pushed back. She had flushed, and her eyes had grown very bright. She got hold of the cuff of his coat. Gently, he eased himself, so that she drew it off. Then he stood in a thin suit, which revealed his vigorous, almost mature form.

"What a weight!" she exclaimed, in a peculiar penetrating voice, as she went out hugging the overcoat. In a moment she came back.

He stood still in the same position, a frown over his fiercely staring eyes. The pain, the fear, the horror in his breast were all burning away in the new, fiercest flame of passion.

"Get your dinner," he said roughly to her.

"I've had all I want," she said. "You come an' have yours."

He looked at the table as if he found it difficult to see things.

"I want no more," he said.

She stood close to his chest. She wanted to touch him and to comfort him. There was something about him now that fascinated her. Berry felt slightly ashamed that she seemed to ignore the presence of others in the room.

The mother came in. She glanced at Sutton, standing planted on the hearthrug, his head ducked, the heavy frown hiding his eyes.

There was a peculiar braced intensity about him that made the elder woman afraid. Suddenly he jerked his head round to his nephew.

"Get on wi' your dinner, lad," he said, and he went to the door. The dogs, which had continually lain down and got up again, uneasy, now rose and watched. The girl went after him, saying, clearly:

"What did you want, Dan?"

Her slim, quick figure was gone, the door was closed behind her.

There was silence. The mother, still more slave-like in her movement, sat down in a low chair. Berry drank some beer.

"That girl will leave him," he said to himself. "She'll hate him like poison. And serve him right. Then she'll go off with somebody else."

And she did.

The Horse-Dealer's Daughter*

"Well, Mabel, and what are you going to do with yourself?" asked Joe, with foolish flippancy. He felt quite safe himself. Without listening for an answer, he turned aside, worked a grain of tobacco to the tip of his tongue, and spat it out. He did not care about anything, since he felt safe himself.

The three brothers and the sister sat round the desolate breakfast-table, attempting some sort of desultory consultation. The morning's post had given the final tap to the family fortunes, and all was over. The dreary dining-room itself, with its heavy mahogany furniture, looked as if it were waiting to be done away with.

But the consultation amounted to nothing. There was a strange air of ineffectuality about the three men, as they sprawled at table, smoking and reflecting vaguely on their own condition. The girl was alone, a rather short, sullen-looking young woman of twenty-seven. She did not share the same life as her brothers. She would have been good-looking, save for the impassive fixity of her face, "bull-dog," as her brothers called it.

There was a confused tramping of horses' feet outside. The three men all sprawled round in their chairs, to watch. Beyond the dark holly-bushes that separated the strip of lawn from the high road,* they could see a cavalcade of shire horses swinging out of their own yard, being taken for exercise. This was the last time. These were the last horses that would go through their hands. The young men watched with critical, callous look. They were all frightened at the collapse of their lives, and the sense of disaster in which they were involved left them no inner freedom.

Yet they were three fine, well-set fellows enough. Joe, the eldest, was a man of thirty-three, broad and handsome in a hot, flushed way. His face was red, he twisted his black moustache over a thick finger, his eyes were shallow and restless. He had a sensual way of uncovering his teeth when he laughed, and his bearing was stupid. Now he watched the horses with a glazed look of helplessness in his eyes, a certain stupor of downfall.

The great draught-horses swung past. They were tied head to tail, four of them, and they heaved along to where a lane branched off from the high road, planting their great hoofs floutingly in the fine black mud, swinging their great rounded haunches sumptuously, and trotting a few sudden steps as they were led into the lane, round the corner. Every movement showed a massive, slumbrous strength, and a stupidity which held them in subjection. The groom at the head looked back, jerking the leading rope. And the cavalcade moved out of sight up the lane, the tail of the last horse, bobbed up tight and stiff, held out taut from the swinging great haunches as they rocked behind the hedges in a motion like sleep.

Joe watched with glazed, hopeless eyes. The horses were almost like his own body to him. He felt he was done for now. Luckily he was engaged to a woman as old as himself, and therefore her father, who was steward of a neighbouring estate, would provide him with a job. He would marry and go into harness. His life was over, he would be a subject animal now.

He turned uneasily aside, the retreating steps of the horses echoing in his ears. Then, with foolish restlessness, he reached for the scraps of bacon-rind from the plates, and, making a faint whistling sound, flung them to the terrier that lay against the fender. He watched the dog swallow them, and waited till the creature looked into his eyes. Then a faint grin came on his face, and in a high, foolish voice he said:

"You won't get much more bacon, shall you, you little b——?"

The dog faintly and dismally wagged its tail, then lowered its haunches, circled round, and lay down again.

There was another helpless silence at the table. Joe sprawled uneasily in his seat, not willing to go till the family conclave was dissolved. Fred Henry, the second brother, was erect, clean-limbed, alert. He had watched the passing of the horses with more *sang-froid*. If he was an animal, like Joe, he was an animal which controls, not one which is controlled. He was master of any horse, and he carried himself with a well-tempered air of mastery. But he was not master of the situations of life. He pushed his coarse brown moustache upwards, off his lip, and glanced irritably at his sister, who sat impassive and inscrutable.

"You'll go and stop with Lucy for a bit, shan't you?" he asked. The girl did not answer.

"I don't see what else you can do," persisted Fred Henry.

"Go as a skivvy,"* Joe interpolated laconically.

The girl did not move a muscle.

"If I was her, I should go in for training for a nurse," said Malcolm, the youngest of them all. He was the baby of the family, a young man of twenty-two, with a fresh, jaunty *museau.**

But Mabel did not take any notice of him. They had talked at her and round her for so many years, that she hardly heard them at all.

The marble clock on the mantelpiece softly chimed the half-hour, the dog rose uneasily from the hearthrug and looked at the party at the breakfast-table. But still they sat on in ineffectual conclave.

"Oh all right," said Joe suddenly, *à propos* of nothing. "I'll get a move on."

He pushed back his chair, straddled his knees with a downward jerk, to get them free, in horsey fashion, and went to the fire. Still he did not go out of the room, he was curious to know what the others would do or say. He began to charge his pipe, looking down at the dog and saying, in a high, affected voice:

"Going wi' me? Going wi' me are ter? Tha'rt goin' further than tha counts on just now, dost hear?"

The dog faintly wagged its tail, the man stuck out his jaw and covered his pipe with his hands, and puffed intently, losing himself in the tobacco, looking down all the while at the dog, with an absent brown eye. The dog looked up at him in mournful distrust. Joe stood with his knees stuck out, in real horsey fashion.

"Have you had a letter from Lucy?" Fred Henry asked of his sister.

"Last week," came the neutral reply.

"And what does she say?"

There was no answer.

"Does she *ask* you to go and stop there?" persisted Fred Henry.

"She says I can if I like."

"Well, then, you'd better. Tell her you'll come on Monday."

This was received in silence.

"That's what you'll do then, is it?" said Fred Henry, in some exasperation.

But she made no answer. There was a silence of futility and irritation in the room. Malcolm grinned fatuously.

"You'll have to make up your mind between now and next Wednesday," said Joe loudly, "or else find yourself lodgings on the kerbstone."

The face of the young woman darkened, but she sat on immutable.

"Here's Jack Fergusson!" exclaimed Malcolm, who was looking aimlessly out of the window.

5   "Where?" exclaimed Joe loudly.

"Just gone past."

"Coming in?"

Malcolm craned his neck to see the gate.

"Yes," he said.

10   There was a silence. Mabel sat on like one condemned, at the head of the table. Then a whistle was heard from the kitchen. The dog got up and barked sharply. Joe opened the door and shouted:

"Come on."

After a moment, a young man entered. He was muffled up in

15   overcoat and a purple woollen scarf, and his tweed cap, which he did not remove, was pulled down on his head. He was of medium height, his face was rather long and pale, his eyes looked tired.

"Hallo, Jack! Well, Jack!" exclaimed Malcolm and Joe. Fred Henry merely said "Jack!"

20   "What's doing?" asked the newcomer, evidently addressing Fred Henry.

"Same. We've got to be out by Wednesday.—Got a cold?"

"I have—got it bad, too."

"Why don't you stop in?"

25   "*Me* stop in? When I can't stand on my legs, perhaps I shall have a chance." The young man spoke huskily. He had a slight Scotch accent.

"It's a knock-out, isn't it," said Joe boisterously, "if a doctor goes round croaking with a cold. Looks bad for the patients, doesn't it?"

30   The young doctor looked at him slowly.

"Anything the matter with *you*, then?" he asked sarcastically.

"Not as I know of. Damn your eyes, I hope not. Why?"

"I thought you were very concerned about the patients, wondered if you might be one yourself."

35   "Damn it, no, I've never been patient to no flaming doctor, and hope I never shall be," returned Joe.

At this point Mabel rose from the table, and they all seemed to become aware of her existence. She began putting the dishes together. The young doctor looked at her, but did not address her.

40   He had not greeted her. She went out of the room with the tray, her face impassive and unchanged.

"When are you off then, all of you?" asked the doctor.

"I'm catching the eleven-forty," replied Malcolm. "Are you goin' down wi' th' trap, Joe?"

"Yes, you young b——, I've told you I'm going down wi' th' trap, haven't I?"

"We'd better be getting her in then.—So long, Jack, if I don't see you before I go," said Malcolm, shaking hands.

He went out, followed by Joe, who seemed to have his tail between his legs.

"Well, this is the devil's own," exclaimed the doctor when he was left alone with Fred Henry. "Going before Wednesday, are you?"

"That's the orders," replied the other.

"Where, to Northampton?"

"That's it."

"The devil!" exclaimed Fergusson with quiet chagrin.

And there was silence between the two.

"All settled up, are you?" asked Fergusson.

"About."

There was another pause.

"Well, I shall miss yer, Freddy boy," said the young doctor.

"And I shall miss thee, Jack," returned the other.

"Miss you like Hell," mused the doctor.

Fred Henry turned aside. There was nothing to say. Mabel came in again, to finish clearing the table.

"What are *you* going to do then, Miss Pervin?" asked Fergusson. "Going to your sister's, are you?"

Mabel looked at him with her steady, dangerous eyes, that always made him uncomfortable, unsettling his superficial ease.

"No," she said.

"Well, what in the name of fortune *are* you going to do? Say what you *mean* to do," cried Fred Henry with futile intensity.

But she only averted her head and continued her work. She folded the white tablecloth, and put on the chenille cloth.

"The sulkiest bitch that ever trod!" muttered her brother.

But she finished her task with perfectly impassive face, the young doctor watching her interestedly all the while. Then she went out.

Fred Henry stared after her, clenching his lips, his blue eyes fixing in sharp antagonism, as he made a grimace of sour exasperation.

"You could bray her into bits, and that's all you'd get out of her," he said in a small, narrowed tone.

The doctor smiled faintly.

"What's she *going* to do then?" he asked.

"Strike me if *I* know!" returned the other.

There was a pause. Then the doctor stirred.

"I'll be seeing you to-night, shall I?" he said to his friend.

5 "Ay—where's it to be? Are we going over to Jessdale?"

"I don't know. I've got such a cold on me. I'll come round to the Moon and Stars,* anyway."

"Let Lizzie and May miss their night for once, eh?"

"That's it—if I feel as I do now."

10 "All's one——"

The two young men went through the passage and down to the back door together. The house was large, but it was servantless now, and desolate. At the back was a small bricked house-yard, and beyond that a big square, gravelled fine and red, and having stables 15 on two sides. Sloping, dank, winter-dark fields stretched away on the open sides.

But the stables were empty. Joseph Pervin, the father of the family, had been a man of no education, who had become a fairly large horse-dealer. The stables had been full of horses, there was a great 20 turmoil and come-and-go of horses and of dealers and grooms. Then the kitchen was full of servants. But of late things had declined. The old man had married a second time, to retrieve his fortunes. Now he was dead and everything was gone to the dogs, there was nothing but debt and threatening.

25 For months Mabel had been servantless in the big house, keeping the home together in penury for her ineffectual brothers. She had kept house for ten years. But previously it was with unstinted means. Then, however brutal and coarse everything was, the sense of money had kept her proud, confident. The men might be foul-mouthed, the 30 women in the kitchen might have bad reputations, her brothers might have illegitimate children. But so long as there was money, the girl felt herself established, and brutally proud, reserved.

No company came to the house, save dealers and coarse men. Mabel had no associates of her own sex, after her sister went away. 35 But she did not mind. She went regularly to church, she attended to her father. And she lived in the memory of her mother, who had died when she was fourteen, and whom she had loved. She had loved her father too, in a different way, depending upon him, and feeling secure in him, until at the age of fifty-four he married again. And 40 then she had set hard against him. Now he had died and left them all hopelessly in debt.

She had suffered badly during the period of poverty. Nothing, however, could shake the curious sullen, animal pride that dominated each member of the family. Now, for Mabel, the end had come. Still she would not cast about her. She would follow her own way just the same. She would always hold the keys of her own situation. Mindless and persistent, she endured from day to day. Why should she think? Why should she answer anybody? It was enough that this was the end, and there was no way out. She need not pass any more darkly along the main street of the small town, avoiding every eye. She need not demean herself any more, going into the shops and buying the cheapest food. This was at an end. She thought of nobody, not even of herself. Mindless and persistent, she seemed in a sort of ecstasy to be coming nearer to her fulfilment, her own glorification, approaching her dead mother, who was glorified.

In the afternoon she took a little bag, with shears and sponge and a small scrubbing brush, and went out. It was a grey, wintry day, with saddened, dark-green fields and an atmosphere blackened by the smoke of foundries* not far off. She went quickly, darkly along the causeway, heeding nobody, through the town to the churchyard.

There she always felt secure, as if no one could see her, although as a matter of fact she was exposed to the stare of everyone who passed along under the churchyard wall. Nevertheless, once under the shadow of the great looming church, among the graves, she felt immune from the world, reserved within the thick churchyard wall as in another country.

Carefully she clipped the grass from the grave, and arranged the pinky-white, small chrysanthemums in the tin cross. When this was done, she took an empty jar from a neighbouring grave, brought water, and carefully, most scrupulously sponged the marble headstone and the coping-stone.

It gave her sincere satisfaction to do this. She felt in immediate contact with the world of her mother. She took minute pains, went through the work in a state bordering on pure happiness, as if in performing this task she came into a subtle, intimate connection with her mother. For the life she followed here in the world was far less real than the world of death she inherited from her mother.

The doctor's house was just by the church. Fergusson, being a mere hired assistant, was slave to the countryside. As he hurried now to attend to the out-patients in the surgery, glancing across the graveyard with his quick eye he saw the girl at her task at the grave. She seemed so intent and remote, it was like looking into another world. Some mystical element was touched in him. He slowed down as he walked, watching her as if spellbound.

She lifted her eyes, feeling him looking. Their eyes met. And each looked away again at once, each feeling in some way found out by the other. He lifted his cap and passed on down the road. There remained distinct in his consciousness, like a vision, the memory of her face, lifted from the tombstone in the churchyard, and looking at him with slow, large, portentous eyes. It *was* portentous, her face. It seemed to mesmerise him. There was a heavy power in her eyes which laid hold of his whole being, as if he had drunk some powerful drug. He had been feeling weak and done before. Now the life came back into him, he felt delivered from his own fretted, daily self.

He finished his duties at the surgery as quickly as might be, hastily filling up the bottles of the waiting people with cheap drugs. Then, in perpetual haste, he set off again to visit several cases in another part of his round before tea-time. At all times he preferred to walk, if he could, but particularly when he was not well. He fancied the motion restored him.

The afternoon was falling. It was grey, deadened, and wintry, with a slow, moist, heavy coldness sinking in and deadening all the faculties. But why should he think or notice? He hastily climbed the hill and turned across the dark-green fields, following the black cinder-track. In the distance, across a shallow dip in the country, the small town was clustered like smouldering ash, a tower, a spire, a heap of low, raw, extinct houses. And on the nearest fringe of the town, sloping into the dip, was Oldmeadow, the Pervins' house. He could see the stables and the outbuildings distinctly, as they lay towards him on the slope. Well, he would not go there many more times! Another resource would be lost to him, another place gone: the only company he cared for in the alien, ugly little town, he was losing. Nothing but work, drudgery, constant hastening from dwelling to dwelling among the colliers and the iron-workers. It wore him out, but at the same time he had a craving for it. It was a stimulant to him to be in the homes of the working people, moving, as it were, through the innermost body of their life. His nerves were excited and gratified. He could come so near, into the very lives of the rough, inarticulate, powerfully emotional men and women. He grumbled, he said he hated the hellish hole. But as a matter of fact it excited him, the contact with the rough, strongly-feeling people was a stimulant applied direct to his nerves.

Below Oldmeadow, in the green, shallow, soddened hollows of fields, lay a square deep pond. Roving across the landscape, the doctor's quick eye detected a figure in black passing through the gates of the field, down towards the pond. He looked again. It would be Mabel Pervin. His mind suddenly became alive and attentive.

Why was she going down there? He pulled up on the path on the slope above, and stood staring. He could just make sure of the small black figure moving in the hollow of the failing day. He seemed to see her in the midst of such obscurity, that he was like a clairvoyant, seeing rather with the mind's eye than with ordinary sight. Yet he could see her positively enough, whilst he kept his eye attentive. He felt, if he looked away from her, in the thick, ugly, falling dusk, he would lose her altogether.

He followed her minutely as she moved, direct and intent, like something transmitted rather than stirring in voluntary activity, straight down the field towards the pond. There she stood on the bank for a moment. She never raised her head. Then she waded slowly into the water.

He stood motionless as the small black figure walked slowly and deliberately towards the centre of the pond, very slowly, gradually moving deeper into the motionless water, and still moving forward as the water got up to her breast. Then he could see her no more in the dusk of the dead afternoon.

"There!" he exclaimed. "Would you believe it?"

And he hastened straight down, running over the wet, soddened fields, pushing through the hedges, down into the depression of callous wintry obscurity. It took him several minutes to come to the pond. He stood on the bank, breathing heavily. He could see nothing. His eyes seemed to penetrate the dead water. Yes, perhaps that was the dark shadow of her black clothing beneath the surface of the water.

He slowly ventured into the pond. The bottom was deep, soft clay; he sank in, and the water clasped dead cold round his legs. As he stirred he could smell the cold, rotten clay that fouled up into the water. It was objectionable in his lungs. Still, repelled and yet not heeding, he moved deeper into the pond. The cold water rose over his thighs, over his loins, upon his abdomen. The lower part of his body was all sunk in the hideous cold element. And the bottom was so deeply soft and uncertain, he was afraid of pitching with his mouth underneath. He could not swim, and was afraid.

He crouched a little, spreading his hands under the water and moving them round, trying to feel for her. The dead cold pond swayed upon his chest. He moved again, a little deeper, and again, with his hands underneath, he felt all around under the water. And he touched her clothing. But it evaded his fingers. He made a desperate effort to grasp it.

And so doing he lost his balance and went under, horribly, suffocating in the foul, earthy water, struggling madly for a few moments. At last, after what seemed an eternity, he got his footing, rose again into the air and looked around. He gasped, and knew he was in the world. Then he looked at the water. She had risen near him. He grasped her clothing, and, drawing her nearer, turned to take his way to land again.

He went very slowly, carefully, absorbed in the slow progress. He rose higher, climbing out of the pond. The water was now only about his legs; he was thankful, full of relief to be out of the clutches of the pond. He lifted her and staggered on to the bank, out of the horror of wet grey clay.

He laid her down on the bank. She was quite unconscious and running with water. He made the water come from her mouth, he worked to restore her. He did not have to work very long before he could feel the breathing begin again in her, she was breathing naturally. He worked a little longer. He could feel her live beneath his hands, she was coming back. He wiped her face, wrapped her in his overcoat, looked round into the dim, dark-grey world, then lifted her and staggered down the bank and across the fields.

It seemed an unthinkably long way, and his burden so heavy he felt he would never get to the house. But at last he was in the stable-yard, and then in the house-yard. He opened the door and went into the house. In the kitchen he laid her down on the hearthrug, and called. The house was empty. But the fire was burning in the grate.

Then again he kneeled to attend to her. She was breathing regularly, her eyes were wide open and as if conscious, but there seemed something missing in her look. She was conscious in herself, but unconscious of her surroundings.

He ran upstairs, took blankets from a bed, and put them before the fire to warm. Then he removed her saturated, earthy-smelling clothing, rubbed her dry with a towel, and wrapped her naked in the blankets. Then he went into the dining-room to look for spirits. There was a little whisky. He drank a gulp himself, and put some into her mouth.

The effect was instantaneous. She looked full into his face, as if she had been seeing him for some time, and yet had only just become conscious of him.

"Dr. Fergusson?" she said.

"What?" he answered.

He was divesting himself of his coat, intending to find some dry clothing upstairs. He could not bear the smell of the dead, clayey water, and he was mortally afraid for his own health.

"What did I do?" she asked.

"Walked into the pond," he replied. He had begun to shudder like one sick, and could hardly attend to her. Her eyes remained full on him; he seemed to be going dark in his mind, looking back at her helplessly. The shuddering became quieter in him, his life came back in him, dark and unknowing, but strong again.

"Was I out of my mind?" she asked, while her eyes were fixed on him all the time.

"Maybe, for the moment," he replied. He felt quiet, because his strength had come back. The strange fretful strain had left him.

"Am I out of my mind now?" she asked.

"Are you?" he reflected a moment. "No," he answered truthfully, "I don't see that you are." He turned his face aside. He was afraid, now, because he felt dazed, and felt dimly that her power was stronger than his, in this issue. And she continued to look at him fixedly all the time. "Can you tell me where I shall find some dry things to put on?" he asked.

"Did you dive into the pond for me?" she asked.

"No," he answered. "I walked in. But I went in overhead as well."

There was silence for a moment. He hesitated. He very much wanted to go upstairs to get into dry clothing. But there was another desire in him. And she seemed to hold him. His will seemed to have gone to sleep, and left him, standing there slack before her. But he felt warm inside himself. He did not shudder at all, though his clothes were sodden on him.

"Why did you?" she asked.

"Because I didn't want you to do such a foolish thing," he said.

"It wasn't foolish," she said, still gazing at him as she lay on the floor, with a sofa cushion under her head. "It was the right thing to do. *I* knew best, then."

"I'll go and shift these wet things," he said. But still he had not the power to move out of her presence, until she sent him. It was as if she had the life of his body in her hands, and he could not extricate himself. Or perhaps he did not want to.

Suddenly she sat up. Then she became aware of her own immediate condition. She felt the blankets about her, she knew her
5 own limbs. For a moment it seemed as if her reason were going. She looked round, with wild eye, as if seeking something. He stood still with fear. She saw her clothing lying scattered.

"Who undressed me?" she asked, her eyes resting full and inevitable on his face.

10 "I did," he replied, "to bring you round."

For some moments she sat and gazed at him awfully, her lips parted.

"Do you love me then?" she asked.

He only stood and stared at her fascinated. His soul seemed to
15 melt.

She shuffled forward on her knees, and put her arms round him, round his legs, as he stood there, pressing her breasts against his knees and thighs, clutching him with strange, convulsive certainty, pressing his thighs against her, drawing him to her face, her throat,
20 as she looked up at him with flaring, humble eyes of transfiguration, triumphant in first possession.

"You love me," she murmured, in strange transport, yearning and triumphant and confident. "You love me. I know you love me, I know."

25 And she was passionately kissing his knees through the wet clothing, passionately and indiscriminately kissing his knees, his legs, as if unaware of everything.

He looked down at the tangled wet hair, the wild, bare, animal shoulders. He was amazed, bewildered, and afraid. He had never
30 thought of loving her. He had never wanted to love her. When he rescued her and restored her, he was a doctor and she was a patient. He had had no single personal thought of her. Nay, this introduction of the personal element was very distasteful to him, a violation of his professional honour. It was horrible to have her there embracing his
35 knees. It was horrible. He revolted from it violently. And yet—and yet—he had not the power to break away.

She looked at him again, with the same supplication of powerful love, and that same transcendent, frightening light of triumph. In view of the delicate flame which seemed to come from her face like a
40 light, he was powerless. And yet he had never intended to love her.

He had never intended. And something stubborn in him could not give way.

"You love me," she repeated, in a murmur of deep, rhapsodic assurance. "You love me."

Her hands were drawing him, drawing him down to her. He was afraid, even a little horrified. For he had really no intention of loving her. Yet her hands were drawing him towards her. He put out his hand quickly to steady himself, and grasped her bare shoulder. A flame seemed to burn the hand that grasped her soft shoulder. He had no intention of loving her: his whole will was against his yielding. It was horrible—— And yet wonderful was the touch of her shoulder, beautiful the shining of her face. Was she perhaps mad? He had a horror of yielding to her. Yet something in him ached also.

He had been staring away at the door, away from her. But his hand remained on her shoulder. She had gone suddenly very still. He looked down at her. Her eyes were now wide with fear, with doubt, the light was dying from her face, a shadow of terrible greyness was returning. He could not bear the touch of her eyes' question upon him, and the look of death behind the question.

With an inward groan he gave way, and let his heart yield towards her. A sudden gentle smile came on his face. And her eyes, which never left his face, slowly, slowly filled with tears. He watched the strange water rise in her eyes, like some slow fountain coming up. And his heart seemed to burn and melt in his breast.

He could not bear to look at her any more. He dropped on his knees and caught her head with his arm and pressed her face against his throat. She was very still. His heart, which seemed to have broken, was burning with a kind of agony in his breast. And he felt her slow, hot tears wetting his throat. But he could not move.

He felt the hot tears wet his neck and the hollows of his neck, and he remained motionless, suspended through one of man's eternities. Only now it had become indispensable to him to have her face pressed close to him, he could never let her go again. He could never let her head go away from the close clutch of his arm. He wanted to remain like that for ever, with his heart hurting him in a pain that was also life to him. Without knowing, he was looking down on her damp, soft brown hair.

Then, as it were suddenly, he smelt the horrid stagnant smell of that water. And at the same moment she drew away from him and looked at him. Her eyes were wistful and unfathomable. He was afraid of them, and he fell to kissing her, not knowing what he was doing. He wanted her eyes not to have that terrible wistful, unfathomable look.

5 When she turned her face to him again, a faint delicate flush was glowing, and there was again dawning that terrible shining of joy in her eyes, which really terrified him, and yet which he now wanted to see, because he feared the look of doubt still more.

"You love me?" she said, rather faltering.

"Yes." The word cost him a painful effort. Not because it wasn't
10 true. But because it was too newly true, the *saying* seemed to tear open again his newly-torn heart. And he hardly wanted it to be true, even now.

She lifted her face to him, and he bent forward and kissed her on the mouth, gently, with the one kiss that is an eternal pledge. And as
15 he kissed her his heart strained again in his breast. He never intended to love her. But now it was over. He had crossed over the gulf to her, and all that he had left behind had shrivelled and become void.

After the kiss, her eyes again slowly filled with tears. She sat still,
20 away from him, with her face dropped aside, and her hands folded in her lap. The tears fell very slowly. There was complete silence. He too sat there motionless and silent on the hearthrug. The strange pain of his heart that was broken seemed to consume him. That he should love her! That this was love! That he should be ripped open
25 in this way!—him, a doctor!—How they would all jeer if they knew!—It was agony to him to think they might know.

In the curious naked pain of the thought he looked again to her. She was sitting there drooped into a muse. He saw a tear fall, and his heart flared hot. He saw for the first time that one of her
30 shoulders was quite uncovered, one arm bare, he could see one of her small breasts; dimly, because it had become almost dark in the room.

"Why are you crying?" he asked in an altered voice.

She looked up at him, and behind her tears the consciousness of
35 her situation for the first time brought a dark look of shame to her eyes.

"I'm not crying, really," she said, watching him half frightened.

He reached his hand, and softly closed it on her bare arm.

"I love you! I love you!" he said in a soft, low, vibrating voice,
40 unlike himself.

She shrank, and dropped her head. The soft, penetrating grip of his hand on her arm distressed her. She looked up at him.

"I want to go," she said, "I want to go and get you some dry things."

"Why?" he said. "I'm all right."

"But I want to go," she said. "And I want you to change your things."

He released her arm, and she wrapped herself in the blanket, looking at him rather frightened. And still she did not rise.

"Kiss me," she said wistfully.

He kissed her, but briefly, half in anger.

Then, after a second, she rose nervously, all mixed up in the blanket. He watched her in her confusion, as she tried to extricate herself and wrap herself up so that she could walk. He watched her relentlessly, as she knew. And as she went, the blanket trailing, and as he saw a glimpse of her feet and her white leg, he tried to remember her as she was when he had wrapped her in the blanket. But he didn't want to remember, because she had been nothing to him then, and his nature revolted from remembering what she was when she was nothing to him.

A tumbling, muffled noise from within the dark house startled him. Then he heard her voice:—"There are clothes." He rose and went to the foot of the stairs, and gathered up the garments she had thrown down. Then he came back to the fire, to rub himself down and dress. He grinned at his own appearance when he had finished.

The fire was sinking, so he put on coal. The house was now quite dark, save for the light of a street-lamp that shone in faintly from beyond the holly trees. He lit the gas with matches he found on the mantelpiece. Then he emptied the pockets of his own clothes, and threw all his wet things in a heap into the scullery. After which he gathered up her sodden clothes, gently, and put them in a separate heap on the copper-top in the scullery.

It was six o'clock on the clock. His own watch had stopped. He ought to go back to the surgery. He waited, and still she did not come down. So he went to the foot of the stairs and called:

"I shall have to go."

Almost immediately he heard her coming down. She had on her best dress of black voile, and her hair was tidy, but still damp. She looked at him—and, in spite of herself, smiled.

"I don't like you in those clothes," she said.

"Do I look a sight?" he answered.

They were shy of one another.

"I'll make you some tea," she said.

"No, I must go."

5   "Must you?" And she looked at him again with the wide, strained, doubtful eyes. And again, from the pain of his breast, he knew how he loved her. He went and bent to kiss her, gently, passionately, with his heart's painful kiss.

"And my hair smells so horrible," she murmured in distraction.
10   "And I'm so awful, I'm so awful! Oh, no, I'm too awful," and she broke into bitter, heart-broken sobbing. "You can't want to love me, I'm horrible."

"Don't be silly, don't be silly," he said, trying to comfort her, kissing her, holding her in his arms. "I want you, I want to marry you;
15   we're going to be married, quickly, quickly—to-morrow if I can."

But she only sobbed terribly, and cried:

"I feel awful. I feel awful. I feel I'm horrible to you."

"No, I want you, I want you," was all he answered, blindly, with that terrible intonation which frightened her almost more than her
20   horror lest he should *not* want her.

The Last Straw*
[Fanny and Annie]

Flame-lurid his face as he turned among the throng of flame-lit and
dark faces upon the platform.* In the light of the furnace she caught
sight of his drifting countenance, like a piece of floating fire. And the 5
nostalgia, the doom of home-coming went through her veins like a
drug. His eternal face, flame-lit now! The pulse and darkness of red
fire from the furnace towers in the sky, lighting the desultory,
industrial crowd on the wayside station, lit him and went out.

Of course, he did not see her. Flame-lit and unseeing! Always the 10
same, with his meeting eyebrows, his common cap, and his red-and-
black scarf knotted round his throat. Not even a collar to meet her!
The flames had sunk, there was shadow.

She opened the door of her grimy, branch-line carriage and began
to get down her bags. The porter was nowhere, of course, but there 15
was Harry, obscure, on the outer edge of the little crowd, missing
her, of course.

"Here! Harry!" she called, waving her umbrella in the twilight.
He hurried forward.

"Tha's come, has ter?" he said, in a sort of cheerful welcome. She 20
got down, rather flustered, and gave him a peck of a kiss.

"Two suit-cases!" she said.

Her soul groaned within her, as he clambered into the carriage
after her bags. Up shot the fire in the twilight sky, from the great
furnace behind the station. She felt the red flame go across her face. 25
She had come back, she had come back for good. And her spirit
groaned dismally. She doubted if she could bear it.

There, on the sordid little station under the furnaces she stood,
tall and distinguished, in her well-made coat and skirt and her broad,
grey velour hat. She held her umbrella, her bead chatelaine, and a 30
little leather case in her grey-gloved hands, while Harry staggered
out of the ugly little train with her bags.

"There's a trunk at the back," she said, in her bright voice. But
she was not feeling bright. The twin black cones of the iron foundry
blasted their sky-high fires into the night. The whole scene was 35

153

lurid. The train waited cheerfully. It would wait another ten minutes. She knew it. It was all so deadly familiar.

Let us confess it at once. She was a lady's maid, thirty years old, come back to marry her first love, a foundry worker, after having kept
5   him dangling, off and on, for a dozen years. Why had she come back—did she love him? No! She didn't pretend to. She had loved her brilliant and ambitious cousin, who had jilted her, and who had died. She had had other affairs which had come to nothing. So here she was, come back suddenly to marry her first-love, who had
10 waited—or remained single—all these years.

"Won't a porter carry those?" she said, as Harry strode with his workman's stride down the platform towards the guard's van.

"I can manage," he said.

And with her umbrella, her chatelaine, and her little leather case,
15 she followed him.

The trunk was there.

"We'll get Heather's greengrocer's cart to fetch it up," he said.

"Isn't there a cab?" said Fanny, knowing dismally enough that there wasn't.
20 "I'll just put it aside o' the penny-in-the-slot, and Heather's greengrocer's 'll fetch it about half past eight," he said.

He seized the box by its two handles and staggered with it across the level-crossing, bumping his legs against it as he waddled. Then he dropped it by the red sweetmeats machine.
25 "Will it be safe there?" she said.

"Ay—safe as houses," he answered. He returned for the two bags. Thus laden, they started to plod up the hill, under the great long black building of the foundry. She walked beside him—workman of workmen, he was, trudging with that luggage. The red lights flared
30 over the deepening darkness. From the foundry came the horrible, slow clang, clang, clang, of iron, a great noise, with an interval just long enough to make it unendurable.

Compare this with the arrival at Gloucester; the carriage for her mistress, the dog-cart for herself with the luggage; the drive out past
35 the river, the pleasant trees of the carriage approach; and herself sitting beside Arthur, everybody so polite to her.

She had come home—for good! Her heart nearly stopped beating as she trudged up that hideous and interminable hill, beside the laden figure. What a come-down! What a come-down! She could
40 not take it with her usual bright cheerfulness. She knew it all too

well. It is easy to bear up against the unusual, but the deadly familiarity of an old stale past!

He dumped the bags down under a lamp-post, for a rest. There they stood, the two of them, in the lamp-light. Passers-by stared at her, and gave good-night to Harry. Her they hardly knew, she had become a stranger.

"They're too heavy for you, let me carry one," she said.

"They begin to weigh a bit by the time you've gone a mile," he answered.

"Let me carry the little one," she insisted.

"Tha can ha'e it for a minute, if ter's a mind," he said, handing over the valise.

And thus they arrived in the street of shops of the little ugly town on top of the hill. How everybody stared at her; my word! how they stared! And the cinema was just going in, and the queues were tailing down the road to the corner. And everybody took full stock of her. "'Night, Harry!" shouted the fellows, in an interested voice.

However, they arrived at her aunt's—a little sweet-shop in a side street. They "pinged" the door-bell, and her aunt came running forward out of the kitchen.

"There you are, child! Dying for a cup of tea, I'm sure. How are you?"

Fanny's aunt kissed her, and it was all Fanny could do to refrain from bursting into tears, she felt so low. Perhaps it was her tea she wanted.

"You've had a drag with that luggage," said Fanny's aunt to Harry.

"Ay, I'm not sorry to put it down," he said, looking at his hand which was crushed and cramped by the bag handle.

Then he departed to see about Heather's greengrocery cart.

When Fanny sat at tea, her aunt, a grey-haired, fair-faced little woman, looked at her with an admiring heart, feeling bitterly sore for her. For Fanny was beautiful: tall, erect, finely coloured, with her delicately arched nose, her rich brown hair, her large lustrous grey eyes. A passionate woman—a woman to be afraid of. So proud, so inwardly violent. She came of a violent race.

It needed a woman to sympathise with her. Men had not the courage. Poor Fanny! She was such a lady, and so straight and magnificent. And yet everything seemed to do her down. Every time she seemed to be doomed to humiliation and disappointment, this handsome, brilliantly sensitive woman, with her nervous over-wrought laugh.

"So you've really come back, child?" said her aunt.

"I really have, Aunt," said Fanny.

5   "Poor Harry! I'm not sure, you know, Fanny, that you're not taking a bit of an advantage of him."

"Oh, Aunt, he's waited so long, he may as well have what he's waited for." Fanny laughed grimly.

"Yes, child, he's waited so long, that I'm not sure it isn't a bit hard
10 on him. You know, I *like* him, Fanny—though, as you know quite well, I don't think he's good enough for you. And I think he thinks so himself, poor fellow."

"Don't you be so sure of that, Aunt. Harry is common, but he's not humble. He wouldn't think the Queen was any too good for him,
15 if he'd a mind to her."

"Well, it's as well if he has a proper opinion of himself."

"It depends what you call proper," said Fanny. "But he's got his good points——"

"Oh, he's a nice fellow, and I like him. I do like him. Only, as I tell
20 you, he's not good enough for you."

"I've made up my mind, Aunt," said Fanny grimly.

"Yes," mused the aunt; "they say all things come to him who waits——"

"More than he's bargained for, eh, Aunt?" laughed Fanny, rather
25 bitterly.

The poor aunt, this bitterness grieved her for her niece.

They were interrupted by the ping of the shop-bell, and Harry's call of "Right?" But as he did not come in at once, Fanny, feeling solicitous for him presumably at the moment, rose and went into the
30 shop. She saw a cart outside, and went to the door.

And the moment she stood in the doorway she heard a woman's common vituperative voice crying from the darkness of the opposite side of the road:

"Tha'rt theer, are ter! I'll shame thee, Mester! I'll shame thee, see
35 if I dunna."

Startled, Fanny stared across the darkness, and saw a woman in a black bonnet go under one of the lamps up the side street.

Harry and Bill Heather had dragged the trunk off the little dray and she retreated before them as they came up the shop step with it.
40 "Wheer shalt ha'e it?" asked Harry.

"Best take it upstairs," said Fanny.

She went up first to light the gas.

When Heather had gone, and Harry was sitting down having tea and pork pie, Fanny asked:

"Who was that woman shouting?"

"Nay, I canna tell thee. To somebody, I s'd think," replied Harry. Fanny looked at him, but asked no more.

He was a fair-haired fellow of thirty-two, with a fair moustache. He was broad in his speech and looked like a foundry-hand, which he was. But women always liked him. There was something of a mother's lad about him—something warm and playful and really sensitive.

He had his attractions, even for Fanny. What she rebelled against so bitterly was that he had no sort of ambition. He was a moulder, but of very commonplace skill. He was thirty-two years old, and hadn't saved twenty pounds. She would have to provide the money for the home. He didn't care. He just didn't care. He had no initiative at all. He had no vices—no obvious ones. But he was just indifferent, spending as he went, and not caring. Yet he did not look happy. She remembered his face in the fire-glow: something haunted, abstracted about it. As he sat there eating his pork pie, bulging his cheek out, she felt he was like a doom to her. And she raged against the doom of him. It wasn't that he was gross. His *way* was common, almost on purpose. But he himself wasn't really common. For instance, his food was not particularly important to him, he was not greedy. He had a charm, too, particularly for women, with his blondness and his sensitiveness and his way of making a woman feel that she was a higher being. But Fanny knew him, knew the peculiar obstinate limitedness of him, that would nearly send her mad.

He stayed till about half-past nine. She went to the door with him.

"When are you coming up?" he said jerking his head in the direction, presumably, of his own home.

"I'll come to-morrow afternoon," she said brightly. Between Fanny and Mrs Goodall, his mother, there was naturally no love lost.

Again she gave him an awkward little kiss, and said good-night.

"You can't wonder, you know, child, if he doesn't seem so very keen," said her aunt. "It's your own fault."

"Oh, Aunt, I couldn't stand him when he was keen. I can do with him a lot better as he is."

The two women sat and talked far into the night. They understood

each other. The aunt, too, had married as Fanny was marrying, a
man who was no companion to her—a violent man, brother of
Fanny's father. He was dead; Fanny's father was dead.

Poor Aunt Lizzie, she cried woefully over her bright niece, when
5 she had gone to bed.

Fanny paid the promised visit to his people the next afternoon.
Mrs Goodall was a large woman with smooth-parted hair, a
common, obstinate woman who had spoiled her four lads and her
one vixen of a married daughter. She was one of those old-fashioned
10 powerful natures that couldn't do with looks or education or any
form of showing off. She fairly hated the sound of correct English.
She *thee'd* and *tha'd* her prospective daughter-in-law, and said:

"I'm none as ormin'* as I look, seest ta."

Fanny did not think her prospective mother-in-law looked at all
15 orming, so the speech was unnecessary.

"I towd him mysen," said Mrs Goodall—"'Er's held back all this
long, let 'er stop as 'er is. 'E'd none ha' had thee for *my* tellin', tha
hears. No, 'e's a fool, an' I know it. I says to him, 'Tha looks a man,
doesn't ter, at thy age, goin' an' openin' to her when ter hears her
20 scrat' at th' gate, after she's done gallivantin' round wherever she'd a
mind. Tha looks rare an' soft.' But it's no use o' any talking; he
answered that letter o' thine, and made his own bad bargain."

But in spite of the old woman's anger, she was also flattered at
Fanny's coming back to Harry. For Mrs Goodall was impressed by
25 Fanny—a woman of her own match. And more than this, everybody
knew that Fanny's Aunt Kate had left her two hundred pounds, this
apart from the girl's savings.

So there was high tea in Princes Street,* when Harry came home
black from work, and a rather acrid odour of cordiality, the vixen
30 Jinny darting in to say vulgar things. Of course, Jinny lived in a house
whose garden end joined the paternal garden. They were a clan who
stuck together, these Goodalls.

It was arranged that Fanny should come to tea again on the
Sunday, and the wedding was discussed. It should take place in a
35 fortnight's time at Morley Chapel.* Morley was a hamlet on the edge
of the real country, and in its little Congregational Chapel Fanny
and Harry had first met.

What a creature of habit he was! He was still in the choir of
Morley Chapel—not very regular. He belonged just because he had
40 a tenor voice and enjoyed singing. Indeed, his solos were only spoilt

to local fame because, when he sang, he handled his aitches so
hopelessly.

> *"And I saw 'eaven hopened*
> *And be'old, a wite 'orse——"**

This was one of Harry's classics, only surpassed by the fine   5
outburst of his heaving:

> *"Hangels—hever bright an' fair——"**

It was a pity, but it was unalterable. He had a good voice, and he
sang with a certain lacerating fire, but his pronunciation made it all
funny. And *nothing* could alter him.   10
So he was never heard save at cheap concerts, and in the little,
poorer chapels. The others scoffed.
Now the month was September, and Sunday was Harvest Festival
at Morley Chapel, and Harry was singing solos. So that Fanny was to
go to afternoon service, and come home to a grand spread of Sunday   15
tea with him. Poor Fanny! One of the most wonderful afternoons
had been a Sunday afternoon service, with her cousin Luther at her
side, Harvest Festival at Morley Chapel. Harry had sung solos
then—ten years ago. She remembered his pale blue tie, and the
purple asters and the great vegetable marrows in which he was   20
framed, and her cousin Luther at her side, young, clever, come down
from London, where he was getting on well, learning his Latin and
his French and German so brilliantly.
However, once again it was Harvest Festival at Morley Chapel,
and once again, as ten years before, a soft, exquisite September day,   25
with the last roses pink in the cottage gardens, the last dahlias
crimson, the last sunflowers yellow. And again the little old chapel
was a bower, with its famous sheaves of corn and corn-plaited pillars,
its great bunches of grapes, dangling like tassels from the pulpit
corners, its marrows and potatoes and pears and apples and   30
damsons, its purple asters and yellow Japanese sunflowers. Just as
before, the red dahlias round the pillars were dropping, weak-
headed, among the oats. The place was crowded and hot, the plates
of tomatoes seemed balanced perilously on the gallery front, the Rev.
Enderby was weirder than ever to look at, so long and emaciated and   35
hairless.
The Rev. Enderby, probably forewarned, came and shook hands
with her and welcomed her, in his broad northern, melancholy

sing-song before he mounted the pulpit. Fanny was handsome in a
gauzy dress and a beautiful lace hat. Being a little late, she sat in a
chair in the side-aisle wedged in, right in the front of the chapel.
Harry was in the gallery above, and she could only see him from the
5 eyes upwards. She noticed again how his eyebrows met, blond and
not very marked, over his nose. He was attractive too: physically
lovable, very. If only—if only her *pride* had not suffered! She felt he
dragged her down.

"Come, ye thankful people, come,
10 *Raise the song of harvest-home.*
All is safely gathered in
Ere the winter storms begin——"*

Even the hymn was a falsehood, as the season had been wet, and
half the crops were still out, and in a poor way.
15 Poor Fanny! She sang little, and looked beautiful through that
inappropriate hymn. Above her stood Harry—mercifully in a dark
suit and a dark tie—looking almost handsome. And his lacerating,
pure tenor sounded well, when the words were drowned in the
general commotion. Brilliant she looked, and brilliant she felt, for
20 she was hot and angrily miserable and inflamed with a sort of fatal
despair. Because there was about him a physical attraction which she
really hated, but which she could not escape from. He was the first
man who had ever kissed her. And his kisses, even while she rebelled
from them, had lived in her blood and sent roots down into her soul.
25 After all this time she had come back to them. And her soul groaned,
for she felt dragged down, dragged down to earth, as a bird which
some dog has got down in the dust. She knew her life would be
unhappy. She knew that what she was doing was fatal. Yet it was her
doom. She had to come back to him.
30 He had to sing two solos this afternoon: one before the "address"
from the pulpit, and one after. Fanny looked up at him, and
wondered he was not too shy to stand up there in front of all the
people. But no, he was not shy. He had even a kind of assurance on
his face as he looked down from the choir gallery at her: the
35 assurance of a common man deliberately entrenched in his com-
monness. Oh, such a rage went through her veins as she saw the air
of triumph, laconic, indifferent triumph which sat so obstinately and
recklessly on his eyelids as he looked down at her. Ah, she despised
him! But there he stood up in that choir gallery like Balaam's ass* in

front of her, and she could not get beyond him. A certain winsomeness also about him. A certain physical winsomeness, and as if
his flesh were new and lovely to touch. The thorn of desire rankled
bitterly in her heart.

He, it goes without saying, sang like a canary this particular
afternoon, with a certain defiant passion which pleasantly crisped the
blood of the congregation. Fanny felt the crisp flames go through her
veins as she listened. Even the curious loud-mouthed vernacular had
a certain fascination. But oh, also, it was so repugnant. He would
triumph over her, obstinately he would drag her right back into the
common people: a doom, a vulgar doom.

The second performance was an anthem, in which Harry sang the
solo parts. It was clumsy, but beautiful, with lovely words:

> *"They that sow in tears shall reap in joy;*
> *He that goeth forth and weepeth, bearing precious seed,*
> *Shall doubtless come again with rejoicing, bringing his sheaves*
> *with him."**

"Shall doubtless come, shall doubtless come," softly intoned the
altos, "Bringing his she-e-eaves with him," the trebles flourished
brightly, and then again began the half-wistful solo:

> *"They that sow in tears shall reap in joy."*

Yes, it was effective and moving.

But at the moment when Harry's voice sank carelessly down to his
close, and the choir, standing behind him, were opening their
mouths for the final triumphant outburst, a shouting female voice
rose up from the body of the congregation. The organ gave one
startled trump, and went silent; the choir stood transfixed.

"You look well standing there, singing in God's holy house,"
came the loud, angry female shout. Everybody turned electrified. A
stoutish, red-faced woman in a black bonnet was standing up
denouncing the soloist. Almost fainting with shock, the congregation
realised it. "You look well, don't you, standing there singing solos in
God's holy house—you, Goodall. But I said I'd shame you. You look
well, bringing your young woman here with you, don't you? I'll let
her know who she's dealing with. A scamp as won't take the
consequences of what he's done." The hard-faced, frenzied woman
turned in the direction of Fanny. "*That's* what Harry Goodall is, if
you want to know."

And she sat down again in her seat. Fanny, startled like all the rest, had turned to look. She had gone white, and then a burning red, under the attack. She knew the woman: a Mrs Nixon, a devil of a woman, who beat her pathetic, drunken, red-nosed second husband,
5   Bob, and her two lanky daughters, grown-up as they were. A notorious character. Fanny turned round again, and sat motionless as eternity in her seat.

There was a minute of perfect silence and suspense. The audience was open-mouthed and dumb; the choir stood like Lot's
10 wife;* and Harry, with his music-sheet uplifted, stood there, looking down with a dumb sort of indifference on Mrs Nixon, his face naïve and faintly mocking. Mrs Nixon sat defiant in her seat, braving them all.

Then a rustle, like a wood when the wind suddenly catches the
15 leaves. And then the tall, weird minister got to his feet, and in his strong, bell-like beautiful voice—the only beautiful thing about him—he said with infinite mournful pathos:

"Let us unite in singing the last hymn on the hymn-sheet; the last hymn on the hymn-sheet, number eleven.

20   *'Fair waved the golden corn*
              *In Canaan's pleasant land.'"**

The organ tuned up promptly. During the hymn the offertory was taken. And after the hymn, the prayer.

Mr Enderby came from Northumberland. Like Harry, he had
25 never been able to conquer his accent, which was very broad. He was a little simple, one of God's fools, perhaps, an odd bachelor soul, emotional, ugly, but very gentle.

"And if, Oh our dear Lord, beloved Jesus, there should fall a shadow of sin upon our harvest, we leave it to Thee to judge, for
30 Thou art Judge. We lift our spirits and our sorrow, Jesus, to Thee, and our mouths are dumb. Oh Lord, keep us from forward speech, restrain us from foolish words and thoughts, we pray Thee, Lord Jesus, who knowest all and judgest all."

Thus the minister said, in his sad, resonant voice, washing his
35 hands before the Lord. Fanny bent forward open-eyed during the prayer. She could see the roundish head of Harry, also bent forward. His face was inscrutable and expressionless. The shock left her bewildered. Anger perhaps was her dominating emotion.

The audience began to rustle to its feet, to ooze slowly and

excitedly out of the chapel, looking with wildly-interested eyes at
Fanny, at Mrs Nixon and at Harry. Mrs Nixon, shortish, stood
defiant in her pew, facing the aisle, as if announcing that, without
rolling her sleeves up, she was ready for anybody. Fanny sat quite
still. Luckily the people did not have to pass her. And Harry, with red
ears, was making his way sheepishly out of the gallery. The loud
noise of the organ covered all the downstairs commotion of exit.

The minister sat silent and inscrutable in his pulpit, rather like a
death's-head, while the congregation filed out. When the last
lingerers had unwillingly departed, craning their necks to stare at the
still seated Fanny, he rose, stalked in his hooked fashion down the
little country chapel, and fastened the door. Then he returned and
sat down by the silent young woman.

"This is most unfortunate, most unfortunate," he moaned. "I am
so sorry, I am so sorry, indeed, indeed, ah! indeed!" he sighed
himself to a close.

"It's a sudden surprise, that's one thing," said Fanny brightly.

"Yes—yes—indeed. Yes, a surprise, yes. I don't know the woman,
I don't know her."

"I know her," said Fanny. "She's a bad one."

"Well, well!" said the minister. "I don't know her. I don't
understand. I don't understand at all. But it is to be regretted, it is
very much to be regretted. I am very sorry."

Fanny was watching the vestry door. The gallery stairs communi-
cated with the vestry, not with the body of the chapel. She knew the
choir members had been peeping for information.

At last Harry came—rather sheepishly, with his hat in his hand.

"Well!" said Fanny, rising to her feet.

"We've had a bit of an extra," said Harry.

"I should think so," said Fanny.

"A most unfortunate circumstance—a most *unfortunate* circumstance. Do you understand it, Harry? I don't understand it at all."

"Ay, I understand it. The daughter's goin' to have a childt, an' 'er
lays it on to me."

"And has she no occasion to?" asked Fanny, rather censorious.

"It's no more mine than it is some other chap's," said Harry,
looking aside.

There was a moment of pause.

"Which girl is it?" asked Fanny.

"Annie, the young one——"

There followed another silence.

"I don't think I know them, do I?" asked the minister.

"I shouldn't think so. Their name's Nixon, mother married old Bob for her second husband. She's a tanger*—'s driven the gel to

5 what she is. They live in Manners Road."

"Why, what's amiss with the girl?" asked Fanny sharply. "She was all right when I knew her."

"Ay, she's all right. But she's always in an' out o' th' pubs, wi' th' fellows," said Harry.

10 "A nice thing!" said Fanny.

Harry glanced towards the door. He wanted to get out.

"Most distressing indeed!" The minister slowly shook his head.

"What about to-night, Mr Enderby?" asked Harry, in rather a small voice. "Shall you want me?"

15 Mr Enderby looked up painedly, and put his hand to his brow. He studied Harry for some time, vacantly. There was the faintest sort of a resemblance between the two men.

"Yes," he said. "Yes, I think. I think we must take no notice, and cause as little remark as possible."

20 Fanny hesitated. Then she said to Harry:

"But *will* you come?"

He looked at her.

"Ay, I s'll come," he said.

Then he turned to Mr Enderby.

25 "Well, good afternoon, Mr Enderby," he said.

"Good afternoon, Harry, good afternoon!" replied the mournful minister. Fanny followed Harry to the door, and for some time they walked in silence through the late afternoon.

"And it's yours as much as anybody else's?" she said.

30 "Ay," he answered, shortly.

And they went, without another word, for the long mile or so, till they came to the corner of the street where Harry lived. Fanny hesitated. Should she go on to her aunt's? Should she? It would mean leaving all this for ever! Harry stood silent.

35 Some obstinacy made her turn with him along the road to his own home. When they entered the house-place, the whole family was there, mother and father and Jinny, with Jinny's husband and children and Harry's two brothers.

"You've been having your ears warmed, th' tell me," said Mrs

40 Goodall grimly.

"Who telled thee?" asked Harry, shortly.

"Maggie and Luke's both been in."

"You look well, don't you!" said interfering Jinny.

Harry went and hung his hat up, without replying.

"Come upstairs and take your hat off," said Mrs Goodall to
Fanny, almost kindly. It would have annoyed her very much if Fanny
had dropped her son at this moment.

"What's 'er say, then?" asked the father secretly, of Harry, jerking
his head in the direction of the stairs whence Fanny had disappeared.

"Nowt yet," said Harry.

"Serve you right if she chucks you now," said Jinny. "I'll bet it's
right about Annie Nixon an' you."

"Tha bets so much," said Harry.

"Yi, but you can't deny it," said Jinny.

"I can if I've a mind."

His father looked at him enquiringly.

"It's no more mine than it is Bill Bowers' or Ted Slaney's, or six or
seven on 'em," said Harry to his father.

And the father nodded silently.

"That'll not get you out of it, in court," said Jinny.

Upstairs Fanny evaded all the thrusts made by his mother, and did
not declare her hand. She tidied her hair, washed her hands, and put
the tiniest bit of powder on her face, for coolness, there in front of
Mrs Goodall's indignant gaze. It was like a declaration of independence. But the old woman said nothing.

They came down to Sunday tea, with sardines and tinned salmon
and tinned peaches, besides tarts and cakes. The chatter was
general. It concerned the Nixon family and the scandal.

"Oh, she's a foul-mouthed woman," said Jinny of Mrs Nixon.
"She may well talk about God's holy house, *she* had. It's first time
she's set foot in it, ever since she dropped off from being converted.
She's a devil and she always was one. Can't you remember how she
treated Bob's children, mother, when we lived down in the Buildings? I can remember when I was a little girl, she used to bathe them
in the yard, in the cold, so that they shouldn't splash the house. She'd
half kill them if they made a mark on the floor—and the language
she'd use. And one Saturday I can remember Garry, that was Bob's
own girl, she ran off when her stepmother was going to bathe
her—ran off without a rag of clothes on—can you remember,

mother? And she hid in Smedley's close—it was the time of mowing grass—and nobody could find her. She hid out there all night, didn't she, mother? Nobody could find her. My word, there was a talk. They found her on Sunday morning——"

5   "Fred Coutts threatened to break every bone in the woman's body if she touched the children again," put in the father.

"Anyhow, they frightened her," said Jinny. "But she was nearly as bad with her own two. And anybody can see that she's driven old Bob till he's gone soft."

10   "Ah, soft as mush," said Jack Goodall. "'E'd never addle* a week's wage, nor yet a day's if th' chaps didn't make it up to him."

"My word, if he didn't bring her a week's wage, she'd pull his head off," said Jinny.

"But a clean woman and respectable, except for her foul mouth,"
15 said Mrs Goodall. "Keeps to herself like a bull-dog. Never lets anybody come near the house, and neighbours with nobody."

"Wanted it thrashing out of her," said Mr Goodall, a silent, evasive sort of man.

"Where Bob gets the money for his drink from is a mystery," said
20 Jinny.

"Chaps treat him," said Harry.

"Well, he's got the pair of frightenedest rabbit-eyes you'd wish to see," said Jinny.

"Ay, with a drunken man's murder in them, *I* think," said Mrs
25 Goodall.

So the talk went on after tea, till it was practically time to start off to chapel again.

"You'll have to be getting ready, Fanny," said Mrs Goodall.

"I'm not going to-night," said Fanny abruptly. And there was a
30 sudden halt in the family. "I'll stop with *you* to-night, Mother," she added.

"Best you had, my gel," said Mrs Goodall, flattered and assured.

UNCOLLECTED STORIES, 1913–22

The Mortal Coil*

I.

She stood motionless in the middle of the room, something tense in her reckless bearing. Her gown of reddish stuff fell silkily about her feet; she looked tall and splendid in the candlelight. Her dark-blond hair was gathered loosely in a fold on top of her head, her young, blossom-fresh face was lifted. From her throat to her feet she was clothed in the elegantly-made dress of silky red stuff, the color of red earth. She looked complete and lovely, only love could make her such a strange, complete blossom. Her cloak and hat were thrown across a table just in front of her.

Quite alone, abstracted, she stood there arrested in a conflict of emotions. Her hand, down against her skirt, worked irritably, the ball of the thumb rubbing, rubbing across the tips of the fingers. There was a slight tension between her lifted brows.

About her the room glowed softly, reflecting the candlelight from its whitewashed walls, and from the great, bowed, whitewashed ceiling. It was a large attic, with two windows, and the ceiling curving down on either side, so that both the far walls were low. Against one, on one side, was a single bed, opened for the night, the white over-bolster* piled back. Not far from this was the iron stove. Near the window closest to the bed was a table with writing materials, and a handsome cactus-plant with clear scarlet blossoms threw its bizarre shadow on the wall. There was another table near the second window, and opposite was the door on which hung a military cloak. Along the far wall, were guns and fishing-tackle, and some clothes too, hung on pegs—all men's clothes, all military. It was evidently the room of a man, probably a young lieutenant.

The girl, in her pure red dress that fell about her feet, so that she looked a woman, not a girl, at last broke from her abstraction and went aimlessly to the writing-table. Her mouth was closed down stubbornly, perhaps in anger, perhaps in pain. She picked up a large seal made of agate, looked at the ingraven coat of arms, then stood

rubbing her finger across the cut-out stone, time after time. At last she put the seal down, and looked at the other things—a beautiful old beer-mug used as a tobacco-jar, a silver box like an urn, old and of exquisite shape, a bowl of sealing wax. She fingered the pieces of
5 wax. This, the dark-green, had sealed her last letter. Ah, well! She carelessly turned over the blotting book, which again had his arms stamped on the cover. Then she went away to the window. There, in the window-recess, she stood and looked out. She opened the casement and took a deep breath of the cold night air. Ah, it was
10 good! Far below was the street, a vague golden milky way beneath her, its tiny black figures moving and crossing and re-crossing with marionette, insect-like intentness. A small horse-car* rumbled along the lines, so belittled, it was an absurdity. So much for the world! . . . he did not come.

15　　She looked overhead. The stars were white and flashing, they looked nearer than the street, more kin to her, more real. She stood pressing her breast on her arms, her face lifted to the stars, in the long, anguished suspense of waiting. Noises came up small from the street, as from some insect-world. But the great stars overhead
20 struck white and invincible, infallible. Her heart felt cold like the stars.

　　At last she started. There was a noisy knocking at the door, and a female voice calling:

　　"Anybody there?"

25　　"Come in," replied the girl.

　　She turned round, shrinking from this intrusion, unable to bear it, after the flashing stars.

　　There entered a thin, handsome dark girl dressed in an extravagantly-made gown of dark purple silk and dark blue velvet. She was
30 followed by a small swarthy, inconspicuous lieutenant in pale-blue uniform.

　　"Ah *you!* . . . alone?" cried Teresa, the newcomer, advancing into the room. "Where's the Fritz, then?"

　　The girl in red raised her shoulders in a shrug, and turned her face
35 aside, but did not speak.

　　"Not here! You don't know where he is? Ach, the dummy, the lout!" Teresa swung round on her companion.

　　"Where is he?" she demanded.

　　He also lifted his shoulders in a shrug.

"He said he was coming in half an hour," the young lieutenant replied.

"Ha!—half an hour! Looks like it! How long is that ago—two hours?"

Again the young man only shrugged. He had beautiful black eye-lashes, and steady eyes. He stood rather deprecatingly, whilst his girl, golden like a young panther, hung over him.

"One knows where he is," said Teresa, going and sitting on the opened bed. A dangerous contraction came between the brows of Marta, the girl in red, at this act.

"Wine, Women and Cards!" said Teresa, in her loud voice. "But they prefer the women on the cards."

> "'My love he has four Queenies,
> Four Queenies has my lo-o-ove.'"*

she sang. Then she broke off, and turned to Podewils. "Was he winning when you left him, Karl?"

Again the young baron raised his shoulders.

"Tant pis que mal,"* he replied, cryptically.

"Ah, *you!*" cried Teresa, "with your *tant pis que mal!* Are *you* tant pis que mal?" She laughed her deep, strange laugh. "Well," she added, "he'll be coming in with a fortune for you, Marta—"

There was a vague, unhappy silence.

"I know his fortunes," said Marta.

"Yes," said Teresa, in sudden sober irony, "he's a horse-shoe round your neck, is that young jockey.—But what are you going to do, Matzen dearest? You're not going to wait for him any longer?—Don't dream of it! The idea, waiting for that young gentleman as if you were married to him!—Put your hat on, dearest, and come along with us . . . Where are we going, Karl, you pillar of salt?*—Eh?—Geier's?—To Geier's, Marta, my dear. Come, quick, up—you've been martyred enough, Marta, my martyr—haw!—haw!!—put your hat on. Up—away!"

Teresa sprang up like an explosion, anxious to be off.

"No, I'll wait for him," said Marta, sullenly.

"Don't be such a fool!" cried Teresa, in her deep voice. "Wait for him! *I'd* give him wait for him. Catch this little bird waiting." She lifted her hand and blew a little puff across the fingers. "Choo-fly!" she sang, as if a bird had just flown.

The young lieutenant stood silent with smiling dark eyes. Teresa was quick, and golden as a panther.

"No, but really, Marta, you're not going to wait any more—really! It's stupid for you to play Gretchen*—your eyes are much too green. Put your hat on, there's a darling."

"No," said Marta, her flower-like face strangely stubborn. "I'll wait for him. He'll have to come some time."

There was a moment's uneasy pause.

"Well," said Teresa, holding her shoulders for her cloak, "so long as you don't wait as long as Lenore-fuhr-ums-Morgen-rot—!* Adieu, my dear, God be with you."

The young lieutenant bowed a solicitous bow, and the two went out, leaving the girl in red once more alone.

She went to the writing table, and on a sheet of paper began writing her name in stiff Gothic characters, time after time:

Marta Hohenest

Marta Hohenest

Marta Hohenest.

The vague sounds from the street below continued. The wind was cold. She rose and shut the window. Then she sat down again.

At last the door opened, and a young officer entered. He was buttoned up in a dark-blue great-coat, with large silver buttons going down on either side of the breast. He entered quickly, glancing over the room, at Marta, as she sat with her back to him. She was marking with a pencil on paper. He closed the door. Then with fine beautiful movements he divested himself of his coat and went to hang it up. How well Marta knew the sound of his movements, the quick light step! But she continued mechanically making crosses on the paper, her head bent forward between the candles, so that her hair made fine threads and mist of light, very beautiful. He saw this, and it touched him. But he could not afford to be touched any further.

"You have been waiting?" he said formally. The insulting futile question! She made no sign, as if she had not heard. He was absorbed in the tragedy of himself, and hardly heeded her.

He was a slim, good-looking youth, clear-cut and delicate in mould. His features now were pale, there was something evasive in his dilated, vibrating eyes. He was barely conscious of the girl, intoxicated with his own desperation, that held him mindless and distant.

To her, the atmosphere of the room was almost unbreathable,

since he had come in. She felt terribly bound, walled up. She rose
with a sudden movement that tore his nerves. She looked to him tall
and bright and dangerous, as she faced round on him.

"Have you come back with a fortune?" she cried, in mockery, her
eyes full of dangerous light. 5

He was unfastening his belt, to change his tunic. She watched him
up and down, all the time. He could not answer, his lips seemed
dumb. Besides, silence was his strength.

"Have you come back with a fortune?" she repeated, in her strong,
clear voice of mockery. 10

"No," he said, suddenly turning. "Let it please you that—that I've
come back at all."

He spoke desperately, and tailed off into silence. He was a man
doomed. She looked at him: he was insignificant in his doom. She
turned in ridicule. And yet she was afraid; she loved him. 15

He had stood long enough exposed, in his helplessness. With
difficulty he took a few steps, went and sat down at the writing-table.
He looked to her like a dog with its tail between its legs.

He saw the paper, where her name was repeatedly written. She
must find great satisfaction in her own name, he thought vaguely. 20
Then he picked up the seal and kept twisting it round in his fingers,
doing some little trick. And continually the seal fell on to the table
with a sudden rattle that made Marta stiffen cruelly. He was quite
oblivious of her.

She stood watching as he sat bent forward in his stupefaction. The 25
fine cloth of his uniform showed the moulding of his back. And
something tortured her as she saw him, till she could hardly bear it:
the desire of his finely-shaped body, the stupefaction and the
abjectness of him now, his immersion in the tragedy of himself, his
being unaware of her. All her will seemed to grip him, to bruise some 30
manly nonchalance and attention out of him.

"I suppose you're in a fury with me, for being late?" he said, with
impotent irony in his voice. Her fury over trifles, when he was lost in
calamity! How great was his real misery, how trivial her small
offendedness! 35

Something in his tone burned her, and made her soul go cold.

"I'm not exactly pleased," she said coldly, turning away to a
window.

Still he sat bent over the table, twisting something with his fingers.
She glanced round on him. How nervy he was! He had beautiful 40

hands, and the big topaz signet-ring on his finger made yellow lights. Ah, if only his hands were really dare-devil and reckless! They always seemed so guilty, so cowardly.

"I'm done for now," he said suddenly, as if to himself, tilting back
5 his chair a little. In all his physical movement he was so fine and poised, so sensitive! Oh, and it attracted her so much!

"Why?" she said, carelessly.

An anger burned in him. She was so flippant. If he were going to be shot, she would not be moved more than about half a pound of
10 sweets.

"Why!" he repeated laconically. "The same unimportant reason as ever."

"Debts?" she cried, in contempt.

"Exactly."
15 Her soul burned in anger.

"What have you done now?—lost more money?"

"Three thousand marks."*

She was silent in deep wrath.

"More fool you!" she said. Then, in her anger, she was silent for
20 some minutes. "And so you're done for, for three thousand marks?" she exclaimed, jeering at him. "You go pretty cheap."

"Three thousand—and the rest," he said, keeping up a manly *sang froid*.

"And the rest!" she repeated in contempt. "And for three
25 thousand—and the rest, your life is over!"

"My career," he corrected her.

"Oh," she mocked, "only your career! I thought it was a matter of life and death. Only your career? Oh, only that!"

His eyes grew furious under her mockery.
30 "My career *is* my life," he said.

"Oh, is it!—You're not a *man* then, you are only a career?"

"I am a gentleman."

"Oh, are you! How amusing! How very amusing, to be a gentleman and not a man!—I suppose that's what it means, to be a
35 gentleman, to have no guts outside your career?"

"Outside my honor—none."

"And might I ask what *is* your honor?" She spoke in extreme irony.

"Yes, you may ask," he replied coolly. "But if you don't know
40 without being told, I'm afraid I could never explain it."

"Oh, you couldn't! No, I believe you—you are incapable of explaining it, it wouldn't bear explaining." There was a long, tense pause. "So you've made too many debts, and you're afraid they'll kick you out of the army, therefore your honor is gone, is it?—And what then—what after that?"

She spoke in extreme irony. He winced again at her phrase "kick you out of the army." But he tilted his chair back with assumed nonchalance.

"I've made too many debts, and I *know* they'll kick me out of the army," he repeated, thrusting the thorn right home to the quick. "After that—I can shoot myself. Or I might even be a waiter in a restaurant—or possibly a clerk, with twenty-five shillings a week."

"Really!—All those alternatives!—Well, why not, why not be a waiter in the Germania? It might be awfully jolly."

"Why not?" he repeated ironically. "Because it wouldn't become me."

She looked at him, at his aristocratic fineness of physique, his extreme physical sensitiveness. And all her German worship for his old, proud family rose up in her. No, he could not be a waiter in the Germania: she could not bear it. He was too refined and beautiful a thing.

"Ha!" she cried suddenly. "It wouldn't come to that, either. If they kick you out of the army, you'll find somebody to get round—you're like a cat, you'll land on your feet."

But this was just what he was not. He was not like a cat. His self-mistrust was too deep. Ultimately he had no belief in himself, as a separate isolated being. He knew he was sufficiently clever, an aristocrat, good-looking, the sensitive superior of most men. The trouble was, that apart from the social fabric he belonged to, he felt himself nothing, a cipher. He bitterly envied the common working-men for a certain manly aplomb, a grounded, almost stupid self-confidence he saw in them. Himself—he could lead such men through the gates of hell—for what did he care about danger or hurt to himself, whilst he was leading? But—cut him off from all this, and what was he? A palpitating rag of meaningless human life.

But she, coming from the people, could not fully understand. And it was best to leave her in the dark. The free indomitable self-sufficient being which a man must be in his relation to a woman who loves him—this he could pretend. But he knew he was not it. He knew that the world of man from which he took his value was his mistress beyond any woman. He wished, secretly, cravingly, almost cravenly, in his heart, it was not so. But so it was.

Therefore, he heard her phrase "you're like a cat," with some bitter envy.

5   "Whom shall I get round?—some woman, who will marry me?" he said.

This was a way out. And it was almost the inevitable thing, for him. But he felt it the last ruin of his manhood, even he.

The speech hurt her mortally, worse than death. She would rather
10 he died, because then her own love would not turn to ash.

"Get married, then, if you want to," she said, in a small broken voice.

"Naturally," he said.

There was a long silence, a foretaste of barren hopelessness.

15 "Why is it so terrible to you," she asked at length, "to come out of the army and trust to your own resources? Other men are strong enough."

"Other men are not me," he said.

Why would she torture him? She seemed to enjoy torturing him.
20 The thought of his expulsion from the army was an agony to him, really worse than death. He saw himself in the despicable civilian clothes, engaged in some menial occupation. And he could not bear it. It was too heavy a cross.

Who was she to talk? She was herself, an actress, daughter of a
25 tradesman. He was himself. How should one of them speak for the other? It was impossible. He loved her. He loved her far better than men usually loved their mistresses. He really cared.—And he was strangely proud of his love for her, as if it were a distinction to him
. . . But there was a limit to her understanding. There was a point
30 beyond which she had nothing to do with him, and she had better leave him alone. Here in this crisis, which was *his* crisis, his downfall, she should not presume to talk, because she did not understand.— But she loved to torture him, that was the truth.

"Why should it hurt you to work?" she reiterated.

35 He lifted his face, white and tortured, his grey eyes flaring with fear and hate.

"Work!" he cried. "What do you think I am worth?—Twenty-five shillings a week, if I am lucky."

His evident anguish penetrated her. She sat dumbfounded,
40 looking at him with wide eyes. He was white with misery and fear; his

hand, that lay loose on the table, was abandoned in nervous ignominy. Her mind filled with wonder, and with deep, cold dread. Did he really care so much? But did it *really* matter so much to him? When he said he was worth twenty-five shillings a week, he was like a man whose soul is pierced. He sat there, annihilated. She looked for him, and he was nothing then. She looked for the man, the free being that loved her. And he was not, he was gone, this blank figure remained. Something with a blanched face sat there in the chair, staring at nothing.

His amazement deepened with intolerable dread. It was as if the world had fallen away into chaos. Nothing remained. She seemed to grasp the air for foothold.

He sat staring in front of him, a dull numbness settled on his brain. He was watching the flame of the candle. And, in his detachment, he realized the flame was a swiftly travelling flood, flowing swiftly from the source of the wick through a white surge and on into the darkness above. It was like a fountain suddenly foaming out, then running on dark and smooth. Could one dam the flood? He took a piece of paper, and cut off the flame for a second.

The girl in red started at the pulse of the light. She seemed to come to, from some trance. She saw his face, clear now, attentive, abstract, absolved. He was quite absolved from his temporal self.

"It isn't true," she said, "is it? It's not so tragic, really?—It's only your pride is hurt, your silly little pride?" She was rather pleading.

He looked at her with clear steady eyes.

"My pride!" he said. "And isn't my pride *me?* What am I without my pride?"

"You are *yourself,*" she said. "If they take your uniform off you, and turn you naked into the street, you are still *yourself.*"

His eyes grew hot. Then he cried:

"What does it mean, *myself!* It means I put on ready-made civilian clothes and do some dirty drudging elsewhere: that is what *myself* amounts to."

She knitted her brows.

"But what are you *to me*—that naked self which you are to me—that is something, isn't it?—everything," she said.

"What is it, if it means nothing?" he said: "What is it, more than a pound of chocolate *dragées?**—It stands for nothing—unless as you say, a petty clerkship, at twenty-five shillings a week."

These were all wounds to her, very deep. She looked in wonder for a few moments.

"And what does it stand for now?" she said. "A magnificent second-lieutenant!"

5 He made a gesture of dismissal with his hand.

She looked at him from under lowered brows.

"And our love!" she said. "It means nothing to you, nothing at all?"

"To me as a menial clerk, what does it mean? What does love 10 mean! Does it mean that a man shall be no more than a dirty rag in the world?—What worth do you think I have in love, if in life I am a wretched inky subordinate clerk?"

"What does it matter?"

"It matters everything."

15 There was silence for a time, then the anger flashed up in her.

"It doesn't matter to you what *I* feel, whether *I* care or not," she cried, her voice rising. "They'll take his little uniform with buttons off him, and he'll have to be a common little civilian, so all he can do is to shoot himself!—It doesn't matter that I'm there—"

20 He sat stubborn and silent. He thought her vulgar. And her raving did not alter the situation in the least.

"Don't you see what value you put on *me*, you clever little man?" she cried in fury. "I've loved you, loved you with all my soul, for two years—and you've lied, and said you loved me. And now, what do I 25 get? He'll shoot himself, because his tuppenny vanity is wounded.—Ah, *fool—!*"

He lifted his head and looked at her. His face was fixed and superior.

"All of which," he said, "leaves the facts of the case quite 30 untouched!"

She hated his cool little speeches.

"Then shoot yourself," she cried, "and you'll be worth *less* than twenty-five shillings a week!"

There was a fatal silence.

35 "*Then* there'll be no question of worth," he said.

"Ha!" she ejaculated in scorn.

She had finished. She had no more to say. At length, after they had both sat motionless and silent, separate, for some time, she rose and went across to her hat and cloak. He shrank in apprehension. 40 Now, he could not bear her to go. He shrank as if he were being whipped. She put her hat on, roughly, then swung her warm plaid cloak over her shoulders. Her hat was of black glossy silk, with a sheeny heap of cocks-feathers, her plaid cloak was dark green and blue, it swung open above her clear harsh-red dress. How beautiful she was, like a fiery Madonna! 5

"Good-bye," she said, in her voice of mockery. "I'm going now."

He sat motionless, as if loaded with fetters. She hesitated, then moved toward the door.

Suddenly, with a spring like a cat, he was confronting her, his 10 back to the door. His eyes were full and dilated, like a cat's, his face seemed to gleam at her. She quivered, as some subtle fluid ran through her nerves.

"Let me go," she said dumbly. "I've had enough." His eyes, with a wide, dark electric pupil, like a cat's, only watched her objec- 15 tively. And again a wave of female submissiveness went over her.

"I want to go," she pleaded. "You know it's no good.—You know this is no good."

She stood humbly before him. A flexible little grin quivered round his mouth. 20

"You know you don't want me," she persisted. "You know you don't really want me.—You only do this to show your power over me—which is a mean trick."

But he did not answer, only his eyes narrowed in a sensual, cruel smile. She shrank, afraid, and yet she was fascinated. 25

"You won't go yet," he said.

She tried in vain to rouse her real opposition.

"I shall call out," she threatened. "I shall shame you before people."

His eyes narrowed again in the smile of vindictive, mocking 30 indifference.

"Call then," he said.

And at the sound of his still, cat-like voice, an intoxication ran over her veins.

"I *will*," she said, looking defiantly into his eyes. But the smile in 35 the dark, full, dilated pupils made her waver into submission again.

"Won't you let me go?" she pleaded sullenly.

Now the smile went openly over his face.

"Take your hat off," he said.

And with quick, light fingers he reached up and drew out the 40

pins of her hat, unfastened the clasp of her cloak, and laid her things
aside.

5 She sat down in a chair. Then she rose again, and went to the
window. In the street below, the tiny figures were moving just the
same. She opened the window, and leaned out, and wept.

He looked round at her in irritation as she stood in her long, clear-
red dress in the window-recess, leaning out. She was exasperating.

"You will be cold," he said.

10 She paid no heed. He guessed, by some tension in her attitude,
that she was crying. It irritated him exceedingly, like a madness.
After a few minutes of suspense, he went across to her, and took her
by the arm. His hand was subtle, soft in its touch, and yet rather cruel
than gentle.

15 "Come away," he said. "Don't stand there in the air—come
away."

He drew her slowly away to the bed, she sat down, and he beside
her.

"What are you crying for?" he said in his strange, penetrating
20 voice, that had a vibration of exultancy in it. But her tears only ran
faster.

He kissed her face, that was soft, and fresh, and yet warm, wet
with tears. He kissed her again, and again, in pleasure of the soft, wet
saltness of her. She turned aside and wiped her face with her handkerchief, and blew her nose. He was disappointed—yet the way she
25 blew her nose pleased him.

Suddenly she slid away to the floor, and hid her face in the side of
the bed, weeping and crying loudly:

"You don't love me—Oh, you don't love me—I thought you did,
and you let me go on thinking it—but you don't, no, you don't, and I
30 can't bear it.—Oh, I can't bear it."

He sat and listened to the strange, animal sound of her crying. His
eyes flickered with exultancy, his body seemed full and surcharged
with power. But his brows were knitted in tension. He laid his hand
softly on her head, softly touched her face, which was buried against
35 the bed.

She suddenly rubbed her face against the sheets, and looked up
once more.

"You've deceived me," she said, as she sat beside him.

"Have I? Then I've deceived myself." His body felt so charged
40 with male vigor, he was almost laughing in his strength.

"Yes," she said enigmatically, fatally. She seen. thoughts. Then her face quivered again.

"And I loved you so much," she faltered, the tea was a clangor of delight in his heart.

"I love *you*," he said softly, softly touching her, softly in a sort of subtle, restrained ecstasy.

She shook her head stubbornly. She tried to draw away. did break away, and turned to look at him, in fear and dou. little, fascinating, fiendish lights were hovering in his eye. like laughter. 10

"Don't hurt me so much," she faltered, in a last protest.

A faint smile came on his face. He took her face between his hands and covered it with soft, blinding kisses, like a soft, narcotic rain. He felt himself such an unbreakable fountain-head of powerful blood. He was trembling finely in all his limbs, with mastery. 15

When she lifted her face and opened her eyes, her face was wet, and her greenish-golden eyes were shining, it was like sudden sunshine in wet foliage. She smiled at him like a child in knowledge, through the tears, and softly, infinitely softly he dried her tears with his mouth and his soft young moustache. 20

"You'd never shoot yourself, because you're mine, aren't you!" she said, knowing the fine quivering of his body, in mastery.

"Yes," he said.

"Quite mine?" she said, her voice rising in ecstasy.

"Yes." 25

"Nobody else but mine—nothing at all—?"

"Nothing at all," he re-echoed.

"But me?" came her last words of ecstasy.

"Yes."

And she seemed to be released free into the infinite of ecstasy. 30

II.

They slept in fulfilment through the long night. But then strange dreams began to fill them both, strange dreams that were neither waking nor sleeping;—only, in curious weariness, through her dreams, she heard at last a continual low rapping. She awoke with 35 difficulty. The rapping began again—she started violently. It was at the door—it would be the orderly rapping for Friedeburg. Everything seemed wild and unearthly. She put her hand on the shoulder

˷ ıe sleeping man, and pulled him roughly, waited a moment, then pushed him, almost violently, to awake him. He woke with a sense of resentment at her violent handling. Then he heard the knocking of the orderly. He gathered his senses.

5   "Yes, Heinrich!" he said.

Strange, the sound of a voice! It seemed a far-off tearing sound. Then came the muffled voice of the servant.

"Half past four, Sir."

"Right!" said Friedeburg, and automatically he got up and made a
10 light. She was suddenly as wide awake as if it were daylight. But it was a strange, false day, like a delirium. She saw him put down the match, she saw him moving about, rapidly dressing. And the movement in the room was a trouble to her. He himself was vague and unreal, a thing seen but not comprehended. She watched all the
15 acts of his toilet, saw all the motions, but never saw him. There was only a disturbance about her, which fretted her, she was not aware of any presence. Her mind, in its strange, hectic clarity, wanted to consider things in absolute detachment. For instance, she wanted to consider the cactus plant. It was a curious object with pure scarlet
20 blossoms. Now, how did these scarlet blossoms come to pass, upon that earthly-looking unliving creature? Scarlet blossoms! How wonderful they were! What were they, then, how could one lay hold on their being? Her mind turned to him. Him, too, how could one lay hold on him, to have him? Where was he, what was he? She seemed
25 to grasp at the air.

He was dipping his face in the cold water—the slight shock was good for him. He felt as if someone had stolen away his being in the night, he was moving about a light, quick shell, with all his meaning absent. His body was quick and active, but all his deep understand-
30 ing, his soul was gone. He tried to rub it back into his face. He was quite dim, as if his spirit had left his body.

"Come and kiss me," sounded the voice from the bed. He went over to her automatically. She put her arms round him, and looked into his face with her clear brilliant, grey-green eyes, as if she too
35 were looking for his soul.

"How are you?" came her meaningless words.

"All right."

"Kiss me."

He bent down and kissed her.
40 And still her clear, rather frightening eyes seemed to be searching

for him inside himself. He was like a bird transfixed by her pellucid, grey-green, wonderful eyes. She put her hands into his soft, thick, fine hair, and gripped her hands full of his hair. He wondered with fear at her sudden painful clutching.

"I shall be late," he said.

"Yes," she answered. And she let him go.

As he fastened his tunic he glanced out of the window. It was still night: a night that must have lasted since eternity. There was a moon in the sky. In the streets below the yellow street-lamps burned small at intervals. This was the night of eternity.

There came a knock at the door, and the orderly's voice.

"Coffee, Sir."

"Leave it there."

They heard the faint jingle of the tray as it was set down outside.

Friedeburg sat down to put on his boots. Then, with a man's solid tread, he went and took in the tray. He felt properly heavy and secure now in his accoutrement. But he was always aware of her two wonderful, clear, unfolded eyes, looking on his heart, out of her uncanny silence.

There was a strong smell of coffee in the room.

"Have some coffee?" His eyes could not meet hers.

"No, thank you."

"Just a drop?"

"No, thank you."

Her voice sounded quite gay. She watched him dipping his bread in the coffee and eating quickly, absently. He did not know what he was doing, and yet the dipped bread and hot coffee gave him pleasure. He gulped down the remainder of his drink, and rose to his feet.

"I must go," he said.

There was a curious, poignant smile in her eyes. Her eyes drew him to her. How beautiful she was, and dazzling, and frightening, with this look of brilliant tenderness seeming to glitter from her face. She drew his head down to her bosom, and held it fast prisoner there, murmuring with tender, triumphant delight: "Dear! Dear!"

At last she let him lift his head, and he looked into her eyes, that seemed to concentrate in a dancing, golden point of vision in which he felt himself perish.

"Dear!" she murmured. "You love me, don't you?"

"Yes," he said mechanically.

The golden point of vision seemed to leap to him from her eyes, demanding something. He sat slackly, as if spellbound. Her hand pushed him a little.

"Mustn't you go?" she said.

5   He rose. She watched him fastening the belt round his body, that seemed soft under the fine clothes. He pulled on his great-coat, and put on his peaked cap. He was again a young officer.

But he had forgotten his watch. It lay on the table near the bed. She watched him slinging it on his chain. He looked down at her.

10 How beautiful she was, with her luminous face and her fine, stray hair! But he felt far away.

"Anything I can do for you?" he asked.

"No, thank you—I'll sleep," she replied, smiling. And the strange golden spark danced on her eyes again, again he felt as if his heart

15 were gone, destroyed out of him. There was a fine pathos too in her vivid, dangerous face.

He kissed her for the last time, saying:

"I'll blow the candles out, then?"

"Yes, my love—and I'll sleep."

20 "Yes—sleep as long as you like."

The golden spark of her eyes seemed to dance on him like a destruction, she was beautiful, and pathetic. He touched her tenderly with his finger-tips, then suddenly blew out the candles, and walked across in the faint moonlight to the door.

25 He was gone. She heard his boots click on the stone stairs—she heard the far below tread of his feet on the pavement. Then he was gone. She lay quite still, in a swoon of deathly peace. She never wanted to move any more. It was finished. She lay quite still, utterly, utterly abandoned.

30 But again she was disturbed. There was a little tap at the door, then Teresa's voice saying, with a shuddering sound because of the cold:

"Ugh!—I'm coming to you, Marta my dear. I can't stand being left alone."

35 "I'll make a light," said Marta, sitting up and reaching for the candle. "Lock the door, will you, Resie, and then nobody can bother us."

She saw Teresa, loosely wrapped in her cloak, two thick ropes of hair hanging untidily. Teresa looked voluptuously sleepy and easy,

40 like a cat running home to the warmth.

"Ugh!" she said, "it's cold!"

And she ran to the stove. Marta heard the chink of the little shovel, a stirring of coals, then a clink of the iron door. Then Teresa came running to the bed, with a shuddering little run, she puffed out the light and slid in beside her friend.

"So cold!" she said, with a delicious shudder at the warmth. Marta made place for her, and they settled down.

"Aren't you glad you're not them?" said Resie, with a little shudder at the thought. "Ugh!—poor devils!"

"I am," said Marta.

"Ah, sleep—sleep, how lovely!" said Teresa, with deep content. "Ah, it's so good!"

"Yes," said Marta.

"Good morning, good night, my dear," said Teresa, already sleepily.

"Good night," responded Marta.

Her mind flickered a little. Then she sank unconsciously to sleep. The room was silent.

Outside, the setting moon made peaked shadows of the high-roofed houses; from twin towers that stood like two dark, companion giants in the sky, the hour trembled out over the sleeping town. But the footsteps of hastening officers and cowering soldiers rang on the frozen pavements. Then a lantern appeared in the distance, accompanied by the rattle of a bullock wagon. By the light of the lantern on the wagon-pole could be seen the delicately moving feet and the pale, swinging dewlaps of the oxen. They drew slowly on, with a rattle of heavy wheels, the banded heads of the slow beasts swung rhythmically.

Ah, this was life! How sweet, sweet each tiny incident was! How sweet to Friedeburg, to give his orders ringingly on the frosty air, to see his men like bears shambling and shuffling into their places, with little dancing movements of uncouth playfulness and resentment, because of the pure cold.

Sweet, sweet it was to be marching beside his men, sweet to hear the great thresh-thresh of their heavy boots in the unblemished silence, sweet to feel the immense mass of living bodies co-ordinated into oneness near him, to catch the hot waft of their closeness, their breathing. Friedeburg was like a man condemned to die, catching at every impression as at an inestimable treasure.

Sweet it was to pass through the gates of the town, the scanty, loose suburb, into the open darkness and space of the country. This was almost best of all. It was like emerging in the open plains of eternal freedom.

They saw a dark figure hobbling along under the dark side of a shed. As they passed, through the open door of the shed, in the golden light were seen the low rafters, the pale, silken sides of the cows, evanescent. And a woman with a red kerchief bound round her head lifted her face from the flank of the beast she was milking, to look at the soldiers threshing like multitudes of heavy ghosts down the darkness. Some of the men called to her, cheerfully, impudently. Ah, the miraculous beauty and sweetness of the merest trifles like these!

They tramped on down a frozen, rutty road, under lines of bare trees. Beautiful trees! Beautiful frozen ruts in the road! Ah, even, in one of the ruts there was a silver of ice and of moon-glimpse. He heard ice tinkle as a passing soldier purposely put his toe in it. What a sweet noise!

But there was a vague uneasiness. He heard the men arguing as to whether dawn were coming. There was the silver moon, still riding on the high seas of the sky. A lovely thing she was, a jewel! But was there any blemish of day? He shrank a little from the rawness of the day to come. This night of morning was so rare and free.

Yes, he was sure. He saw a colorless paleness on the horizon. The earth began to look hard, like a great, concrete shadow. He shrank into himself. Glancing at the ranks of his men, he could see them like a company of rhythmic ghosts. The pallor was actually reflected on their livid faces. This was the coming day! It frightened him.

The dawn came. He saw the rosiness of it hang trembling with light, above the east. Then a strange glamor of scarlet passed over the land. At his feet, glints of ice flashed scarlet, even the hands of the men were red as they swung, sinister, heavy, reddened.

The sun surged up, her rim appeared, swimming with fire, hesitating, surging up. Suddenly there were shadows from trees and ruts, and grass was hoar and ice was gold against the ebony shadow. The faces of the men were alight, kindled with life. Ah, it was magical, it was all too marvellous! If only it were always like this!

When they stopped at the inn for breakfast, at nine o'clock, the smell of the inn went raw and ugly to his heart: beer and yesterday's tobacco!

He went to the door to look at the men biting huge bites from their hunks of grey bread, or cutting off pieces with their clasp-knives. This made him still happy. Women were going to the fountain for water, the soldiers were chaffing them coarsely. He liked all this.

But the magic was going, inevitably, the crystal delight was thawing to desolation in his heart, his heart was cold, cold mud. Ah, it was awful. His face contracted, he almost wept with cold, stark despair.

Still he had the work, the day's hard activity with the men. Whilst this lasted, he could live. But when this was over, and he had to face the horror of his own cold-thawing mud of despair: ah, it was not to be thought of. Still, he was happy at work with the men: the wild desolate place, the hard activity of mock warfare. Would to God it were real: war, with the prize of death!

By afternoon the sky had gone one dead, livid level of grey. It seemed low down, and oppressive. He was tired, the men were tired, and this let the heavy cold soak in to them like despair. Life could not keep it out.

And now, when his heart was so heavy it could sink no more, he must glance at his own situation again. He must remember what a fool he was, his new debts like half thawed mud in his heart. He knew, with the cold misery of hopelessness, that he would be turned out of the army. What then?—what then but death? After all, death was the solution for him. Let it be so.

They marched on and on, stumbling with fatigue under a great leaden sky, over a frozen dead country. The men were silent with weariness, the heavy motion of their marching was like an oppression. Friedeburg was tired too, and deadened, as his face was deadened by the cold air. He did not think any more; the misery of his soul was like a frost inside him.

He heard someone say it was going to snow. But the words had no meaning for him. He marched as a clock ticks, with the same monotony, everything numb and cold-soddened.

They were drawing near to the town. In the gloom of the afternoon he felt it ahead, as unbearable oppression on him. Ah the hideous suburb! What was his life, how did it come to pass that life was lived in a formless, hideous grey structure of hell! What did it all mean? Pale, sulphur-yellow lights spotted the livid air, and people, like soddened shadows, passed in front of the shops that were lit up ghastly in the early twilight. Out of the colorless space, crumbs of snow came and bounced animatedly off the breast of his coat.

At length he turned away home, to his room, to change and get warm and renewed, for he felt as cold-soddened as the grey, cold, heavy bread which felt hostile in the mouths of the soldiers. His life was to him like this dead, cold bread in his mouth.

5   As he neared his own house, the snow was peppering thinly down. He became aware of some unusual stir about the house-door. He looked—a strange, closed-in wagon, people, police. The sword of Damocles* that had hung over his heart, fell. O God, a new shame, some new shame, some new torture! His body moved on. So it would

10 move on through misery upon misery, as is our fate. There was no emergence, only this progress through misery unto misery, till the end. Strange, that human life was so tenacious! Strange, that men had made of life a long, slow process of torture to the soul. Strange, that it was no other than this! Strange, that but for man, this misery

15 would not exist. For it was not God's misery, but the misery of the world of man.

He saw two officials push something white and heavy into the cart, shut the doors behind with a bang, turn the silver handle, and run round to the front of the wagon. It moved off. But still most of the

20 people lingered. Friedeburg drifted near in that inevitable motion which carries us through all our shame and torture. He knew the people talked about him. He went up the steps and into the square hall.

There stood a police-officer, with a note-book in his hand, talking

25 to Herr Kapell, the housemaster. As Friedeburg entered through the swing door, the housemaster, whose brow was wrinkled in anxiety and perturbation, made a gesture with his hand, as if to point out a criminal.

"Ah!—the Herr Baron von Friedeburg!" he said, in self-

30 exculpation.

The police officer turned, saluted politely, and said, with the polite, intolerable *suffisance** of officialdom:

"Good evening! Trouble here!"

"Yes?" said Friedeburg.

35 He was so frightened, his sensitive constitution was so lacerated, that something broke in him, he was a subservient, murmuring ruin.

"Two young ladies found dead in your room," said the police-official, making an official statement. But under this cold impartiality of officialdom, what obscene unction! Ah, what obscene exposures

40 now!

"Dead!" ejaculated Friedeburg, with the wide eyes of a child. He became quite child-like, the official had him completely in his power. He could torture him as much as he liked.

"Yes." He referred to his note-book. "Asphyxiated by fumes from the stove." 5

Friedeburg could only stand wide-eyed and meaningless.

"Please—will you go upstairs?"

The police-official marshalled Friedeburg in front of himself. The youth slowly mounted the stairs, feeling as if transfixed through the base of the spine, as if he would lose the use of his legs. The 10 official followed close on his heels.

They reached the bedroom. The policeman unlocked the door. The housekeeper followed with a lamp. Then the official examination began.

"A young lady slept here last night?" 15

"Yes."

"Name, please?"

"Marta Hohenest."

"H-o-h-e-n-e-s-t," spelled the official. "—And address?"

Friedeburg continued to answer. This was the end of him. The 20 quick of him was pierced and killed. The living dead answered the living dead in obscene antiphony. Question and answer continued, the note-book worked as the hand of the old dead wrote in it the replies of the young who was dead.

The room was unchanged from the night before. There was her 25 heap of clothing, the lustrous, pure-red dress lying soft where she had carelessly dropped it. Even, on the edge of the chair-back, her crimson silk garters hung looped.

But do not look, do not see. It is the business of the dead to bury their dead.* Let the young dead bury their own dead, as the old dead 30 have buried theirs. How can the dead remember, they being dead? Only the living can remember, and are at peace with their living who have passed away.

The Thimble

She had not seen her husband for ten months, not since her fortnight's honeymoon with him, and his departure for France. Then, in those excited days of the early war, he was her comrade, her counterpart in a sort of Bacchic revel before death. Now all that was shut off from her mind, as by a great rent in her life.

Since then, since the honeymoon, she had lived and died and come to life again. There had been his departure to the front. She had loved him then.

"If you want to love your husband," she had said to her friends, with splendid recklessness, "you should see him in khaki." And·she had really loved him, he was so handsome in uniform, well-built, yet with a sort of reserve and remoteness that suited the neutral khaki perfectly.

Before, as a barrister with nothing to do, he had been slack and unconvincing, a sort of hanger-on, and she had never come to the point of marrying him. For one thing they neither of them had enough money.

Then came the great shock of the war, his coming to her in a new light, as lieutenant in the artillery. And she had been carried away by his perfect calm manliness and significance, now he was a soldier. He seemed to have gained a fascinating importance, that made her seem quite unimportant. It was she who was insignificant and subservient, he who was dignified, with a sort of indifferent lordliness.

So she had married him, all considerations flung to the wind, and had known the bewildering experience of their fortnight's honeymoon, before he left her for the front.

And she had never got over her bewilderment. She had, since then, never thought at all, she seemed to have rushed on in a storm of activity and sensation. There was a home to make, and no money to make it with: none to speak of. So, with the swift, business-like aptitude of a startled woman, she had found a small flat in Mayfair,* had attended sales and bought suitable furniture, had made the place complete and perfect. She was satisfied. It was small and insignificant, but it was a complete unity.

Then she had had a certain amount of war-work to do, and she had kept up all her social activities. She had not had a moment which was not urgently occupied.

All the while, came his letters from France, and she was writing her replies. They both sent a good deal of news to each other, they both expressed their mutual passion.

Then suddenly, amid all this activity, she fell ill with pneumonia, and everything lapsed into delirium. And whilst she was ill, he was wounded, his jaw smashed and his face cut up by the bursting of a shell. So they were both laid by.

Now, they were both better, and she was waiting to see him. Since she had been ill, whilst she had lain or sat in her room in the castle in Scotland, she had thought, thought very much. For she was a woman who was always trying to grasp the whole of her context, always trying to make a complete thing of her own life.

Her illness lay between her and her previous life like a dark night, like a great separation. She looked back, she remembered all she had done, and she was bewildered, she had no key to the puzzle. Suddenly she realized that she knew nothing of the man she had married, he knew nothing of her. What she had of him, vividly, was the visual image. She could *see* him, the whole of him, in her mind's eye. She could remember him with peculiar distinctness, as if the whole of his body were lit up by an intense light, and the image fixed on her mind.

But he was an impression, only a vivid impression. What her own impression was, she knew most vividly. But what *he* was *himself*: the very thought startled her, it was like looking into a perilous darkness. All that she knew of him was her own affair, purely personal to her, a subjective impression. But there must be a *man*, another being, somewhere in the darkness which she had never broached.

The thought frightened her exceedingly, and her soul, weak from illness, seemed to weep. Here was a new peril, a new terror. And she seemed to have no hope.

She could scarcely bear to think of him as she knew him. She could scarcely bear to conjure up that vivid image of him which remained from the days of her honeymoon. It was something false, it was something which had only to do with herself. The man himself was something quite other, something in the dark, something she dreaded, whose coming she dreaded, as if it were a mitigation of her own being, something set over against her, something that would annul her own image of herself.

Nervously she twisted her long white fingers. She was a beautiful woman, tall and loose and rather thin, with swinging limbs, one for whom the modern fashions were perfect.* Her skin was pure and clear, like a Christmas rose, her hair was fair and heavy. She had large, slow, unswerving eyes, that sometimes looked blue and open with a childish candour, sometimes greenish and intent with thought, sometimes hard, sea-like, cruel, sometimes grey and pathetic.

Now she sat in her own room, in the flat in Mayfair, and he was coming to see her. She was well again: just well enough to see him. But she was tired as she sat in the chair whilst her maid arranged her heavy, fair hair.

She knew she was a beauty, she knew it was expected of her that she should create an impression of modern beauty. And it pleased her, it made her soul rather hard and proud; but also, at the bottom, it bored her. Still, she would have her hair built high, in the fashionable mode, she would have it modelled to the whole form of her head, her figure. She lifted her eyes to look. They were slow, greenish, and cold like the sea at this moment, because she was so perplexed, so heavy with trying, all alone, always quite coldly alone, to understand, to understand, and to adjust herself. It never occurred to her to expect anything of the other person: she was utterly self-responsible.

"No," she said to her maid, in her slow, laconic, plangent voice, "don't let it swell out over the ears, lift it straight up, then twist it under—like that— so it goes clean from the side of the face. Do you see?"

"Yes my lady."

And the maid went on with the hair-dressing, and she with her slow, cold musing.

She was getting dressed now to see her bridegroom. The phrase, with its association in all the romances of the world, made her snigger involuntarily to herself. She was still like a schoolgirl, always seeing herself in her part. She got curious satisfaction from it too. But also she was always humorously ironical when she found herself in these romantic situations. If brigands and robbers had carried her off, she would have played up to the event perfectly. In life, however, there was always a certain painful, laborious heaviness, a weight of self-responsibility. The event never carried her along, a helpless protagonist. She was always responsible, in whatever situation.

Now, this morning, her husband was coming to see her, and she was dressing to receive him. She felt heavy and inert as stone, yet inwardly trembling convulsively. The known man, he did not affect her. Heavy and inert in her soul, yet amused, she would play her part in his reception. But the unknown man, what was he? Her dark, unknown soul trembled apprehensively.

At any rate he would be different. She shuddered. The vision she had of him, of the good-looking, clean, slightly tanned, attractive man, ordinary and yet with odd streaks of understanding that made her ponder, this she must put away. They said his face was rather horribly cut up.* She shivered. How she hated it, coldly hated and loathed it, the thought of disfigurement. Her fingers trembled, she rose to go downstairs. If he came he must not come into her bedroom.

So, in her fashionable but inexpensive black silk dress, wearing her jewels, her string of opals, her big, ruby brooch, she went downstairs. She knew how to walk, how to hold her body according to the mode. She did it almost instinctively, so deep was her consciousness of the impression her own appearance must create.

Entering the small drawing-room she lifted her eyes slowly and looked at herself: a tall, loose woman in black, with fair hair raised up, and with slow, greenish, cold eyes looking into the mirror. She turned away with a cold, pungent sort of satisfaction. She was aware also of the traces of weariness and illness and age, in her face. She was twenty-seven years old.

So she sat on the little sofa by the fire. The room she had made was satisfactory to her, with its neutral, brown grey walls, its deep brown, plain, velvety carpet, and the old furniture done in worn rose brocade, which she had bought from Countess Ambersyth's sale. She looked at her own large feet,* upon the rose-red Persian rug.

Then nervously, yet quite calm, almost static, she sat still to wait. It was one of the moments of deepest suffering and suspense, which she had ever known. She did not want to think of his disfigurement, she did not want to have any preconception of it. Let it come upon her. And the man, the unknown strange man who was coming now to take up his position over against her soul, her soul so naked and exposed from illness, the man to whose access her soul was to be delivered up!—she could not bear it. Her face set pale, she began to lose her consciousness.

Then something whispered in her:

"If I am like this, I shall be quite impervious to him, quite
5   oblivious of anything but the surface of him." And an anxious sort of hope sent her hands down on to the sofa at her side, pressed upon the worn brocade, spread flat. And she remained in suspense.

But could she bear it, could she bear it? She was weak and ill in a sort of after-death. Now what was this that she must confront, this
10   other being? Her hands began to move slowly backwards and forwards on the sofa bed, slowly, as if the friction of the silk gave her some ease.

She was unaware of what she was doing. She was always so calm, so self-contained, so static; she was much too stoically well-bred to
15   allow these outward nervous agitations. But now she sat still in suspense in the silent drawing room, where the fire flickered over the dark brown carpet and over the pale rose furniture and over the pale face and the black dress and the white, sliding hands of the woman, and her hands slid backwards and forwards, backwards and
20   forwards like a pleading, a hope, a tension of madness.

Her right hand came to the end of the sofa and pressed a little into the crack, the meeting between the arm and the sofa bed. Her long white fingers pressed into the fissure, pressed and entered rhythmically, pressed and pressed further and further into the tight depths of
25   the fissure, between the silken, firm upholstery of the old sofa, whilst her mind was in a trance of suspense, and the firelight flickered on the yellow chrysanthemums that stood in a jar in the shadows.*

The working, slow, intent fingers pressed deeper and deeper in the fissure of the sofa, pressed and worked their way intently, to the
30   bottom. It was the bottom. They were there, they made sure. Making sure, they worked all along, very gradually, along the tight depth of the fissure.

Then they touched a little extraneous object, and a consciousness awoke in the woman's mind. Was it something? She touched again. It
35   was something hard and rough. The fingers began to ply upon it. How firmly it was embedded in the depths of the sofa-crack. It had a thin rim, like a ring, but it was not a ring. The fingers worked more insistently. What was the little hard object?

The fingers pressed determinedly, they moved the little object.
40   They began to work it up to the light. It was coming, there was

success. The woman's heart relaxed from its tension, now her aim was being achieved. Her long, strong, white fingers brought out the little find.

It was a thimble* set with brilliants; it was an old, rather heavy thimble of tarnished gold, set round the base with little diamonds or rubies. Perhaps it was not gold, perhaps they were only paste.

She put it on her sewing finger. The brilliants sparkled in the firelight. She was pleased. It was a vulgar thing, a gold thimble with ordinary pin-head dents, and a belt of jewels round the base. It was large too, big enough for her. It must have been some woman's embroidery thimble, some bygone woman's, perhaps some Lady Ambersyth's. At any rate, it belonged to the days when women did stitching as a usual thing. But it was heavy, it would make one's hand ache.

She began to rub the gold with her handkerchief. There was an engraved monogram, an Earl's, and then Z, Z, and a date 15 Oct. 1801. She was very pleased, trembling with the thought of the old romance. What did Z. stand for? She thought of her acquaintance, and could only think of Zouche. But he was not an Earl. Who would give the gift of a gold thimble set with jewels, in the year 1801? Perhaps it was a man come home from the wars: there were wars then.

The maid noiselessly opened the door and saw her mistress sitting in the soft light of the winter day, polishing something with her handkerchief.

"Mr Hepburn has come, my lady."

"Has he!" answered the laconic, slightly wounded voice of the woman.

She collected herself and rose. Her husband was coming through the doorway, past the maid. He came without hat or coat or gloves, like an inmate of the house. He was an inmate of the house.

"How do you do?" she said, with stoic, plangent helplessness. And she held out her hand.

"How are *you*?" he replied, rather mumbling, with a sort of muffled voice.

"All right now, thanks," and she sat down again, her heart beating violently. She had not yet looked at his face. The muffled voice terrified her so much. It mumbled rather mouthlessly.

Abstractedly, she put the thimble on her middle finger, and continued to rub it with her handkerchief. The man sat in silence opposite, in an arm-chair. She was aware of his khaki trousers and his brown shoes. But she was intent on burnishing the thimble.

Her mind was in a trance, but as if she were on the point of waking, for the first time in her life, waking up.

5   "What are you doing? What have you got?" asked the mumbling, muffled voice. A pang went through her. She looked up at the mouth that produced the sound. It was broken in, the bottom teeth all gone, the side of the chin battered small, whilst a deep seam, a deep, horrible groove ran right into the middle of the cheek. But the mouth
10   was the worst, sunk in at the bottom, with half the lip cut away.

"It is treasure-trove," answered her plangent, cold-sounding voice. And she held out the thimble.

He reached to take it. His hand was white, and it trembled. His nerves were broken. He took the thimble between his fingers.

15   She sat obsessed, as if his disfigurement were photographed upon her mind, as if she were some sensitive medium to which the thing had been transferred. There it was, her whole consciousness was photographed into an image of his disfigurement, the dreadful sunken mouth that was not a mouth, which mumbled in talking to
20   her, in a disfigurement of speech.

It was all accident, accident had taken possession of her very being. All she was, was purely accidental. It was like a sleep, a thin, taut, overfilming sleep in which the wakefulness struggles like a thing as yet unborn. She was sick in the thin, transparent membrane of her
25   sleep, her overlying dream-consciousness, something actual but too unreal.

"How treasure-trove?" he mumbled. She could not understand. "How what?"

She felt his moment's hesitation before he tried again, and a hot
30   pain pierced through her, the pain of his maimed crippled effort.

"Treasure-trove, you said," he repeated, with a sickening struggle to speak distinctly.

Her mind hovered, then grasped, then caught the threads of the conversation.

35   "I found it," she said. Her voice was clear and vibrating as bronze, but cold. "I found it just before you came in."

There was a silence. She was aware of the purely accidental condition of her whole being. She was framed and constructed of accident, accidental association. It was like being made up of
40   dream-stuff, without sequence or adherence to any plan or purpose.

Yet within the imprisoning film of the dream was herself, struggling unborn, struggling to come to life.

It was difficult to break the inert silence that had succeeded between them. She was afraid it would go on forever. With a strange, convulsive struggle, she broke into communication with him. 5

"I found it here, in the sofa," she said, and she lifted her eyes for the first time to him.

His forehead was white, and his hair brushed smooth, like a sick man's. And his eyes were like the eyes of a child that has been ill, blue and abstract, as if they only listened from a long way off, and did 10 not see any more. So far-off, he looked, like a child that belongs almost more to death than to life. And her soul divined, that he was waiting vaguely where the dark and the light divide, whether he should come in to life, or hesitate, and pass back.

She lowered her eyelids, and for a second she sat erect like a mask, 15 with closed eyes, whilst a spasm of pure unconsciousness passed over her. It departed again, and she opened her eyes. She was awake.

She looked at him. His eyes were still abstract and without answer, changing only to the dream-psychology of his being. She contracted as if she were cold and afraid. They lit up now with a superficial 20 over-flicker of interest.

"Did you really? Why how did it come there?"

It was the same voice, the same stupid interest in accidental things, the same man as before. Only the enunciation of the words was all mumbled and muffled, as if the speech itself were disinte- 25 grating.

Her heart shrank, to close again like an over-sensitive new-born thing, that is not yet strong enough in its own being. Yet once more she lifted her eyes, and looked at him.

He was flickering with his old, easily-roused, spurious interest in 30 the accidentals of life. The film of separateness seemed to be coming over her. Yet his white forehead was somewhat deathly, with its smoothly brushed hair. He was like one dead. He was within the realm of death. This over-flicker of interest was only extraneous.

"I suppose it had got pushed down by accident," she said, 35 answering from her mechanical mind.

But her eyes were watching him who was dead, who was there like Lazarus* before her, as yet unrisen.

"How did it happen?" she said, and her voice was changed, penetrating with sadness and approach. He knew what she meant. 40

"Well, you see I was knocked clean senseless, and that was all I knew for three days. But it seems that it was a shell fired by one of our own fellows, and it hit me because it was faultily made."

Her face was very still as she watched.

5   "And how did you feel when you came round?"

"I felt pretty bad, as you can imagine: there was a crack on the skull as well as this on the jaw."

"Did you think you were going to die?"

There was a long pause, whilst the man laughed self-consciously.
10 But he laughed only with the upper part of his face: the maimed part remained still. And though the eyes seemed to laugh, just as of old, yet underneath them was a black, challenging darkness. She waited whilst this superficial smile of reserve passed away.

Then came the mumbling speech, simple, in confession.

15   "Yes, I lay and looked at it."

The darkness of his eyes was now watching her, her soul was exposed and new-born. The triviality was gone, the dream-psychology, the self-dependence. They were naked and new-born in soul, and dependent on each other.

20   It was on the tip of her tongue to say: "And why didn't you die?" But instead, her soul, weak and new-born, looked helplessly at him.

"I couldn't while you were alive," he said.

"What?"

"Die."

25   She seemed to pass away into unconsciousness. Then, as she came to, she said, as if in protest:

"What difference should *I* make to you! You can't live off me."

He was watching her with unlighted, sightless eyes. There was a long silence. She was thinking, it was not her consciousness of him
30 which had kept *her* alive. It was her own will.

"What did you hope for, from me?" she asked.

His eyes darkened, his face seemed very white, he really looked like a dead man as he sat silent and with open, sightless eyes. Between his slightly-trembling fingers was balanced the thimble,
35 that sparkled sometimes in the firelight. Watching him, a darkness seemed to come over her. She could not see, he was only a presence near her in the dark.

"We are both of us helpless," she said, into the silence.

"Helpless for what?" answered his sightless voice.
40   "To live," she said.

They seemed to be talking to each other's souls, their eyes and minds were sightless.

"We are helpless to live," he repeated.

"Yes," she said.

There was still a silence. 5

"I know," he said, "we are helpless to live. I knew that when I came round."

"I am as helpless as you are," she said.

"Yes," came his slow, half-articulate voice. "I know that. You're as helpless as I am." 10

"Well then?"

"Well then, we are helpless. We are as helpless as babies," he said.

"And how do you like being a helpless baby?" came her ironic voice. 15

"And how do *you* like being a helpless baby?" he replied.

There was a long pause. Then she laughed brokenly.

"I don't know," she said. "A helpless baby can't know whether it likes being a helpless baby."

"That's just the case. But I feel *hope*, don't you?" 20

Again there was an unwilling pause on her part.

"Hope of what?"

"If I am a helpless baby now, that I shall grow into a man."

She gave a slight, amused laugh.

"And I ought to hope that I shall grow into a woman?" she said. 25

"Yes, of course."

"Then what am I now?" she asked, humorously.

"Now you're a helpless baby, as you said."

It piqued her slightly. Then again, she knew it was true.

"And what was I before—when I married you?" she asked, 30
challenging.

"Why, then—I don't know what you were. I've had my head cracked and some dark let in, since then. So I don't know what you were, because it's all gone, don't you see."

"I see." 35

There was a pause. She became aware of the room about her, of the fire burning low and red.

"And what are we doing together?" she said.

"We're going to love each other," he said.

"Didn't we love each other before?" challenged her voice. 40

"No, we couldn't. We weren't born."

"Neither were we dead," she answered.

He seemed struck.

"Are we dead now?" he asked in fear.

5   "Yes, we are."

There was a suspense of anguish, it was so true.

"Then we must be born again,"* he said.

"Must we?" said her deliberate, laconic voice.

"Yes, we must—otherwise— —"

10   He did not finish.

"And do you think we've got the power to come to life again, now we're dead?" she asked.

"I think we have," he said.

There was a long pause.

15   "Resurrection?" she said, almost as if mocking. They looked slowly and darkly into each other's eyes. He rose unthinking, went over and touched her hand.

"'Touch me not, for I am not yet ascended unto the Father',"*'she quoted, in her level, cold-sounding voice.

20   "No," he answered; "it takes time."

The incongruous plainness of his statement made her jerk with laughter. At the same instant her face contracted and she said in a loud voice, as if her soul was being torn from her:

"Am I going to love you?"

25   Again he stretched forward and touched her hand, with the tips of his fingers. And the touch lay still, completed there.

Then at length he noticed that the thimble was stuck on his little finger. In the same instant she also looked at it.

"I want to throw it away," he said.

30   Again she gave a little jerk of laughter.

He rose, went to the window, and raised the sash. Then, suddenly, with a strong movement of the arm and shoulder, he threw the thimble out into the murky street. It bounded on the pavement opposite. Then a taxi-cab went by, and he could not see it any more.

Adolf

When we were children our father often worked on the night-shift. Once it was spring-time, and he used to arrive home, black and tired, just as we were downstairs in our nightdresses. Then night met morning face to face, and the contact was not always happy. Perhaps it was painful to my father to see us gaily entering upon the day into which he dragged himself soiled and weary. He didn't like going to bed in the spring morning sunshine.

But sometimes he was happy, because of his long walk through the dewy fields in the first daybreak. He loved the open morning, the crystal and the space, after a night down pit.* He watched every bird, every stir in the trembling grass, answered the whinneying of the pee-wits and tweeted to the wrens. If he could he also would have whinnied and tweeted and whistled in a native language that was not human. He like non-human things best.

One sunny morning we were all sitting at table when we heard his heavy slurring walk up the entry.* We became uneasy. His was always a disturbing presence, trammelling. He passed the window darkly, and we heard him go into the scullery and put down his tin bottle. But directly he came into the kitchen. We felt at once that he had something to communicate. No one spoke. We watched his black face for a second.

"Give me a drink," he said.

My mother hastily poured out his tea. He went to pour it out into his saucer. But instead of drinking he suddenly put something on the table among the teacups. A tiny brown rabbit! A small rabbit, a mere morsel, sitting against the bread as still as if it were a made thing.

"A rabbit! A young one! Who gave it you, father?"

But he laughed enigmatically, with a sliding motion of his yellow-grey eyes, and went to take off his coat. We pounced on the rabbit.

"Is it alive? Can you feel its heart beat?"

My father came back and sat down heavily in his armchair. He

dragged his saucer to him, and blew his tea, pushing out his red lips
under his black moustache.

"Where did you get it, father?"

"I picked it up," he said, wiping his naked forearm over his mouth
5   and beard.

"Where?"

"Is it a wild one?" came my mother's quick voice.

"Yes, it is."

"Then why did you bring it?" cried my mother.

10   "Oh, we wanted it," came our cry.

"Yes, I've no doubt you did——" retorted my mother. But she
was drowned in our clamour of questions.

On the field path my father had found a dead mother rabbit and
three dead little ones—this one alive, but unmoving.

15   "But what had killed them, daddy?"

"I couldn't say, my child. I s'd think she'd aten something."

"Why did you bring it!" again my mother's voice of condem-
nation. "You know what it will be."

My father made no answer, but we were loud in protest.

20   "He must bring it. It's not big enough to live by itself. It would
die," we shouted.

"Yes, and it will die now. And then there'll be *another* outcry."

My mother set her face against the tragedy of dead pets. Our
hearts sank.

25   "It won't die, father, will it? Why will it? It won't."

"I s'd think not," said my father.

"You know well enough it will. Haven't we had it all before—!"
said my mother.

"They dunna always pine," replied my father testily.

30   But my mother reminded him of other little wild animals he had
brought, which had sulked and refused to live, and brought storms of
tears and trouble in our house of lunatics.

Trouble fell on us. The little rabbit sat on our lap, unmoving, its
eye wide and dark. We brought it milk, warm milk, and held it to its
35   nose. It sat as still as if it were far away, retreated down some deep
burrow, hidden, oblivious. We wetted its mouth and whiskers with
drops of milk. It gave no sign, did not even shake off the wet white
drops. Somebody began to shed a few secret tears.

"What did I say?" cried my mother. "Take it and put it down in
40   the field."

Her command was in vain. We were driven to get dressed for school. There sat the rabbit. It was like a tiny obscure cloud. Watching it, the emotions died out of our breast. Useless to love it, to yearn over it. Its little feelings were all ambushed. They must be circumvented. Love and affection were a trespass upon it. A little wild thing, it became more mute and asphyxiated still in its own arrest, when we approached with love. We must not love it. We must circumvent it, for its own existence.

So I passed the order to my sister and my mother. The rabbit was not to be spoken to, nor even looked at. Wrapping it in a piece of flannel I put it in an obscure corner of the cold parlour, and put a saucer of milk before its nose. My mother was forbidden to enter the parlour whilst we were at school.

"As if I should take any notice of your nonsense," she cried, affronted. Yet I doubt if she ventured into that parlour.

At midday, after school, creeping into the front room, there we saw the rabbit still and unmoving in the piece of flannel. Strange grey-brown neutralisation of life, still living! It was a sore problem to us.

"Why won't it drink its milk, mother?" we whispered. Our father was asleep.

"It prefers to sulk its life away, silly little thing." A profound problem. Prefers to sulk its life away! We put young dandelion leaves to its nose. The sphinx was not more oblivious. Yet its eye was bright.

At tea-time, however, it had hopped a few inches, out of its flannel, and there it sat down again, uncovered, a little solid cloud of muteness, brown, with unmoving whiskers. Only its side palpitated slightly with life.

Darkness came; my father set off to work. The rabbit was still unmoving. Dumb despair was coming over the sisters, a threat of tears before bedtime. Clouds of my mother's anger gathered as she muttered against my father's wantonness.

Once more the rabbit was wrapped in the old pit-singlet. But now it was carried into the scullery and put under the copper fireplace,* that it might imagine* itself inside a burrow. The saucers were placed about, four or five, here and there on the floor, so that if the little creature *should* chance to hop abroad, it could not fail to come across some food. After this my mother was allowed to take from the scullery what she wanted and then she was forbidden to open the door.

When morning came and it was light, I went downstairs. Opening the scullery door, I heard a slight scuffle. Then I saw dabbles of milk all over the floor and tiny rabbit-droppings in the saucers. And there the miscreant, the tips of his ears showing behind a pair of boots. I
5 peeped at him. He sat bright-eyed and askance, twitching his nose and looking at me while not looking at me.

He was alive—very much alive. But still we were afraid to trespass much on his confidence.

"Father!" My father was arrested at the door. "Father, the
10 rabbit's alive."

"Back your life it is," said my father.

"Mind how you go in."

By evening, however, the little creature was tame, quite tame. He was christened Adolf. We were enchanted by him. We couldn't
15 really love him, because he was wild and loveless to the end. But he was an unmixed delight.

We decided he was too small to live in a hutch—he must live at large in the house. My mother protested, but in vain. He was so tiny. So we had him upstairs, and he dropped his tiny pills on the bed and
20 we were enchanted.

Adolf made himself instantly at home. He had the run of the house, and was perfectly happy, with his tunnels and his holes behind the furniture.

We loved him to take meals with us. He would sit on the table
25 humping his back, sipping his milk, shaking his whiskers and his tender ears, hopping off and hobbling back to his saucer, with an air of supreme unconcern. Suddenly he was alert. He hobbled a few tiny paces, and reared himself up inquisitively at the sugar-basin. He fluttered his tiny fore-paws, and then reached and laid them on the
30 edge of the basin, whilst he craned his thin neck and peeped in. He trembled his whiskers at the sugar, then did his best to lift down a lump.

"*Do* you think I will have it! Animals in the sugar pot!" cried my mother, with a rap of her hand on the table.

35 Which so delighted the electric Adolf that he flung his hind-quarters and knocked over a cup.

"It's your own fault, mother. If you had left him alone——"

He continued to take tea with us. He rather liked warm tea. And he loved sugar. Having nibbled a lump, he would turn to the butter.
40 There he was shooed off by our parent. He soon learned to treat her

shooing with indifference. Still, she hated him to put his nose in the
food. And he loved to do it. And so one day between them they
overturned the cream-jug. Adolf deluged his little chest, bounced
back in terror, was seized by his little ears by my mother and bounced
down on the hearth-rug. There he shivered in momentary discom-   5
fort, and suddenly set off in a wild flight to the parlour.

This last was his happy hunting ground. He had cultivated the bad
habit of pensively nibbling certain bits of cloth in the hearth-rug.
When chased from this pasture he would retreat under the sofa.
There he would twinkle in Buddhist meditation until suddenly, no   10
one knew why, he would go off like an alarm clock. With a sudden
bumping scuffle he would whirl out of the room, going through the
doorway with his little ears flying. Then we would hear his thunder-
bolt hurtling in the parlour, but before we could follow, the wild
streak of Adolf would flash past us, on an electric wind that swept   15
him round the scullery and carried him back, a little mad thing,
flying possessed like a ball round the parlour. After which ebullition
he would sit in a corner composed and distant, twitching his whiskers
in abstract meditation. And it was in vain we questioned him about
his outbursts. He just went off like a gun, and was as calm after it as a   20
gun that smokes placidly.

Alas, he grew up rapidly. It was almost impossible to keep him
from the outer door.

One day, as we were playing by the stile, I saw his brown shadow
loiter across the road and pass into the field that faced the houses.   25
Instantly a cry of "Adolf!" a cry he knew full well. And instantly a
wind swept him away down the sloping meadow, his tail twinkling
and zig-zagging through the grass. After him we pelted. It was a
strange sight to see him, ears back, his little loins so powerful,
flinging the world behind him. We ran ourselves out of breath, but   30
could not catch him. Then somebody headed him off, and he sat
with sudden unconcern, twitching his nose under a bunch of nettles.

His wanderings cost him a shock. One Sunday morning my father
had just been quarrelling with a pedlar, and we were hearing the
aftermath indoors, when there came a sudden unearthly scream   35
from the yard. We flew out. There sat Adolf cowering under a
bench, whilst a great black and white cat glowered intently at him, a
few yards away. Sight not to be forgotten. Adolf rolling back his eyes
and parting his strange muzzle in another scream, the cat stretching
forward in a slow elongation.   40

Ha, how we hated that cat! How we pursued him over the chapel wall and across the neighbours' gardens.

Adolf was still only half grown.

"Cats!" said my mother. "Hideous detestable animals, why do
5 people harbour them?"

But Adolf was becoming too much for her. He dropped too many pills. And suddenly to hear him clumping downstairs when she was alone in the house was startling. And to keep him from the door was impossible. Cats prowled outside. It was worse than having a child to
10 look after.

Yet we would not have him shut up. He became more lusty, more callous than ever. He was a strong kicker, and many a scratch on face and arms did we owe him. But he brought his own doom on himself. The lace curtains in the parlour—my mother was rather proud of
15 them—fell on to the floor very full. One of Adolf's joys was to scuffle wildly through them as though through some foamy undergrowth. He had already torn rents in them.

One day he entangled himself altogether. He kicked, he whirled round in a mad nebulous inferno. He screamed—and brought down
20 the curtain-rod with a smash, right on the best beloved pelargonium, just as my mother rushed in. She extricated him, but she never forgave him. And he never forgave either. A heartless wildness had come over him.

Even we understood that he must go. It was decided, after a long
25 deliberation, that my father should carry him back to the wild-woods. Once again he was stowed into the great pocket of the pit-jacket.

"Best pop him i' th' pot," said my father, who enjoyed raising the wind of indignation.

30 And so, next day, our father said that Adolf, set down on the edge of the coppice, had hopped away with utmost indifference, neither elated nor moved. We heard it and believed. But many, many were the heartsearchings. How would the other rabbits receive him? Would they smell his tameness, his humanised degradation, and
35 rend him? My mother pooh-poohed the extravagant idea.

However, he was gone, and we were rather relieved. My father kept an eye open for him. He declared that several times passing the coppice in the early morning, he had seen Adolf peeping through the nettlestalks. He had called him, in an odd, high-voiced, cajoling
40 fashion. But Adolf had not responded. Wildness gains so soon upon

its creatures. And they become so contemptuous then of our tame presence. So it seemed to me. I myself would go to the edge of the coppice, and call softly. I myself would imagine bright eyes between the nettlestalks, flash of a white, scornful tail, past the bracken. That insolent white tail, as Adolf turned his flank on us! It reminded me always of a certain rude gesture, and a certain unprintable phrase, which may not even be suggested.

But when naturalists discuss the meaning of the white rabbit's tail, that rude gesture and still ruder phrase always come to my mind. Naturalists say that the rabbit shows his white tail in order to guide his young safely after him, as a nursemaid's flying strings are the signal* to her toddling charges to follow on. How nice and naïve! I only know that my Adolf wasn't naïve. He used to whisk his flank at me, push his white feather in my eye, and say *Merde!** It's a rude word—but one which Adolf was always semaphoring at me, flag-wagging it with all the derision of his narrow haunches.

That's a rabbit all over—insolence, and the white flag of spiteful derision. Yes, and he keeps his flag flying to the bitter end, sporting, insolent little devil that he is. See him running for his life. Oh, how his soul is fanned to an ecstasy of fright, a fugitive whirlwind of panic. Gone mad, he throws the world behind him, with astonishing hind legs. He puts back his head and lays his ears on his sides and rolls the white of his eyes in sheer ecstatic agony of speed. He knows the awful approach behind him; bullet or stoat. He knows! He knows, his eyes are turned back almost into his head. It is agony. But it is also ecstasy. Ecstasy! See the insolent white flag bobbing. He whirls on the magic wind of terror. All his pent-up soul rushes into agonised electric emotion of fear. He flings himself on, like a falling star swooping into extinction. White heat of the agony of fear. And at the same time, bob! bob! bob! goes the white tail, *merde! merde! merde!* it says to the pursuer. The rabbit can't help it. In his utmost extremity he still flings the insult at the pursuer. He is the inconquerable fugitive, the indomitable meek. No wonder the stoat becomes vindictive.

And if he escapes, this precious rabbit! Don't you see him sitting there, in his earthly nook, a little ball of silence and rabbit-triumph? Don't you see the glint on his black eye? Don't you see, in his very immobility, how the whole world is *merde* to him? No conceit like the conceit of the meek. And if the avenging angel in the shape of the ghostly ferret steals down on him, there comes a shriek of terror out of that little hump of self-satisfaction sitting motionless in a corner.

Falls the fugitive. But even fallen, his white feather floats. Even in death it seems to say: "I am the meek, I am the righteous, I am the rabbit. All you rest, you are evil doers, and you shall be *bien emmerdés*!"*

Rex*

Since every family has its black sheep, it almost follows that every man must have a sooty uncle. Lucky if he hasn't two. However, it is only with my mother's brother that we are concerned. She had loved him dearly when he was a little blond boy. When he grew up black, she was always vowing she would never speak to him again. Yet when he put in an appearance, after years of absence, she invariably received him in a festive mood, and was even flirty with him.

He rolled up one day in a dog-cart, when I was a small boy. He was large and bullet-headed and blustering, and this time, sporty. Sometimes he was rather literary, sometimes coloured with business. But this time he was in checks, and was sporty. We viewed him from a distance.

The upshot was, would we rear a pup for him. Now my mother detested animals about the house. She could not bear the mix-up of human with animal life. Yet she consented to bring up the pup.

My uncle had taken a large, vulgar public-house in a large and vulgar town. It came to pass that I must fetch the pup. Strange for me, a member of the Band of Hope,* to enter the big, noisy, smelly plate-glass and mahogany public-house. It was called The Good Omen. Strange to have my uncle towering over me in the passage, shouting "Hello Johnny, what d'yer want?" He didn't know me. Strange to think he was my mother's brother, and that he had his bouts when he read Browning aloud with emotion and *éclat*.

I was given tea in a narrow, uncomfortable sort of living-room, half kitchen. Curious that such a palatial pub. should show such miserable private accommodation, but so it was. There was I, unhappy, and glad to escape with the soft fat pup. It was winter-time, and I wore a big-flapped black overcoat, half cloak. Under the cloak-sleeves I hid the puppy, who trembled. It was Saturday, and the train was crowded, and he whimpered under my coat. I sat in mortal fear of being hauled out for travelling without a dog-ticket. However, we arrived, and my torments were for nothing.

The others were wildly excited over the puppy. He was small and fat and white, with a brown-and-black head: a fox terrier. My father said he had a lemon head—some such mysterious technical phraseology. It wasn't lemon at all, but coloured like a field bee. And he had a black spot at the root of his spine.

5   It was Saturday night—bath-night. He crawled on the hearth-rug like a fat white tea-cup, and licked the bare toes that had just been bathed.

"He ought to be called Spot," said one. But that was too ordinary. It was a great question, what to call him.

10   "Call him Rex—the King," said my mother, looking down on the fat, animated little tea-cup, who was chewing my sister's little toe and making her squeal with joy and tickles. We took the name in all seriousness.

"Rex—the King!" We thought it was just right. Not for years did I
15   realise that it was a sarcasm on my mother's part. She must have wasted some twenty years or more of irony, on our incurable naïveté.

It wasn't a successful name, really. Because my father, and all the people in the street failed completely to pronounce the monosyllable *Rex*. They all said *Rax*. And it always distressed me. It always
20   suggested to me seaweed, and rack-and-ruin. Poor Rex!

We loved him dearly. The first night we woke to hear him weeping and whinneying in loneliness at the foot of the stairs. When it could be borne no more, I slipped down for him, and he slept under the sheets.

25   "I won't have that little beast in the beds. Beds are not for dogs," declared my mother callously.

"He's as good as *we* are!" we cried, injured.

"Whether he is or not, he's not going in the beds."

I think now, my mother scorned us for our lack of pride. We were
30   a little *infra dig.*, we children.

The second night, however, Rex wept the same and in the same way was comforted. The third night we heard our father plod downstairs, heard several slaps administered to the yelping, dismayed puppy, and heard the amiable, but to us heartless voice saying
35   "Shut it then! Shut thy noise, 'st hear? Stop in thy basket, stop there!"

"It's a shame!" we shouted, in muffled rebellion, from the sheets.

"*I'll* give you shame, if you don't hold your noise and go to sleep," called our mother from her room. Whereupon we shed angry tears
40   and went to sleep. But there was a tension.

"Such a houseful of idiots would make me detest the little beast, even if he was better than he is," said my mother.

But as a matter of fact, she did not detest Rexie at all. She only had to pretend to do so, to balance our adoration. And in truth, she did not care for close contact with animals. She was too fastidious.—My father, however, would take on a real dog's voice, talking to the puppy: a funny, high, sing-song falsetto which he seemed to produce at the top of his head.—"'s a pretty little dog! 's a pretty little doggy!—ay!—yes!—he is, yes!—Wag thy strunt,* then! Wag thy strunt, Raxie!—Ha-ha!—Nay, tha munna—"—This last as the puppy, wild with excitement at the strange falsetto voice, licked my father's nostrils and bit my father's nose with his sharp little teeth.

"'E makes blood come," said my father.

"Serves you right for being so silly with him," said my mother.

It was odd to see her as she watched the man, my father, crouching and talking to the little dog and laughing strangely when the little creature bit his nose and toused* his beard. What does a woman think of her husband at such a moment?—

My mother amused herself over the names we called him.

"He's an angel—he's a little butterfly—Rexie, my sweet!"

"Sweet! A dirty little object!" interpolated my mother.

She and he had a feud from the first. Of course he chewed boots and worried our stockings and swallowed our garters. The moment we took off our stockings he would dart away with one, we after him. Then as he hung, growling vociferously, at one end of the stocking, we at the other, we would cry:

"Look at him mother! He'll make holes in it again."

Whereupon my mother darted at him and spanked him sharply.

"Let go, Sir, you destructive little fiend."

But he didn't let go. He began to growl with real rage, and hung on viciously. Mite as he was, he defied her with a manly fury. He did not hate her, nor she him. But they had one long battle with one another.

"I'll teach you, my Jockey! Do you think I'm going to spend my life darning after your destructive little teeth! I'll show you if I will."

But Rexie only growled more viciously. They both became really angry, whilst we children expostulated earnestly with both. He would not let *her* take the stocking from him.

"You should tell him properly, mother. He won't be driven," we said.

"I'll drive him further than he bargains for. I'll drive him out of *my* sight for ever, that I will," declared my mother, truly angry. He would put her into a real temper, with his tiny, growling defiance.

"He's sweet! A Rexie, a little Rexie!"

5   "A filthy little nuisance! Don't think I'll put up with him."

And to tell the truth, he *was* dirty at first. How could he be otherwise, so young? But my mother hated him for it. And perhaps this was the real start of their hostility. For he lived in the house with us. He would wrinkle his nose and show his tiny dagger-teeth in fury

10 when he was thwarted, and his growls of real battle-rage against my mother rejoiced us as much as they angered her. But at last she caught him *in flagrante.** She pounced on him, rubbed his nose in the mess, and flung him out into the yard. He yelped with shame and disgust and indignation. I shall never forget the sight of him as he

15 rolled over, then tried to turn his head away from the disgust of his own muzzle, shaking his little snout with a sort of horror, and trying to sneeze it off. My sister gave a yell of despair, and dashed out with a rag and a pan of water, weeping wildly. She sat in the middle of the yard with the befouled puppy, and shedding bitter tears she wiped

20 him and washed him clean. Loudly she reproached my mother. "Look how much bigger you are than he is. It's a shame, it's a shame!"

"You ridiculous little lunatic, you've undone all the good it would do him, with your soft ways. Why is my life made a curse with

25 animals! Haven't I enough as it is—"

There was a subdued tension afterwards. Rex was a little white chasm between us and our parent.

He became clean. But then another tragedy loomed. He must be docked. His floating puppy-tail must be docked short. This time my

30 father was the enemy. My mother agreed with us, that it was an unnecessary cruelty. But my father was adamant. "The dog'll look a fool all his life if he's not docked." And there was no getting away from it. To add to the horror, poor Rex's tail must be *bitten* off. Why bitten?, we asked aghast. We were assured that biting was the only

35 way. A man would take the little tail and just nip it through with his teeth, at a certain joint. My father lifted his lips and bared his incisors, to suit the description. We shuddered. But we were in the hands of fate.

Rex was carried away, and a man called Rowbotham bit off the

40 superfluity of his tail in the *Nags Head*, for a quart of best and bitter.

We lamented our poor diminished puppy, but agreed to find him more manly and *comme il faut*. We should always have been ashamed of his little whip of a tail, if it had not been shortened. My father said it had made a man of him.

Perhaps it had. For now his true nature came out. And his true nature, like so much else, was dual. First he was a fierce, canine little beast, a beast of rapine and blood. He longed to hunt, savagely. He lusted to set his teeth in his prey. It was no joke with him. The old canine Adam stood first in him, the dog with fangs and glaring eyes. He flew at us when we annoyed him. He flew at all intruders, particularly the postman. He was *almost* a peril to the neighbourhood. But not quite. Because close second in his nature stood that fatal need to love, the *besoin d'aimer** which at last makes an end of liberty. He had a terrible, terrible necessity to love, and this trammelled the native, savage hunting beast which he was. He was torn between two great impulses: the native impulse to hunt and kill, and the strange, secondary, supervening impulse to love and obey. If he had been left to my father and mother, he would have run wild and got himself shot. As it was, he loved us children with a fierce, joyous love. And we loved him.

When we came home from school we would see him standing at the end of the entry, cocking his head wistfully at the open country in front of him, and meditating whether to be off or not: a white, inquiring little figure, with green savage freedom in front of him. A cry from a far distance from one of us, and like a bullet he hurled himself down the road, in a mad game. Seeing him coming, my sister invariably turned and fled, shrieking with delighted terror. And he would leap straight up her back, and bite her and tear her clothes. But it was only an ecstasy of savage love, and she knew it. She didn't care if he tore her pinafores. But my mother did.

My mother was maddened by him. He was a little demon. At the least provocation, he flew. You had only to sweep the floor, and he bristled and sprang at the broom. Nor would he leave go. With his scruff erect and his nostrils snorting rage, he would turn up the whites of his eyes at my mother, as she wrestled at the other end of the broom. "Leave go, Sir, leave *go*!" She wrestled and stamped her foot, and he answered with horrid growls. In the end it was *she* who had to let go. Then *she* flew at him, and he flew at her. All the time we had him, he was within a hair's-breadth of savagely biting her. And she knew it. Yet he always kept sufficient self-control.

We children loved his temper. We would drag the bones from his mouth, and put him into such paroxysms of rage that he would twist his head right over and lay it on the ground upside-down, because he didn't know what to do with himself, the savage was so strong in
5 him and he *must* fly at us. "He'll fly at your throat one of these days," said my father. Neither he nor my mother dared have touched Rex's bone. It was enough to see him bristle and roll the whites of his eyes when they came near. How near he must have been to driving his teeth right into *us*, cannot be told. He was a
10 horrid sight snarling and crouching at us. But we only laughed and rebuked him. And he would whimper in the sheer torment of his need to attack us.

He never did hurt us. He never hurt anybody, though the neighbourhood was terrified of him. But he took to hunting. To my
15 mother's disgust, he would bring large dead bleeding rats and lay them on the hearth-rug, and she had to take them up on a shovel. For he would not remove them. Occasionally he brought a mangled rabbit, and sometimes, alas, fragmentary poultry. We were in terror of prosecution. Once he came home bloody and feathery and rather
20 sheepish-looking. We cleaned him and questioned him and abused him. Next day we heard of six dead ducks. Thank heaven no one had seen him.

But he was disobedient. If he saw a hen he was off, and calling would not bring him back. He was worst of all with my father, who
25 would take him walks on Sunday morning. My mother would not walk a yard with him. Once, walking with my father, he rushed off at some sheep in a field. My father yelled in vain. The dog was at the sheep, and meant business. My father crawled through the hedge, and was upon him in time. And now the man was in a paroxysm of
30 rage. He dragged the little beast into the road and thrashed him with a walking stick.

"Do you know you're thrashing that dog unmercifully?" said a passer-by.

"Ay, an' mean to," shouted my father.

35 The curious thing was that Rex did *not* respect my father any the more, for the beatings he had from him. He took much more heed of us children, always.

But he let us down also. One fatal Saturday he disappeared. We hunted and called, but no Rex. We were bathed, and it was
40 bed-time, but we would not go to bed. Instead we sat in a row in our

night-dresses on the sofa, and wept without stopping. This drove our mother mad.

"*Am* I going to put up with it? *Am* I! And all for that hateful little beast of a dog! He shall go! If he's not gone now, he shall go."

Our father came in late, looking rather queer, with his hat over his eye. But in his staccato tippled fashion he tried to be consoling.

"Never mind, my duckie, I s'll look for him in the morning."

Sunday came—Oh, such a Sunday. We cried, and didn't eat. We scoured the land, and for the first time realised how empty and wide the earth is, when you're looking for something. My father walked for many miles—all in vain. Sunday dinner, with rhubarb pudding, I remember, and an atmosphere of abject misery that was unbearable.

"Never," said my mother, "never shall an animal set foot in this house again, while *I* live. I knew what it would be! I knew."

The day wore on, and it was the black gloom of bed-time, when we heard a scratch and an impudent little whine at the door. In trotted Rex, mud-black, disreputable, and impudent. His air of off-hand 'How d'ye do!' was indescribable. He trotted round with *suffisance*, wagging his tail as if to say "Yes, I've come back. But I didn't need to. I can carry on remarkably well by myself." Then he walked to his water, and dranked noisily and ostentatiously. It was rather a slap in the eye for us.

He disappeared once or twice in this fashion. We never knew where he went. And we began to feel that his heart was not so golden as we had imagined it.

But one fatal day re-appeared my uncle and the dog-cart. He whistled to Rex, and Rex trotted up. But when he wanted to examine the lusty, sturdy dog, Rex became suddenly still, then sprang free. Quite jauntily he trotted round—but out of reach of my uncle. He leaped up, licking our faces, and trying to make us play.

"Why what ha' you done wi' the dog—You've made a fool of him. He's softer than grease. You've ruined him. You've made a damned fool of him," shouted my uncle.

Rex was captured and hauled off to the dog-cart and tied to the seat. He was in a frenzy. He yelped and shrieked and struggled, and was hit on the head, hard, with the butt-end of my uncle's whip, which only made him struggle more frantically. So we saw him driven away, our beloved Rex, frantically, madly fighting to get to us from the high dog-cart, and being knocked down, whilst we stood in the street in mute despair.

After which, black tears, and a little wound which is still alive in our hearts.

I only saw Rex once again, when I had to call just once at the *Good Omen*. He must have heard my voice, for he was upon me in the passage before I knew where I was. And in the instant I knew *how* he loved us. He really loved us. And in the same instant there was my uncle with a whip, beating and kicking him back, and Rex cowering, bristling, snarling.

My uncle swore many oaths, how we had ruined the dog for ever, made him vicious, spoiled him for showing purposes, and been altogether a pack of mard-soft* fools not fit to be trusted with any dog but a gutter-mongrel.

Poor Rex! We heard his temper was incurably vicious, and he had to be shot.

And it was our fault. We had loved him too much, and he had loved us too much. We never had another pet.

It is a strange thing, love. Nothing but love has made the dog lose his wild freedom, to become the servant of man. And this very servility or completeness of love makes him a term of deepest contempt.—"You dog!"

We should not have loved Rex so much, and he should not have loved us. There should have been a measure. We tended, all of us, to overstep the limits of our own natures. He should have stayed outside human limits, we should have stayed outside canine limits. Nothing is more fatal than the disaster of too much love. My uncle was right, we had ruined the dog.

My uncle was a fool, for all that.

APPENDIX
'England, My England', 1915 version

Note on the text

The earliest surviving version of 'England, My England' is the uncorrected galley proofs (GP), located in the Nottinghamshire County Libraries, of the text in the *English Review* (xxi, October 1915, pp. 238–252) (Per1). GP is base-text and is emended twice from Per1. The variants for Per1 and for the *Metropolitan* magazine (April 1917) (Per 2) are recorded in the Textual apparatus.

The following forms in Per2 are not recorded unless in conjunction with another variant: 'while' for 'whilst', 'toward' for 'towards', 'forever' for 'for ever', 'highroad' for 'high-road'.

'England, My England', 1915 version

I.

The dream was still stronger than the reality. In the dream he was at home on a hot summer afternoon, working on the edge of the common, across the little stream at the bottom of the garden, carrying the garden path in continuation on to the common. He had cut the rough turf and the bracken, and left the grey, dryish soil bare. He was troubled because he could not get the path straight. He had set up his sticks, and taken the sights between the big pine-trees, but for some unknown reason everything was wrong. He looked again, strained and anxious, through the strong, shadowy pine-trees as through a doorway, at the green garden-path rising from the log bridge between sunlit flowers, tall purple and white columbines, to the butt-end of the old, beautiful cottage. Always, tense with anxiety, he saw the rising flowery garden and the sloping old roof of the cottage, beyond the intervening shadow, as in a mirage.

There was the sound of children's voices calling and talking: high, childish, girlish voices, plaintive, slightly didactic, and tinged with hard authoritativeness. "If you don't come soon, Nurse, I shall run out there where there are snakes."

Always this conflict of authority, echoed even in the children! His heart was hard with disillusion. He worked on in the gnawing irritation and resistance.

Set in resistance, he was all the time clinched upon himself. The sunlight blazed down upon the earth; there was a vividness of flamy vegetation and flowers, of tense seclusion amid the peace of the commons. The green garden-path went up between tall, graceful flowers of purple and white; the cottage with its great sloping roofs slept in the for-ever sunny hollow, hidden, eternal. And here he lived, in this ancient, changeless, eternal hollow of flowers and sunshine and the sloping-roofed house. It was balanced like a nest in a tree, this hollow home, always full of peace, always under heaven only. It had no context, no relation with the world; it held its cup under heaven alone, and was filled for ever with peace and sunshine and loveliness.

The shaggy, ancient heath that rose on either side, the downs that were pale against the sky in the distance, these were the extreme rims
5 of the cup. It was held up only to heaven; the world entered in not at all.

And yet the world entered in and goaded the heart. His wife, whom he loved, who loved him—she goaded the heart of him. She was young and beautiful and strong with life like a flame in the
10 sunshine; she moved with a slow grace of energy like a blossoming, red-flowered tree in motion. She, too, loved their hollow with all her heart. And yet she was like a weapon against him, fierce with talons of iron, to push him out of the nest-place he had made. Her soul was hard as iron against him, thrusting him away, always away. And his
15 heart was hard as iron against her in resistance.

They never put down their weapons for a day now. For a few hours, perhaps, they ceased to be in opposition; they let the love come forth that was in them. Then the love blazed and filled the old, silent hollow where the cottage stood, with flowers and magnificence
20 of the whole universe.

But the love passed in a few hours; only the cottage with its beauty remained like a mirage. He would abide by the mirage. The reality was the tension of the silent fight between him and his wife. He and she, as if fated, they were armed and exerting all their force to
25 destroy each other.

There was no apparent reason for it. He was a tall, thin, fair, self-contained man of the middle class, who, never very definite or positive in his action, had now set in rigid silence of negation. He kept rigid within himself, never altering nor yielding, however much
30 torture of repression he suffered.

Her ostensible grievance against him was that he made no money to keep his family; that, because he had an income of a hundred and fifty a year, he made no effort to do anything at all—he merely lived from day to day. Not that she accused him of being lazy; it was not
35 that; he was always at work in the garden; he had made the place beautiful. But was this all it amounted to? They had three children; she had said to him, savagely, she would have no more. Already her father was paying for the children's nurse, and helping the family at every turn. What would they do without her father? Could they
40 manage on a hundred and fifty a year, with a family of three children,

when they had both been brought up in plenty, and could not
consider pennies? Living simply as they did, they spent two hundred
and fifty a year; and now the children were tiny; what would it be
when they had to go to school? Yet Evelyn would not stir to obtain
any more.   5

Winifred, beautiful and obstinate, had all her passion driven into
her conscience. Her father was of an impoverished Quaker family.*
He had come down from Newcastle to London when he was a young
man, and there, after a hard struggle, had built up a moderate
fortune again. He had ceased to be a Quaker, but the spirit persisted   10
in him. A strong, sensual nature in himself, he had lived according to
the ideas of duty inculcated upon him, though his active life had been
inspired by a very worship of poetry and of poetic literature. He was a
business man by tradition, but by nature he was sensual, and he was
on his knees before a piece of poetry that really gratified him.   15
Consequently, whilst he was establishing a prosperous business, a
printing house and a small publishing house, at home he diffused the
old Quaker righteousness with a new, æsthetic sensuousness, and
his children were brought up in this sensuous heat, which was
always, at the same time, kept in the iron grate of conventional ethics.   20

Winifred had loved her husband passionately. He came of an old
south-of-England family,* refined and tending towards dilettantism.
He had a curious beauty of old breeding, slender and concentrated,
coupled with a strange inertia, a calm, almost stoic indifference
which her strong, crude, passionate, ethical nature could not   25
understand. She could not bear it that their marriage, after all the
tremendous physical passion that had convulsed them both, should
resolve gradually into this nullity. Her passion gradually hardened
into ethical desire. She wanted some result, some production, some
new vigorous output into the world of man, not only the hot physical   30
welter, and children.

Gradually she began to get dissatisfied with her husband. What
did he stand for? She had started with a strange reverence for him.
But gradually she fell away. A sense of meaninglessness came up
strong in her. He was so strangely inconclusive. Her robust,   35
undeveloped ethical nature was negated by him.

Then came the tragedy. They had three children, three fair-
haired flitting creatures, all girls. The youngest was still a baby. The
eldest, their love-child, was the favourite. They had wanted a boy in
place of the others.   40

Then one day this eldest child fell on a sharp old iron in the garden and cut her knee. Because they were so remote in the country she did not have the very best attention. Blood-poisoning set in. She was driven in a motor-car to London, and she lay, in dreadful
5 suffering, in the hospital, at the edge of death. They thought she must die. And yet in the end she pulled through.

In this dreadful time, when Winifred thought that if only they had had a better doctor at the first all this might have been averted, when she was suffering an agony every day, her husband only seemed to
10 get more distant and more absent and exempt. He stood always in the background, like an exempt, untouched presence. It nearly drove her mad. She had to go to her father for all advice and for all comfort. Her father brought the specialist to the child; her father came to Winifred and held his arm round her, and called her his darling, his
15 child, holding her safe, whilst all the time her husband stood aloof, silent, neutral. For this horrible neutrality, because of the horrible paralysis that seemed to come over him in these crises, when he could do nothing, she hated him. Her soul shrank from him in a revulsion. He seemed to introduce the element of horror, to make
20 the whole thing cold and unnatural and frightful. She could not forgive him that he made the suffering so cold and rare. He seemed to her almost like a pale creature of negation, detached and cold and reserved, with his abstracted face and mouth that seemed shut in eternity.
25 The child recovered, but was lame. Her leg was stiff and atrophied. It was an agony to both the parents, they who lived wholly by the physical life. But to the mother it was an open, active grief; to him it was silent and incommutable, nihilistic. He would not speak of the child if he could help it, and then only in an off-hand, negligent
30 fashion. So the distance was finally unsheathed between the parents, and it never really went away. They were separate, hostile. She hated his passivity as if it were something evil.

She taunted him that her father was having to pay the heavy bills for the child, whilst he, Evelyn, was idle, earning nothing. She asked
35 him, did he not intend to keep his own children; did he intend her father to support them all their lives? She told him, her six brothers and sisters* were not very pleased to see all the patrimony going on her children.

He asked her what could he do? She had talked all this out with
40 her father, who could easily find a suitable post for Evelyn; Evelyn

ought to work, everybody said. He was not idle; why, then, would he not do some regular work? Winifred spoke of another offer—would he accept that? He would not. But why? Because he did not think it was suitable, and he did not want it. Then Winifred was very angry. They were living in London, at double expense; the child was being massaged by an expensive doctor; her father was plainly dissatisfied; and still Evelyn would not accept the offers that were made him. He just negated everything, and went down to the cottage.

Something crystallised in Winifred's soul. She alienated herself from him. She would go on alone with her family, doing everything, not counting her negative husband.

This was the state of affairs for almost a year. The family continued chiefly in London; the child was still being massaged, in the hope of getting some use back into the leg. But she was a cripple; it was horrible to see her swing and fling herself along, a young, swift, flame-like child working her shoulders like a deformed thing. Yet the mother could bear it. The child would have other compensation. She was alive and strong; she would have her own life. Her mind and soul should be fulfilled. That which was lost to the body should be replaced in the soul. And the mother watched over, endlessly and relentlessly brought up the child when she used the side of her foot, or when she hopped, things which the doctor had forbidden. But the father could not bear it; he was nullified in the midst of life. The beautiful physical life was all life to him. When he looked at his distorted child, the crippledness seemed malignant, a triumph of evil and of nothingness. Henceforward he was a cipher. Yet he lived. A curious corrosive smile came on his face.

II.

It was at this point in their history that the war broke out. A shiver went over his soul. He had been living for weeks fixed without the slightest sentience. For weeks he had held himself fixed, so that he was impervious. His wife was set fast against him. She treated him with ignoring contempt; she ignored his existence. She would not mend his clothes, so that he went about with his shirt-shoulders slit into rags. She would not order his meals. He went to the kitchen and got his own. There was a state of intense hard hatred between them. The children were tentative and uncertain, or else defiant and ugly. The house was hard and sterile with negation. Only the mother gave herself up in a passion of ethical submission to her duty, and to a religion of physical self-sacrifice: which even yet she hardly believed in.

Yet the husband and wife were in love with each other. Or, rather, each held all the other's love dammed up.

The family was down at the cottage when war was declared. He took the news in his indifferent, neutral way. "What difference does it make to me?" seemed to be his attitude. Yet it soaked in to him. It absorbed the tension of his own life, this tension of a state of war. A flicker had come into his voice, a thin, corrosive flame, almost like a thin triumph. As he worked in the garden he felt the seethe of the war was with him. His consciousness had now a field of activity. The reaction in his soul could cease from being neutral; it had a positive form to take. There, in the absolute peace of his sloping garden, hidden deep in trees between the rolling of the heath, he was aware of the positive activity of destruction, the seethe of friction, the waves of destruction seething to meet, the armies moving forward to fight. And this carried his soul along with it.

The next time he went indoors he said to his wife, with the same thin flame in his voice:

"I'd better join, hadn't I?"

"Yes, you had," she replied; "that's just the very thing. You're just the man they want. You can ride and shoot, and you're so healthy and strong, and nothing to keep you at home."

She spoke loudly and confidently in her strong, pathetic, slightly deprecating voice, as if she knew she was doing what was right, however much it might mean to her.

The thin smile narrowed his eyes; he seemed to be smiling to himself, in a thin, corrosive manner. She had to assume all her impersonal righteousness to bear it.

"All right——" he said in his thin, jarring voice.

"We'll see what father says," she replied.

It should be left to the paternal authority to decide. The thin smile fixed on the young man's face.

The father-in-law approved heartily; an admirable thing for Evelyn to do, he thought; it was just such men as the country wanted. So it was the father-in-law who finally overcame the young man's inertia and despatched him to the war.

Evelyn Daughtry enlisted in a regiment which was stationed at Chichester,* and almost at once he was drafted into the artillery. He

hated very much the subordination, the being ordered about, and the having no choice over quite simple and unimportant things. He hated it strongly, the contemptible position he occupied as a private. And yet, because of a basic satisfaction he had in participating in the great destructive motion, he was a good soldier. His spirit acqui-   5
esced, however he despised the whole process of becoming a soldier.

Now his wife altered towards him and gave him a husband's dignity; she was almost afraid of him; she almost humbled herself before him. When he came home, an uncouth figure in the rough khaki, he who was always so slender and clean-limbed and beautiful   10
in motion, she felt he was a stranger. She was servant to his new arrogance and callousness as a soldier. He was now a quantity in life; he meant something. Also he had passed beyond her reach. She loved him; she wanted his recognition. Perhaps she had a thrill when he came to her as a soldier. Perhaps she too was fulfilled by him, now   15
he had become an agent of destruction, now he stood on the side of the Slayer.

He received her love and homage as tribute due. And he despised himself even for this. Yet he received her love as tribute due, and he enjoyed it. He was her lover for twenty-four hours. There was even a   20
moment of the beautiful tenderness of their first love. But it was gone again. When he was satisfied he turned away from her again. The hardness against her was there just the same. At the bottom of his soul he only hated her for loving him now he was a soldier. He despised himself as a soldier, ultimately. And she, when he had been   25
at home longer than a day, began to find that the soldier was a man just the same, the same man, only become callous and outside her ethical reach, positive now in his destructive capacity.

Still they had their days of passion and of love together when he had leave from the army. Somewhere at the back was the death he   30
was going to meet. In face of it they were oblivious of all but their own desire and passion for each other. But they must not see each other too often, or it was too great a strain to keep up, the closeness of love and the memory of death.

He was really a soldier. His soul had accepted the significance. He   35
was a potential destructive force, ready to be destroyed. As a potential destructive force he now had his being. What had he to do with love and the creative side of life? He had a right to his own satisfaction. He was a destructive spirit entering into destruction. Everything, then, was his to take and enjoy, whilst it lasted; he had   40

the right to enjoy before he destroyed or was destroyed. It was pure logic. If a thing is only to be thrown away, let anybody do with it what he will.

She tried to tell him he was one of the saviours of mankind. He listened to these things; they were very gratifying to his self-esteem. But he knew it was all cant. He was out to kill and destroy; he did not even want to be an angel of salvation. Some chaps might feel that way. He couldn't; that was all. All he could feel was that at best it was a case of kill or be killed. As for the saviour of mankind: well, a German was as much mankind as an Englishman. What are the odds? We're all out to kill, so don't let us call it anything else.

So he took leave of his family and went to France. The leave-taking irritated him, with its call upon his loving constructive self, he who was now a purely destructive principle. He knew he might not see them again, his wife and children. But what was the good of crying about it even then. He hated his wife for her little fit of passion at the last. She had wanted it, this condition of affairs; she had brought it about; why, then, was she breaking up at the last? Let her keep a straight face and carry it on as she had begun!

There followed the great disorder of the first days in France, such a misery of chaos that one just put up with it. Then he was really engaged. He hated it, and yet he was fulfilling himself. He hated it violently, and yet it gave him the only real satisfaction he could have in life now. Deeply and satisfactorily it fulfilled him, this warring on men. This work of destruction alone satisfied his deepest desire.

He had been twice slightly wounded in the two months. Now he was again in a dangerous position. There had been another retreat to be made, and he remained with three machine-guns covering the rear. The guns were stationed on a little bushy hillock just outside a village. Only occasionally—one could scarcely tell from what direction—came the sharp crackle of rifle fire, though the far-off thud of cannon hardly disturbed the unity of the winter afternoon.

Evelyn was working at the guns. Above him, in the sky, the lieutenant stood on the little iron platform at the top of the ladders, taking the sights and giving the aim, calling in a high, tense voice to the gunners below. Out of the sky came the sharp cry of the directions, then the warning numbers, then "Fire!" The shot went, the piston of the gun sprang back, there was a sharp explosion, and a very faint film of smoke in the air. Then the other two guns were

fired, and there was a lull. The officer on the stand was uncertain of
the enemy's position. Only in the far distance the sound of heavy
firing continued, so far off as to give a sense of peace.

The gorse bushes on either hand were wintry and dark, but there
was still the flicker of a few flowers. Kissing was never out of favour.   5
Evelyn, waiting suspended before the guns, mused on the abstract
truth. Things were all abstract and keen. He did not think about
himself or about his wife, but the abstract fact of kissing being always
in favour interested and elated him. He conceived of kissing as an
abstraction. Isolated and suspended, he was with the guns and the   10
other men. There was the physical relationship between them all,
but no spiritual contact. His reality was in his own perfect isolation
and abstraction. The comradeship, which seemed so close and real,
never implicated his individual soul. He seemed to have one physical
body with the other men; but when his mind or soul woke, it was   15
supremely and perfectly isolated.

Before him was the road running between the high banks of grass
and gorse. Looking down, he saw the whitish, muddy tracks, the
deep ruts and scores and hoof-marks on the wintry road, where the
English army had gone by. Now all was very still. The sounds that   20
came, came from the outside. They could not touch the chill, serene,
perfect isolation of the place where he stood.

Again the sharp cry from the officer overhead, the lightning,
perfectly mechanical response from himself as he worked at the
guns. It was exhilarating, this working in pure abstraction. It was a   25
supreme exhilaration, the finest liberty. He was transported in the
keen isolation of his own abstraction, the physical activity at the guns
keen as a consummation.

All was so intensely, intolerably peaceful that he seemed to be
immortalised. The utter suspension of the moment made it eternal.   30
At the corner of the high-road, where a little country road joined on,
there was a wayside crucifix knocked slanting. So it slanted in all
eternity. Looking out across the wintry fields and dark woods, he felt
that everything was thus for ever; this was finality. There appeared a
tiny group of cavalry, three horsemen, far off, very small, on the crest   35
of a field. They were our own men. So it is for ever. The little group
disappeared. The air was always the same—a keen frost immovable
for ever.

Of the Germans nothing was to be seen. The officer on the

platform above waited and waited. Then suddenly came the sharp orders to train the guns, and the firing went on rapidly, the gunners grew hot at the guns.

Even so, even amid the activity, there was a new sound. A new,
5 deep "Papp!" of a cannon seemed to fall on his palpitating tissue. Himself he was calm and unchanged and inviolable. But the deep "Papp!" of the cannon fell upon the vulnerable tissue of him. Still the unrelenting activity was kept up at his small guns.

Then, over the static inviolability of the nucleus, came a menace,
10 the awful, faint whistling of a shell, which grew into the piercing, tearing shriek that would tear up the whole membrane of the soul. It tore all the living tissue in a blast of motion. And yet the cold, silent nerves were not affected. They were beyond, in the frozen isolation that was out of all range. The shell swung by behind, he heard the
15 thud of its fall and the hoarseness of its explosion. He heard the cry of the soldier to the horses. And yet he did not turn round to see. He had not time. And he was cold of all interest, intact in his isolation. He saw a twig of holly with red berries fall like a gift on to the road below and remain lying there.

20 The Germans had got the aim with a big gun. Was it time to move? His superficial consciousness alone asked the question. The real *he* did not take any interest. He was abstract and absolute.

The faint whistling of another shell dawned, and his blood became still to receive it. It drew nearer, the full blast was upon him,
25 his blood perished. Yet his nerves held cold and untouched, in inviolable abstraction. He saw the heavy shell swoop down to earth, crashing into the rocky bushes away to the right, and earth and stones poured up into the sky. Then these fell to the ground again; there was the same peace, the same inviolable, frozen eternality.

30 Would they move now? There was a space of silence, followed by the sudden explosive shouts of the officer on the platform, and the swift training of the guns, and the warning and the shout to "Fire!" In the eternal dream of this activity a shell passed unnoticed. And then, into the eternal silence and white immobility of this activity,
35 suddenly crashed a noise and a darkness and a moment's flaring agony and horror. There was an instantaneous conflagration of life and eternity, then a profound weight of darkness.

When faintly something began to struggle in the darkness, a consciousness of pain and sick life, he was at home in the cottage
40 troubling about something, hopelessly and sickeningly troubling,

but hopelessly. And he tried to make it out, what it was. It was something inert and heavy and hopeless. Yet there was the effort to know.

There was a resounding of pain, but that was not the reality. There was a resounding of pain. Gradually his attention turned to the noise. What was it? As he listened, the noise grew to a great clanging resonance which almost dazed him. What was it, then?

He realised that he was out at the front. He remembered the retreat, the hill. He knew he was wounded. Still he did not open his eyes; his sight, at least, was not free. A very large, resounding pain in his head rang out the rest of his consciousness. It was all he could do to lie and bear it. He lay quite still to bear it. And it resounded largely. Then again there returned the consciousness of the pain. It was a little less. The resonance had subsided a little. What, then, was the pain? He took courage to think of it. It was his head. He lay still to get used to the fact. It was his head. With new energy he thought again. Perhaps he could also feel a void, a bruise, over his brow. He wanted to locate this. Perhaps he could feel the soreness. He was hit, then, on the left brow. And, lying quite still and sightless, he concentrated on the thought. He was wounded on the left brow, and his face was wet with stiffening blood. Perhaps there was the feel of hot blood flowing; he was not sure. So he lay still and waited. The tremendous sickening, resounding ache clanged again, clanged and clanged like a madness, almost bursting the membrane of his brain.

And again, as he lay still, there came the knowledge of his wife and children, somewhere in a remote, heavy despair. This was the second, and deeper, reality. But it was very remote.

How deep was the hurt to his head? He listened again. The pain rang now with a deep boom, and he was aware of a profound feeling of nausea. He felt very sick. But how deep was the wound in his head? He felt very sick, and very peaceful at the same time. He felt extraordinarily still. Soon he would have no pain, he felt so finely diffused and rare.

He opened his eyes on the day, and his consciousness seemed to grow more faint and dilute. Lying twisted, he could make out only jumbled light. He waited, and his eyes closed again. Then he waked all of a sudden, in terror lest he were able to see nothing but the jumbled light. The terror lest he should be confronted with nothing but chaos roused him to an effort of will. He made a powerful effort to see.

And vision came to him. He saw grass and earth; then he made out a piece of high-road with its tufts of wintry grass; he was lying not far from it, just above. After a while, after he had been all the while unrelaxed in his will to see, he opened his eyes again and saw the
5 same scene. In a supreme anguish of effort he gathered his bearings and once more strove for the stable world. He was lying on his side, and the high-road ran just beneath. The bank would be above. He had more or less made his bearings. He was in the world again. He lifted his head slightly. That was the high-road, and there was the
10 body of the lieutenant, lying on its face, with a great pool of blood coming from the small of the back and running under the body. He saw it distinctly, as in a vision. He also saw the broken crucifix lying just near. It seemed very natural.

Amid all the pain his head had become clear and light. He seemed
15 to have a second being, very clear and rare and thin. The earth was torn. He wanted to see it all.

In his frail, clear being he raised himself a little to look, and found himself looking at his own body. He was lying with a great mass of bloody earth thrown over his thighs. He looked at it vaguely, and
20 thought it must be heavy over him. He was anxious, with a very heavy anxiety, like a load on his life. Why was the earth on his thighs so soaked with blood? As he sat faintly looking, he saw that his leg beyond the mound was all on one side. He went sick, and his life went away from him. He remained neutral and dead. Then,
25 relentlessly, he had to come back, to face the fact of himself. With fine, delicate fingers he pushed the earth from the sound leg, then from the wounded one. But the soil was wet with blood. The leg lay diverted. He tried to move a little. The leg did not move. There seemed a great gap in his being. He knew that part of his thigh was
30 blown away. He could not think of the great bloody mess. It seemed to be himself, a wet, smashed, red mass. Very faintly the thin being of his consciousness hovered near. A frail, fine being seemed to be distilled out of the gaping red horror. As he sat he was detached from his wounds and his body.

35 Beyond his knowledge of his mutilation he remained faint and isolated in a cold, unchanging state. His being had become abstract and immutable. He sat there isolated, pure, abstract, in a state of supreme logical clarity. This he was now, a cold, clear abstraction. And as such he was going to judge. The outcome should be a pure,
40 eternal, logical judgment: whether he should live or die. He

examined his thought of his wife, and waited to see whether he should move to her. He waited still. Then his faintly beating heart died. The decision was no. He had no relation there. He fell away towards death. But still the tribunal was not closed. There were the children. He thought of them and saw them. But the thought of them did not stir the impulse back to life. He thought of them, but the thought of them left him cold and clear and abstract; they remained remote, away in life. And still he waited. Was it, then, finally decided? And out of the cold silence came the knowledge. It was decided he remained beyond, clear and untouched, in death.

In this supreme and transcendent state he remained motionless, knowing neither pain nor trouble, but only the extreme suspension of passing away.

Till the horrible sickness of dissolution came back, the over-whelming cold agony of dissolution.

As he lay in this cold, sweating anguish of dissolution, something again startled his consciousness, and, in a clear, abstract movement, he sat up. He was now no longer a man, but a disembodied, clear abstraction.

He saw two Germans who had ridden up, dismount by the body of the lieutenant.

"*Kaput?*"

"*Jawohl!*"*

In a transcendent state of consciousness he lay and looked. They were turning over the body of the lieutenant. He saw the muscles of their shoulders as they moved their arms.

Clearly, in a calm, remote transcendence, he reached for his revolver. A man had ridden past him up the bank. He knew, but he was as if isolated from everything in this distinct, fine will of his own. He lay and took careful, supreme, almost absolute aim. One of the Germans started up, but the body of the other, who was bending over the dead lieutenant, pitched forward and collapsed, writhing. It was inevitable. A fine, transcendent spirituality was on the face of the Englishman, a white gleam. The other German, with a curious, almost ludicrous bustling movement had got out his revolver and was running forwards, when he saw the wounded, subtle Englishman luminous with an abstract smile on his face. At the same instant two bullets entered his body, one in the breast, and one in the belly. The body stumbled forward with a rattling, choking, coughing noise, the revolver went off in the air, the body fell on to its knees. The

Englishman, still luminous and clear, fired at the dropped head. The bullet broke the neck.

Another German had ridden up, and was reining his horse in terror. The Englishman aimed at the red, sweating face. The body
5 started with horror and began slipping out of the saddle, a bullet through its brain.

At the same moment the Englishman felt a sharp blow, and knew he was hit. But it was immaterial. The man above was firing at him. He turned round with difficulty as he lay. But he was struck again,
10 and a sort of paralysis came over him. He saw the red face of a German with blue, staring eyes coming upon him, and he knew a knife was striking him. For one moment he felt the searing of steel, another final agony of suffocating darkness.

The German cut and mutilated the face of the dead man as if he
15 must obliterate it. He slashed it across, as if it must not be a face any more; it must be removed. For he could not bear the clear, abstract look of the other's face, its almost ghoulish, slight smile, faint but so terrible in its suggestion, that the German was mad, and ran up the road when he found himself alone.

EXPLANATORY NOTES

EXPLANATORY NOTES

England, My England

5:1 **England, My England** The title is a refrain from the patriotic poem 'England' (1900) by William Ernest Henley (1849–1903), which begins: 'What have I done for you, / England, my England? / What is there I would not do, / England, my own?'

DHL wrote this story while he and Frieda were living in a cottage on the estate of the 'formidable and poetic Meynell family' (*Letters*, ii. 255), at Greatham, Sussex. He uses precise details of the place for the setting of the story. Although he transfers it to the neighbouring county, Hampshire (5:13), he still refers to the foot of the South Downs (5:28) in central Sussex.

DHL drew not only on the place but also on members of the family for his story. Godfrey Marshall and his 'literary' wife are loosely modelled on Wilfrid and Alice Meynell – the former an author, editor and publisher (1852–1948), the latter a Catholic poet and essayist (1847–1922). (See Appendix, p. 221 and note on 221:7.) Two daughters, Monica (1880–1929) and Viola (1885–1956), are models for Magdalen and Priscilla in the story (6:33, 37). A third daughter, Madeline (1884–1975), married Perceval Drewett Lucas (1879–1916) in 1907: they are the models for DHL's fictional characters Winifred and Egbert.

Wilfred Meynell 'proceeded to give each of his children a cottage' at Greatham, DHL noted (*Letters*, ii. 259), and in the story he accurately portrays these (6:3–7; 6:29–7:3). In 1912 Meynell gave the Lucases a remote cottage known as Rackham Cottage (the 'Crockham' of the story) some half-mile from the main farmhouse (6:38ff.). Perceval Lucas built up its garden of which he was especially fond. Sylvia ('Joyce' in the story), the eldest of the Lucases' three daughters, had an accident to her leg in the summer of 1913: while her father was away in Italy, she fell on a sickle left lying in long grass by a visitor. DHL saw the Lucas children in April 1915 when they were staying with their mother at Greatham, though not in their own cottage, which was let. He observed and talked to the limping eldest child. Perceval Lucas had enlisted in September 1914, and was commissioned in the Infantry on 22 June 1915, after DHL had completed the first version of the story (see Appendix). He visited his family at Greatham on his few days of leave. See note on 30:15. He died of wounds in France on 6 July 1916. DHL saw him at Greatham and may have met him; he certainly met and talked with Madeline Lucas. In his story, DHL includes the two younger daughters, Christian and Barbara Lucas, naming them Annabel (11:39) and Barbara (17:33). See Barbara Lucas, 'Apropos of "England, My England"' in *Twentieth Century*, clxix (1961), 288–93, and *Letters*, ii. 386, 635.

5:29 **the Saxons** Sussex, homeland of the 'South Saxons', was occupied during the Anglo-Saxon invasions of the fifth century A.D.

5:32 **mulleins** Herbaceous plants. See also 30:17ff. Evidently the Great or Common Mullein (*Verbascum thapsus*), popularly known as 'Aaron's Rod'. DHL had himself worked in the garden at Rackham Cottage with something of Egbert's joy (5:30): *Letters*, ii. 344.

6:32 **long barn or shed** The Meynells had converted a cowshed, which they called jocularly 'Shed Hall', for Viola. DHL stayed there from January to July 1915.

7:15 **Morris-dance and the old customs.** Perceval Lucas played an important part in the revival of Morris dancing early in the twentieth century and was a member of Cecil Sharp's original team which travelled widely, demonstrating folk-dancing. He edited the first two numbers of the *Journal of the English Folk Dance Society* (1914, 1915) to which he contributed 'A Bibliography of the Morris Dance'. See A. H. Fox Strangways, *Cecil Sharp* (Oxford, 1933), especially pp. 112–13.

10:1 **back of her** For DHL's use of this phrase see Introduction, p. xxviii and footnote 25.

12:30 **casus belli,** Immediate cause of war (Latin).

12:33 **consider the lilies ... they spin,** Matthew vi. 28. Cf. 12:40.

14:19 **bring an ass to the water,** DHL's variant of the English proverb ['you may lead a horse to water'].

15:36 **basta!** Enough! (Italian). See Introduction, p. xxx.

15:40 **will-to-power.** DHL frequently used this term from Friedrich Nietzsche – 'Wille zur Macht': see, e.g. *Women in Love*, ed. David Farmer, Lindeth Vasey and John Worthen (Cambridge, 1987), p. 150.

16:18 **psychoanalysts ... complex ... word invented.** DHL had just completed his revision of *Fantasia of the Unconscious* (*inter alia* a critique of psychoanalysis) just before rewriting this story late in 1921. See, for instance, chap. 1; also his *Psychoanalysis and the Unconscious*, chap. 1, and *Letters*, i. 543. 'Complex' had been established as a psychanalytic term by Carl Jung earlier in the century. DHL's acquaintance Godwin Baynes, an assistant to Jung 1919–22, edited his writings.

16:20 **like Isaac.** Genesis xxii. 1–13.

16:40 **"A little child shall lead them —"** Isaiah xi. 6.

18:23 **you left lying about** See note on 5:1. The involvement of the father in the accident is DHL's invention.

19:9 **Mater Dolorata.** Mother of Sorrows (Italian). One of the devotional names for the Virgin Mary. In art (usually with the Latin title *Mater Dolorosa*) she is shown sorrowing for the passion of her son, with clasped hands and in tears, and sometimes wearing her own crown of thorns. See 23:21ff.

19:13 **four miles to the village** Pulborough village is 4 miles from Greatham. The doctor who treated Sylvia Lucas came from Storrington, a mile closer.

22:19 **take Joyce up to London,** When Sylvia Lucas had her accident, the local doctor had been unable to treat the complications. Maitland Radford (1884–1944), a medical doctor and son of DHL's friend Dollie Radford, was at the time staying at Greatham with Viola Meynell. He arranged for Sylvia to be taken to his London hospital, thus saving her life. During DHL's residence at Greatham, the Radfords spent some weeks at the Lucases' cottage, where DHL constantly visited them.

26:18   **like Ishmael,** Genesis xxi. 9–21.

27:10   **Baal and Ashtaroth?** Semitic fertility god and goddess.

28:10   **"conquests of peace"** An allusion to Milton's sonnet 'To the Lord Generall Cromwell May 1652' (1673): '... yet much remaines / To conquer still; peace hath her victories / No less renownd then warr...' (ll. 9–11). Cf. Shakespeare, *2 Henry IV*, iv. ii. 89: 'A peace is of the nature of a conquest...'

28:34   *canaille* Rabble, literally a pack of dogs (French).

30:15   **he came alone** On several occasions Perceval Lucas came alone to Greatham to see his garden. There is a record of one such visit on 23 June 1915, in a notebook written under DHL's guidance by Mary Saleeby (cousin of Sylvia Lucas); see Nehls, i. 304.

32:7   **Wither thou goest I will go.** Ruth i. 16 ['... goest, I ...'].

Tickets Please

34:1   **Tickets Please** DHL's original title 'John Thomas' was changed editorially to 'Tickets, Please!' (Per1) and to 'The Eleventh Commandment' (Per2) probably on grounds of decency (see note on 36:21). He subsequently adopted 'Tickets Please'. See Introduction, pp. xxxiv–xxxv. In facetious colloquial usage an eleventh commandment 'Thou shalt not be found out' is added to the ten of Moses in Genesis xx.

34:2   **a single-line tramway system** DHL makes use in this story of the Nottingham–Ripley tramway, opened in August 1913, which passed through his home town, Eastwood. See Introduction, p. xxxiv.

34:10   **the terminus,** Ripley, Derbyshire, where DHL's sister Ada lived, on the edge of the Peak District.

34:14   **the Co-operative Wholesale Society's Shops** The co-operative movement, deriving from the ideas of Robert Owen (1771–1858), took its present form of shops returning profits to customers in the 1840s. DHL refers here to the Ripley branch. Cf. 'Return to Bestwood', *Phoenix II* 257.

34:17   **the hill-top market-place:** A reference to Eastwood market-place at the intersection of the Nottingham and Mansfield roads: 'the draughty little market-place where my mother shopped on Friday evenings...' ('Return to Bestwood', *Phoenix II* 259).

34:23   **city cars,** I.e. tram-cars on the Nottingham city lines.

34:28   **cripples and hunchbacks ... the devil in them.** Cf. the popular belief that devils or evil spirits inhabited the mis-shapen bodies of cripples. See John B. Vickery, *The Literary Impact of 'The Golden Bough'* (Princeton, 1973), p. 298.

35:14 **Trams that pass in the night.** DHL's adaptation of the proverbial 'Ships that pass in the night...' See 'Tales of A Wayside Inn', III (1874) by Henry Wadsworth Longfellow (1807–82).

35:36 **Thermopylae.** DHL appears to imply a mock-heroic identification with Leonidas the Spartan, remembered for his heroic defence during the Persian war in 480 B.C. at Thermopylae – literally 'the hot gates' (Greek) – a narrow pass in eastern Greece.

36:21 **John Thomas ... Coddy.** John Thomas – penis (slang) – was editorially changed and Coddy – from 'cods', testicles (slang) – omitted in Per1 probably on grounds of decency. 'Jontom' (Per2) ('Coddy' in A1) may perhaps have been in MS. See Textual apparatus and note on 34:1.

37:5 **Statutes fair,** One of two annual fairs held in November in Church Street and the market-place, near the Sun Inn, Eastwood. (Cf. 34:17.)

37:16 **[of new-]fried** This editorial conjecture makes sense of the odd reading in A1 and E1. DHL appears to have revised this passage, and the easy misreading of 'of new' as 'a few' could have been Mrs Carmichael's or the A1 typesetter's. See Textual apparatus and Introduction, p. xxxv.

38:9 **the cinema,** The fairground cinema and its spruiker: the patrons 'climb the boards' to enter. The reading in A1 (and E1) is a simple error.

39:32 **Hasn't he got a face on him!"** Isn't he cheeky! (slang).

39:35 **He'll get dropped on** I.e. someone will take revenge on him.

40:31 **Birkin.** For DHL's use of this name see *Women in Love*, ed. Farmer, Vasey and Worthen, p. 531, note on 16:6.

41:12 **the tune having got into her mind.** The song 'I'm afraid to come home in the dark' by Americans Harry Williams, Jack Judge and Egbert van Alstyne was popularised in England about 1909 by Hetty King, music-hall singer and male impersonator. DHL's punctuation indicates the rhythm of the music.

41:16 **all on my lonely-O."** From the popular song by C. W. Murphy and Dan Lipton: 'O, O, Antonio, / He's gone away. / Left me on my ownio / All all alonio.'

43:3 **Strange, wild creatures,** Reminiscent of the maenads ('mad women'), votaries of Dionysos, tearing animals to pieces, in a state of possession. The legendary poet Orpheus was said by one tradition to have been torn to pieces by the maenads for interfering with their worship.

The Blind Man

46:2 **Isabel Pervin** Based on DHL's friend Catherine Carswell. 'There was nothing superficially like me in her, and nothing that could not be easily refuted. Yet somewhere the truth smote me...' (Catherine Carswell, *The Savage Pilgrimage*, 1932, p. 106).

46:11 **The Grange** Suggested by the vicarage at Upper Lydbrook in the Forest of Dean, Monmouthshire, where DHL visited the Carswells in August 1918, and where the story was first conceived. See Catherine Carswell, *Savage Pilgrimage*, pp. 100–6.

46:17 **a Scottish newspaper,** Catherine Carswell had reviewed for the *Glasgow Herald.*

47:35 **Bertie Reid** This character, Bertram Reid, was possibly suggested by Bertrand Russell, whose friendship with DHL in 1915–16 had by this time lapsed. See *Letters*, ii. 282, etc.

Monkey Nuts

64:1 **Monkey Nuts** Another name for peanuts, often used colloquially to indicate a thing or a person of little value. But DHL may also be punning on the name of Violet Monk (see note on 65:10), especially at 69:1–3. In letters and diary DHL gives the title as 'Monkey Nuts', as in A1 and E1, although within the story he uses the compound 'Monkey-nuts'. In Per the title is 'MONKEY-NUTS' but within the text it appears once without hyphen (76:15) and several times in lower case. In the absence of the MS, DHL's own recorded form of the title is retained.

The setting for the story fairly closely recreates Hermitage, some 5 miles n.e. of Newbury ('Belbury', 66:14), Berkshire, where the Lawrences lived at various times during 1918–19. There was then a rural branch railway serving the village.

64:2 **O. K.** DHL's use of this term is the first cited for the twentieth century in *OED Supplement.*

64:4 **billeted in a cottage** Soldiers on leave from the front during the First World War, and for some time afterwards, were sent to rural areas as farm-labourers, especially to assist with the harvest and with haymaking. Three soldiers, a corporal and two privates, were billeted at a cottage in Hermitage, the home of Hilda Brown (Cotterell) and her family during DHL's residence late in 1918. As a result, the child was obliged to sleep in the adjoining cottage, which DHL had rented. See her memoir in Nehls, i. 454ff.

64:31 **Playcross** DHL's name for Longlane, a hamlet just s. of Hermitage and the postal address for Grimsbury Farm, home of his friend Cecily Lambert (see note on 65:10), where DHL stayed in September 1919.

64:33 **land-girls** During the War women worked as farm-hands to replace men serving in the forces.

65:10 **Miss Stokes,"** A character probably based on Violet Monk, cousin of Cecily Lambert, who was assisting with the work at Grimsbury Farm. See Cecily Lambert's memoir in Nehls, i. 463ff. DHL used both women as models for the principal characters in 'The Fox', a contemporaneous story.

66:31 **pictures.** This word, from Per, is more likely to have been DHL's, at this time, than 'movies'. The latter may have been substituted by Seltzer's editor. Cf. 68:26: 'go' (A1) for 'do' (Per) and see Introduction, p. xxxvii.

67:19 **coming it quick,** Being provocative (colloquial).

67:40 **cotton on,** Understand (colloquial).

68:15 **Handsome is as handsome looks,"** Albert's adaptation of the English proverb 'Handsome is as handsome does'.

69:8   **The circus** In her memoir, Hilda Brown Cotterell recalls Frieda taking her to Sanger's Circus in Newbury, and later reporting the details to DHL (Nehls, i. 457).

69:20   **sensational drama of the cinema.** For DHL's contrasting of circus and cinema, see his poem 'When I Went to the Circus' in *The Complete Poems of D. H. Lawrence*, ed. Vivian de Sola Pinto and Warren Roberts (1967), i. 444; see also *The Lost Girl*, ed. John Worthen (Cambridge, 1981), chap. VII.

69:40   **rattler,"** Bicycle (slang).

70:22   **Miss Stokes should turn off.** Grimsbury Farm was in a lane off the Hermitage–Newbury road.

70:33   **grid,** Bicycle (slang); *OED Supplement* gives this as the first recorded use of the word.

71:24   ***Daily Mirror ... Daily Sketch,*** London popular newspapers.

73:39   **your mettle ... to temper it.** A pun on the word 'metal'. Steel is tempered or hardened by being plunged in cold water when hot.

74:11   **Beeley.** Probably DHL's name for Bucklebury.

74:31   **"I'm Gilbert ... the nuts."** From the popular song by Arthur Wimperis (1874–1953), 'Gilbert, the Filbert, / The Colonel of the Knuts'. Cf. *Letters*, iii. 502. 'Filbert' is another name for the hazelnut or cobnut; 'knut' (or 'nut') was contemporary slang for an extravagantly elegant or superior person. Hence the puns on 'knuts' – 'nuts' and 'colonel' – 'kernel'.

74:35   **variety's the salt of life** Albert's adaption of 'Variety's the very spice of life, / That gives it all its flavour' from William Cowper (1731–1800), 'The Task' (1785), II. ll. 6–7. Now proverbial.

74:37   **Am I my brother's keeper?** Genesis iv. 9.

75:28   **Gord love ... in it."** 'God love us, she's too lively for you.' 'Beans': from 'full of beans', energetic, vital (colloquial).

76:27   **the armistice** The armistice was signed at 11 a.m. on 11 November 1918.

Wintry Peacock

77:1   **Wintry Peacock** The story may have its origins in a dream DHL reported to Lady Cynthia Asquith in the summer of 1918, six months before writing the story. The dream concerned an injured peacock and a protective lady in a nearby cottage; see *Letters*, iii. 247–8. Richard Aldington claimed that the Goytes were based on a butcher and his wife in Hermitage, Berks., where DHL had been living; see Nehls, i. 594 n. 482. (The river Goyt, which rises near Buxton, Derbyshire, may have suggested the name.)

For the additions to the title in Per and E1 see Introduction, pp. xxxviii, xl.

Before the first publication in the *Metropolitan*, DHL had deleted a long passage from the opening of the story, presumably in the missing TS. See Introduction, p. xxxix. The MS (pp. 1–2) begins:

I had always wondered why they had peacocks in Tible. Tible is a village—not a village, but a knot of three or four stone farms, and a couple of stone cottages, and a tiny stone chapel, lying on the brow of a bare hill, half-sheltered in a cluster of ash-trees, in the Peak. Away below, in the valley, winds a beautiful highroad, where an occasional pony trots, or a motor-car buzzes. But the real traffic all passes through a valley away to the right, six miles off. So that Tible, stranded on the brow of the hill high above its own steel ribbon of road, is as remote as only an English hamlet can be, forgotten of life.

But crossing the table-land, bare, with an intricate network of stone fences with naked hills swelling all round in the distance, it is pleasant to incline downhill and suddenly find oneself in the rich shade of a group of ash-trees, among stone farm-buildings. So I had thought, the first time, in the summer. I was a little uneasy, thinking I had taken a private farm-road. But I kept on. In a rough garden to the right, raised above the road, tall blue bell-flowers rose. And a little further, a very lovely peacock was stepping among the stones, swelling its blue neck and trailing its bronze and green. All round was the cow-splashed sordidness of a farm, strong smelling. I stopped to look at the peacock as he stepped and pecked and made his crest tremble. And then I glanced ·back. A woman was standing out from the end of the wall to watch me. She wore a print bonnet. Seeing me look at her she walked across the road to the opposite cart-shed.

The next time I went through Tible was autumn, and I had been blackberry-ing. It was the same knot of ash-shaded stone walls—but many ash-leaves were on the ground. I saw two peacocks walking in the raised garden, between the red-hot-poker flowers. They were rather draggled, as the garden was draggled, grass-grown. I stood to look at them.

"Plenty of blackberries this year," said a ringing voice near to me. It was a rather short woman, "glegging" up at me from under her cotton bonnet, with fine, black, furtive eyes. She was sallow and long-faced, with crisp black hair. Her skirts were very short. She would be about thirty years old. She spoke with a rolling west-country burr impossible in Derbyshire. I listened to the roll of her "ye-urrr," and looked at her. She averted her face.

"Plenty for the picking," I said.

She turned again to me with a wry laugh.

"Yes, if you've the patience for it," she said. "I haven't."

"You see how far my patience goes," I said, holding out my basket.

"About a pound and a half," she said, with a slight derisive laugh.

"It'll do," I said.

"I don't suppose I've picked a quart this season," she said. "Oh, I can't be bothered with the nasty fiddling things." Then she cocked her eyes up at me again. "Are you staying round about?"

"Living over at Scargill for the present—my wife and I."

"Oh yes—oh, I know the house—"

So we chattered—and so I left her, trying to fix her dialect. It was either Wiltshire, Berkshire, or Oxfordshire, I decided. As I went down the hill I wished I had asked her about the peacocks.

When I saw her again it was winter.

77:5 **Tible.** Based on the hamlet Ible, a couple of miles n.w. from DHL's cottage at Middleton. He described it (see note on 77:1) as lying between two roads, identifiable as the Via Gellia and the highroad 6 miles e. In MS (p. 8) DHL altered 'Ible' to 'Tible'.

77:20 **I had ... the summer.** DHL must have added this sentence to TS consequent upon his earlier deletion (see note on 77:1), but neglected to change 'the' to 'a' in 'the cotton bonnet' (77:23).

78:33 **addressed from France** In the MS (p. 3), DHL went on to confirm that Elise was 'a girl in North France' which he changed, presumably in TS, to 'a French-speaking girl' (78:36). In the following paragraph he added the first of three references to Elise as Belgian. By not altering the words 'addressed from France' at this point, he left an inconsistency which has troubled some critics of the story.

78:34 **Mon cher** My dear (French).

80:4 **the South African War.** The Boer War, 1899–1901. DHL slightly altered this reference for E1, making Goyte not only go to the South African War, but stay in the country for a further five years as a member of the Cape Mounted Police. Goyte is more of a drifter and a 'rake' in that version. See Textual apparatus for 79:37 and 80:11.

80:29 **'bu-rrd.'** This allusion to Mrs Goyte's dialect has more point in the light of the deleted opening of the story. See note on 77:1 above.

82:36 **downy** Knowing (slang).

83:17 **said I. "He'd** The paragraph break here in Per1 (p. 22), and in A1 which used it as setting-copy, was perhaps inadvertent. In the *Metropolitan* magazine twenty-six pages separate 'said I.' from the continuation (on p. 48) of the narrator's speech.

84:1 **groove** Pit, cave (dialect). DHL replaced 'world' in MS (p. 8) with 'groove' which was misread as 'grove', presumably by Pinker's typist.

86:3 **nesh,** Sensitive (dialect).

86:24 **Griff Low."** Apparently DHL's creation. Griffe Grange is not far from Middleton, and Low (hill) is a common topographical term in the vicinity, e.g. Blake Low close to Ible.

87:20 **smite** Small portion (dialect).

87:35 **us.** The breaks in the text of A1 and E2 at this point and in A1 at 88:24 were carried over from page breaks in the *Metropolitan* text.

90:11 **Figure-toi ... suis désolée————'"** Imagine how broken-hearted I am (French).

90:33 **"Yes," said [88:39] ... he murmured.** This passage was considerably revised in TS. MS (pp. 14–16) reads:
"Alfred Goyte, Lance-Corporal—" I said.
He cocked up his eyes, seemed to fumble a moment in his mind, then answered sharply "Yes."

"Yes," said I. "She asked me to read it to her."

He looked square at me, with hatred.

"What did it say?" he asked, sharply.

"You know as well as I do," I said.

"What?" he barked.

"You know as well as I do—probably better. So why ask me?" I replied.

Again he fumbled in his mind for some minutes. Then he coloured deeply, perhaps with anger, and his eyes looked hot. It seemed to me he was on the point of tears: what kind of tears I could not say.

"I don't know. No, I don't know—" he stammered.

I looked at him closely. Suddenly he jerked up his head.

"She burnt the blasted thing before I saw it," he said.

Mentally, I gave a long whistle.

"But what did she say was in it?" I asked.

"Any blasted thing," he replied, confusedly. Then, with a jerk, he recovered himself. "I don't know what to make of what she says," he added, rapidly.

"What did she say?" I repeated.

"Here!" he suddenly jerked out. "You know what was in it. Why can't you spit it out!"

"What do you know already?" I said.

His eyes looked at me hotly. Then he wavered, and came to. He flushed again, and hot water seemed to come in his eyes.

"I know it was from Elise. But that hell-cat won't tell me anything straight.— What about a baby? Is it the mother's, or is it Elise's, or what?"

"I told your wife it was the mother's—but it was Elise's," I replied—and he stared at me.

"What the hell did you do that for?"

"I can't say. I suddenly began lying, and went on. I read as if you had been a general benefactor of the household—and as if Elise had a new baby brother, that the family were going to name Alfred after you, out of gratitude to you: and as if Elise was piously in love with you."

He stared at me blankly for some minutes. Then he began to laugh. Then he roared with laughter, roared and roared, till the valley rang again. Then he clapped me on the shoulder, and said:

"It's a knock-out—a fair knock-out."

After which he stared at me for some moments, fixedly. At the end of which he asked, half tremulously:

"And what did she really say?"

"Who?"

He hesitated to pronounce the name.

"Elise."

I then went over, as far as I could remember, the exact terms of the letter—in French as far as I could. He watched me fixedly.

"Mon Dieu!" he murmured at the end. "Oh my God!" And his eyes swam with hot water. "Elise!" he murmured.

Then he looked at me sharply.

"She said the baby was mine?" he asked, precipitate.

"She *said* so," I replied.

Again he fixed me.

"What do you mean?" he barked.

But I did not answer this query.

"I loved that girl," he said sentimentally.

I suppose I must have laughed.

"Don't you believe it?" he demanded fiercely.

"I'm quite impartial," I said.

He stared at me.

"I don't love that hell-cat up yonder," he said at length. Then suddenly he broke off on a new line.

"Hey!" he said. "Why didn't you wring that b— peacock's neck—that b— Joey?"

"I had no grudge against him," I said, laughing.

He stared at me.

"By Jove, though, I have," he said. "He haunts me. I believe there's the devil in him.—I hate the brute. He cleared out when I made a grab at him—"

I laughed. He stood and mused.

"Poor little Elise," he murmured. "Poor old girl!"

Hadrian [You Touched Me]

92:2 **[You Touched Me]** DHL clearly preferred 'Hadrian' as the title of this story: see Introduction, p. xlii. If the new title was passed on in Seltzer's setting-copy, it was ignored. DHL saw no proofs and there is no record of his reaction.

92:3 **The Pottery House** Based on the 'Pottery House', in Lynn Croft, Eastwood, down the hill from the house, no. 97, in which the Lawrence family lived from 1903 when DHL was aged 18. The Pottery kilns were in the fields behind the house. See Roy Spencer, *D. H. Lawrence Country* (1980), p. 13.

93:6 **Mary ... Martha:** Luke x. 38–42.

94:34 **the armistice** See note on 76:27.

96:24 **Mannie!"** A diminutive man. The term is used endearingly of young boys, in this case sarcastically of Hadrian. See 96:29, 105:26.

101:14 **Rawsley."** DHL's recreation of Eastwood in this story. There is a 'Rowsley' about 6 miles n.w. of Matlock, Derbyshire.

103:10 **sliving** Scheming, stealthy (dialect).

Samson and Delilah

108:1 **Samson and Delilah** See Judges xvi. For DHL's earlier title see Introduction, p. xlii.

108:3 **Penzance to St. Just-in-Penwith,** In this, the only story he set in Cornwall, DHL uses actual place names. The road, in the extreme s.w. of Cornwall, runs from Penzance on the s. coast to St Just close to the w. coast, a distance of about 8 miles.

108:6 **the lighthouse below the cliffs** The Longships Lighthouse at Land's End, named at 108:25.

108:10 **ruined power-houses of tin-mines** The Botallack mines, n. of St Just, visible from the Penzance road. Many Cornish mines were abandoned from the nineteenth century on, and Cornish miners (like Willie Nankervis) emigrated to America and Australia.

108:13 **The man [108:8] ... Celtic night.** Per2, in addition to the substantive variants listed in the Textual apparatus, made many small cuts. These were 108:8–13; 108:20–29; 109:12–16, 35–110:6; 110:13–14, 17, 19–20; 110:39–111:7, 13–14, 17, 18, 22–3, 28–30, 35–6; 113:1, 3–5, 8, 23–4, 30; 113:39–114:2; 114:7–9, 22–4, 29–31; 115:11–12, 24–5, 33–4; 116:3–4, 14–15, 30; 117:12–14, 20–1; 118:37, 119:6; 120:16–23, 27–8, 32–3, 36; 121:7–9, 22–3. They were always complete sentences, with the exception of the phrase 'of a German' at 117:9 and 117:19. Otherwise the text follows Per1. See Introduction, p. xlii and footnote 68.

108:33 **"The Tinners Rest."** DHL's recreation of 'The Tinners Arms', Zennor, which is set back from the road some 10 miles n.e. of St Just. DHL and Frieda stayed there (February–March 1916) before moving into their cottage at Tregerthen. He described it as 'a good little inn' (*Letters*, iii. 200).

110:32 *aplomb* The word is underlined in MS (p. 9) possibly because DHL considered it still to be foreign (French).

112:7 **New Army,** Lord Kitchener's intensive recruitment campaigns produced the so-called New Army in 1915–16, in preparation for the summer offensive of 1916. The Derby Scheme in late 1915 reorganised recruitment while avoiding direct conscription. DHL noted in January 1916: 'the war has come' to Cornwall; see *Letters*, ii. 495 and n. 3, 496.

117:26 **"Get the rope boys,** Cf. Samson in Judges xvi. 11–12.

117:34 **Laocoon** The group of statues (Rhodes, *c.* 25 B.C.) portraying Laocoön, a Trojan priest of Apollo, and his two sons wrestling with the sea-serpents which killed them. See *Letters*, i. 137 and nn. 1 and 2.

120:7 **yellowish American cloth,** Glazed or waterproofed cotton cloth.

120:31 **Butte City** More likely to be the mining town n. of Sacramento, California than Butte City, Montana; see note on 108:10.

121:7 **I dessay,"** I dare say (colloquial).

121:38 **'struth** Aphetic form of 'God's truth' (colloquial).

122:10 **by Ga-ard,"** By God. DHL's indication of an American accent.

122:15 **Damn me, you** The MS ends with these words as the final page is missing; see Textual apparatus.

122:20 **fet** Fought (dialect).

The Primrose Path

123:1 **The Primrose Path** From *Hamlet* I. iii. 45–9, where Ophelia admonishes her brother: 'Do not, as some ungracious pastors do, / Show me the steep and thorny way to heaven, / Whilst, like a puff'd and reckless libertine, / Himself the primrose path of dalliance treads, / And recks not his own rede.'

This story was completed about a week before DHL went to Eastwood to attend his sister Ada's wedding. This was to be his first visit to his native town since he had eloped with Frieda to Germany the year before. The similarity with his uncle's experience (see note on 123:15) cannot have eluded him and may perhaps have inspired the story.

123:2 **Victoria station,** Nottingham's main station on the Eastern Railway.

123:14 **as if** For the typist Douglas Clayton's interference with the text of TS, see Introduction p. xliii.

123:15 **you are my uncle,"** Daniel Sutton is closely based on DHL's maternal uncle, Herbert Beardsall (b. 1871). DHL's mother was twenty years older than Herbert (cf. 125:16), the youngest of the large family of George Beardsall, a zealous Wesleyan lay preacher and ardent teetotaller. (See *Letters*, i. xxiv–xxv.) Like Sutton, Herbert was considered the black sheep of the family (124:40): he had once been publican of the 'Lord Belper', Sneinton, Nottingham, had worked for a sporting paper (125:28) and had an unhappy marriage (125:31ff.) from which he eloped to Australia with another woman (126:16) who, he believed, tried to poison him (127:12–13). He later managed a taxi service in Nottingham. Like Daniel Berry, DHL shared his uncle's name (Herbert). In MS, Berry was at first called David (DHL's first name).

124:3 **She died at Christmas,"** DHL's mother had died of cancer on 9 December 1910.

124:5 **that's three of 'em gone!"** Herbert Beardsall had six sisters: Emma died in 1907, Ellen in 1908, Lydia in 1910 (see previous note).

124:7 **Trinity Church.** Directly opposite Victoria Station in Nottingham.

124:11 **sermon-lapping** I.e. drinking in sermons as a cat laps milk. Cf. note on 123:15.

124:33 *danse macabre* The dance of death (French).

125:6 **road—"** In MS (p. 4) DHL inserted this speech over a cancelled question but failed to delete the punctuation. His typist supplied a full stop (see Textual apparatus), but there seems no reason not to retain the dash of the original punctuation.

125:7 **Watmore,"** DHL's recreation of Watnall, 3 miles s.e. of Eastwood.

125:24 **Daniel Sutton** This editorial substitution follows DHL's revised character name. In MS (p. 5) he first wrote 'David', then deleted it and wrote 'John' above it in an attempt to find the right name. Having later decided on 'Daniel', he neglected to revise this instance. The last two letters of 'John' were blurred by the dot on the cancelled 'i' and the stem of the cancelled 'd' of 'David'. Douglas Clayton misread the word as 'Joky', and, believing it to be a nickname, typed it in inverted commas. In revising TS DHL did not correct this oddity, which appears nowhere else as Daniel Sutton's name. DHL's frequent changing of names in MS led to two main characters being called 'Daniel' (see note on 123:15).

126:24 **past the cemetery** The route from Victoria Station past Nottingham General Cemetery towards Eastwood is accurately depicted in this account of the taxi-ride.

128:3 **the Railway Arms ... Rollin's Mill Crossing.** The Wheatsheaf Inn at the Bobber's Mill level crossing just outside Nottingham.

128:32 **Red Seal,** 'Red Seal' Scotch whisky, a product of James Buchanan and Co.

129:1 **Cinderhill—,"** Four miles n.w. from the centre of Nottingham.

130:37 **Winnie,"** Herbert Beardsall's elder daughter was named Winnie, the younger, Maud.

133:10 **Elaine ... poetic name** After Elaine, heroine of Tennyson's 'Lancelot and Elaine' (1859).

134:11 **dining room.** In MS (p. 17) DHL wrote 'kitchen', apparently forgetting that Berry and the woman were in the dining room. Douglas Clayton typed 'dining-room', correcting this oversight. The editorial form here follows DHL's only other use of it at 132:39.

The Horse-Dealer's Daughter

137:1 **The Horse-Dealer's Daughter** For DHL's change of title from 'The Miracle', see Introduction, p. xlv. His most frequent spelling 'Horse-Dealer's' in letters and diary has been adopted editorially in the absence of the manuscript. The Pervins' house, Oldmeadow (144:26), is based on Hill Top House in the Nottingham Road, Eastwood, home of DHL's school friend Duncan Meakin whose father, John Thomas Meakin, was a farmer and horse-dealer. The family provided models for the Pervin family, as they had for the Mayhews in *The White Peacock*, ed. Andrew Robertson (Cambridge, 1983), p. 279ff.

137:21 **the dark holly-bushes ... high road,** Cf. *The White Peacock*, ed. Robertson, p. 279, where the Meakin house is called The Hollies.

139:1 **skivvy,"** A derogatory term for a female general domestic servant.

139:5 *museau.* Literally 'muzzle' (French), but used to indicate a person's face.

142:7 **the Moon and Stars,** Probably the 'Three Tuns' in Eastwood. But see *The Lost Girl*, ed. Worthen, p. 373.

143:18 **smoke of foundries** The Bennerley iron works were just s. of Eastwood towards Cossall. See *Letters*, i. 206 and n. 1.

The Last Straw [Fanny and Annie]

153:1 **The Last Straw** On 29 December 1921 DHL told Secker he wanted this to be the title; there is no record of similar advice to Seltzer. DHL's original title was used in A1 and E1. See Introduction, p. xlvi.

153:4 **Flame-lurid his face ... platform.** Cf. DHL's experience on 30 November 1918:

> The week-end I was at Ripley. Going, on Sat. night, the train runs just above the surface of Butterley reservoir, and the iron-works on the bank were flaming, a massive roar of flame and burnt smoke in the black sky, flaming and waving again on the black water round the train. On Butterley platform – where I got out – everything was lit up red – there was a man with dark brows, odd, not a human being. I could write a story about him. He made me think of Ashaburnipal.
>
> (*Letters*, iii. 302)

158:13 **ormin'** Clumsy, shambling (dialect).

158:28 **Princes Street,** Princes Street in Eastwood adjoins Victoria Street where DHL was born.

158:35 **Morley Chapel.** The Congregational Chapel in Moorgreen is the model for this chapel. Morley is a village, w. of Ilkeston, Derbyshire, and DHL is probably switching names.

159:4 **"And I ... a wite 'orse——"** The words of this unidentified solo are from Revelation xix. 11.

159:7 **"Hangels—hever bright an' fair——"** 'Angels ever bright and fair' is an aria from the oratorio 'Theodora' (first perf. 1750) by George Frederick Handel (1685–1759).

160:12 **"Come, ye ... storms begin——"** Hymn by Henry Alford (1810–71), commonly sung at Harvest Festivals.

160:39 **like Balaam's ass** Numbers xxii. 20–34.

161:17 **"They that ... joy; He ... with him."** Psalm cxxvi. 5–6 ['... joy. He ... shall ...', AV].

162:10 **like Lot's wife;** Genesis xix. 26. Cf. *Letters*, i. 98.

162:21 **'Fair waved ... pleasant land.'"** Hymn by John Hampden Gurney (1802–62).

164:4 **a tanger** Literally something which stings (dialect): a sharp-tongued, 'stinging' person.

166:10 **addle** Earn (dialect).

Uncollected Stories, 1913–22
The Mortal Coil

169:1 **The Mortal Coil** The title derives from *Hamlet* III. i. 64–8. 'To die, to sleep; / To sleep, perchance to dream. Ay, there's the rub; / For in that sleep of death what dreams may come, / When we have shuffled off this mortal coil, / Must give us pause.' The story is based on an experience from the youth of Frieda Lawrence's father, Friedrich Freiherr von Richthofen (1845–1915). See Introduction, p. xlvii.

169:21 **over-bolster** Continental quilt or duvet.

170:12 **horse-car** A horse-drawn tram-car.

171:14 **" 'My love … my lo-o-ve.' "** Probably Teresa's own words to a popular Venetian tune (early nineteenth century) known in English as 'The Carnival of Venice', one version of which goes 'My hat it has three corners…'

171:18 **Tant pis que mal,"** So much the worse (French).

171:29 **pillar of salt?** Immovable object. See note on 162:10 above.

172:4 **Gretchen** The pure heroine of Goethe's *Faust* (Part I, 1808). Marta is much too inclined to jealousy (green-eyed) to play such a role.

172:11 **Lenore-fuhr-ums-Morgenrot—!** 'Lenore started up at dawn!' is the opening line of the poem 'Lenore' (1773) by the German poet Gottfried August Bürger (1747–94). Lenore awakes from troubled dreams asking where her lover can be, not yet aware that he is dead.

174:17 **Three thousand marks."** An amount equivalent to about £150 in 1913.

177:39 **chocolate *dragées?*** Chocolate-coated sugar-plums.

188:8 **The sword of Damocles** Closely impending disaster (proverbial), from the legend of Damocles who was forced to sit under a sword suspended by a hair.

188:32 ***suffisance*** Complacent self-sufficiency (French).

189:30 **to bury their dead.** Cf. Matthew viii. 22.

The Thimble

190:33 **Mayfair,** An exclusive upper-class area of London bordering the e. side of Hyde Park.

192:6 **She was a beautiful woman … perfect.** This and other details of Mrs Hepburn are modelled on Lady Cynthia Asquith (1887–1960). She thought that 'some of his character hints are damnably good. He has kept fairly close to the model in the circumstances' (*Letters*, ii. 420 n.1); see also Introduction, p. xlviii. See Lady Cynthia Asquith, *Diaries: 1915–1918* (1968), pp. 89, 94, 95.

193:14 **his face was rather horribly cut up.** Lady Cynthia's husband, Herbert Asquith (1881–1947), had been slightly wounded earlier in 1915: 'three teeth knocked out' (*Letters*, ii. 359).

193:33 **her own large feet,** See Introduction, p. xlviii.

194:27 **shadows.** DHL first wrote 'opposite her' in MS (p. 11), deleted it and wrote above it 'in the shadows'. A typist could easily misread the last word as 'window', hence the reading of Per (p. 440); see Textual apparatus.

195:4 **a thimble** The thimble buried deep in the chair may have been suggested by an anecdote of Jessie Chambers about a pair of scissors discovered in a chair after her family purchased it. See Helen Corke, *D. H. Lawrence: The Croydon Years* (Austin, 1965), p. 26, and *The Prussian Officer*, ed. Worthen, p. 261.

197:38   **like Lazarus** John xi–xii. 2.

200:7   **we must be born again,"** John iii. 7. Cf. parts vii and viii of DHL's poem 'New Heaven and Earth', also written at Greatham, in *Complete Poems of D. H. Lawrence*, ed. Pinto and Roberts, i. 260–1.

200:18   **"'Touch me ... the Father',"** John xx. 17 ['...not; for...', RV].

Adolf

201:11   **down pit.** DHL's father worked at Brinsley pit about 1 mile n. of Eastwood across the fields. The events seem to date from the time the Lawrences were living at 3 Walker Street (1891–1903).

201:17   **the entry.** A passage between two terrace houses.

203:34   **copper fireplace,** I.e. the fireplace under the copper boiler used for washing clothes.

203:35   **imagine** See Textual apparatus. A word was omitted from TS2 and 'think' was inserted in ink by an unidentified hand. At 203:37, the 'upon' in TS2 is in the typing and may be a misreading.

207:12   **nursemaid's flying strings are the signal** A reference to the long (sometimes starched) ties with which a nursemaid's apron was fastened behind.

207:14   **white feather ...** *Merde!* A common symbol of cowardice. In England during the First World War white feathers, as a mark of shame, were often handed to young men apparently not serving in the army ... Shit! (French).

208:4   *bien emmerdés!"* Thoroughly contemptible (French).

Rex

209:1   **Rex** Cf. DHL's account in this story with his sister's recollection in Ada Lawrence and Stuart Gelder, *Early Life of D. H. Lawrence* (1932), pp. 33–4. She remembered DHL himself naming the dog Rex. The uncle of the story was Herbert Beardsall, Mrs Lawrence's youngest brother, who at the time described in the story kept the 'Lord Belper' (Cf. the 'Good Omen', 209:20); see 'The Primrose Path' and notes.

209:19   **the Band of Hope,** A temperance association for young people who signed a pledge never to drink alcohol.

211:9   **Wag thy strunt,** Wag your tail (dialect), referring to the fleshy stump of the terrier's tail.

211:17   **toused** Tousled, tangled (dialect).

212:12   **in flagrante.** From 'in flagrante delicto' – red-handed, [caught] in the act (Latin). Literally, 'with the crime still blazing'.

213:13   **the** *besoin d'aimer* The need to love (French).

216:11   **mard-soft** Spoiled, namby-pamby (dialect).

Appendix
England, My England, 1915 version

Note: Annotation has not been provided when the notes on 'England, My England' above provide the necessary equivalent information.

221:7 impoverished Quaker family. Wilfrid Meynell was born into a Quaker family in Newcastle on Tyne where his father was a small colliery owner; he later became a Catholic. As a young man in London he made a modest living as a journalist.

221:22 old south-of-England family, Perceval Lucas came of a Sussex family which, like the Meynells, had Quaker connections.

222:37 six brothers and sisters Wilfrid and Alice Meynell had seven children.

224:40 stationed at Chichester, Perceval Lucas had been stationed at Epsom and Nottinghamshire before his commission, which was in the infantry and not the artillery.

231:23 *Kaput?...Jawohl!'* Dead? ... Yes, indeed! (German).

TEXTUAL APPARATUS

TEXTUAL APPARATUS

The following symbols are used throughout:

MS = Manuscript
TS = Typescript
Per = Periodical
A1 = American First Edition (Seltzer, 1922)
E1 = English First Edition (Secker, 1924) except for 'Wintry Peacock', 'Adolf' and 'Rex' (see separate entries)

The Note on the texts, pp. 2–3 specifies which symbols are used for each story.

In the apparatus for each story the adopted reading appears to the left of the square bracket, with identification of the source if it is other than the base-text; all variants, together with their sources, are given in chronological order on the right of the bracket. In the absence of information to the contrary, the reader should assume that a particular variant recurs in all subsequent states. The sequence is separately indicated for each story.

The following symbols are used editorially:

Ed. = Editor
~ = Repeated word in recording a punctuation variant
Om. = Omitted
/ = Line or page break resulting in a punctuation, hyphenation or spelling error
P = Paragraph division
= Internal division
R = Autograph correction by DHL to a state of the text, e.g. *TSR* in 'The Primrose Path'

England, My England

The sequence is *A1*, *E1*, and the base-text is *A1*.

5:20	always] ~, *E1*		13:28	garden] ~, *E1*
5:32	chaps,] ~ *E1*		13:32	slim] ~, *E1*
6:20	archer,] ~ *E1*		13:38	ah ... ah] ~, ... ~, *E1*
6:20	long,] ~ *E1*		16:17	psychoanalysts] psycho-analyst
6:26	energy] ~, *E1*			*E1*
10:1	back of] behind *E1*		16:24	willynilly] willy-/ nilly *E1*
11:39	Joyce— *E1*] ~; *A1*		16:38	try ... possible] ~, ... ~, *E1*
12:7	oh] ~, *E1*		17:2	it—] ~. *E1*
12:8	He] he *E1*		17:11	So,] ~ *E1*
12:29	and she] that she *E1*		17:13	death.—] ~. *E1*
13:6	But] ~, *E1*		17:22	and after all] ~, ~ ~, *E1*

255

18:10 deer.—] ~. *E1*

18:14 oh] ~, *E1*

18:17 Oh] ~, *E1*

18:19 knee.—] ~. *E1*

18:32 guilty—] ~? *E1*

19:6 Oh ... Oh] ~, ... ~, *E1*

19:26 Joyce] ~, *E1*

20:17 down] ~, *E1*

20:20 But] ~, *E1*

20:23 Oh ... Oh ... Well] ~, ... ~, ... ~, *E1*

20:27 Well] ~, *E1*

21:18 nothing] ~, *E1*

21:27 powerful] ~, *E1*

21:30 Joyce] ~, *E1*

21:32 —The] ~ *E1*

21:34 Well] ~, *E1*

22:11 And] ~, *E1*

22:24 Oh] ~, *E1*

22:33 Oh] ~, *E1*

23:2 thick] ~, *E1*

23:11 knee] ~, *E1*

23:14 wonderful] ~, *E1*

23:16 sensual!] ~. *E1*

24:31 food,] ~ *E1*

25:24 menad] mænad *E1*

25:29 menad] mænad *E1*

26:24 wicked] ~, *E1*

26:40 baby Barbara] ~, ~, *E1*

27:24 its *E1*] his *A1*

28:5 also,] ~ *E1*

30:21 clothes,] ~ *E1*

31:20 serene;] ~: *E1*

33:17 no!] No! *E1*

33:19 oh] ~, *E1*

Tickets Please

The sequence is *Per1*, *Per2*, *A1*, *E1*, and *Per2* is the base-text. (*Per1* agrees with *Per2* unless otherwise indicated.)

34:1 Tickets Please *Ed.*] "TICKETS, PLEASE!" *Per1* The Eleventh Commandment *Per2* TICKETS, PLEASE *A1* see notes

34:2 Midlands *A1*] North *Per1*

34:2 tramway system *A1*] system of tram-cars *Per1* system *Per2*

34:3 county *Per1*, *A1*] country *Per2*

34:6 stark *A1*] dark *Per1*

34:9 church,] ~ *Per1*

34:9 ash trees] ash-trees *Per1*

34:9 rush] bolt *Per1*

34:12 green] blue *Per1*

34:12 creamy-coloured *Ed.*] creamy coloured *Per1*, *A1* creamy-colored *Per2*

34:14 Co-operative] Coöperative *A1*

34:14 Shops] shops *Per1*

34:16 loops:] ~; *Per1*

34:20 beyond *A1*] ~, *Per1*

34:20 gas works] gasworks *Per1* gas-works *A1*

34:21 town, once ... [34:25] colliery garden. *A1*] town, once ... still jerky ... dare-devil, pert as a blue-tit out of ... colliery garden. *Per1* town. *Per2*

34:26 Since we are in war-time, the *A1*] The *Per1*

34:27 are] are often *Per1*

34:29 steeplechase] steeple-chase *A1*

34:29 Hurray!—] Hurrah! *Per1* Hurray! *A1*

34:29 leapt *Per1*, *A1*] leaped *Per2*

34:29 clean] clear *A1*

34:30 corner.] ~! *Per1*

34:31 sure,] ~ *Per1*

34:33 car] ~, *Per1*, *A1*

34:34 people] ~, *Per1*, *A1*

35:2 girl conductor] girl-conductor *Per1*

35:2 call—] ~: *Per1* ~, *A1*

35:2 fire.] ~! *A1*

35:2 Instead, however, *A1*] Instead *Per1*

35:4 on.] ~! *A1*

35:7 wind-swept *Per1*] wind-/swept *Per2* windswept *A1*

35:8   travel, *Per1, A1*] ~ *Per2*

35:11   notice—] ~ *Per1, A1*

35:11   "Depot Only"— *Per1*] ~- ~— *Per2* "~ ~," *A1*

35:12   wrong:] ~; *Per1* ~! *A1*

35:13   derision.] ~? *Per1*

35:14   night.] ~! *Per1*

35:15   tram service] tram-service *Per1, A1*

35:16   declare] ~, *Per1, A1*

35:16   girls] ~, *Per1, A1*

35:17   a little ... young men, *A1*] or else by invalids *Per1 Om. Per2*

35:19   uniforms] uniform *A1*

35:20   *sang froid*] sang-froid *Per1 sang-froid A1*

35:22   hymns *Per1, A1*] hyenas *Per2*

35:27   Halloa *Per1*] Hello *Per2*

35:28   Halloa *Per1*] Hello *Per2*

35:29   Stone.] ~! *Per1*

35:35   The step ... Thermopylae.] *Om. Per1* The ... Thermopylæ. *A1*

35:38   time for soft romance *A1*] romantic time *Per1* time for this *Per2*

35:40   market day] market-/ day *Per1* market-day *E1*

36:1   Then] Thus *A1*

36:2   her] the *A1*

36:4   shipmates] shipments *A1*

36:5   stormy] hilly *Per1*

36:5   land.] ~? *Per1*

36:6   during *A1*] in *Per1*

36:6   hours,] ~ *Per1*

36:10   wet] ~, *Per1, A1*

36:10   oil-skin] oilskin *Per1*

36:12   faint] ~, *Per1*

36:13   water-proof] waterproof *Per1, A1*

36:15   Halloa *Per1*] Hello *Per2*

36:15   Annie—keeping] ~! Keeping *Per1, A1*

36:18   foot-board— *Per1*] foot-board, *Per2, E1* foot-/ board, *A1*

36:20   Thomas] Joseph *Per1 see notes*

36:20   Raynor:] ~— *A1*

36:21   Thomas,] Joseph. *Per1*

36:21   except ... Coddy *A1*] *Om. Per1* except ... Jontom *Per2*

36:21   sets *Per1, A1*] gets *Per2*

36:23   half a dozen] half-a-dozen *Per1*

36:24   girl conductors] girl-conductors *Per1*

36:25   night,] ~ *Per1*

36:26   course] ~, *Per1, A1*

36:26   quit *Per1, A1*] leave *Per2*

36:27   the new-comer] a new-comer *Per1* the newcomer *A1*

36:31   port.] ~? *Per1*

36:33   tartar] Tartar *A1*

36:35   more:] ~; *Per1*

36:39   other,] ~ *Per1*

36:39   A fine ... he was.] *Om. Per1* A fine cock of the walk he was. *A1*

37:1   their] this *A1*

37:1   antagonism,] ~ *A1*

37:1   friends,] ~; *Per1*

37:3   sufficiently *A1*] fully *Per1*

37:5   Bestwood] Middleton *Per1*

37:6   drizzling] ~, *Per1*

37:10   side shows] side-shows *Per1*

37:11   cocoa-nut] coco-nut *Per1* cocoanut *A1*

37:11   cocoa-nuts] coco-nuts *Per1* cocoanuts *A1*

37:12   war-time *A1*] *Om. Per1*

37:16   [of new-]fried *Ed.*] fried *Per1* a few fried *A1 see notes*

37:16   potatoes,] ~ *Per1*

37:16   of electricity *A1*] electricity *Per1*

37:17   show ground] show-ground *Per1, E1* show-/ ground *A1*

37:18   Thomas.] Joseph! *Per1*

37:20   hardy *Per1*] handy *Per2*

37:24   Dragons] dragons *Per1*

37:25   tram-car,] ~ *A1*

37:25   But] ~, *A1*

37:26   shaking] ~, *E1*

37:28   Thomas,] Joseph *Per1* Thomas *A1*

37:28   was after all] ~, ~ ~, *Per1*

37:32   for shame *A1*] for shame to *Per1* for-shame to *Per2*

37:39   she *A1*] *Om. Per1*

37:39 He of course] ~, ~ ~, *Per1, A1*

37:40 sideways, *A1*] ~ *Per1* side-/ ways, *Per2*

38:1 But of course] ~, ~ ~, *Per1*

38:5 half lying] half-lying *Per1*

38:6 happy,] ~; *Per1, A1*

38:8 her] for her *A1*

38:8 pale blue] pale-blue *Per1, A1*

38:9 hat-pins] hatpins *Per1*

38:9 cinema] cinemas *A1*

38:11 performances,] ~ *A1*

38:16 And] ~, *Per1, E1*

38:16 all] ~, *Per1, A1*

38:16 held:] ~; *Per1*

38:18 hair, she] ~. She *Per1* ~; ~ *A1*

38:19 And] ~, *Per1, E1*

38:21 up,] ~; *A1*

38:22 nonchalant] nonchalantly *A1*

38:34 rich] pleasant *Per1*

38:34 herself,] ~ *A1*

38:34 whenever *Per1, E1*] wherever *A1*

38:37 good] gratifying *Per1*

38:40 man,] ~; *Per1, A1*

39:2 *mere*] mere *A1*

39:2 presence:] ~— *Per1* ~, *A1*

39:6 presence, *Per1, E1*] ~; *A1*

39:12 was no] is no *A1*

39:15 desolation] ~, *Per1, A1*

39:18 head *A1*] eyes *Per1*

39:19 else,] ~ *A1*

39:21 Thomas] William *Per1*

39:22 rather] somewhat *Per1*

39:24 her:] ~; *A1*

39:24 then] ~, *Per1*

39:24 softly:] ~, *A1*

39:29 do] ~, *Per1, A1*

39:31 is] ~, *A1*

39:33 cheek!] ~. *A1*

39:33 foot-board] footboard *Per1, A1* foot-/ board *E1*

39:34 at me.] me! *Per1*

39:35 dropped on] dropped-on *A1*

39:36 will] ~, *E1*

40:1 What? Don't] ~! don't *Per1*

40:4 fact,] ~ *Per1*

40:8 *qui vive*] qui-vive *A1*

40:13 10.15] ten-fifteen *Per1*

40:17 half dozen] half-dozen *Per1*

40:18 So] ~, *A1*

40:19 in,] ~ *Per1*

40:19 in to] into *Per1, A1*

40:20 home,] ~ *Per1*

40:20 round] around *A1*

40:21 Outside was ... war-time. *A1*] *Om. Per1*

40:25 Prayer meeting] Prayer-meeting *A1*

40:26 Ladies only] Ladies' effort *Per1*

40:31 Birkin *A1*] Birken *Per1*

40:32 in,] ~ *Per1, A1*

40:33 circle,] ~ *Per1*

40:34 great-coat *Per1, A1*] great coat *Per2*

40:35 tea-pot] teapot *Per1, A1*

40:36 Purdy *A1*] *Om. Per1*

40:37 drippin' *A1*] dripping *Per1*

40:39 give us a bit] all's welcome *Per1*

41:6 Me!] ~? *Per1*

41:6 am.] ~! *Per1*

41:7 minutes,] ~ *Per1, A1*

41:8 Houselay *A1*] Housely *Per1*

41:9 duck,] ~! *Per1, A1*

41:11 "'But—*Ed.*] "'~ *Per1* "~ *Per2* "~—*A1*

41:11 to,] ~ *Per1*

41:11 in, *A1*] ~ *Per1*

41:11 dark,'" *Per1*] ~," *Per2*

41:13 John Thomas] Mr. Raynor *Per1*

41:15 Thomas] Joseph *Per1*

41:15 myself,] ~ *Per1, A1*

41:16 lonely-O *A1*] lonely-o *Per1* lonely—O *Per2*

41:17 ejaculation. *P* The *A1*] ~. The *Per1*

41:21 overcoat *A1*] coat *Per1*

41:24 manner. *P* They *A1*] ~. They *Per1*

41:26 Muriel, "don't] ~. Don't *Per1, A1*

41:26 leave us ... one! *A1*] disappoint us all. *Per1* disappoint us all, John Thomas. *Per2*

41:28 responded *Per2, E1*] ~, *Per1, A1*

41:29   company,] ~; *Per1, A1*
41:31   Nay,] ~—*A1*
41:32   one *Per1*] *Om. A1*
41:33   Ay,] ~! *Per1*
41:33   Pick *A1*] Choose *Per1*
41:34   Thomas,] Joseph— *Per1* ~;*A1*
41:35   tonight. *Ed.*] to-night." *Per1*
        tonight." *Per2* to-night. *A1*
41:35   Feeling good, for once." *A1*]
        He frowned at the use of his
        double name. *Per1 Om. Per2*
41:37   Whereabouts *A1*] Who says
        Per1
41:37   Take a good un, then. *A1*] *Om.*
        Per1
41:37   But tha's ... of us! *A1*] Tha's
        got to ta'e one. *Per1* Tha's got
        to tac' one. *Per2*
41:39   one,] ~? *Per1*
42:1   Annie.] Annie, grimly. *Per1*
42:2   added *A1*] said *Per1*
42:2   Laura.] Laura. A laugh went
        up. *Per1*
42:3   Oh] ~, *Per1, A1*
42:3   ay *Per1*] my *Per2*
42:3   turning,] ~ *Per1*
42:4   Well,] ~—*A1*
42:4   good-night.] ~! *Per1*
42:5   make your pick *A1*] take one
        Per1
42:7   us—go] ~. Go *Per1, A1*
42:9   He was ... break away. *A1*]
        Om. Per1
42:12   He looked around uneasily.
        A1] *Om. Per1*
42:17   flying, and himself staggering.]
        flying. *Per1*
42:20   He however] ~, ~, *Per1, A1*
42:25   was distinctly afraid] became
        suddenly pale *Per1*
42:29   chosen,] ~! *A1*
42:31   going *A1*] *Om. Per1*
42:31   replied. *P* He *A1*] replied. The
        girls stood back in a silent,
        attentive group. *P* He *Per1*
        replied. He *Per2*
42:32   moment:— *Per1*] ~. *Per2*
42:33   blasted] confounded *Per1*

42:35   choose,] ~! *A1*
42:35   girls. *P* "Come on!" cried ...
        on!" *A1*] girls. *P* He hung a
        moment; then he went sud-
        denly red, and his eyes flashed.
        P "Come on! Come on!" cried
        Annie. *Per1* girl. "Come on!
        Come on!" *Per2*
42:38   forward, rather vaguely *A1*]
        forward, threatening *Per1*
        forward to lay hold on her *Per2*
42:38   belt, and] ~ ~, *Per1*
42:39   head,] ~ *Per1, A1*
42:40   sprang and seized her *A1*]
        rushed with lifted hand *Per1*
        rushed and seized her *Per2*
43:1   rushed upon] flew at *Per1*
43:1   and tearing *A1*] him and
        pushing *Per1* him and tearing
        Per2
43:2   thoroughly] *Om. Per1*
43:5   back.] ~, *A1*
43:6   button] button-hole *Per1*
43:8   simply] *Om. Per1*
43:8   back,] back as they dragged
        him, *Per1*
43:8   shirt-sleeves *Per1, A1*] shirt
        sleeves *Per2*
43:8   his arms were] one arm was
        Per1
43:9   girls *A1*] girls simply *Per1*
43:9   on him *A1*] *Om. Per1*
43:10   him:] ~; *Per1*
43:11   might: or ... more intense. *A1*]
        might. *Per1*
43:13   rushed on] rushed *Per1*
43:15   scratch, his ... bruised. *A1*]
        scratch. *Per1*
43:19   captor. Sometimes *A1*] ~. *P*
        Sometimes *Per1*
43:21   torn] scratched and bleeding
        Per1
43:22   Now then,] ~, ~, *A1*
43:22   length. "Now] ~. *P* "Now
        Per1
43:27   now] ~, *A1*
43:27   then—!] ~! *Per1, A1*
43:27   length. *P* And] ~. And *Per1*

43:28 heart-beating *Per2, E1*]
heartbeating *Per1* heart-/
beating *A1*

43:38 in a ... it now! *A1*] recovering
her senses a little. *P* "Yes, you
may well lie there! *Per1* recovering her ... there!— *Per2*

43:39 *You*] You *A1*

43:39 you?—] ~? *Per1, A1*

44:1 eyes,] ~ *Per1*

44:6 Oh-h-hs] oh-h-h's *Per1*

44:8 said] ~, *Per1*

44:9 Oh, yes *A1*] Yes *Per1*

44:11 she *A1*] he *Per1*

44:12 him. *P* But *A1*] ~. But *Per1*

44:13 quite *A1*] *Om. Per1*

44:14 started, *A1*] ~ *Per1*

44:14 Then his ... after all. *A1*] *Om.
Per1*

44:17 He only ... near his. *A1*] *Om.
Per1*

44:19 said, *A1*] said, bewildered,
Per1

44:20 *choose! Ed.*] ~, *Per1 choose! A1*

44:21 menace, and ... exact more.
A1] menace. *Per1*

44:23 your girl ... settled now. *A1*]
which of us you'll have, do you
hear, and stop your little
games. We'll settle you. *Per1*

44:27 He did ... to bits. *A1*] *Om.
Per1*

44:29 right] ~, *A1*

44:29 said,] ~. *Per1*

44:29 Annie." His ... [44:32] in
chorus. *A1*] Annie." *P* "Three
cheers for Annie!" cried
Laura. *Per1*

44:33 She was ... [44:36] bitter
accent. *A1*] Her face was very
white, her eyes like coal.

"Me——!" *Per1* Her face ...
coals. "Me!——" *Per2*

44:37 drawing away ... bitterness *A1*]
pushing him away from her
with a strange disgust *Per1*

44:40 But her face ... turned aside.
A1] The other girls rose also.
Per1

45:2 floor, with ... averted face. *A1*]
floor. *Per1*

45:4 again] another *Per1*

45:5 hopelessness *A1*] disgust *Per1*

45:6 up." *P* He *Per1, A1*] ~." He
Per2

45:7 ragged] ~, *Per1, A1*

45:9 Laura] ~, *Per1, A1*

45:10 contempt] derision *Per1*

45:10 Yet each ... broken in her. *A1*]
Om. Per1

45:13 He, however ... [45:37] stupefied faces. *A1*] And they began
to put themselves tidy, taking
down their hair, and arranging
it. Annie unlocked the door.
John Joseph looked round for
his things. He picked up the
tatters, and did not quite know
what to do with them. Then he
found his cap, and put it on,
and then his overcoat. He
rolled his ragged tunic into a
bundle. And he went silently
out of the room, into the night.
P The girls continued in
silence to dress their hair and
adjust their clothing, as if he
had never existed. *Per1* And
they ... hair and ... John
Thomas looked vaguely round
... existed. *Per2*

The Blind Man

The sequence is *Per1, Per2, A1, E1*. Thus *Per2* follows *Per1* and *E1* follows *A1*
unless indicated.

46:20 place,] ~—— *A1*

47:18 prattling *E1*] rattling *Per1*

48:31 fact:] ~; *A1*

49:3 an emotional *A1*] a feeling *Per1*

50:19 eye-lids] eyelids *Per2*

50:37 tea-pot] teapot *A1*

51:26 Tartan] tartan *A1*

51:29 outhouses *A1*] out-/ houses *Per1* out-houses *Per2*

52:16 in *E1*] *Om. Per1*

53:17 boots,] ~ *A1*

53:26 familiar] ~, *E1*

53:38 said,] ~ *E1*

54:33 throw-back *A1*] throw-/ back *Per1* throwback *Per2*

55:3 visitors' *Per1*, *A1*] visitor's *Per2*, *E1*

56:4 scar] scars *E1*

56:15 eat." *P* Bertie *Per1*, *A1*] ~. "Bertie *Per2*

56:33 plate] place *E1*

57:33 quick,] ~ *A1*

58:21 patronised *A1*] despised *Per1*

58:24 uptilted *Per1*, *A1*] uplifted *Per2*

60:9 night] evening *E1*

60:9 clock. *P* "I] ~ "I *A1*

62:28 terror-struck *Ed.*] terror-/ struck *Per1*, *A1* terrorstruck *Per2*

Monkey Nuts

The sequence is *Per, A1, E1*, and the base-text is *Per.*

64:1 Monkey Nuts *A1*] MONKEY-NUTS *Per see notes*

64:4 billeted] billetted *E1*

64:4 station;] ~, *A1* ~: *E1*

64:5 masters;] ~: *A1* ~, *E1*

64:10 Albert] ~, *A1*

64:11 Flanders] ~, *A1*

64:11 heaven *A1*] Heaven *Per*

64:15 decent,] ~ *A1*

64:19 pleasant-looking] pleasant looking *A1*

64:23 goods-yard: *A1*] ~; *Per*

64:28 station-master *Per, E1*] station master *A1*

65:1 overalls *Ed.*] overall *Per* over-/ alls *A1*

65:3 Now,] ~ *A1*

65:3 us] ~, *A1*

65:5 corporal,] ~: *A1*

65:7 pal.— *A1*] ~. *Per, E1*

65:20 certainty!] ~, *A1*

65:23 strong] ~, *A1*

65:25 Now,] ~! *A1*

65:30 absorbed] ~, *A1*

65:34 attitudes] ~, *E1*

65:38 fresh— *A1*] ~, *Per*

66:3 Always after this] ~, ~ ~, *A1*

66:3 team] ~, *A1*

66:9 jokes but] ~. But *A1*

66:12 afternoon] ~, *A1*

66:13 telegram: *P* "Meet] ~: "Meet *A1*

66:14 6 p.m.] 6.00 p. m. *A1* 6.00 P.M. *E1*

66:14 to-day.—] ~. *A1*

66:14 S." *P* He] ~." He *A1*

66:21 then,] ~; *A1*

66:31 pictures] movies *A1 see notes*

67:1 6] *6.00 A1*

67:1 S."] S.," *E1*

67:11 Well] ~, *A1*

67:13 Wha-at] Wha—at *A1*

67:18 him with *Per, E1*] with with *A1*

67:19 blazes—what] ~! What *A1*

67:37 haughtily,] ~. *A1*

67:40 Well— *A1*] ~, *Per*

68:1 *women*— *A1*] ~, *Per*

68:17 Now] ~, *A1*

68:18 waiting— *A1*] ~, *Per*

68:20 on,] ~ *E1*

68:26 do] go *A1 see note to* 66:31

68:28 No] ~, *A1*

68:34 said] ~, *A1*

68:40 Stokes. *A1*] ~: *Per*

68:41 said] ~, *A1*

69:3 Monkey nuts] Monkey-nuts *A1*

69:10 ticket caravan] ticket-caravan *A1*

69:17 legs,] ~ *A1*

69:18 horse,] ~; *A1*

69:19 strength] ~, *E1*

69:21 Half-way *A1*] Halfway *Per*

69:24 clown; *Per, E1*] ~: *A1*

69:24 she also *A1*] ~, ~, *Per*

69:29   dark] ~, *E1*

69:34   villages,] ~; *A1*

69:36   village,] ~ *E1*

69:38   bicycle—a land-girl—] ~; a
        land girl; *A1*

70:3   words? *A1*] ~! *Per*

70:3   Albert. "That's *A1*] ~. *P*
        "That's *Per*

70:3   what I call cruel, now,] cruel of
        you, *A1*

70:7   replied] ~, *A1*

70:10   What!—you *A1*] ~! You *Per*

70:17   pine wood] pine-wood *A1*

70:17   village, *A1*] ~ *Per*

70:18   road, was *A1*] road were *Per*

70:19   hand,] ~ *A1*

70:22   cross-roads] cross-road *A1*

70:24   home, *A1*] ~? *Per*

70:28   No *A1*] ~, *Per*

70:31   pal!] ~. *A1*

70:34   Joe] ~, *A1*

70:37   that.] ~! *A1*

71:12   nearer, and] ~ ~ *A1*

71:15   silence— *A1*] ~, *Per*

71:16   trill] ~, *A1*

71:23   malarial *A1*] malaria *Per*

71:35   monkey-nuts]   Monkey-nuts
        A1

71:35   corporal. *P* But] ~. But *A1*

71:38   taciturn,] ~ *A1*

72:8   wain—] ~: *A1*

72:10   good-looking;] ~, *A1*

72:11   Joe *A1*] ~, *Per*

72:13   her. He *A1*] ~. *P* He *Per*

72:14   tender] ~, *A1*

72:21   monkey-nuts]   Monkey-nuts
        A1

72:23   like!] ~, *A1*

72:28   dark-red] dark red *A1*

73:2   puttees] ~, *A1*

73:10   asked] ~, *A1*

73:13   quiet, *A1*] quite *Per*

73:15   daylight— *A1*] ~, *Per*

73:17   continued:] ~. *A1*

73:22   murdered?— *A1*] ~, *Per*

73:23   murdering?— *A1*] ~— *Per*

73:24   while] ~, *A1*

73:26   aside, *A1*] ~ *Per*

73:33   'er!] ~, *A1*

73:34   a while] awhile *A1*

73:37   pondered— *A1*] ~, *Per*

73:39   water] ~, *A1*

73:39   soft-hearted—— *A1*] ~. *Per*

74:13   walked,] ~ *A1*

74:34   change;] ~: *E1*

74:39   know!] ~? *A1*

74:39   Not *Per, E1*] No *A1*

74:40   stopped,] ~ *A1*

75:2   road,] ~ *A1*

75:3   side] ~, *A1*

75:5   he *A1*] *Om. Per*

75:12   you, *A1*] ~ *Per*

75:27   boy,] ~; *A1*

75:27   Monkey-nuts *A1*] monkey-
        nuts *Per*

75:33   usual:] ~; *A1*

75:36   Joe?] ~! *A1*

75:38   He] he *A1*

76:8   half-averted] half averted *A1*

76:9   you,] ~! *A1*

76:15   Monkey nuts] Monkey-nuts
        A1

76:16   white— *A1*] ~, *Per*

Wintry Peacock

Additional symbols used in this story are:
     PPr = Proofs of *Per* authorially revised for *E1*
     E1 = *New Decameron*
     E2 = English edition of *England, My England* (Secker)
The sequence is *MS, Per, PPr, E1, A1, E2*, and the base-text is *Per*.

77:1   Wintry Peacock *MS, A1*]
        Wintry Peacock / The Lance-
        Corporal Comes Home from
        the War *Per* The Poet's Tale /
        Wintry Peacock *PPr* THE
        POET'S TALE / WINTRY

PEACOCK *E1 see notes*
77:8 tail-less] tailless *E1*
78:8 cartshed,] cart-shed *A1*
78:15 me, *MS*] ~ *Per*
78:25 French, *Per, A1*] ~? *E1*
78:33 Lance-Corporal *Per, A1*] M. Alfred *PPr*
78:37 English soldier *Per, A1*] Englishman *PPr*
78:38 me. "— *MS*] ~." *Per* ~?" *E1*
78:40 private! *Per, A1*] ~? *E1*
79:1 world, *Per, A1*] ~ *E1*
79:4 on] ~, *E1*
79:12 you.] ~? *E1*
79:14 no. You *MS*] ~, you *Per*
79:15 you. I can] you, *A1*
79:17 father, *Per, A1*] ~ *E1*
79:20 Alfred,] ~ *A1*
79:21 money, *Per, A1*] ~. *E1*
79:23 baby— — *MS, E2*] ~—— *Per*
79:31 Oh yes.—] ~, ~—— *A1*
79:31 Eliza?— *MS*] ~? *Per*
79:35 Post-man *MS*] Postman *Per*
79:37 tonight] to-night *E1*
79:37 He's been ... [80:4] fed up.—] He had an accident and hurt his leg. He's been abroad most of his time for this last four years. He's chauffeur to a gentleman who travels about in one country and another, on some sort of business.— Married?—We married? Why six years. And I tell you, I've seen little enough of him for four of them.—But he always was a rake. He went through the South African War, and stopped out there for five years. *PPr* He had ... business. Married? We married? Why, six ... you I've ... them. But ... years. *E1 see also following entries to 80:4*
79:39 then.—] ~. *A1*
80:2 will.—] ~. *A1*
80:3 war.—] ~. *A1*
80:4 War.— *MS*] ~. *Per*

80:4 up.—] ~. *A1*
80:5 mother.—] ~. *E1* ~— *A1*
80:7 no.— *MS*] ~. *Per*
80:8 Oh] ~, *A1*
80:9 daughters.—] ~. *A1*
80:10 like.— *MS*] ~. *Per*
80:11 home.—] ~. *E1*
80:11 Before the ... a long time—" *MS*] Before the ... time——" *Per* Always a chauffeur? No, he's been all sorts of things: was to be a farm-bailiff by rights. He's had a good education—but he liked the farming better.—Then he was five years in the Cape Mounted Police. I met him when he came back from there, and married him—more · fool me——" *PPr* Always a ... the motors better ... me——" *E1* Before the ... better. Then ... time——" *A1* Before the ... better. Then ... time—" *E2*
80:17 Hello] ~, *E1*
80:19 Joey] ~, *A1*
80:20 voice." You're *MS*] ~: "You're *Per* ~: "you're *E1* ~, "you're *A1*
80:21 you. *MS*] ~? *Per*
80:21 forward *Per, A1*] downward *E1*
80:25 does—" *MS*] ~," *Per, A1* ~" *E1*
80:26 I?] ~. *A1*
80:29 'bu-rrd.' *MS*] "bir-rrd." *Per*
80:32 *dee-urrr? MS*] *dee-urr? Per*
80:40 enough—all these four years. *Per, A1*] enough. *E1*
81:2 grumble.— *MS*] ~. *Per*
81:4 'My dear Alfred.' *MS*] "~ ~ ~." *Per, A1* "'~ ~ ~.'" *E1*
81:5 Alfred— *MS*] ~. *Per*
81:10 "'I *MS, E1*] "~ *Per, A1*
81:11 me—'" *MS*] ~?"— *Per, A1* ~?'" *E1*
81:12 besides *MS*] beside *Per*
81:14 continued—"'A *MS*] ~."~ *Per, A1* ~. "'~ *E1*

81:16 arms—'" *MS*] ~——" *Per, A1*
~——'" *E1*
81:19 me *MS*] *Om. Per*
81:21 said, "it's] ~. "It's *E1*
81:21 mother's.—'He *MS*] ~. " *Per*
~. '~ *E1* ~." "~ *A1*
81:22 eyes—'" *MS, E1*] ~——" *Per,*
A1
81:28 Oh *Per*] ~, *A1*
81:28 very.— *MS*] ~! *Per*
81:28 *Joey Per*] ~, *A1*
81:30 "— Er] —"~ *A1*
81:30 'We *E1*] ~ *Per, A1*
81:31 Alfred, *MS*] ~ *Per*
81:33 you—'" *Ed.*] ~—" *MS*
~——" *Per* ~——'" *E1*
81:35 said I *MS*] I said *Per*
81:35 mother's. Er— 'My] ~." Er—
"~ *A1*
81:36 on leave *Per, A1*] from Lille
PPr
82:1 father?— *MS*] ~? *Per*
82:2 wound *Per, A1*] leg *PPr*
82:2 walk—'" *MS*] ~'—" *Per*
~——'" *E1* ~——" *A1*
82:3 Goyte.—] ~. *E1*
82:4 her *Per, A1*] her that *E1*
82:4 one.—] ~. *E1*
82:5 "'We *MS, E1*] "~ *Per, A1*
82:5 all *MS*] *Om. Per*
82:6 well—'" *MS*] ~——" *Per, A1*
~——" *E1* ~—" *E2*
82:7 *Eh*] *eh, E1* eh, *E2*
82:7 *Joey!— MS*] ~! *Per*
82:8 "'If *MS, E1*] "~ *Per, A1*
82:11 comfort *Per, A1*] comforter *E1*
82:13 for ever—'" *MS*] forever.'" *Per*
for ever.'" *E1* for ever." *A1*
82:15 shame, *Per, A1*] ~ *E1*
82:16 hopes.— *MS*] ~— *Per*
82:21 wanted *Per, A1*] wanted to *E1*
82:22 said. "We] ~, "we *A1*
82:23 different!—] ~! *A1*
82:24 Tommy-rot] tommy-rot *A1*
82:24 life!—] ~?— *E1* ~! *A1*
82:26 'We] ~ *A1*
82:26 England.— *MS*] ~. *Per*
82:29 Elise.'"] ~." *A1*

82:33 that. *Per, E2*] ~! *A1*
83:2 Oh] ~, *A1*
83:2 said,— *MS*] ~— *Per*
83:3 that— *MS, E2*] ~—— *Per, A1*
~——? *E1*
83:5 said. *P* She *MS*] ~. She *Per*
83:8 Oh] ~, *A1*
83:9 end.—] ~. *A1*
83:9 And *Per*] ~, *A1*
83:11 Oh— *Per, A1*] ~—— *E1*
83:12 it—me *Per, A1*] ~. Me *E1*
83:13 hand *Per, A1*] hands *E1*
83:14 parcels *Per, A1*] nice little cakes
and bits I thought he'd fancy
PPr
83:15 parcels *Per, A1*] things *PPr*
83:15 him.— *Per*] ~. *A1*
83:17 I. "He'd *MS, E1, E2*] ~. *P*
"He'd *Per, A1 see notes*
83:19 face.—] ~. *E1*
83:22 Then *Per, A1*] ~, *E1*
83:30 glistering *MS*] glistening *Per*
83:32 whiteness, *MS*] ~ *Per*
83:38 valley,] ~ *E2*
84:1 groove *MS*] grove *Per see notes*
84:3 black,] ~ *A1*
84:4 one *MS*] me *Per*
84:6 of] of the *A1*
84:13 valley-side *MS, E1*] valley-/
side *Per* valleyside *A1*
84:15 birds, *Per, A1*] ~— *E1*
84:20 Yes, *MS, E1*] ~ *Per*
84:22 Joey] ~, *E2*
84:25 eye *Per, A1*] eyes *E1*
84:30 tired, *MS, E1*] ~ *Per, A1*
84:36 stretching *MS*] stretched *Per*
84:37 put] *put A1*
85:6 night however] ~, ~, *E1*
85:14 shadow *Per, A1*] shadows *E1*
85:15 valley-side] valleyside *A1*
85:16 pine trees *Per, A1*] pine-trees
E1
85:17 snowy, *Per, A1*] ~ *E1*
85:18 wide,] ~ *A1*
85:18 eye *Per, A1*] eyes *E1*
85:19 township,] ~ *E2*
85:28 Joey! *Per, A1*] ~? *E1*
85:30 snow,] ~ *E2*

85:30   up, *Per, A1*] ~ *E1*
85:39   Ah *MS, E1*] ah *Per, A1*
86:2   ⸱ life.— *MS*] ~. *Per*
86:2   must 'a *Per*] must/'a' *E1* must'a *A1*
86:2   —Tha *MS*] ~ *Per*
86:3   Maggie, 'e'd *MS*] ~. 'E'd *Per*
86:3   froze.— *MS*] ~. *Per*
86:4   concluded,] ~ *E1*
86:14   debonair *Per, A1*] debonnair *E1*
86:16   turning, *MS*] ~ *Per*
86:17   called: "Alfred *Per, A1*] ~: *P* "Alfred *E1*
86:19   up then *Per, A1*] ~, ~ *E1*
86:21   wearing rough khaki *Per, A1*] limping, wearing a thick short coat *PPr*
86:22   Danish looking *Per, A1*] Danish-looking *E1*
86:23   'E's *MS*] I's *Per*
86:23   back *Per, A1*] ~, *E1*
86:23   son—] ~; *E2*
86:24   back. *MS*] ~,' *Per* ~, *E1*
86:24   'E flyed ower ter *MS*] flyed ower the *Per*
86:28   Master? *MS, E1*] ~, *Per, A1*
86:31   carryin' *MS, E1*] carrin' *Per, A1*
86:32   living room *Per, A1*] living-room *E1*
86:33   cosy, *Per, A1*] ~ *E1*
86:36   again, *Per, A1*] ~ *E1*
86:37   'Er's *MS, E1*] 'er's *Per, A1* 'ers *E2*
86:39   did.— *MS*] ~. *Per*
86:39   yer.— *MS*] ~. *Per*
87:2   they *MS*] then *Per* there *PPr*
87:3   flushed] ~, *A1*
87:5   quiet] ~, *E1*
87:7   'Er's *Ed.*] Er's *MS* 'er's *Per* 'Er's *E1* 'Ers *E2*
87:8   us *MS*] 'er *Per*
87:9   north-east *MS, E1*] northeast *Per, A1*
87:13   Ah'n *MS*] Ah've *Per*
87:13   it.— *MS*] ~. *Per*
87:14   Alfred—? *MS*] ~? *Per*
87:16   'E's *MS, A1*] 'e's *Per* 'Es *E2*

87:16   's *MS*] 'is *Per*
87:16   back, *Per, A1*] ~ *E2*
87:17   Mother, *Per, A1*] ~ *E1*
87:18   tom-foolery *Per, A1*] tomfoolery *E1*
87:18   makkin' *Per, A1*] makin' *E1*
87:19   ower] over *A1*
87:20   use.— *MS*] ~. *Per*
87:20   'Er *MS, E1*] 'er *Per*
87:21   on't.— *MS*] ~. *Per*
87:21   Ay] Ty *A1*
87:21   y' expect *MS, A1*] y'expect *Per*
87:29   there: *MS*] ~— *Per*
87:34   hulked, *MS*] ~ *Per*
87:35   us. *P* The *MS, E1*] ~. # *P* The *Per, A1 see notes*
88:1   hulked *Per, A1*] huddled *E1*
88:1   seeming] seemingly *A1*
88:9   longer?— *MS*] ~ ? *Per*
88:9   today] to-day *E1*
88:13   neck, *Per, A1*] ~ *E1*
88:15   Oh *Per, A1*] ~, *E1, E2*
88:20   went *Per, A1*] was *E1*
88:22   abstractedness, *MS*] ~ *Per*
88:24   her. *P* The *MS, E1, E2*] ~. # *P* The *Per, A1*
88:25   yellowish, when *MS*] ~. When *Per*
88:25   out, *MS*] ~ *Per*
88:26   sun, *MS*] ~; *Per*
88:29   striding *Per, A1*] striding awkwardly *PPr*
88:29   scarp, *MS*] ~ *Per*
88:31   farmer of the hills: *MS*] farmer ... hills; *Per, A1* knock-about fellow. *PPr*
88:33   said, *MS*] ~ *Per*
88:34   him, *MS*] ~ *Per*
88:38   mine—? *MS, E2*] ~——? *Per, A1* ~? *E1*
89:13   —he was a horse-soldier. Then *Per, A1*] and *PPr*
89:20   flushed *Per, A1*] flushed out *E1*
90:11   "'Mon *Ed.*] "~ *Per*
90:11   Alfred— Figure-toi *Per, A1*] ~,— Figure-toi *E1*
90:11   désolée——'" *Ed.*] desolée——"

Per, *A1 désolée*——" *E1*
desolée—" *E2*

90:12 finished *E1*] ~, *Per*
90:13 remember, *E1*] ~ *Per*
90:18 Oh *E1*] ~, *Per, A1*
90:28 Hey! *MS*] Why? *Per*
90:28 b— *Per, A1*] b—— *E1, E2*
90:29 b— *Per, A1*] b—— *E1, E2*
90:31 had a shot at him— —] let fly at
him the night I got back— *PPr*

had a ... him——*A1* had a ...
him— *E2*

90:34 *petite MS*] petite *Per*
90:34 asked. *P* He *MS*] ~. He *Per*
90:38 off *MS*] Om. *Per*
91:1 knock-out, *MS*] knockout! *Per*
91:1 amused. *P* Then *MS*] ~. Then
Per
91:5 in— *Per, A1*] ~—— *E1*
91:6 also] Om. *A1*

Hadrian [You Touched Me]

The sequence is *Per, A1, E1*, and the base-text is *A1*.

92:1 Hadrian *Ed.*] Om. *Per*
92:2 [You Touched Me] *Ed.*] "~ ~
~" *Per* YOU TOUCHED ME
A1
92:6 works:] ~; *Per*
92:8 pottery,] ~; *Per*
92:9 out-houses] outhouses *E1*
92:11 pottery] Pottery *E1*
92:12 crates,] ~ *E1*
92:15 pottery-lasses] pottery lasses
Per
92:29 district,] ~ *Per*
92:32 workmen.] workmen. And
unfortunately the tradespeople
and well-to-do men seemed to
produce strings of ill-fated
daughters who were too good
to marry working-men, and
who could find nobody else, for
the supply of bank-clerks and
chemists and doctors' assist-
ants was quite inadequate. So
that for two or three generations Rawsley had raised its
crop of old maids of all sorts,
most of them having just
enough money to live and die
on. *Per*
92:33 died:] ~; *Per*
92:35 at:] ~; *Per*
93:2 nonconformist] Nonconformist *Per*
93:5 graceful] ~, *Per*
93:6 Martha:] ~; *Per*

93:8 housekeeping *Ed.*] house-/
keeping *A1* housekeep-/ ing
Per
93:8 plumper] ~, *Per*
93:16 been ... whiskey-drinker]
drunk a good deal *Per*
93:24 daughters,] ~ *Per*
93:25 household] houseful *Per*
93:26 Charity Institution] charity
institution *Per*
93:27 fourteen] twenty *Per*
93:27 sixteen] twenty-two *Per*
93:30 hair] ~, *Per*
93:30 eyes] ~, *Per*
93:30 ordinary] ~, *Per*
93:31 cockney] Cockney *Per*
94:2 Pottery premises] pottery ~ *Per*
94:10 High School ... County] high
school ... county *Per*
94:14 He] So he *Per*
94:24 Institution] institution *Per*
94:25 seemed] ~, *Per*
94:26 them:] ~; *Per*
94:38 father.] father, who was
becoming swelled with water.
Per
95:4 morning] ~, *Per*
95:8 lather] lather of Lux *Per*
95:13 sewing machine]
sewing-machine *Per*
95:14 Charity Institution] charity
institution *Per*
95:18 hands *Per*] hand *A1*
95:25 best:] ~; *Per*

95:26 pink-and-white] pink and white *Per*

95:35 exclaimed,] ~ *Per*

95:35 today] to-day *Per, E1*

95:36 voice ... unexpected] ~, ... ~, *Per*

95:38 said,] ~ *Per*

96:3 apple-trees] apple trees *Per*

96:3 as] so *Per*

96:12 round—] ~, *Per*

96:16 kitchen,] ~ *Per*

96:18 *sotto voce*] sotto voce *Per*

96:19 he!] ~? *Per*

96:20 grimace,] ~ *Per*

96:29 Emmie, "but] ~. "But *Per*

96:34 Matilda,] ~ *Per*

96:35 *Sly—!*] *Sly! Per*

97:18 narrowly,] ~ *Per*

97:23 confab] "~" *Per*

97:28 men,] ~ *Per*

97:30 Oh] ~, *Per, E1*

97:32 drily] dryly *Per*

97:35 garden,] ~ *Per*

97:39 Emmie] ~, *E1*

98:2 plebeian] plebian *E1*

98:3 classes,] ~ *Per*

98:9 dark-blue] dark blue *Per*

99:11 *he—*] ~ *Per*

99:28 Gently,] ~ *Per*

99:28 leaned] leant *Per*

99:32 bed. "Yes] ~. *P* "Yes *Per*

99:33 answered. It] ~. *P* It *Per*

99:33 Instantly,] ~ *Per*

100:5 it.] ~? *Per*

100:7 laid] lain *Per*

100:9 mistake:] ~; *Per*

100:17 eyes,] ~ *Per*

100:21 drugged] sleepy *Per*

100:22 eyes,] ~ *Per*

100:24 But she ... [100:40] secretly plotting.] *Om. Per*

101:5 breeding] psyche *Per*

101:7 felt:] ~; *Per*

101:19 Uncle] uncle *Per*

101:21 A good bit] Nigh on twenty years *Per*

101:22 thirty] forty *Per*

101:23 Well] No *Per*

101:23 thirty-two] thirty-seven *Per*

101:27 "Do you ... father, restive.] *Om. Per*

101:30 said] cried *Per*

101:31 you wanted me to] you'd let me *Per*

101:32 The sick ... the window.] *Om. Per*

101:38 father,] ~ *Per*

101:38 I don't think ... the youngest.] I'm not against it. *Per*

101:40 more alive] young *Per*

102:1 ask] tell *Per*

102:3 ask] tell *Per*

102:14 still.—] ~. *Per, E1*

102:14 Hadrian——] ~. *Per*

102:15 rose,] ~ *Per*

102:16 you.] you. I want you to marry Hadrian. *Per*

102:17 "But you ... enough.—I ... tell you."] *Om. Per* "But ... enough. I ... you." *E1*

102:21 you,] ~? *Per*

102:30 replied,] ~ *Per*

102:31 said] ~, *E1*

102:33 erect,] ~ *Per, E1*

102:35 you're a ... you see?] you'll get nothing from me. *Per*

103:3 enough:] ~; *Per*

103:5 Hadrian:] ~; *Per*

103:13 impossible] horrible *Per*

103:20 will?] ~. *Per*

103:27 office,] ~ *Per*

103:29 will-form.] ~? *Per*

103:39 Uncle] uncle *Per*

103:40 Yes,] ~ *Per*

104:18 Matilda,] ~ *Per*

104:23 arrangements] arrangement *Per*

104:25 refused] ~, *Per*

104:37 aside:] ~; *Per*

104:40 immovable, they ... notice.] immovable. *Per*

105:6 came] come *E1*

105:12 Why,] ~ *Per*

105:16 He too ... of all.] *Om. Per*

105:25 with it] *Om. Per*

105:27 noiselessly] *Om. Per*

105:27 tired. ....] ~. *Per*
105:28 on] ~, *Per, E1*
105:30 father bluntly ... Go on."]
father. *Per*
105:37 everything] anything *E1*
106:7 Then] The *E1*
106:10 successful:] ~; *Per*
106:13 me] ~, *E1*
106:13 said,] ~ *Per*
106:13 subtle,] ~ *Per*
106:27 money?] ~. *E1*

106:35 She felt ... again despised.]
Om. Per
106:37 evening,] ~ *Per, E1*
106:39 at her] *Om. Per*
106:39 pain,] ~ *Per*
106:40 said,] ~ *Per*
107:17 Hadrian,—you've got her]
Hadrian—my son-in-law *Per*
107:17 said,] ~ *Per*
107:21 Let's] Let me *Per*

Samson and Delilah

The sequence is *MS, Per1, (Per2), A1, E1*, and the base-text is *MS*
For *Per2* only its eleven substantive variants are recorded; see the Explanatory note on 108:13 for its omissions.

108:1 Samson and Delilah *Per1*] The
Prodigal Husband *MS*
SAMSON AND DELILAH
A1 see notes
108:9 cautious *A1*] *Om. MS*
108:9 power-houses *Per1*]
power-house *MS*
108:10 tin-mines *MS, A1*] tin mines
Per1
108:11 by-gone *MS, A1*] bygone *Per1*
108:12 darkness,] ~ *Per1*
108:13 the lonely ... night. *A1*] home.
So, this was what it looked like!
MS home. *Per1*
108:14 watchful *A1*] alert *MS*
108:16 stiff, *MS, A1*] ~; *Per1*
108:18 shoulders:] ~; *Per1*
108:20 stumpy] stump *A1*
108:21 goodnight] good night *Per1*
good-night *A1*
108:21 to insist ... intonation. *A1*] the
familiarity pleased him. *MS*
108:27 a little ... conflict *A1*]
extremely pleased with himself,
with his own situation *MS*
108:30 road, *MS, A1*] ~; *Per1*
108:31 village, *MS, A1*] ~ *Per1*
108:32 road, *MS, A1*] highway *Per1*
108:33 There *Per1*] Ay, there *MS*
108:33 Tinners] Tinners' *Per1*
109:3 little, *MS, A1*] ~ *Per1*

109:6 men, miners, *MS, A1*]
~—~— *Per1*
109:9 Good-evening *MS, A1*] Good
evening *Per1*
109:9 landlady, *MS, A1*] ~ *Per1*
109:11 Good-evening.—] Good
evening. *Per1* Good-evening.
A1
109:14 assented, *MS, A1*] ~ *Per1*
109:15 weather. *Per1*] weather,
though. *MS*
109:16 seasonable, *MS, A1*] ~— *Per1*
109:17 lips, *MS, A1*] ~ *Per1*
109:23 dressed, *MS, A1*] ~— *Per1*
109:23 stranger. But *Ed.*] ~. / But *MS*
~. *P* But *Per1*
109:27 well-coloured] well coloured
Per1
109:27 eye-brows] eyebrows *Per1*
109:28 bright, mindless *Per1*] inexpressive *MS*
109:29 abstracted *Per1*] absorbed *MS*
109:31 vigour, *MS, A1*] ~; *Per1*
109:32 men, *MS, A1*] ~; *Per1*
109:32 shouted, *MS, A1*] ~ *Per1*
109:35 Oh] ~, *A1*
109:35 Now] ~, *E1*
109:38 Why *MS, A1*] ~, *Per1*
109:38 unfair!] ~? *Per1*
109:39 me, *MS, A1*] ~ *Per1*
109:40 it] ~, *Per1*

109:40 Queen of Spades] queen of spades *A1*

110:1 —Now] ~ *Per1* ~, *E1*

110:2 queen *MS, A1*] Queen *Per1*

110:3 Alice, *MS, A1*] ~ *Per1*

110:3 it— *MS, E1*] ~—— *Per1*

110:4 Ay *MS, A1*] ~, *Per1, E1*

110:4 say!] ~? *Per1*

110:5 Missis] missis *Per1* missus *A1*

110:7 khaki, *MS, A1*] ~— *Per1*

110:7 sergeant,] ~ *Per1*

110:10 Oh] ~, *E1*

110:10 back: *MS, A1*] ~; *Per1*

110:12 Ma *MS, A1*] ma *Per1*

110:13 private, *MS, A1*] ~ *Per1*

110:15 dears.—] ~. *Per1*

110:17 We *Per1*] Yes, we *MS*

110:22 kitchen.] ~? *Per1*

110:26 sixteen came in. She was *A1*] sixteen, *MS* sixteen entered, *Per2*

110:27 dark, young, expressionless *MS, A1*] dark, living young *Per1* dark young *Per2*

110:30 Ho—Maryann ... Maryann, now! *Ed.*] Ho—Mabel! Evenin' Mabel! How's Mabel! *MS* Ho, Mabel! Evenin', Mabel! How's Mabel? *Per1* Ho, Maryann ... now? *A1*

110:32 voice, *MS, A1*] ~— *Per1*

110:34 as if ... modesty. *A1*] like a stiff young animal. *MS*

110:39 him, *MS, A1*] ~ *Per1*

110:39 unreasoning *Per1*] mindless *MS*

111:1 said. Her ... sing-song. *Ed.*] said, in her soft-breathing, gently sing-song voice. *MS* said in her soft-breathing gently singsong voice. *Per1* said. Her ... singsong. *A1*

111:5 What have you got? *Per1*] What you've got, *MS*

111:5 he] she *E1*

111:5 said, *MS, A1*] ~ *Per1*

111:5 in to] into *Per1*

111:6 meat—] ~—— *Per1*

111:8 table, *MS, A1*] ~ *Per1*

111:10 on] in *Per1*

111:10 large, *MS, A1*] ~ *Per1*

111:13 blouse, *MS, A1*] ~ *Per1*

111:15 asked, *MS, A1*] ~; *Per1*

111:18 Oh, *MS, A1*] Om. *Per1*

111:20 soldiers, *MS, A1*] ~ *Per1*

111:25 —But] ~ *Per1* —but *A1*

111:28 seemed ... agate *A1*] had no human meaning in them *MS, Per1*

111:29 brows] brow *Per1*

111:31 *thought Per1*] thought *MS*

111:31 not.—But] ~—but *Per1*

111:34 said, "you've] ~. "You've *Per1*

111:35 her into silence *A1*] for his own answer there *MS*

111:38 did not say any *A1*] would say no *MS*

111:38 with a flounce *A1*] in a pet *MS*

112:1 her, *MS, A1*] ~; *Per1*

112:5 Goodnight, Ma. Goodnight, Maryann *Ed.*] Good-night, Mother. Goodnight, Mabel *MS* Good night, ma. Good night, Mabel *Per1* Good-night, Ma. Good night, Maryann *A1*

112:6 sergeant,] ~ *Per1*

112:7 New Army *Per1*] new army *MS, A1*

112:9 looks at him *Per1*] glances at the stranger *MS*

112:10 storm swelled] storms welled *Per1* storm welled *A1*

112:11 suppressed, *MS, A1*] ~ *Per1*

112:18 fidgeting spasmodically with the newspaper *A1*] stitching spasmodically *MS* fidgetting ... newspaper *Per1*

112:21 Gentlemen ... goodnight all!" *Ed.*] Time, my dears," she said, in a voice of repressed fury. *MS* Gentlemen ... said in ... please." *Per1* Gentlemen ... good-night all!" *A1*

112:22 goodnight] good night *Per1* good-night *A1*

112:26 stood] ~, *Per1*

112:29 Sir *MS, A1*] sir *Per1, E1*

112:33 Closing-time] Closing time *Per1*

112:34 turned *Per1*] swung *MS*

112:35 jewel-like *A1*] meaningless *MS*

112:36 said, *MS, A1*] ~ *Per1*

112:36 laconic,] ~ *Per1*

112:40 Oh ... Oh] ~, ... ~, *Per1* ~! ... ~, *E1*

112:40 —And] ~ *Per1*

113:3 door, *MS, A1*] ~ *Per1*

113:7 my] the *Per1*

113:9 At least ... you are *MS, A1*] Anyway, I know you *Per1*

113:10 Oh do you! Oh do you!] ~, ~ ~? ~, ~ ~? *Per1*

113:10 if you'll ... tell me? *Per1*] at your service. *MS*

113:12 bright, *MS, A1*] ~ *Per1*

113:13 Missis *MS, A1*] missis *Per1*

113:13 you know it, as well as I do *A1*] I know it, and you know it *MS* you know it as ... do *Per1*

113:15 her. Her] ~. P Her *Per1*

113:17 *Do Per1*] Do *MS*

113:17 it] ~, *A1*

113:19 Missis *MS, A1*] missis *Per1*

113:19 him?— *MS, A1*] ~? *Per1*

113:21 Missis *MS, A1*] missis *Per1*

113:21 house, *MS, A1*] ~ *Per1*

113:25 What you say, eh? You *A1*] What, you *MS*

113:25 said, *MS, A1*] ~ *Per1*

113:25 sing-song *E1*] steady *MS* singsong *A1*

113:26 emotionless, *Per1*] ~ *MS*

113:26 smothered and pressing: *A1*] reasonable and curious: *MS* smothered and pressing; *Per1*

113:27 *you* anywhere ... don't you? *Ed.*] *you* anywhere. *MS* you anywhere. *Per1* you anywhere ... don't you? *A1*

113:30 baffled *Per1*] baffled rather *MS*

113:31 replied, *MS, A1*] ~ *Per1*

113:32 known, and respected, *MS, A1*] ~ ~ ~ *Per1*

113:33 round.—] ~. *Per1*

113:33 you." Her] ~." *P Her Per1* ~." *P Her A1*

113:35 tonight *Ed.*] this minute *MS* to-night *Per1*

113:36 flexible *A1*] nasty *MS*

113:37 Yes] ~, *Per1*

113:37 man, *MS, A1*] ~ *Per1*

113:37 Yes] ~, *Per1*

113:38 Your name's ... Nankervis. *A1*] You've got my name, and you've had a child by me— —You're my missis right enough. *MS* Your name's ... girl Mabel ... girl. You're my missis right enough. *Per1*

114:1 fixity of intention *A1*] detachment *MS*

114:6 Ay *MS, A1*] Aye *Per1*

114:6 said] ~, *A1*

114:6 unmoved *Per1*] ironically *MS*

114:6 He was uneasy before *A1*] But he was also frightened of *MS* But he was frightened of *Per1*

114:7 Only he ... as agate. *A1*] *Om. MS*

114:9 towered, *MS, A1*] ~ *Per1*

114:10 you—" she] ~?" She *Per1*

114:11 madness "*this minute!*] ~. "*This minute! Per1*

114:13 said, with suppressed emphasis *A1*] barked suddenly *MS*

114:13 you, *MS, A1*] ~ *Per1*

114:17 wincing *Per1*] frightened *MS*

114:24 boys!] ~? *Per1*

114:24 you,] ~. *A1*

114:25 overcoat, *MS, A1*] ~ *Per1*

114:28 dark-grey] dark grey *Per1*

114:34 missis] Missis *A1*

114:36 "She's that, sure enough." *A1*] *Om. MS*

115:2 sheepishly, *MS, A1*] ~ *Per1*

115:3 bar, *MS, A1*] ~ *Per1*

115:6 I have *MS, A1*] I've *Per1*

115:8 all!—] ~! *Per1*

115:9 dying *Per1*] last *MS*

115:9 breath.—] ~. *Per1*
115:11 pink. *MS, A1*] pink, she breathed with difficulty. *Per1*
115:19 declare I never *Per1*] don't believe I ever *MS*
115:20 else, *MS, A1*] ~— *Per1*
115:21 Why *MS, A1*] ~, *Per1, E1*
115:21 saying *MS, A1*] to say *Per1*
115:23 Maryann *A1*] Mabel *MS*
115:23 you had by me *MS, A1*] is mine *Per1*
115:24 soldiers] soldier *Per1*
115:25 unperturbed] imperturbed *A1*
115:27 it!] ~? *Per1*
115:27 But you see *MS, A1*] ~, ~ ~, *Per1*
115:30 watched] watched her *Per2*
115:32 Oh ... Oh yes *MS, A1*] ~, ...~, ~, *Per1*
115:32 sir, *MS, A1*] ~; *Per1*
115:33 landlady's] lady's *Per1*
115:35 fire, she] ~. She *Per1*
115:36 bar, *MS, A1*] ~; *Per1*
115:37 half way] half-way *Per1* halfway *A1*
115:37 them, *MS, A1*] ~; *Per1*
116:1 —Is] ~ *Per1*
116:1 sergeant, *MS, A1*] ~ *Per1*
116:3 great,] ~ *Per1*
116:5 pocket-handkerchief] pocket handkerchief *Per1*
116:6 Maryann *A1*] Mabel *MS*
116:8 me *MS, A1*] *Om. Per2*
116:8 penny bit *MS, A1*] penny-bit *Per1*
116:8 villain.—] ~. *Per1*
116:12 bewildered, *MS, A1*] ~; *Per1*
116:16 better go, for *A1*] go *MS* better go *Per1*
116:17 bit, *MS, A1*] ~ *Per1*
116:18 you.—] ~. *Per1*
116:19 woman, I ... sudden-like. *A1*] woman if you've treated her like that. *MS* woman if you've been gone like that. *Per1*
116:22 shaken *MS, A1*] shake *Per1*
116:23 matter!] ~, *Per1*
116:24 stop in my own home,— *A1*]

stop,— *MS* stop ... home— *Per1*
116:25 There *MS, A1*] ~, *Per1*
116:31 man, *MS, A1*] ~ *Per1*
116:32 moving *MS, A1*] going *Per1*
116:33 her, *MS, A1*] ~ *Per1*
116:33 said,] ~ *A1*
116:35 boys?— *MS, A1*] ~? *Per1*
116:37 *mention, A1*] mention, *MS* mention *Per1*
116:37 American mining-camps *MS, A1*] America mining camps *Per1*
116:40 might?—] ~? *Per1*
116:41 shame—] ~—— *Per1*
117:1 soldiers, ... sergeant,] ~ ... ~ *Per1*
117:2 stooped *MS, A1*] stopped *Per1*
117:5 soldiers, *MS, A1*] ~ *Per1*
117:7 man, *MS, A1*] ~ *Per1*
117:9 —You] ~ *Per1*
117:10 with,] *Om. Per1*
117:13 spell-bound or ... intention *A1*] bewitched *MS*
117:17 Well] ~, *Per1*
117:17 coaxed, *MS, A1*] ~ *Per1*
117:20 him, *MS, A1*] ~ *Per1*
117:20 challenging *MS, A1*] ~, *Per1*
117:22 No] ~, *Per1*
117:22 thing.—] ~. *Per1*
117:24 I!] ~? *Per1*
117:26 rope] ~, *Per1*
117:26 Alfred—John, quick now—— *A1*] *Om. MS*
117:32 breast, *MS, A1*] ~; *Per1*
117:32 back his head *Per1*] his face *MS*
117:32 frantically, *MS, A1*] ~ *Per1*
117:34 Laocoon *MS, A1*) Laocoön *Per1*
117:34 swaying *A1*] writhing *MS*
117:36 me *A1*] *Om. MS*
117:36 here!] ~, *Per1*
117:38 table, *MS, A1*] ~ *Per1*
117:39 cuttle-fish] cuttlefish *A1*
117:40 And he ... furniture bumping. *A1*] *Om. MS*

118:2   lower, *MS, A1*] ~; *Per1*
118:5   genius, *MS, A1*] ~ *Per1*
118:6   a *MS, Per2*] the *Per1, A1*
118:8   sides *Per1*] side *MS*
118:9   the *Per1*] a *MS*
118:12 over-turned] overturned *A1*
118:13 and pulled up *A1*] *Om. MS*
118:14 dazed, but excited with the
        row. *A1*] dazed. *MS*
118:16 great] ~, *A1*
118:17 surcharged, *MS, A1*] ~; *Per1*
118:19 his *MS, A1*] to his *Per2*
118:21 man, *MS, A1*] ~ *Per1*
118:24 strong, *MS, A1*] ~ *Per1*
118:27 triumphed *A1*] was appeased
        MS
118:28 watched fascinated *MS, A1*] ~,
        ~, *Per1*
118:29 large, *MS, A1*] ~ *Per1*
118:32 moments, *MS, A1*] ~ *Per1*
118:33 sergeant,] ~ *Per1*
118:34 you, *MS, A1*] ~ *Per1*
118:34 trouble. *MS, A1*] ~? *Per1*
118:38 outside, *MS, A1*] ~ *Per1*
118:39 policeman, *MS, A1*] ~ *Per1*
119:1   sergeant. "We *MS, A1*] ~, "we
        Per1
119:2   prisoner:] ~. *A1*
119:2   outside, *MS, A1*] ~ *Per1*
119:5   answer, *MS, A1*] ~; *Per1*
119:6   bright] ~, *E1*
119:8   Well *MS, A1*] ~, *Per1, E1*
119:9   up *MS, A1*] *Om. Per2*
119:10 man, *MS, A1*] ~ *Per1*
119:14 stocking-feet   *MS,   A1*]
        stockinged feet *Per1*
119:14 outside *Per1*] *Om. MS*
119:17 sergeant, *MS, A1*] ~ *Per1*
119:18 knot, *MS, A1*] ~ *Per1*
119:18 you'll] you *Per1*
119:18 Missis *MS, A1*] missis *Per1*
119:19 man, *MS, A1*] ~ *Per1*
119:26 He had various contusions. *A1*]
        Om. MS
119:27 arms *MS, A1*] hands *Per2*
119:31 crystal] ~, *A1*
119:33 church-yard *MS, A1*]
        churchyard *Per1*

119:34 wall, *MS, A1*] ~ *Per1*
119:36 together, *MS, A1*] ~ *Per1*
119:36 night, *MS, A1*] ~ *Per1*
119:36 inn. The] ~. *P* The *Per1*
119:38 Then, very quietly,] ~ ~ ~
        Per1
119:39 entered, *MS, A1*] ~ *Per1*
119:40 bar-counter, *MS, A1*] ~ *Per1*
120:6   table,] ~ *A1*
120:7   seat *MS, A1*] ~, *Per1*
120:9   fender,] ~ *A1*
120:9   fire, *MS, A1*] ~ *Per1*
120:11 silent] ~, *A1*
120:18 night, *MS, A1*] ~ *Per1*
120:19 well-shapen *MS, A1*] ~, *Per1*
120:24 picked you out among thou-
        sands *A1*] knowed you among
        thousands *MS* picked you out
        among a thousand *Per1*
120:25 "Though you're ... made."
        A1] *Om. MS*
120:30 this] this *E1*
120:30 year?—] ~? *Per1*
120:31 Butte *A1*] Bute *MS*
120:34 goes.—] ~— *Per1*
120:39 'sept] 'cept *Per1*
121:1   warily *A1*] easy *MS*
121:1   her, *MS, A1*] ~ *Per1, E1*
121:7   Ay *MS, A1*] Aye *Per1*
121:7   in *MS, A1*] into *Per1*
121:11 woman *MS, A1*] ~, *Per1*
121:12 fashion, *MS, A1*] ~ *Per1*
121:14 and *MS, A1*] ~, *Per1*
121:15 fire, *MS, A1*] ~ *Per1*
121:16 head, *MS, A1*] ~ *Per1*
121:16 hair, she ... bite her. *A1*] hair!
        She could scarcely refrain from
        touching it. *MS* hair she ...
        touching it. *Per1*
121:18 man!] ~? *Per1* ~? *A1*
121:20 finger,] fingers. *Per1*
121:20 It's no good ... know of. *A1*]
        Om. MS
121:24 yourself! *MS, A1*] ~? *Per1*
121:24 exclaimed, *MS, A1*] ~ *Per1*
121:25 a *MS, A1*] *Om. Per2*
121:27 her,] ~. *A1*
121:27 I'll answer ... for theirs *A1*] it

takes my sort to make up all sorts *MS*

121:31 cried, *MS, A1*] ~ *Per1*
121:31 helplessness *A1*] distress *MS*
121:32 lifted *MS, A1*] ~, *Per1*
121:34 said, *MS, A1*] ~ *Per1*
121:35 the deuce ... I shouldn't. *A1*] a damn fine woman—damn me if you're not as fine a built woman as I've seen, handsome with it an' all. *MS* a fine woman—as fine a built woman as I've seen, handsome with it as well. *Per1*
121:39 hot, as ... fixedly. *A1*] hot. *MS*
122:1 Been very *A1*] Not *MS*
122:1 you, for ... replied *A1*] you," she said cryptically *MS*
122:5 said, *MS, A1*] ~ *Per1*
122:6 laconic *MS, A1*] soft *Per1*
122:7 here *MS, A1*] ~, *Per1*
122:9 cowed, *MS, A1*] ~ *Per1*
122:10 by Ga-ard," he drawled *MS, A1*] they have," he said abstractedly *Per1*
122:13 You was ... Damn me, you *Ed.*] It wasn't a bad dodge of yours

to hang on to me like that," he said, "and get me tied up—not half a bad dodge. Damn me, you *MS* "Wasn't half a bad dodge ... dodge. You *Per1* You was ... Darn me, you *A1*
122:16 He leaned ... [122:34] my Missis..." *A1*] *Om. MS* He went behind her chair and put his hands over her shoulders on to her full soft breasts. She shrank as if struck. *P* "But I don't think no harm of you for it," came his balanced, soft, absent voice, as his strong fingers seemed to move her very heart. "You're a darn sight too fine a women for me to bear you any grudge, you are that!" *P* He put his hand under her soft, full chin and lifted her face. Almost a groan of helpless, desirous resentment came from her lips as he kissed her. *Per1* He went ... hands over her full ... her. *Per2 see note on* 122:15

The Primrose Path

The sequence is *MS, TS, TSR, A1, E1*, and *MS* is the base-text.

123:4 glass roof] glass-roof *E1*
123:4 greatcoats] great-coats *A1*
123:7 Berry however] ~, ~, *A1*
123:10 Sir] sir *E1*
123:14 as if] *Om. TS, A1 see notes*
123:23 Well] ~, *A1*
123:23 kid." Rather] ~." *P* Rather *A1*
123:24 awkwardly,] ~ *A1*
123:24 hour,] ~ *A1*
123:28 things—" *P* He] ~,"—he *TS* ~"—he *E1*
123:29 taxicab] taxi-cab *A1*
123:32 more.—You] ~; you *TS*
124:4 Our] our *TS*
124:9 —I] ~ *TS*
124:11 are:] ~, *TS*
124:11 Maud,—] ~, *TS*
124:12 nephew.—] ~. *E1*
124:16 Fifty five] Fifty-five *TS*
124:17 Fifty five—] Fifty-five ... *TS*
124:18 him.] ~: *TS*
124:18 it] ~, *E1*
124:18 again—] ~, *E1*
124:20 Julia *A1*] Emma *MS*
124:21 family.—] ~. *TS*
124:21 Oh] ~, *E1*
124:22 What] ~, *TS*
124:24 blue eyed] blue-eyed *TS*
124:26 taxi-driver] taxi driver *TS*
124:30 society.] ~? *A1*
124:31 him.—] ~. ... *TS*

124:35 ever you] you ever *E1*
124:35 crew *TSR*] stew *MS*
124:35 about.] ~! *A1*
124:37 'em,] ~ *TS*
124:38 come— *MS, E1*] ~——— *TS*
124:40 darling,] ~ *TS*
125:3   however, *TS*] ~ *MS*
125:6   road— *Ed.*] ~—? *MS* ~. *TS see notes*
125:10 Come on] ~ ~, *A1*
125:17 dearly.— *TSR*] ~. *MS, E1*
125:20 God] god *TS*
125:24 Daniel *Ed.*] John *MS* "Joky" *TS see notes*
125:27 parents,] ~ *TS*
125:28 on to *TSR*] onto *MS*
125:29 uplift *A1*] kindliness *MS*
125:34 cold *TSR*] sterile *MS*
125:35 close *A1*] mean *MS* stingy *TSR*
125:39 his own *TSR*] *Om. MS*
126:1   caresses,] ~ *TS*
126:3   he and his wife *A1*] they *MS*
126:11 With a ... love him. *A1*] *Om. MS*
126:16 allowance,] ~ *TS*
126:19 quiet *TSR*] cold *MS*
126:38 alone] ~, *A1*
127:4   "The one ... with."—At which *TSR*] Then, *MS* "The ... with." At which *A1*
127:8   ship.—] ~. ... *TS*
127:15 Sydney— *Ed.*] Sidney— *MS* Sydney—— *A1*
127:17 live—.] ~. *TS*
127:19 time.—] ~— *TS*
127:20 coffee—] ~. *TS*
127:28 marvel—] ~.— *TS*
127:29 us—] ~? *TS*
127:33 your—] ~ ... *TS*
127:35 "How] "—~ *TS*
127:35 twenty one—] twenty-one. *TS*
127:38 divorce—] ~—— *A1*
127:39 her—] ~. *TS*
128:1   Aunt *A1*] *Om. MS*
128:3   Crossing.—] ~. ... *TS*
128:4   time—] ~. *TS*

128:5   Lord.] ~! *A1*
128:6   Yes—] ~—— *A1*
128:11 town,] ~ *E1*
128:17 an' *TSR*] an *MS*
128:23 in] *Om. TS*
128:27 quick] ~, *A1*
128:28 withdrawal] ~, *TS*
128:31 "—Are] "~ *A1*
128:31 George? *TSR*] ~, *MS*
128:32 Berry.—] ~. *E1*
128:32 Red *A1*] a Red *MS*
128:35 bar]door *TS*
128:37 "'s] "—'s *TS*
128:40 you don't] don't you *TS*
128:40 out there] *Om. TS*
129:1   Cinderhill] Cinder Hill *TS*
129:3   in] it in *TS*
129:6   and] an' *TS*
129:12 brown red] brown-red *TS*
129:27 She] She's *A1*
130:1   eiderdown] eider-down *A1*
130:8   Hello Maud,] ~, ~! *TS*
130:8   yer] ye *A1*
130:8   doin'—!] ~? *TS*
130:16 ivy-leaves] ivy leaves *TS*
130:18 ivy-leaves] ivy leaves *TS*
130:19 them,] ~ *E1*
130:22 youth:] ~/ *TS* ~, *A1*
130:24 till] until *TS*
130:37 Winnie,] ~? *TS*
130:37 interpreted,] ~ *TS*
131:3   wash-stand] washstand *TS*
131:3   three-star] Three Star *TS*
131:4   There] And there *TS*
131:11 her] ~, *TS*
131:18 want? *TS*] ~. *MS*
131:26 had had] had *TS*
131:37 allotment gardens *Ed.*] alottment gardens *MS* allotment-gardens *TS*
131:39 dwelling houses] dwelling-houses *TS*
132:1   onto] on to *A1*
132:16 high-road] highroad *A1*
132:17 old,] ~ *A1*
132:25 house-keeper] house-/ keeper *A1* housekeeper *E1*
132:29 Oh] ~, *A1*

132:30 elderly *A1*] elder *MS*
132:39 dining room] dining-room *TS*
132:39 tall] ~, *A1*
132:40 ladylike] lady-/like *TS* lady-like *A1*
133:1 than *TSR*] that *MS*
133:18 room too] ~, ~, *A1*
133:20 he *TS*] I *MS*
133:21 showing *TSR*] almost showing *MS*
133:22 them] ~, *E1*
133:23 Yes." She] ~,"—she *TS* ~"—she *A1*
133:24 Sally—] ~—— *TS*
133:29 crumpling] crumbling *TS*

133:32 soup-plates *TS*] soupplates *MS*
134:5 less;] ~, *A1*
134:11 dining room *Ed.*] kitchen *MS* dining-room *TS see notes*
134:13 Oh] ~, *A1*
134:14 Hello] ~, *A1*
134:15 half challenging] half-challenging *TS*
134:37 Oh] ~, *A1*
134:39 pretence. Which] ~, which *TS*
135:4 ate] he ate *A1*
136:10 "She'll hate … else." *P* And she did. *A1*] *Om. MS* "She'll hate … else." *P* Which was what happened. *TSR*

The Horse-Dealer's Daughter

The sequence is *Per, A1, E1*, and the base-text is *Per*.

137:1 Horse-Dealer's *Ed.*] Horse-dealer's *Per* HORSE DEALER'S *A1 see notes*
137:7 breakfast-table] breakfast table *A1*
137:20 chairs,] ~ *A1*
137:21 high road] highroad *A1*
138:3 high road] highroad *A1*
138:11 motion like] motionlike *A1* motion-/like *E1*
138:12 glazed,] ~ *A1*
138:20 and,] ~ *A1*
139:8 mantelpiece] mantel-piece *A1*
139:10 breakfast-table] breakfast table *A1*
139:15 room,] ~; *A1*
139:39 Joe] ~, *A1*
140:18 Hallo,] Hello *A1* Hello, *E1*
140:19 said] ~, *E1*
140:22 —Got *A1*] ~ *Per*
140:29 cold. *A1*] ~? *Per*
140:31 asked *Per, E1*] ~, *A1*
141:4 you young b——,] *Om. A1*
141:6 then.— *A1*] ~. *Per*
141:10 doctor] ~, *A1*
141:15 Fergusson] ~, *A1*
141:22 Hell] hell *A1*
141:31 Henry] ~, *A1*

141:32 head] ~, *A1*
141:33 tablecloth] table-cloth *A1*
141:40 said] ~, *A1*
142:19 horse-dealer] horse dealer *A1*
142:25 months] ~, *A1*
142:27 previously] ~, *A1*
142:38 father] ~, *A1*
143:30 coping-stone *A1*] coping/stone *Per*
143:33 work] park *A1*
143:38 countryside] country-/side *A1*
143:39 out-patients] outpatients *A1*
143:40 eye] ~, *A1*
144:2 spellbound] spell-bound *A1*
144:4 away] *Om. A1*
144:4 feeling in some way] ~, ~ ~ ~, *A1*
144:16 tea-time] teatime *A1*
144:23 cinder-track *A1*] cinder/track *Per*
144:30 town,] ~ *A1*
144:34 moving, as it were,] ~ ~ ~ ~ *A1*
145:2 square] ~, *A1*
145:4 gates] gate *A1*
145:12 ugly,] ~ *A1*
145:32 clay;] ~, *A1*

146:8 foul,~ *A1*
146:12 and,] ~ *A1*
146:18 wet] ~, *A1*
146:22 her,] ~; *A1*
146:24 hands,] ~; *A1*
146:39 dining-room] dining-room, *A1* dining room, *E1*
147:12 him;] ~, *A1*
147:21 afraid,] ~ *E1*
148:14 her] ~, *A1*
148:25 knees] ~, *A1*
148:31 doctor] ~, *A1*
148:35 it] ~, *A1*
149:6 had really] ~, ~, *A1*
149:11 horrible——] ~. *E1*
149:12 shoulder] shoulders *E1*
149:24 melt] melt away *A1*
149:26 arm] arms *A1*
149:33 him,] ~; *A1*
150:2 terrible] ~, *A1*

150:20 dropped] drooped *A1*
150:24 her! *Ed.*] ~? *Per*
150:25 him] Him *A1*
150:25 doctor!— *A1*] ~! *Per*
150:26 knew!— *A1*] ~! *Per*
150:33 asked] ~, *A1*
151:11 her, *A1*] ~ *Per*
151:18 remember] remember then *A1*
151:19 what] her as *A1*
151:22 voice:— *A1*] ~: *Per*
151:25 appearance] ~, *A1*
151:29 mantelpiece] mantel-piece *A1*
151:39 and,] ~ *A1*
151:40 don't *Per, E1*] don't look *A1*
152:10 awful," and] ~." And *A1*
152:11 heart-broken] heartbroken *A1* heart-/ broken *E1*
152:14 you;] ~, *A1*

The Last Straw [Fanny and Annie]

The sequence is *Per, A1, E1,* and the base-text is *Per.*

153:1 The Last Straw *Ed.*] *Om. Per see notes*
153:2 [Fanny and Annie] *Ed.*] Fanny and Annie *Per* FANNY AND ANNIE *A1*
153:10 course,] ~ *A1*
153:10 Flame-lit *Per, E1*] ~, *A1*
153:14 carriage] ~, *A1*
153:28 furnaces] ~, *A1*
153:29 broad,] ~ *A1*
153:33 at *A1*] in *Per*
153:33 said,] ~ *A1*
154:4 first love] first-love *A1*
154:4 worker,] ~: *A1*
154:6 —did] Did *A1*
154:6 No!] ~. *A1*
154:21 greengrocer's 'll] greengrocers 'll *A1* greengrocers'll *E1*
154:21 half past] half-past *A1*
154:26 Ay— *A1*] Aye, *Per*
154:29 workmen,] ~ *A1*
154:31 clang, of] ~ ~ *A1*
154:33 Gloucester;] ~: *A1*

154:35 carriage approach] carriage-approach *A1*
155:13 street] streets *A1*
155:14 word!] ~, *A1*
155:15 cinema *A1*] Cinema *Per*
155:17 "'Night] "Night *A1*
155:28 Ay,] ~— *A1*
155:30 greengrocery] green-grocery *A1*
156:10 though,] ~ *A1*
156:16 Well, it's] ~—It's *A1*
156:18 points—— *A1*] ~. *Per*
156:19 him. I] ~, ~ *A1*
156:21 Fanny] ~, *A1*
156:22 aunt; "they] ~. "They *A1*
156:24 Fanny,] ~ *A1*
156:28 Right?] ~! *A1*
156:31 doorway] ~, *A1*
156:34 ter!] ~? *A1*
156:34 Mester! *Ed.*] Harry! *Per* Mester. *A1*
156:38 dray] ~, *A1*
157:6 somebody *A1*] some/ body *Per*

157:6 I s'd] I's'd *A1* Is'd *E1*

157:9 speech] ~, *A1*

157:13 attractions,] ~ *A1*

157:18 no vices *A1*] vices *Per*

157:25 to him *A1*] Om. *Per*

157:26 He had ... [157:29] sent her *A1*] The peculiar obstinate limitedness of him sent her almost *Per*

157:31 said] ~, *A1*

157:32 direction, *Per, E1*] ~ *A1*

158:1 marrying,] ~: *A1*

158:2 her—] ~, *A1*

158:3 dead;] ~, *A1*

158:8 woman] ~, *A1*

158:16 Goodall—] ~, *A1*

158:17 tellin',] ~— *A1*

158:19 goin' an' openin' to her *A1*] whistlin' her back *Per*

158:20 she's done ... a mind *A1*] her's done a' the gallivantin' in her power *Per*

158:21 talking;] ~: *A1*

158:22 thine,] ~ *A1*

158:26 pounds,] ~: *A1*

158:28 Street,] ~ *A1*

158:30 Jinny *A1*] Susie *Per*

158:30 course,] ~ *A1*

158:30 Jinny *A1*] Susie *Per*

158:40 voice] ~, *A1*

158:40 Indeed,] ~ *A1*

158:40 spoilt to *A1*] debarred from *Per*

159:1 sang,] ~ *A1*

159:3 *hopened / And be'old, A1*] ~, *and* ~ *Per*

159:7 *Hangels*— ... *fair*——" *A1*] ~ ... ~ " *Per*

159:8 unalterable] inalterable *A1*

159:11 concerts,] ~ *A1*

159:13 Harvest Festival *A1*] harvest festival *Per*

159:15 afternoon *A1*] the afternoon *Per*

159:18 Harvest Festival *A1*] harvest festival *Per*

159:23 brilliantly *A1*] rapidly *Per*

159:24 Harvest Festival *A1*] harvest

festival *Per*

159:32 weak-headed,] ~ *A1*

159:34 perilously] perilous *A1*

160:1 sing-song] singsong *A1*

160:6 He was ... her down. *A1*] Om. *Per*

160:12 *begin*—— *A1*] ~. *Per*

160:17 tie—] ~, *A1*

160:21 despair. Because ... [160:30] afternoon: *A1*] despair. *P* Harry was down for two solos, *Per*

160:31 pulpit,] ~ *A1*

160:31 looked up at ... [161:4] her heart. *E1*] sat in pain through the first of these performances. She hardly noticed his voice, but was thinking to herself. "What if X heard this! Or Y! Or Z!" What if they heard this deadly game of skittles with the aspirate and knew that the performer was her husband-to-be! She might have spared herself the comparison for it was as good as impossible that either X or Y or Z *should* hear. Still, she had some ground for distress. There must be something wanting in a man who lives to the age of thirty-two without being able, upon occasion, to handle an aitch. It was not more snobbing on her part than it was crossness on his. *Per* looked at ... heart. *A1*

161:6 crisped *A1*] curdled *Per*

161:7 Fanny felt ... [161:11] vulgar doom. *A1*] Fanny, unfortunately, had her pleasant curdling turned acid by the shocks of mispronunciation. *Per*

161:13 words:] ~. *A1*

161:14 *joy*;] ~, *A1*

161:15 *seed,*] ~ *A1*

161:17 *him.*] ~—— *A1*

161:18 shall] Shall *A1*

161:18 come,"] ~—" *A1*
161:19 altos,] ~— *A1*
161:21 *joy.*] ~—— *A1*
161:23 carelessly *A1*] gently *Per*
161:23 his *A1*] its *Per*
161:25 voice *A1*] *Om. Per*
161:33 house—] ~, *A1*
162:10 uplifted, stood there,] stood there uplifted, *A1*
162:11 indifference *A1*] wonder *Per*
162:12 faintly mocking *A1*] expressionless *Per*
162:16 bell-like] ~, *A1*
162:20 '*Fair A1*] "~ *Per*
162:20 *corn*] ~, *A1*
162:21 *land.*'"*A1*] ~." *Per*
162:26 odd bachelor ... gentle *A1*] old, weird bachelor, emotional and sensitive *Per*
162:28 Oh *Ed.*] Oh, *Per* O *A1*
162:30 Judge] judge *A1*
162:31 Oh *Ed.*] Oh, *Per* O *A1* O, *E1*
162:32 pray Thee *A1*] enquire of thee *Per*
162:34 said,] ~ *A1*
162:34 washing] washed *A1*
162:37 inscrutable *A1*] calm *Per*
162:38 bewildered *A1*] dumbfounded *Per*
163:2 Nixon] ~, *A1*
163:12 chapel,] ~ *E1*
163:14 unfortunate,"] ~!" *A1*
163:15 ah!] ~, *A1*
163:18 Yes—yes— *A1*] ~, ~, *Per*
163:20 bad one *A1*] beastly woman *Per*
163:21 Well, well] ~! Well *A1*
163:27 sheepishly,] ~— *A1*
163:29 Harry. *A1*] Harry, sheepishly. *Per*
163:33 'er *A1*] er' *Per*
163:36 chap's *A1*] chaps' *Per*
163:40 Annie,] ~— *A1*
164:3 Nixon,] ~— *A1*
164:8 Ay,] ~— *A1*
164:20 Harry:] ~ *E1*

164:23 Ay *A1*] Ah *Per*
164:25 good afternoon] good-afternoon *A1*
164:26 Good afternoon ... good afternoon!] Good-afternoon ... good-afternoon, *A1*
164:30 answered,] ~ *A1*
164:31 went,] ~ *A1*
164:34 this] ~, *A1*
164:35 obstinacy *A1*] precise obstinacy *Per*
164:37 Jinny, *A1*] Susie *Per*
164:37 Jinny's *A1*] Susie's *Per*
164:39 th'] they *A1*
165:1 Harry,] ~ *A1*
165:3 Jinny *A1*] Susie *Per*
165:8 secretly,] ~ *A1*
165:12 Jinny *A1*] Susie *Per*
165:15 Yi,] ~— *A1*
165:15 Jinny *A1*] Susie *Per*
165:18 Bowers'] Bower's, *A1*
165:21 Jinny *A1*] Susie *Per*
165:30 Jinny *A1*] Susie *Per*
165:31 house, *she A1*] ~. She *Per*
165:35 bathe *A1*] bath *Per*
165:37 floor—] ~, *A1*
165:38 use.] used. *A1* use! *E1*
165:39 stepmother] step-mother *A1*
165:39 bathe *A1*] bath *Per*
166:1 close] closes *A1*
166:1 mowing grass] mowing-grass *A1*
166:5 body] ~, *A1*
166:7 Jinny *A1*] Susie *Per*
166:10 addle *A1*] 'andle *Per*
166:11 day's] ~, *A1*
166:12 her *A1*] *Om. Per*
166:13 Jinny *A1*] Susie *Per*
166:14 woman] ~, *A1*
166:17 thrashing] thrashed *A1*
166:20 Jinny *A1*] Susie *Per*
166:21 treat] treats *A1*
166:23 Jinny *A1*] Susie *Per*
166:26 on after tea, till *A1*] on. After tea *Per*
166:32 gel *A1*] gal *Per*

The Mortal Coil

Per is the only text for this story.

169:16 candlelight *Ed.*] candle-/ light *Per*

171:12 cards." *Ed.*] ~. *Per*

172:10 Lenore- *Ed.*] Lenora- *Per*

The Thimble

The sequence is *MS*, *Per*, and the base-text is *MS*.

190:22 importance,] ~ *Per*
190:29 her] the *Per*
191:6 while,] ~ *Per*
191:9 pneumonia,] ~ *Per*
191:21 the] this *Per*
191:23 mind's *Per*] minds' *MS*
192:18 proud;] ~: *Per*
192:24 understand, and] ~ ~ *Per*
192:31 Yes] ~, *Per*
192:37 it] ~, *Per*
193:30 brown grey] brown-grey *Per*
193:35 suspense,] ~ *Per*
194:1 —she] She *Per*
194:6 on to] onto *Per*
194:16 drawing room] drawing-room *Per*
194:26 firelight] fire-light *Per*
194:27 shadows] window *Per see notes*
194:38 the] this *Per*
195:5 round] around *Per*
195:11 thimble *Per*] needle *MS*
195:16 date] ~, *Per*
195:16 Oct.] ~., *Per*

195:18 acquaintance] acquaintances *Per*
196:11 her] the *Per*
196:27 treasure-trove *Per*] treasure trove *MS*
196:28 "How what?"] *Om. Per*
197:11 far-off,] ~ *Per*
197:12 divined,] ~ *Per*
197:22 Why] ~, *Per*
197:30 easily-roused] easily roused *Per*
197:34 This] His *Per*
198:6 imagine:] ~; *Per*
198:19 dependent] depended *Per*
199:14 baby?] ~, *Per*
199:14 her] the *Per*
199:20 case] same *Per*
199:25 woman?] ~, *Per*
199:28 Now] ~, *Per*
200:9 otherwise— —" *P* He] ~—" He *Per*
200:16 other's *Per*] others *MS*
200:18 Father',"] ~,'" *Per*
200:31 suddenly,] ~ *Per*

Adolf

The sequence is *TS1*, *TS2*, *Per*, *E1*, and the base-text is *TS1*.

201:4 nightdresses *TS1, E1*] night-dresses *TS2*
201:14 whistled *TS1, E1*] ~, *TS2*
201:25 his *TS1, E1*] the *Per*
201:25 drinking *TS1, E1*] ~, *TS2*
201:26 table *TS1, E1*] ~, *TS2*
201:26 teacups *TS1, E1*] tea-cups *TS2*
202:29 you *TS2*] to you *TS1*
201:34 armchair *TS1, E1*] arm-chair *TS2*
202:11 did—— *TS1, Per*] ~—— *TS2*
202:13 path *TS1, E1*] ~, *TS2*
202:15 daddy *TS1, E1*] Daddy *TS2*

202:16 say, *TS2*] ~ *TS1*
202:16 aten *TS1, E1*] eaten *TS2*
202:22 *another TS2, E1*] another *TS1, Per*
202:27 before—! *TS2*] ~! *TS1, E1*
202:35 were] was *TS2*
202:39 in *TS1, E1*] *Om. TS2*
203:9 my mother *TS1, E1*] mother *TS1, Per*
203:11 flannel *TS1, E1*] ~, *TS2*
203:14 cried, *TS2, Per*] ~/ *TS1* ~ *E1*
203:24 Yet its eye was bright. *TS1, E1*] *Om. Per*

203:29 came; *TS1, E1*] ~, *TS2*
203:31 bedtime *TS1, E1*] bed-time *TS2*
203:31 gathered *TS1, E1*] ~, *TS2*
203:34 fireplace *TS1, E1*] fire-place *TS2* fire-/ place *Per*
203:35 imagine *TS1, E1*] think *TS2 see notes*
203:37 *should TS2, E1*] should *TS1, Per*
203:37 across] upon *TS2*
204:1 came *TS1, E1*] ~, *TS2*
204:2 door, *TS1, E1*] ~ *TS2*
204:30 of *TS2*] on *TS1*
204:33 *Do TS2, E1*] Do *TS1, Per*
204:37 had *TS1*] *Om. TS2*
204:37 alone—— *TS1, E1*] ~—— *TS2*
205:8 hearth-rug *TS2*] hearthrug *TS1, E1* heart-rug *Per*
205:9 pasture *TS1, E1*] ~, *TS2*
205:11 alarm *TS1, E1*] alarum *TS2*
205:12 bumping *TS2*] dumping *TS1*
205:13 thunderbolt *TS1, E1*] thunder-bolt *TS2*

205:32 unconcern, *TS2*] ~/ *TS1*
206:2 gardens. *P* Adolf *TS1, E1*] ~. Adolf *TS2*
206:5 them? *TS1, E1*] ~! *TS2*
206:13 him] to him *TS2*
206:23 over *TS1, Per*] *Om. TS2*
206:24 decided, *TS1, E1*] ~; *Per*
206:33 heartsearchings *TS1, E1*] heart searchings *TS2*
206:37 times *TS1, E1*] ~, *TS2*
207:4 nettlestalks] nettle-stalks *TS2*
207:4 tail,] ~ *TS2*
207:11 nursemaid's *TS1, E1*] nurse-maid's *TS2*
207:14 *Merde! TS2*] "Merde"! *TS1, E1*
207:30 *merde! merde! merde TS2*] merde! merde! merde *TS1, E1*
207:37 *merde TS2*] merde *TS1, E1*
207:39 him *TS2*] his *TS1*
208:3 evil doers *TS1, E1*] evil-doers *TS2*
208:3 *bien emmerdés! Ed.*] bien emmerdes! *TS1 bien emmerdé. TS2* bien emmerdés! *E1*

Rex

The sequence is *MS, TS, Per, E1*, and the base-text is *MS*.

209:26 pub.] pub *Per*
209:27 accommodation] accomodations *TS* accommodations *E1*
209:28 winter-time] winter-/ time *Per* wintertime *E1*
210:19 *Rex*] Rex *TS*
210:19 *Rax*] Rax *TS*
210:27 *we*] we *TS*
210:30 *infra dig.*] infra dig. *TS*
210:38 *I'll*] I'll *TS*
211:5 fastidious.—] ~. *TS*
211:8 —"'s] "S *TS* "'S *Per*
211:10 Ha-ha!—] ~! *TS*
211:10 —This] ~ *TS*
211:14 mother. *P* It] ~. It *TS*
211:18 moment?—] ~? *TS*
211:21 mother. *P* She] ~. She *TS*
211:27 him] ~, *TS*
211:27 again." *P* Whereupon] ~. Whereupon *TS*

211:34 Jockey] Jocky *E1*
211:35 will.] ~! *TS*
211:38 *her*] her *TS*
212:1 *my*] my *TS*
212:3 defiance *MS, Per*] defence *TS*
212:6 *was*] was *TS*
212:7 young?] ~! *TS*
212:12 *in flagrante MS, Per*] in flagrante *TS*
212:29 puppy-tail *MS, Per*] puppy tail *TS*
212:30 us,] ~ *TS*
212:33 *bitten MS, Per*] bitten *TS*
212:34 bitten?,] ~? *TS*
212:40 *Nags Head*] Nags Head *TS*
213:2 *comme il faut MS, Per*] comme il faut *TS*
213:11 *almost*] almost *TS*
213:13 *besoin d'aimer MS, Per*] besoin d'aimer *TS*

213:17 strange,] ~ *E1*
213:33 leave] let *TS*
213:36 *go*] go *TS*
213:37 *she ... she*] she ... she *TS*
214:5 *must*] must *TS*
214:9 *us*] us *TS*
214:35 *not*] not *TS*
215:3 *Am ... Am* I!] Am ... Am I? *TS*

215:14 *I*] I *TS*
215:18 'How] "how *TS*
215:18 do!'] ~!" *TS*
215:18 *suffisance MS, Per*] suffisance *TS*
216:3 only saw Rex] saw Rex only *TS*
216:3 the *Good Omen*] The Good Omen *TS*
216:5 *how*] how *TS*

England, My England, 1915 version

The sequence is *GP, Per1, Per2,* and the base-text is *GP.*

219:1 England,] ~ *Per2*
219:2 I.] *Om. Per2*
219:4 on the ... common, *GP, Per2*] *Om. Per1*
219:10 again, strained and anxious, *GP, Per2*] again *Per1*
219:11 strong,] ~ *Per2*
219:11 pine-trees] ~, *Per2*
219:12 from the log bridge *GP, Per2*] *Om. Per1*
219:13 columbines, to ... cottage. *GP, Per2*] columbines. *Per1*
219:19 Nurse] nurse *Per2*
219:25 earth;] ~, *Per2*
219:26 tense] fierce *Per2*
219:26 peace] savage peace *Per2*
219:27 green garden-path ... white; the] *Om. Per1* green ... white, the *Per2*
219:29 for-ever] forever *Per2*
219:30 changeless, eternal *GP, Per2*] changeless *Per1*
219:32 tree *GP, Per2*] bank *Per1*
219:32 home] where he lived *Per2*
220:3 ancient] savage *Per2*
220:7 the world ... heart.] it was none of it true. *Per1* the world ... heart of him. *Per2*
220:8 him—] ~, *Per2*
220:8 the heart of *GP, Per2*] *Om. Per1*
220:9 life like ... sunshine;] life; *Per1* life like ... sunshine, *Per2*
220:10 blossoming, red-flowered *GP, Per2*] blossoming *Per1*

220:12 like a weapon *GP, Per2*] *Om. Per1*
220:14 hard *GP, Per2*] fierce *Per1*
220:19 flowers and ... universe] satisfaction and magnificence *Per1* the flowers and ... universe *Per2*
220:21 the love *GP, Per2*] it *Per1*
220:22 He would ... mirage. *GP, Per2*] *Om. Per1*
220:24 they *GP, Per2*] *Om. Per1*
220:27 self-contained *GP, Per2*] attractive *Per1*
220:28 silence *GP, Per2*] obstinacy *Per1*
220:33 all—] ~; *Per2*
220:36 beautiful] a very joy of beauty *Per2*
220:36 all it amounted to] to go on forever *Per2*
220:37 to him] in her heart *Per2*
220:37 more] more of his children *Per2*
221:2 simply] ~, *Per2*
221:6 obstinate] warm *Per2*
221:6 driven into] in *Per2*
221:7 family. He] family, who *Per2*
221:9 there] who *Per2*
221:10 spirit] spirit of his fathers *Per2*
221:11 A *GP, Per2*] Of *Per1*
221:11 sensual nature in himself,] sensual nature, *Per1* sensuous nature in himself, *Per2*
221:12 the ideas ... upon him, *GP, Per2*] rigid ideas of duty, *Per2*

221:12 though *GP, Per2*] but *Per1*

221:13 inspired *GP, Per2*] coloured *Per1*

221:14 by tradition] *Om. Per1* by nature *Per2*

221:14 by nature he was sensual, and] he was *Per2*

221:15 gratified] moved *Per2*

221:16 a printing ... publishing house, *GP, Per2*] *Om. Per1*

221:17 diffused] fired *Per2*

221:18 sensuousness] passion *Per2*

221:19 sensuous heat] sensuous, æsthetic heat *Per1* passion *Per2*

221:20 always, at ... ethics] always stoically ethical, and at the same time always cravingly reverential to esthetic beauty *Per2*

221:21 had] *Om. Per2*

221:25 ethical] yearning *Per2*

221:26 She could ... into ethical desire ... new vigorous output ... and children.] She could ... into dissatisfaction ... new active output ... children. *Per1* She felt one *must* be doing one's best, one should be doing one's very utmost in life, all the time. She *could* not understand idleness. To her it was simply nihilistic. *Per2*

221:32 Gradually] Then gradually *Per2*

221:32 get dissatisfied with *GP, Per2*] reject *Per1*

221:34 she fell ... strong in] a sense of frustration came up strong in *Per1* she fell away. Her sense of duty to the world was too strong for *Per2*

221:35 inconclusive] neutral *Per2*

221:36 undeveloped ethical] undeveloped, conscience-stricken *Per2*

221:36 negated] foiled *Per1* frustrated *Per2*

221:37 children,] ~— *Per2*

221:37 fair-haired] ~, *Per2*

221:39 They had ... the others.] *Om. Per2*

222:2 remote in the country] remote, *Per2*

222:10 distant and more absent and exempt] futile and more false *Per1* distant and more silent and reserved *Per2*

222:11 background,] ~ *Per2*

222:11 an exempt] a silent *Per2*

222:11 presence. *GP, Per2*] presence. Or when he came near her, he only wanted the physical contact with her, the passion. *Per1*

222:12 had to go *GP, Per2*] went *Per1*

222:13 specialist] great doctor *Per2*

222:14 Winifred] her, Winifred, and *Per2*

222:16 silent *GP, Per2*] futile *Per1*

222:21 rare] deathly *Per2*

222:22 negation, detached] death, hard *Per2*

222:24 eternity *GP, Per2*] aversion *Per1*

222:26 an agony *Per1*] an agony grief *GP* a cruel grief *Per2*

222:26 parents, they ... physical life.] parents. *Per2*

222:28 incommutable, nihilistic] passive *Per2*

222:29 off-hand] offhand *Per2*

222:35 him,] ~ *Per2*

222:36 him,] ~ *Per2*

222:40 Evelyn;] ~. *Per2*

223:1 said. He] ~; he *Per2*

223:2 do] take *Per2*

223:2 work] job *Per2*

223:4 suitable,] ~ *Per2*

223:6 dissatisfied;] ~, *Per2*

223:8 negated] dodged *Per1* stubbornly refused *Per2*

223:9 Something ... Winifred's soul] Hard as a weapon Winifred was with anger *Per2*

223:11 not counting] betrayed by *Per2*

223:11 husband. *GP, Per2*] husband,

who could only be physical. Yet she wanted him. *Per1*

223:16 flame-like child] flamelike being *Per2*

223:16 thing. Yet] ~. *P* Yet *Per2*

223:18 strong;] ~, *Per2*

223:18 Her mind ... the soul.] *Om. Per2*

223:23 was nullified ... [223:26] he lived.] wanted to go away. He was like a thing buried alive, that is going mad. *Per2*

223:27 corrosive] little *Per2*

223:28 II.] *Om. Per2*

223:30 He had ... sentience. *GP, Per2*] *Om. Per1*

223:32 impervious *GP, Per2*] impervious to attack *Per1*

223:33 ignoring *GP, Per2*] *Om. Per1*

223:33 contempt; she ignored his existence. *GP, Per2*] contempt. *Per1*

223:36 them. *GP, Per2*] them. All the time, he let himself be despised. *Per1*

223:38 Only the ... believed in.] Only the mother gave herself up with ethical rigour to look after the children and to discipline her own flesh. *Per1 Om. Per2*

224:5 each] each one *Per2*

224:8 in to] into *Per2*

224:9 this] the *Per2*

224:11 triumph] smile *Per2*

224:11 he felt] *Om. Per2*

224:14 There,] ~ *Per2*

224:15 hidden deep ... heath, *GP, Per2*] *Om. Per1*

224:17 meet,] ~ *Per2*

224:18 And this ... with it. *GP, Per2*] *Om. Per1*

224:31 right——] ~, *Per2*

224:31 said] ~, *Per2*

224:33 It should ... decide. *GP, Per2*] *Om. Per1*

224:35 heartily;] ~: *Per2*

224:36 as] *Om. Per1* as he whom *Per2*

224:40 almost at once he was] was almost at once *Per2*

225:4 participating ... great destructive motion] participating ... great warrior motion *Per1* the preparation for the destructive purposes for which he was destined *Per2*

225:5 spirit acquiesced] heart was really in it *Per2*

225:7 Now] ~, *Per2*

225:7 altered towards] loved *Per2*

225:8 humbled herself before him] entreated for his love *Per2*

225:10 beautiful] so beautiful *Per2*

225:11 a] almost a *Per2*

225:12 arrogance] hardness *Per2*

225:12 life;] ~, *Per2*

225:13 Also] ~, *Per2*

225:14 him;] ~, *Per2*

225:15 she too] ~, ~, *Per2*

225:16 agent ... of the Slayer] independent Self, military and of free licence *Per1* agent ... of death *Per2*

225:20 a moment of] *Om. Per2*

225:21 was gone again] soon passed away *Per2*

225:28 reach, positive ... capacity.] reach. *Per2*

225:29 together] ~, *Per2*

225:31 it] ~, *Per2*

225:32 desire] love *Per2*

225:36 be destroyed] become destructive *Per2*

225:38 life?] life? His hand was against life. *Per2*

225:40 Everything, then,] ~ ~ *Per2*

225:40 whilst] while *Per2*

226:2 do with ... he will] take out of it what he can *Per2*

226:5 listened to] liked to be told *Per2*

226:6 cant] a falsehood, that kind of thing *Per2*

226:7 even want] pretend *Per2*

226:7 feel that way] bring that sort of thing off *Per2*

226:8 couldn't;] ~, *Per2*

226:9   mankind:] ~— *Per2*
226:11   else. *P* So] ~. So *Per2*
226:13   irritated him ... principle] left
         him just as cold as any other
         leave-taking *Per2*
226:15   good] use *Per2*
226:16   then.] ~? *Per2*
226:16   passion] hysterics *Per2*
226:19   begun!] ~. *Per2*
226:24   satisfactorily] ~, *Per2*
226:25   destruction *GP, Per2*] inflicting
         death *Per1*
226:28   machine-guns] machine guns
         Per2
226:30   occasionally—] ~, *Per2*
226:31   direction—] ~, *Per2*
226:31   rifle fire] rifle-fire *Per2*
227:11   physical] mathematical *Per2*
227:12   spiritual] human *Per2*
227:13   The comradeship ... perfectly
         isolated.] *Om. Per2*
227:17   road] highroad *Per2*
227:27   physical] abstract *Per2*
227:31   high-road] highroad *Per2*
227:32   it slanted ... eternity] it slanted
         in the absolute *Per1* would it
         slant through all eternity *Per2*
227:34   for ever;] forever, *Per2*
227:36   our own men] Englishmen *Per2*
227:36   it is] would it be *Per2*
227:37   same—] ~, *Per2*
228:2   rapidly,] ~; *Per2*
228:5   Papp] papp *Per2*
228:7   Papp] papp *Per2*
228:9   Then,] ~ *Per2*
228:10   piercing *GP, Per2*] rushing
         Per1
228:11   the soul] life *Per2*
228:12   a] its *Per2*
228:18   red berries] bright red berries
         on it *Per2*
228:19   below] ~, *Per2*
228:27   crashing] crushing *Per2*
228:29   inviolable,] ~ *Per2*
228:31   platform, and] platform; *Per2*
228:34   then,] ~ *Per2*
228:34   activity,] ~ *Per2*
228:38   When faintly] ~, ~, *Per2*

229:4   There was ... of pain.] *Om.*
         Per2
229:6   listened,] ~ *Per2*
229:7   resonance] ~, *Per2*
229:7   it,] ~ *Per2*
229:10   sight, at least,] ~ ~ ~ *Per2*
229:17   void, a bruise] soreness, a
         smart *Per2*
229:18   hit, then,] ~ ~ *Per2*
229:19   And,] ~ *Per2*
229:27   second, and deeper,] ~ ~ ~
         Per2
229:31   peaceful] light *Per2*
229:32   still] light *Per2*
229:32   finely diffused and rare] light
         Per2
229:37   terror] ~, *Per2*
229:39   chaos] jumbled light *Per2*
230:2   a piece of high-road] a piece of
         whiteness *Per1* the highroad
         Per2
230:5   effort] ~, *Per2*
230:6   once more ... stable world] was
         able to think *Per2*
230:12   also saw] also saw, suddenly,
         Per2
230:13   It seemed very natural.] *Om.*
         Per2
230:14   pain *GP, Per2*] ~, *Per1*
230:17   clear being] bodiless clarity,
         Per2
230:19   vaguely,] ~ *Per2*
230:24   Then, relentlessly,] ~ ~ *Per2*
230:25   back,] ~ *Per2*
230:31   smashed,] ~ *Per2*
230:33   sat] ~, *Per2*
230:36   isolated] ~, *Per2*
231:3   He fell ... towards death.] *Om.*
         Per1 He fell ... toward death.
         Per2
231:8   it, then,] ~ ~ *Per2*
231:9   knowledge.] knowledge, it was.
         Per2
231:9   decided] ~, *Per2*
231:14   Till] Then *Per2*
231:17   and,] ~ *Per2*
231:17   movement,] ~ *Per2*
231:20   up, *Per1*] ~ *GP*

231:22 *Kaput*] *Tod Per2*
231:26 arms.] arms. He must shoot them. *Per2*
231:27 calm *GP, Per2*] fine *Per1*
231:29 in] but just *Per2*
231:35 ludicrous] ~, *Per2*
231:35 movement] ~, *Per2*
231:36 forwards] forward *Per2*
231:38 breast,] ~ *Per2*
231:39 noise,] ~; *Per2*

231:40 air,] ~; *Per2*
232:3 up,] ~ *Per2*
232:4 aimed] carefully aimed *Per2*
232:7 blow,] ~ *Per2*
232:12 steel] steel in his throat *Per2*
232:14 man] ~, *Per2*
232:17 ghoulish,] ~ *Per2*
232:17 faint] ~, *Per2*
232:18 suggestion,] ~ *Per2*
232:18 mad,] ~ *Per2*

Of the compound words which are hyphenated at the end of a line in this edition, only the following hyphenated forms should be retained in quotation:

5:27	snake-infested	111:40	good-humoured
6:22	white-skinned	112:36	Cornish-Yankee
15:32	will-to-succeed	116:5	pocket-handkerchief
29:28	hazel-bushes	137:7	breakfast-table
30:31	machine-guns	153:11	red-and-black
36:9	good-looking	156:1	over-wrought
66:18	dark-blue	159:32	weak-headed
66:31	nothing-in-particular	175:30	working-men
72:8	Monkey-nuts	175:31	self-confidence
72:33	black-browed	175:37	self-sufficient
73:39	soft-hearted	180:6	clear-red
82:28	ever-grateful	185:19	high-roofed
85:39	daughter-in-law	188:29	self-exculpation
86:21	knee-breeches	188:37	police-official
86:36	father-in-law	198:17	dream-psychology
87:7	father-in-law	204:35	hind-quarters
94:16	school-fellows	206:25	wild-woods
95:11	self-possessed	207:15	flag-wagging
108:22	west-Cornish	221:37	fair-haired
109:27	eye-brows	226:12	leave-taking